Senses of Place

Publication of the Advanced Seminar Series is made possible by
generous support from the Brown Foundation, Inc., of Houston, Texas.

School of American Research Advanced Seminar Series
Douglas W. Schwartz, General Editor

Senses of Place

CONTRIBUTORS

Keith H. Basso
Department of Anthropology
University of New Mexico

Karen I. Blu
Department of Anthropology
New York University

Edward S. Casey
Department of Philosophy
State University of New York, Stony Brook

Steven Feld
Anthropology Board of Studies
University of California, Santa Cruz

Charles O. Frake
Department of Anthropology
State University of New York, Buffalo

Clifford Geertz
School of Social Science
Institute for Advanced Study
Princeton, New Jersey

Miriam Kahn
Department of Anthropology
University of Washington

Kathleen C. Stewart
Department of Anthropology
University of Texas at Austin

*"We come and go,
but the land is always here.
And the people who love it
and understand it are the people
who own it—for a little while."*

Willa Cather, *O Pioneers!*

Senses of Place

Edited by Steven Feld and Keith H. Basso

SCHOOL OF AMERICAN RESEARCH PRESS I SANTA FE I NEW MEXICO

School of American Research Press
Post Office Box 2188
Santa Fe, New Mexico 87504-2188
www.press.sarweb.org

Director of Publications: Joan K. O'Donnell
Editor: June-el Piper
Designer: Deborah Flynn Post
Indexer: Douglas J. Easton
Typographer: Tseng Information Systems, Inc.
Printer: Thomson-Shore, Inc.

Library of Congress Cataloging-in-Publication Data:

Senses of place / edited by Steven Feld and Keith H. Basso.
p. cm. — (School of American Research advanced seminar series)
Includes bibliographical references and index.
ISBN 0-933452-94-2 (cloth). — ISBN 0-933452-95-0 (pbk.)
1. Human geography—Philosophy. 2. Ethnology—Philosophy.
3. Geographical perception. I. Feld, Steven. II. Basso, Keith, 1940–   . III.
Series.
GF21.S45   1996
304.2'3—dc20   93-31354
                                                    CIP

Cover: "Road Taken. 95," by Carol Anthony. Craypas and enamel on ges-
soed panel. © 1996 Carol Anthony. Courtesy of the Gerald Peters Gallery,
Santa Fe. Photo by Dan Morse.

Contents

Illustrations

Acknowledgments

The essays presented here were first written for a School of American Research advanced seminar titled "Place, Expression, and Experience," held in March–April 1993. Because of length constraints, this volume omits one paper prepared for the advanced seminar, "Creating a Heterotopia: An Analysis of the Spacetime of Olmsted's and Vaux's Central Park," by Nancy D. Munn.

Speaking from our position as conveners, we thank the seminar participants for their essays, for their spirited discussions, and for their patience through the rewriting and publishing phase of the project. Their enthusiasm helped enlarge what was, for us at least, a more circumscribed dialogue about matters of place and making place matter.

For their generous support of the advanced seminar, we thank the School of American Research and the Wenner-Gren Foundation for Anthropological Research. The hospitality of SAR president Douglas Schwartz, conference coordinator Cecile Stein, and their staff made the meeting relaxed and enjoyable. For help with manuscript preparation, we are grateful to Frances Terry and to the staff of the SAR Press.

Senses of Place

Introduction

Steven Feld and Keith H. Basso

A recent spate of writings on the subject of place, both within and across academic disciplines, obliges us to begin with a simple question: What is meant to be the contribution of this book? How does it differ from and how does it mesh with developing trends in contemporary scholarship? In particular, what were the aims of this group of authors in circulating their papers prior to an advanced seminar at the School of American Research in 1993, coming together in Santa Fe to discuss them, and then rethinking and revising them in light of the group meeting, readers' responses, and further attention to the growing body of literature?

First, the broader setting. Readers interested in place are no doubt aware of valuable contributions made lately by cultural geographers, many of whom have adopted interpretive frameworks similar to those familiar to anthropologists. Some of these frameworks are pointedly humanistic (Buttimer 1993; Entrikin 1991; J. Jackson 1994), emerging from a lineage of inquiry into place and lived experiences, particularly experiences of rootedness, uprootedness, or transrootedness (Bachelard 1964; Buttimer and Seamon 1980; Cosgrove 1984; Lowenthal 1985; Relph 1976; Tuan 1977). The cultural geographers' work, which tends to incorporate a good deal of modern philosophical thought, is often guided by ideas on "dwelling" described in the phenomenology of Martin Heidegger (1971). These ideas are variously blended with social theory, sometimes producing syntheses bearing affinities to the sociological notion of "placeways" developed in the work of E. V. Walter (1988), and at other times producing critical and deconstructive analyses for application in the fields of environmental design, urban planning, and architecture (Mugerauer 1994; Seamon 1992).

An equally prominent trend in cultural geography is centrally concerned with neo-Marxist cultural critique and with global postmodern theory (Harvey 1989; P. Jackson 1989; Soja 1989). Accordingly, many of its proponents position their writing in relation to geographies of struggle and resistance, especially those writers who embrace issues of representation, gender, and political action (Duncan and Ley 1993; Keith and Pile 1993; Massey 1994). Most of these authors are clearly indebted to Michel Foucault's exposition (1970, 1979, 1986) of panopticism and heterotopias, and they take as their starting points his spatial analyses of repression, institutional power, and social control.

Perspectives in cultural geography articulate in varying degrees with other humanistic studies of place written by historians, critics, and artists: in literature and biography (Hiss 1990; Turner 1989), in folklore (Ryden 1993), in music (Stokes 1994), and in literary theory and art history (Mitchell 1994). And the cultural geography literature now includes perspectives from anthropology and archaeology in works exploring the relationships between landscape and authority (Bender 1993) and dialogues with indigenous peoples and heritage conservationists about the importance of protecting sacred sites (Carmichael et al. 1994; Kelley and Francis 1994).

Alongside these trends, and often enough in juxtaposition to them, the recent topicalization of place by cultural anthropologists has mostly been concerned with theorizing social identities. An important jumping-off point for this enterprise was a short collection of essays titled *Place: Experience and Symbol* that brought together ethnographers and humanistic geographers. Most of these essays focused on the social well-being attached to the sense of rootedness in place—so much so that in the end editor Miles Richardson lamented that the emphasis they gave to the rooted over the unrooted or the uprooted, to the in-place over the out-of-place, was at best problematical and perhaps "inauthentic" (1984:66).

Subsequent work in anthropology has taken several steps beyond that starting point by theorizing place largely from the standpoint of its contestation and its linkage to local and global power relations. Whatever else may be involved, this development surely reflects the now acute world conditions of exile, displacement, diasporas, and inflamed borders, to say nothing of the increasingly tumultuous struggles by indigenous peoples and cultural minorities for ancestral homelands, land rights, and retention of sacred places. These days, narratives of place once presented under such gentle rubrics as "national integration" and "political evolution" are being framed in decidedly harsher terms: as economic development by state invasion and occupation, or as the extraction of transnational wealth at escalating costs in human suffering, cultural destruction, and environmental degradation (Bodley 1988; Burger 1990; Cultural Survival 1993).

In this light it is hardly surprising that anthropologists have come to worry less about place in broad philosophical or humanistic terms than about places as sites of power struggles or about displacement as histories of annexation, absorption, and resistance. Thus, ethnography's stories of place and places are increasingly about contestation. And this makes them consistent with a larger narrative in which previously absent "others" are now portrayed as fully present, no longer a presumed and distant "them" removed from a vague and tacit "us." These stories are placed and in motion on a world map whose once black-lined borders and boundaries are increasingly smudged by vagueness, erased by chaos, or clouded by uncertainty (Appadurai and Breckenridge 1988; Deleuze and Guattari 1986; Kapferer 1988; Rosaldo 1988).

Arjun Appadurai considers these and related matters in his introduction to a 1988 theme issue of *Cultural Anthropology*, "Place and Voice in Anthropological Theory." At the outset, Appadurai contrasts the practice of explicitly naming the locations to which ethnographers travel with the tendency to ignore or assume the locations from which they come. Then he links this practice to the rhetorical problem of embedding a multiplicity of local voices in the more singular and synthetic voice of anthropological authorship. Joining those two concerns, Appadurai and other authors in the symposium examine the metonymy of place and idea, arguing that in the realm of representations, geographical regions are not so much physically distinct entities as discursively constructed settings that signal particular social modalities: India becomes hierarchy, New Guinea exchange, Africa segmentation, and so forth.

In a similar vein, Margaret C. Rodman's *American Anthropologist* article, "Empowering Place: Multilocality and Multivocality" (1992), reviews and critiques the power positions and assumptions underlying equations of "place" and "location." Rodman recommends studies of place that take discontinuities and multiplicities of voice and action into greater account. Such studies, she contends, must reject "boundedness" models of culture and the ways they privilege the authority of persons in positions of power.

In a more recent theme issue of *Cultural Anthropology* titled "Space, Identity, and the Politics of Difference," editors Akhil Gupta and James Ferguson likewise see the need for a reevaluation of the "assumed isomorphism of space, place and culture" (1992:7), a reassessment based on critical theorizations of space "embodied in such notions as surveillance, panopticism, simulacra, deterritorialization, postmodern hyperspace, borderlands, and marginality" (1992:6). Joining with other critics of anthropology's historical tendency to favor representations of contained people, places, and identities, Gupta and Ferguson call for an anthropology of space grounded in an understanding of the realities of boundary erosion, diasporas and dispersal, mobility and movement. They imagine this space as one "beyond culture," where stabilized territories are replaced by hybrid and fluid zones such as borderlands, which are characterized by place indeterminacy (see also Gupta, Ferguson, and Rouse 1992; Appadurai 1992 proposes the notion of "ethnoscapes" as a response to the bounded culture syndrome; Clifford 1992 critiques anthropology's privileging of dwelling over travel).

More recently still, an anthology titled *The Anthropology of Landscape: Perspectives on Place and Space* (Hirsch and O'Hanlon 1995) has appeared, showing how different lines of thought on these topics have been developing in British social anthropology. Derived from a conference at the London School of Economics in 1989, the collection begins with an essay on the concept of landscape by an art historian. It is followed by nine ethnographic chapters treating dimensions of place concepts and spatial history in the Amazon, Madagascar, India, Israel, Mongolia, Fiji, aboriginal Australia, and Papua New Guinea. As Eric Hirsch indicates in his introductory overview, ethnography can contribute much to unpacking the Western landscape concept, not only as it has influenced artistic visual representations of distant worlds but also as it shapes the imagination of rural places as fixed and immutable "elsewheres." In doing so, Hirsch suggests, anthropology might provide—contra more static, absolute, or predominantly visual approaches—a theorization of landscape as cultural process that is dynamic, multisensual, and constantly oscillating between a "foreground" of everyday lived emplacement and a "background" of social potential (see also Tilley 1994).

Few of the works just mentioned had been published in the spring of 1990, when we conceived the idea of a School of American Research advanced seminar on "Place, Expression, and Experience." Most of the themes we have cited were familiar to us then, as were some of their antecedents, but these were not what we talked about. Rather, we were struck by something more basic: that while cultural anthropologists had certainly done useful research on place and places, ethnographic accounts that were centered on native constructions of particular localities—which is to say, the perception and experience of place—were few and far between. This impression remained intact until the time of our meeting during the last days of March and the first days of April 1993, although by then some welcome exceptions to it, such as Fred Myers's *Pintupi Country, Pintupi Self* (1991) and James Weiner's *The Empty Place* (1991), had become well known.

Because long-term ethnographic fieldwork with a strong linguistic focus was the main shared feature of our own intellectual biographies, we found ourselves imagining a project that would honor the basic anthropological commonplace that where meaning and experience are concerned, careful ethnography—and with it careful attention to language and language use—is basic and essential. To that end we invited our colleagues to explore in close detail cultural processes and practices through which places are rendered meaningful—through which, one might say, places are actively sensed. We asked for lengthy essays (at least by anthology standards) that gave top priority to forms of local knowledge and to localized forms of expression. And we expected the essays, when considered all together, to serve as a springboard for profitable discussions about the complex ways in which places anchor lives in social formations ranging widely in geographical location, in economic and political scale, and in accompanying realms of gender, race, class, and ethnicity.

Because the two of us would be writing about peoples typically viewed as among anthropology's most traditional and stereotypically exotic interlocutors—Apache Indians and rainforest Papuans—we felt strongly that the book should contain contrastive essays about very different groups of Native Americans and Papua New Guineans, particularly those whose renderings of place relied less on highly aestheticized narrative and poetic forms. Thus we invited Karen I. Blu to present her research on the history of multiple claims to place held by Lumbee Indians and their African-American and Anglo-American neighbors in North Carolina, and Miriam Kahn to discuss the Papuan world of the coastal Wamirans, a world where myths and memories are voiced in material ways, including the placement of stones. The essays by Blu and Kahn showed us conspicuously different modes of imagining and enacting place, making it clear, among other things, that there were no monolithic Native American or Melanesian modes of dwelling.

A more radical way to create sharp textual juxtapositions, we felt, was to emphasize places and populations whose geographical closeness and presumed familiarity made them, ironically, *more,* not less, "other" and remote, at least in terms of conventional ethnographic writing. With this in mind we invited Kathleen C. Stewart to discuss her work on Appalachian material and narrative voicings of ruined places as tropes of marginality. We also asked Nancy D. Munn to present her research on the history of creating New York City's famed Central Park, and Charles O. Frake to discuss his work on the history and ethnography of the English countryside. All three essays presented us, again, with stylistic and substantive differences in the activities, practices, and imaginations involved in making places both meaningful and multidimensional.

Motivated by our interest in securing fine-grained ethnographic descriptions from our authors, we did not direct them to theorize place in abstract ways. At the same time, we feared that without some attention to the historical and philosophical underpinnings of writings on place, our discussions might descend into a welter of particulars. For this reason we invited two distinguished theorists to speak to and through our more ethnographic explorations. One, Edward S. Casey, is a philosopher long concerned with the phenomenological account of place, and his recent writing on the topic (Casey 1993) is strongly engaged in dialogue with both social theory and ethnographic inquiry. The other, Clifford Geertz, is well known for his ethnographic writings on Indonesia and Morocco and for his theoretical influence on symbolic and interpretive trends in cultural anthropology. By having Casey and Geertz bracket and criss-cross our ethnographic accounts, we were sure to draw out the tensions between phenomenological and hermeneutic positions in social theory, particularly the tensions inherent in the contrastive ways in which they account for perception, meaning, experience, and invention. Additionally, we hoped, Casey's and Geertz's perspectives would help us confront and clarify assumptions about the familiar and the exotic, the nearby and the remote, the central and the peripheral, the "modern" and the "traditional," the universal and the particular, the local and the global, the emplaced and the displaced.

In general then, our book is ethnographic, its primary purpose being to describe and interpret some of the ways in which people encounter places, perceive them, and invest them with significance. We seek to move beyond facile generalizations about places being culturally constructed by describing specific ways in which places naturalize different worlds of sense. Further, we aim to equate such ethnographic evocations with local theories of dwelling—which is not just living in place but also encompasses ways of fusing setting to situation, locality to life-world. We take seriously the challenge to ground these ethnographies closely in the dialogues with local voices that animated them in the first place—that is, we take seriously the challenge to register a full range of discursive and nondiscursive modes of expression through which everyday and poetically heightened senses of place are locally articulated. We asked for essays that described how specific expressive practices and performances imbued acts, events, and objects with significance, thus illuminating different ways in which place is voiced and experienced. In the process of illustrating, performing, mimicking, and evoking such descriptions, our authors draw upon a broad range of local symbolic materials—verbal, visual, musical, oral, graphic, and written—and present them through a variety of essay writing styles. In doing so they locate the intricate strengths and fragilities that connect places to social imagination and practice, to memory and desire, to dwelling and movement.

Having so strongly announced our commitment to ethnography, it may perhaps seem contradictory that we started our discussions at the advanced seminar, and now begin this book, not with an ethnographic essay but with a philosophical account of place. This is not meant to privilege a specific theoretical vantage point but rather to invoke the necessity of a deeper and more engaged anthropological dialogue with the philosophy of place. Toward this end, Edward S. Casey reminds us, in ways yet different from those he took up in *Remembering* (1987) and *Getting Back into Place* (1993), of how the intimate relationship between embodiment and emplacement brings the problem of place into close resonance with the anthropological problem of knowing "local knowledge." Following the lead of Merleau-Ponty, Casey examines how to be in place is to know, is to become aware of one's very consciousness and sensuous presence in the world. From there Casey argues that the experience of place is no secondary grid overlaid on the presumed primacy of space. Rather, he contends, place is the most fundamental form of embodied experience—the site of a powerful fusion of self, space, and time.

Drawing on some of the same phenomenological works that compel Casey, we ourselves continue the dialogue in separate essays exploring the implications of what Western Apache and Kaluli people have in mind when they say that their lives are "like a trail" or "like a path." In the distinct and distant social and physical worlds of Southwestern desert and Papuan rainforest, places are evoked through poetic means. We find Apache stories and Kaluli songs that hold and unleash wisdom, that embody memories in manners of voicing, and that animate the sensuality of place as both landscape and soundscape. Our essays also emphasize the significance of local placenames, and how it is that toponyms, when employed in certain contexts, contribute to the creation of senses of place rich in moral, cosmological, and biographical texture.

Kathleen C. Stewart's contribution on Appalachia deals too with the felt intensity of places and their complex sensuous components. But she describes a different sense of place—gritty, edgy, troublesome—as she travels through spaces of loss and marginality in the "hollers" of West Virginia. Stewart challenges us to picture a rather close-by world made increasingly remote by class and power cleavages, a world where history lies inscribed in mined landscapes of trash and is performed daily in hard talk and sad songs. Evoking the hyperreal spaces of poetic intensification that she hears in Appalachian voices and sees in local yards of rubbish, Stewart writes against the flatness of ethnographic realism, dispelling any easy naturalization of place as rooted contentment, any simple naturalization of nostalgia as romantic desire. Hers is a disturbing confrontation with ways in which emplacement and displacement involve distractions, excesses, and heightened anxieties.

Miriam Kahn begins with a common and often taken-for-granted aspect of place: the scenario of going and coming, the public exhibition of entangling and disentangling. Asking why the management of arriving and leaving is sometimes so poignant, Kahn proceeds to explore the emotional contours situated in her own experiences of settling into, taking leave of, returning to, and again departing Wamira village in Papua New Guinea. Not surprisingly, Wamirans had their own complicated ideas about how these dramatic displays should be publicly enacted. Kahn's essay uses the autobiographical voice to articulate her engagement with Wamiran sentimentality and sociability, arguing for additional ways in which people and places are bonded through feelingful speech and actions.

Karen I. Blu's essay explores the history and ethnography of three spatially and interactionally overlapped and interlocked communities in eastern North Carolina. There, in Robeson County, groups of Lumbee Indians, African Americans, and Whites all stake claims for a "home place," for group identities tied to particular towns and landscapes. These resilient identities—and the locales to which they are attached—are more than a little complex, having been shaped by shared yet separate histories, unequal access to economic and political power, and different degrees of involvement in local, county, and national events. Blu takes us up and around the roads of a place thick with impacts, a region whose inhabitants live deeply immersed in personifications, ambiences, and memories. She reveals how struggles and uprooted moments are endlessly countered with actions meant to ensure a sense of home.

Charles O. Frake ends the collection by musing over a "troublesome tribe"—the English—and their rural world of East Anglia, where the countryside is locally constituted as a unique and telling quaintness. Frake interprets a variety of local materials—from placenames to local pub talk, from guide books to Ordnance Survey maps, from county records to English novels—to present a complex representation of place. He concludes with an ethnographic reading of "improvement" that reveals how local ideas of restoration and planning are imagined to oppose other notions of modernization.

In his afterword to the book, Clifford Geertz reflects on some issues our ethnographies of place entail. First, because place "makes a poor abstraction," exploring its local specificities and resonances is likely to prove more fruitful than searching for common denominators. Second, and parallel to the first, no matter how strongly current world conditions argue for the primacy of places as sites of power struggles and disaggregation, senses of place are "barely diminished in the modern world." Indeed, displacement is no less the source of powerful attachments than are experiences of profound rootedness. And last, in a phrase thick enough to serve as this volume's epigraph and bumper sticker, "no one lives in the world in general." What could be truer of placed experience—secure or fragile, pleasurable or repugnant, comforting or unsettling—than the taken-for-granted quality of its intense particularity?

Senses of place: the terrain covered here includes the relation of sensation to emplacement; the experiential and expressive ways places are known, imagined, yearned for, held, remembered, voiced, lived, contested, and struggled over; and the multiple ways places are metonymically and metaphorically tied to identities. We begin by asking how people are dwelling and how ethnographic accounts of their modes of dwelling might enrich our sense of why places, however vague, are lived out in deeply meaningful ways.

Forging an intellectual path of their own alongside humanistic and critical postmodern tendencies, these essays reveal that as people fashion places, so, too, do they fashion themselves. People don't just dwell in comfort or misery, in centers or margins, in place or out of place, empowered or disempowered. People everywhere act on the integrity of their dwelling. Thus, allegories that inform and guide the conduct of wayward Apaches, puzzled songs and refigured gender positions flowing from waterfalls in a Papuan rainforest, aggravated lives in the West Virginia hollers, anthropologists and locals embracing each other's homesickness in Papua New Guinea, remembered fables and hegemonic accomodations in multiethnic North Carolina, protection societies and leaving the right things off of maps in rural East Anglia—all these are as instructive for geographies of disruption and contestation as for histories of creativity and resilience. Whether they are embedded in discourses of sensuous beauty or ugliness (Feld and Stewart), in discourses of morality and theft (Basso and Blu), or in discourses of nostalgia and longing (Kahn and Frake), struggles arising from loss and desires for control are always placed. Our essays find those placements in cartographies mapped, sung, or storied, in environments piled high in trash or meticulously hedged, in local knowledge of well-attended paths or roads made vague by having no names or too many, and in the voicings of deep aphorism, memorial poesis, heated backtalk, letters from home, speeches with choked-back tears, humorous quips, true-to-life fictions, and what goes without saying.

1

How to Get from Space to Place in a Fairly Short Stretch of Time

Phenomenological Prolegomena
Edward S. Casey

All existing things are either in place or not without place.
— *Archytas, as cited by Simplicius*

The power of place will be remarkable.
— *Aristotle*, Physics, Book IV

Space is a society of named places.
— *Claude Lévi-Strauss*, The Savage Mind

Nothing could extinguish the fact and claim of estate.
— *W. E. H. Stanner, "Aboriginal Territorial Organization"*

It is sensible, perhaps even irresistible, to assume that human experience begins with space and time and then proceeds to place. Are not space and time universal in scope, and place merely particular? Can place do anything but specify what is already the case in space and time? Or might it be that place is something special, with its own essential structures and modes of experience, even something universal in its own way?

These are questions I shall address in this chapter, and I will do so by way of phenomenology. The insistently descriptive character of the phenomenological enterprise in philosophy rejoins the emphasis in anthropology on precise description in the field (which has never prevented considerable speculation in the chair!). There is much more that could be said about the convergence of anthropology and phenomenology, but in the limitations of this essay I shall attempt only to show how phenomenology as I practice it treats the question of place; anthropological implications will be adumbrated but nowhere fully pursued.

Phenomenology began as a critique of what Husserl called the "natural attitude," that is, what is taken for granted in a culture that has been influenced predominantly by modern science — or, more precisely, by scientism and its many offshoots in materialism, naturalism, psychologism, and so forth. (And anthropologism: in the Prolegomena to his *Logical Investigations* [1970], Husserl addresses "transcendental anthropologism.")

One belief endemic to the natural attitude concerns the way places relate to what is commonly called "space." Once it is assumed (after Newton and Kant) that space is absolute and infinite as well as empty and a priori in status, places become the mere apportionings of space, its compartmentalizations.

Indeed, that places are the determinations of an already existing monolith of Space has become an article of scientific faith, so much so that two recent books in anthropology that bear expressly on place—both quite valuable works in many regards—espouse the view that place is something *posterior to space,* even *made from space.* By "space" is meant a neutral, pre-given medium, a tabula rasa onto which the particularities of culture and history come to be inscribed, with place as the presumed result. We find this view, for example, in James F. Weiner's richly suggestive ethnography of the Foi of Papua New Guinea, *The Empty Place:* "A society's place names schematically image a people's intentional transformation of their habitat from a sheer physical terrain into a pattern of historically experienced and constituted space and time. . . . The bestowing of place names constitutes Foi existential space out of a blank environment" (Weiner 1991:32).

The idea of transformation from a "sheer physical terrain" and the making of "existential space"—which is to say, place—out of a "blank environment" entails that to begin with there is some empty and innocent spatial spread, waiting, as it were, for cultural configurations to render it placeful. But when does this "to begin with" exist? And where is it located? Answers to both questions will generate a vicious regress of the kind at stake in Kant's first antinomy: to search for a first moment in either time or space is to incur shipwreck on the shoals of Pure Reason.[1]

Or consider the following claim from Fred R. Myers's otherwise remarkable ethnography of desert aboriginal people of Central Australia, *Pintupi Country, Pintupi Self:* "The process by which space becomes 'country,' by which a story gets attached to an object, is part of the Pintupi habit of mind that looks behind objects to events and sees in objects a sign of something else" (Myers 1991:67). Here we are led to ask, What are these "objects" behind which events lurk and to which stories get attached? The neutrality of the term *object* suggests that the first-order items in the universe are denuded things—denuded of the very "secondary qualities" (in the demeaning term of Galilean-Cartesian-Lockian discourse) that would make them fit subjects of events and stories. We wonder, further, what is this "process by which space becomes 'country,'" by which space is "culturalized," and by which "impersonal geography" becomes "a home, a *ngurra*" (Myers 1991:54).[2]

Myers intimates that all such transformations are a matter of the "projection"—or, alternatively, of the "reproduction"—of determinate social actions and structures. "Country" is the system of significant places as specified by the Dreaming, which represents "a projection into symbolic space of various social processes" (Myers 1991:47). And the structure of the Dreaming in turn—a structure isomorphic with the landscape of the country—is "a product of the way Pintupi society reproduces itself in space and time" (Myers 1991:48). The phrase "in space and time" is telling: the reproduction is in some preexisting medium. Having no inherent configurations of its own, this presumptively empty medium must be populated after the fact (but the fact of what? what fact?) by processes that impute to empty space the particularities that belong to the Dreaming. Generality, albeit empty, belongs to space; particularity, albeit mythic, belongs to place; and the twain meet only by an appeal to a procedure of superimposition that is invoked ex post facto.

But the Pintupi themselves think otherwise, as Myers himself avers: "To the Pintupi, then, a place itself with its multiple features is logically prior or central" (Myers 1991:59). Whom are we to believe? The theorizing anthropologist, the arsenal of his natural attitude bristling with explanatory projectiles that go off into space? Or the aborigine on the ground who finds this ground itself to be a coherent collocation of pre-given places—pre-given at once in his experience and in the Dreaming that sanctions this experience? For the anthropologist, Space comes first; for the native, Place; and the difference is by no means trivial.

It is not, of course, simply a matter of choosing between the anthropologist's vantage point and that of the natives—as if the Pintupi had chosen to participate in a debate on the comparative primacy of space versus place. Nor is any such primacy Myers's own express concern. As an anthropologist in the field, his task is not to argue for space over against place but to set forth as accurately as possible what being-in-place means to the Pintupi. Just there, however, is the rub: even when treating a culture for which place is manifestly paramount, the anthropologist leans on a concept that obscures what is peculiar to place and that (by an implicit cultural fiat) even implies its secondariness. The anthropologist's theoretical discourse—in which the priority of space over place is virtually axiomatic—runs athwart his descriptive commitment.

The question is not so much *whom* we are to believe—both anthropologist and natives are trustworthy enough—but *what* we are to believe. Are we to believe that human experience starts from a mute and blank "space" to which placial modifiers such as "near," "over there," "along that way," and "just here" are added, sooner or later: presumably sooner in perception and later in culture? Or are we to believe that the world comes configured in odd protuberances, in runs, rills, and flats, in *fele* and *do:m,* as the Kaluli might put it (Feld, this volume)—all of which are traits of places? (Ironically, in this view flatness and, more generally, "featurelessness" belong to place to begin with.)

I take the second view as just stated to be both more accurate as a description and more valuable as a heuristic in the understanding of place. In doing so, I join not only the Pintupi and the Kaluli but also certain early and late figures in Western thought. Both Archytas and Aristotle proclaimed that place is prior to space, and, more recently, Bachelard and Heidegger have reembraced the conviction. All four thinkers subscribe to what could be called the Archytian Axiom: "Place is the first of all things."[3] In between the ancients and the postmoderns there was a period of preoccupation with space—as well as with time, conceived of as space's cosmic partner. But how may we retrieve a sense of the priority of place by means other than arguing from authority (as I have just done in citing certain congenial Western thinkers) or arguing against authority (as occurs when modern science is pilloried, which Husserl does in attacking the natural attitude)?

My suggestion is that we can retrieve such a sense by considering what a phenomenological approach to place might tell us. Even if such an approach is not without its own prejudicial commitments and ethnocentric stances, it is an approach that, in its devotion to concrete description, has the advantage of honoring the actual experience of those who practice it. In this regard it rejoins not only the anthropologist in the field but the native on the land: both have no choice but to begin with experience. As Kant insisted, "there can be no doubt that all our knowledge begins with experience" (1950 [1787]: B1).

For Kant, *to begin with* means *to be instigated by.* Thus he must add the qualification that "though all our knowledge begins with experience, it does not follow that it all arises out of experience" (Kant 1950 [1787]: B1). Knowledge of any rigorous sort does not *derive from* experience. Kant makes this perfectly clear in his *Anthropology from a Pragmatic Point of View,* arguably the first theoretical treatise on anthropology in the West: "General knowledge must always precede local knowledge . . . [because] without [general knowledge], all acquired knowledge can only be a fragmentary experiment and not a science."[4] This paradigmatic Enlightenment statement sets the stage—indeed, still holds the stage in many ways —for the idea that space precedes place. Space, being the most pervasive of cosmic media, is considered that about which we must have general knowledge, whereas we possess merely local knowledge about place.

But what if things are the other way around? What if the very idea of space is posterior to that of place, perhaps even derived from it? What if local knowledge—which, in Geertz's appropriately pleonastic

locution, "presents locally to locals a local turn of mind" (1983:12) —
precedes knowledge of space? Could place be general and "space" particular? Phenomenology not only moves us to ask these impertinent anti-
Enlightenment questions but also provides reasons for believing that the
answers to them are affirmative.

In a phenomenological account, the crux in matters of place is the
role of perception. Is it the case, as Kant believes (along with most modern epistemologists), that perception provides those bare starting-points
called variously "sensations," "sense data," "impressions," and so forth? Or
is something else at work in perception that conveys more about place
than mere sensory signals can ever effect? It is certainly true—and this
is what Kant emphasizes in the idea of "beginning with"—that sensory
inputs are the *occasions* of the perception (eventually the knowledge) of
concrete places. These impingements—as connoted in the term *Empfin-
dungen,* Kant's word for "sensations"—alert us to the fact that we are
perceiving, and they convey certain of the very qualities (including the
secondary qualities) of the surfaces of what we perceive. But their poin-
tillistic character ill equips them for supplying anything like the sense
of *being in a place.* Yet we do always find ourselves in places. We find
ourselves in them, however different the places themselves may be and
however differently we construe and exploit them. But how do we grasp
this *in* of being in a particular place: this preposition which is literally a
"pre-position" inasmuch as we are always already in a place, never not
emplaced in one way or another?[5]

If perception is "primary" (as both Husserl and Merleau-Ponty insist), then a significant part of its primariness must be its ability to give
to us more than bits of information about the phenomenal and epiphenomenal surfaces of things—and more, too, than a conviction that
we are merely in the presence of these surfaces. Beyond what Husserl
calls the "hyletic" factor, and Merleau-Ponty, "sensing," there must be, as
an ingredient in perception from the start, a conveyance of what being
in places is all about. Merleau-Ponty considers this conveyance to be
depth—a "primordial depth" that, far from being imputed to sensations
(as Berkeley [1934], for example, had held), already situates them in a
scene of which we ourselves form part. Husserl's way of putting it is
that "every experience has its own horizon" and that we continually find
ourselves in the midst of perceptual horizons, both the "internal" horizons of particular things (i.e., their immediate circumambience) and the
"external" horizons that encompass a given scene as a whole.[6]

But precisely as surrounded by depths and horizons, the perceiver
finds herself in the midst of an entire teeming place-world rather than in
a confusing kaleidoscope of free-floating sensory data. The coherence of

perception at the primary level is supplied by the depth and horizons of the *very place* we occupy as sentient subjects. That is why we can trust this coherence with what Santayana (1955) called "animal faith," and Husserl (1982: section 103), "primal belief (*protodoxa*)." We come to the world—we come into it and keep returning to it—as already placed there. Places are not added to sensations any more than they are imposed on spaces. Both sensations and spaces are themselves emplaced from the very first moment, and at every subsequent moment as well.

There is no knowing or sensing a place except by being in that place, and to be in a place is to be in a position to perceive it. Knowledge of place is not, then, subsequent to perception—as Kant dogmatically assumed—but is ingredient in perception itself. Such knowledge, genuinely local knowledge, is itself experiential in the manner of *Erlebnis*, "lived experience," rather than of *Erfahrung*, the already elapsed experience that is the object of analytical or abstract knowledge. (Kant, significantly, speaks only of *Erfahrung*.) Local knowledge is at one with lived experience if it is indeed true that this knowledge is of the localities in which the knowing subject lives. To live is to live locally, and to know is first of all to know the places one is in.

I am not proposing a merely mute level of experience that passively receives simple and senseless data of place. Perception at the primary level is synesthetic—an affair of the whole body sensing and moving. Thanks to its inherent complexity, bodily perceiving is directed at (and is adequate to) things and places that come configured, often in highly complicated ways. Moreover, the configuration and complication are already meaningful and not something internally registered as sensory givens that lack any sense of their own: the sensory is senseful. Nor does the inherent meaningfulness of what we perceive require the infusion of determinate concepts located higher up the epistemic ladder. The perceived possesses a core of immanent sense, a "noematic nucleus" in Husserl's technical term (1982: section 91). Because this senseful core is actively grasped, it follows that perception is never entirely a matter of what Kant calls "receptivity," as if the perceiving subject were merely passive. Not only is primary perception inseparable from myriad modes of concrete action, but it is itself "a kind of *passivity in activity*" (Husserl 1973:108; his italics). To perceive synesthetically is to be actively passive; it is to be absorptive yet constitutive, both at once.

It is also to be *constituted*: constituted by cultural and social structures that sediment themselves into the deepest level of perception. The primacy of perception does not mean that human sensing and moving are precultural or presocial. No more than perception is built up from atomic sensations is it constructed from brute givens unaffected by cultural practices and social institutions. On the contrary: these practices and institutions pervade every level of perception, from the quite implicit (e.g., tacitly grasped outer horizons) to the extremely explicit (e.g., the thematic thing perceived). The permeation occurs even—indeed, especially—when a given perception is preconceptual and prediscursive. To be not yet articulated in concept or word is not to be nonculturally constituted, much less free from social constraints. Hence, the primacy of perception does not entail the priority of perception to the givens of culture or society, as if the latter were separable contents of our being and experience: these givens become infusions into the infrastructures of perception itself. The primacy of perception is ultimately a primacy of the lived body—a body that, as we shall see in more detail later, is a creature of habitual cultural and social processes.

But perception remains as *constitutive* as it is constituted. This is especially evident when we perceive places: our immersion in them is not subjection to them, since we may modify their influence even as we submit to it. This influence is as meaningful as it is sensuous. Not only is the sensuous senseful, it is also placeful. As Feld (this volume) puts it, "as place is sensed, senses are placed; as places make sense, senses make place." The dialectic of perception and place (and of both with meaning) is as intricate as it is profound, and it is never-ending.

Given that we are never without perception, the existence of this dialectic means that we are never without emplaced experiences. It signifies as well that we are not only *in* places but *of* them. Human beings—along with other entities on earth—are ineluctably place-bound. More even than earthlings, we are placelings, and our very perceptual apparatus, our sensing body, reflects the kinds of places we inhabit. The ongoing reliability and general veracity of perception (a reliability and veracity that countenance considerable experiential vicissitudes) entail a continual attunement to place (also experienced in open-ended variation). But if this is true, it suggests that place, rather than being a mere product or portion of space, is as primary as the perception that gives access to it. Also suggested is the heretical—and quite ancient—thought that place, far from being something simply singular, is something general, perhaps even universal: a thought to which we shall return.

> Nature makes itself specific.
> —*Kant,* The Critique of Judgment

It is characteristic of the modern Western mind to conceive of space in terms of its formal essence—hence the insistent search for mathematical expressions of pure spatial relations. For Newton, More, Gassendi,

Descartes, and Galileo, space was homogeneous, isotropic, isometric, and infinitely (or, at least, indefinitely) extended. Within the supremely indifferent and formal scene of space, local differences did not matter. Place itself did not matter. It was not for nothing that Descartes proposed in his *Principles of Philosophy* that matter and space were the same thing—which meant that space had no qualities not present in matter, whose own primary property was a metrically determinable pure extension. Place was simply a creature of such extension, either its mere subdivision ("internal place" or volume) or a relationally specified location in it ("position").[7] In his *Mathematical Principles of Natural Philosophy*, Newton still recognized "absolute" and "relative" places, but both kinds of places were only "portions" of absolute space, which was where all the action (e.g., gravitational action) was to be found. On the basis of absolute space, places were apportioned and mapped out: just there is the conceptual root of the paralogism I detect in certain recent anthropological treatments of place and space.

In this early modern paradigm shift, there was little space for place as a valid concept in its own right. As a result, place was disempowered: all the power now resided in space—and in time, the second colossal concern of modern thought. Although time was held to have direction, it was as essentially devoid of content as was space. A century after Newton described space and time as "God's infinite sensoria," Kant considered them to be "pure forms of intuition" located within the finite human subject. By this act of internalization, Kant sealed the fate of place even more drastically: at most, the human subject had "position" in the space and time of its own making. But place was of almost no concern in the *Critique of Pure Reason*.[8]

One way to avoid the high road of modernism as it stretches from the abstract physics of Newton to the critical philosophy of Kant and beyond is to reoccupy the low land of place. For place can be considered either premodern or postmodern; it serves to connect these two far sides of modernity. To reinstate place in the wake of its demise in modern Western thought—where space and time have held such triumphant and exclusive sway—one can equally well go to the premodern moments described in ethnographic accounts of traditional societies or to the postmodern moment of the increasingly nontraditional present, where place has been returning as a reinvigorated *revenant* in the writings of ecologists and landscape theorists, geographers and historians, sociologists and political thinkers—and now, in this volume, anthropologists.

> Do we not sense from the outset a certain difference, by virtue of which *locality belongs to me somewhat more essentially* [than, for example, size and weight]? . . . Men and animals are *spatially localized;* and even what is psychic about them, at least in virtue of its essential foundedness in what is bodily, partakes of the spatial order.
> —*Husserl,* Ideas Pertaining to a Pure Phenomenology and to a Phenomenological Philosophy, *Second Book; his italics*

How, then, do we get back into place? In the very way by which we are always already there—by *our own lived body.* Ironically, Kant was the first Western thinker to point to the importance of bodily structure for emplacement. In his remarkable precritical essay of 1768, "On the First Ground of the Distinction of Material Regions in Space," he argued that the two-sidedness—especially the two-handedness—of the human body was essential for orientation in "cosmic regions" of surrounding sky or earth:

> Even our judgments about the cosmic regions are subordinated to the concept we have of regions in general, insofar as they are determined in relation to the sides of the body. . . . However well I know the order of the cardinal points, I can determine regions according to that order only insofar as I know towards which hand this order proceeds. . . . Similarly, our geographical knowledge, and even our commonest knowledge of the position of places, would be of no aid to us if we could not, by reference to the sides of our bodies, assign to regions the things so ordered and the whole system of mutually relative positions. (Kant 1928 [1768]: 22–23)[9]

The bilateral body is singled out, then, just when it is a question of orientation in *regions (Gegenden),* where places are concatenated in formations that resist the ascription of pinpointed location. Could it be that the body is *essentially,* and not just contingently, involved in matters of emplacement?

Kant's prescient observations about the body in its basic bilaterality anticipated and complemented Robert Hertz's brilliant speculations on the cultural significance of right- versus left-handedness (Hertz 1973 [1909]: 3–31) Both Kant and Hertz subscribed, tacitly if not explicitly, to a more general principle: that the human body's brachiated and multiply articulated structure renders it a uniquely valuable vehicle in the establishment of place. Precisely by allowing us to make a diverse entry into a given place—through hands and feet, knees and hips, elbows and shoulders—the body insinuates itself subtly and multiply into encompassing regions. If the body were an inert and intact thing with no moving parts, a fleshly monolith, it could be grasped as something sheerly physical that is punctually located at a given position in space and does not reach out farther. This is how Galileo construed *all* bodies: as inert, non-self-moving entities submitting to the laws of gravitation and motion.

But once a *Körper* (body as physical object) has become a *Leib* (body as lived)—once there is resurrection in the body, as it were—more than merely punctiform positioning in empty space (and at an equally stigmatic moment in time) is at stake. This is what Kant discovered—and then quickly forgot. It is also what Husserl and Hertz rediscovered a century and a half later.

The several members of a lived body move not randomly but by what Merleau-Ponty calls "corporeal intentionality." Thanks to this intentionality, the lived body integrates itself with its immediate environment, that is to say, its concrete place. The integration is effected by various "intentional threads" that bind body and place in a common complex of relations.[10] But none of this pervasive integumentation between body and place would be possible without the freely moving members of the body as it situates itself in a particular place, remembers itself in that place, and so forth. The lived body—the body living (in) a place—is thus "the natural subject of perception" (Merleau-Ponty 1962:208). The experience of perceiving that I discussed earlier requires a corporeal subject who lives *in* a place *through* perception. It also requires a place that is amenable to this body-subject and that extends its own influence back onto this subject. A place, we might even say, has its own "operative intentionality" that elicits and responds to the corporeal intentionality of the perceiving subject. Thus place integrates with body as much as body with place. It is a matter of what Basso calls "interanimation."[11]

Other aspects of the lived body are at stake in being-in-place, each of them specifying further what first caught Kant's keen eye. First, various kinesthesias and synesthesias—as well as sonesthesias, as Feld insists in this volume—allow bodily self-motion to be registered and enriched, ultimately constituting what Husserl terms the "aesthesiological body." This body itself serves as a "field of localization" for the manifold sensuous presentations (including sonorous ones) that stem from a particular place but are registered by (or with) a lived body that finds itself in that place.[12] Second, immanent bodily dimensionalities of up/down, front/back, right/left—explicitly recognized by Kant, who was inclined, however, to reduce them to the three Cartesian coordinates—help to connect body with the placial settings of these same three dyads.[13]

Third, the concreteness of a lived body, its density and mass, answers to the thick concreteness of a given place, but the difference between the two concretions is just as critical because it sets up a "coefficient of adversity" (Sartre 1965:590) that makes ordinary perception itself possible. Fourth, a given lived body and a given experienced place tend to present themselves as particular: as just this body in just this place. Each thus actively partakes in the "this-here"—which does not, however, exclude significant variations, ranging from bi-gendered to bi-located bodies.[14] And fifth, the porosity of the skin of an organic body rejoins, even as it mimics, the openness of the boundaries of places; there is a fleshlike, pneumatic structure shared in a common "flesh of the world."[15] Were the body a windowless monad, it could neither negotiate the varieties nor grasp the valences of the places in which it found itself. And these same places have to have their own windows if the body is to enter them in turn.

In addition to these five factors, we need to recognize the crucial interaction between body, place, and *motion*. A given place may certainly be perduring and consistent, but this does not mean that it is simply something inactive and at rest—as is all too often assumed. Part of the power of place, its very dynamism, is found in its encouragement of motion in its midst, its "e-motive" (and often explicitly emotional) thrust. Indeed, we may distinguish among three kinds of bodily motion pertinent to place. The first and most limited case is *staying in place.* Here the body remains in place, in one single place. Yet such a body in such a situation is never entirely stationary except in extreme circumstances of paralysis or rigor mortis. Even when staying in place, the body changes the position of some of its parts, however modestly: moving its limbs, rotating its head, twiddling its thumbs. The body twitches in place. Moreover, an unmoving body may still move if it is transported by another moving body: the driver of a car, the rider on horseback. Toynbee remarks that Bedouins riding on horses "move by not moving."[16] We might say that the body of the Bedouin stays in one position, yet the locus of this position—where "locus" signifies a position in its capacity to change places in space—itself changes as the mount moves between different places.[17]

The second case, *moving within a place,* is the circumstance in which I move my whole body about a given place while still remaining in it. Insofar as I am typing this manuscript, I am in one position; but when I get up to pace, I move around in the room I am in. I move within a circumscribed "space" defined by the walls of the room. The whole body moves in the whole room. Similarly, much ceremonial action is taken by bodies moving in set ways within entire prescribed places: kivas, plazas, longhouses, temples.

Finally, *moving between places* denotes the circumstance in which bodies travel between different places. No longer is movement circumscribed by the restrictions of a single position or one place; now it ranges among a number of places. In this case, the motion is a genuine transition and not just a transportation.[18] The most salient instance is the journey, and cases in point are emigrations, pilgrimages, voyages of exchange, and nomadic circulations. In all of these, the bodies of the journeyers follow more or less preordained routes between particular places: for example, the pilgrimage route to Santiago de Compostela as it connects various interim places throughout western Europe. The body's active role is most evident in the literal legwork of circumambulations and other forms of peregrination, but it is no less present in the building of homesteads in the land of emigration or in the setting up of temporary nomadic encampments. Just as staying in place corresponds to *position,* and moving the whole body within one locus answers to *place* proper, so moving between places corresponds to an entire *region,* that is, an area concatenated by peregrinations between the places it connects.

There is much more to be said about the role of the body in place, especially about how places actively solicit bodily motions. At the very least, we can agree that the living-moving body is essential to the process of emplacement: *lived bodies belong to places* and help to constitute them. Even if such bodies may be displaced in certain respects, they are never placeless; they are never *only* at discrete positions in world time or space, though they may *also* be at such positions. By the same token, however, *places belong to lived bodies* and depend on them. If it is true that "the body is our general medium for having a world" (Merleau-Ponty 1962:146), it ensues that the body is the specific medium for experiencing a place-world. The lived body is the material condition of possibility for the place-world while being itself a member of that same world. It is basic to place and part of place. Just as there are no places without the bodies that sustain and vivify them, so there are no lived bodies without the places they inhabit and traverse. (Even imaginary places bring with them virtual bodies—"subtle bodies" in an earlier nomenclature.) Bodies and places are connatural terms. They interanimate each other.

> We may suggest that the day will come when we will not shun the question whether the opening, the free open, may not be that within which alone pure space and ecstatic time and everything present and absent in them have the place which gathers and protects everything.
> —Heidegger, *"The End of Philosophy and the Task of Thinking"*

Places gather: this I take to be a second essential trait (i.e., beyond the role of the lived body) revealed by a phenomenological topoanalysis. Minimally, places gather things in their midst—where "things" connote various animate and inanimate entities. Places also gather experiences and histories, even languages and thoughts. Think only of what it means to go back to a place you know, finding it full of memories and expectations, old things and new things, the familiar and the strange, and much more besides. What else is capable of this massively diversified holding action? Certainly not individual human subjects construed as sources of "projection" or "reproduction"—not even these subjects as they draw upon their bodily and perceptual powers. The power belongs to place itself, and it is a power of gathering.

By "gathering" I do not mean merely amassing. To gather placewise is to have a peculiar hold on what is presented (as well as represented) in a given place. Not just the contents but the very mode of containment is held by a place. "The hold is held."[19] The hold of place, its gathering action, is held in quite special ways. First, it is a holding *together* in a particular configuration: hence our sense of an ordered arrangement of things in a place even when those things are radically disparate and quite conflictual. The arrangement allows for certain things—people, ideas, and so forth—to overlap with, and sometimes to occlude, others as they recede or come forward together. Second, the hold is a holding *in* and a holding *out*. It retains the occupants of a place within its boundaries: if they were utterly to vanish and the place to be permanently empty, it would be no place at all but a void. But, equally, a place holds out, beckoning to its inhabitants and, assembling them, making them manifest (though not necessarily manifest to each other, or to the same degree). It can move place-holders toward the margins of its own presentation while, nevertheless, holding them within its own ambiance.

Third, the holding at issue in the gathering of a place reflects the layout of the local landscape, its continuous contour, even as the outlines and inlines of the things held in that place are respected. The result is not confusion of container with contained but a literal *con*figuration in which the form of the place—for example, "mountain," "mesa," "gulley"—joins up with the shapes of the things in it. Being in a place is being in a configurative complex of things. Fourth, intrinsic to the holding operation of place is *keeping*. What is kept in place primarily are experiencing bodies regarded as privileged residents rather than as orchestrating forces (much less as mere registrants). My body-in-place is less the *metteur en scène* than itself *mise en scène*—or rather, it is both at once, "passivity in activity" (Husserl 1973).

And last, places also keep such unbodylike entities as thoughts and memories. When I revisit my hometown of Topeka, Kansas, I find this place more or less securely holding memories for me. In my presence, it releases these memories, which belong as much to the place as to my brain or body. This kind of keeping is especially pertinent to an intensely gathered landscape such as that of aboriginal Australia—a landscape that holds ancestral memories of the Dreaming. Yet even when I recall people and things and circumstances in an ordinary place, I have the sense that these various recollecta have been kept securely in place, harbored there, as it were.[20]

Gathering gives to place its peculiar perduringness, allowing us to return to it again and again as *the same place* and not just as the same position or site.[21] For a place, in its dynamism, does not age in a systematically changing way, that is, in accordance with a preestablished schedule of growth and decline; only its tenants and visitors, enactors and witnesses (including myself and others in these various roles) age and grow old in this way. A place is generative and regenerative on its own schedule. From it experiences are born and to it human beings (and other organisms) return for empowerment, much like Antaeus touching the earth for renewed strength. Place is the generatrix for the collection, as well as the recollection, of all that occurs in the lives of sentient beings, and even for the trajectories of inanimate things. Its power consists in gathering these lives and things, each with its own space and time, into one arena of common engagement.

> Husserl's essences are destined to bring back all the living relationships of experience, as the fisherman's net draws up from the depths of the ocean quivering fish and seaweed.
> —*Merleau-Ponty,* Phenomenology of Perception

It should be clear by now that I do not take place to be something simply physical. A place is not a mere patch of ground, a bare stretch of earth, a sedentary set of stones. What kind of thing is it then? The "what is" locution—Aristotle's *ti esti* question—combined with "kind of" suggests that there is some single sort of thing that place is, some archetype of Place. But whatever place is, it is not the kind of thing that can be subsumed under already given universal notions—for example, of space and time, substance or causality. A given place may not permit, indeed it often defies, subsumption under given categories. Instead, a place is something for which we continually have to discover or invent new forms of understanding, new concepts in the literal sense of ways of "grasping-together."

A place is more an *event* than a *thing* to be assimilated to known categories. As an event, it is unique, idiolocal. Its peculiarity calls not for assumption into the already known—that way lies site, which lends itself to predefined predications, uses, and interpretations—but for the imaginative constitution of terms respecting its idiolocality (these range from placenames to whole discourses). The "kind" at stake in "kind of" is neither a genus nor a species, that is, a determinate concept that rules *over* its instances, but something operating *across* margins, laterally, by means of homology or similitude. Yet place qua kind remains something specific inasmuch as it alters in keeping with its own changing constituents. The kind in question, the answer pertinent to the "what is" question, is more a *type* or a *style* than a pure concept or formal universal. While such a concept or universal is fixed in definition (if not always in application), a type or style connotes an open manifoldness, a unity-in-diversity, and not a self-identical unity. Further, a type or style admits of degrees — so sensitively that a change of a few degrees may bring with it a change in identity, as when analytical Cubism gave way imperceptibly but suddenly to synthetic Cubism.

In the case of place, then, the kind is itself *kind of something,* rather than a definite sort of something. This is why we speak of places in phrases like "a clean well-lit place," "a place for recovering one's sanity," "a Southwestern landscape," or "a Southern plantation." The indefinite article employed in these locutions bespeaks the indefiniteness of the kind of thing a place or region is. Such indefiniteness — not to be confused with indeterminacy, much less with chaos — is in no way incompatible with the ostensive definiteness of demonstrative pronouns and adverbial locatives, that is, those "essentially occasional expressions" that are so frequently used to refer to particular places or regions: "just here," "in this place," and so forth. I would even say that the open-endedness of place, its typological status as morphologically vague, its *de*-finition, creates the semantic space within which definite demonstrations and exact localizations can arise.[22]

Rather than being one definite sort of thing — for example, physical, spiritual, cultural, social — a given place takes on the qualities of its occupants, reflecting these qualities in its own constitution and description and expressing them in its occurrence as an event: places not only *are,* they *happen.* (And it is because they happen that they lend themselves so well to narration, whether as history or as story.) Just as a particular place is at least several kinds of things, so there are many sorts of places and not one basic kind only — one supposedly supreme genus. Sorts of places depend on the kinds of things, as well as the actual things, that make them up. A biochore or biotope directly reflects the character of its constituents, that is, its soils and flora and fauna; an agora is qualified by the people who pass through it or linger there; a dwelling is characterized less by its architecture than by the quality of the life that is sustained in it. If, as Wallace Stevens put it, "a mythology reflects its region", then a region reflects both what is held together there (its "contents," its co-tenants) and how it is so held.

A place or region is metaphysically neutral inasmuch as it does not possess some given substrate, a "ground" that would be metaphysically definite enough to determine the place or region as just one kind of entity. And if there is no such preexisting ground, then the model of adding successive strata of meaning (added by cultures or minds, actions or words) is of dubious application.[23] Even to call such a putative ground "the earth" is already to regionalize, or rather to geologize, at the most basic level. The fact is that there is not any "most basic level" to be presumed as simply there, "*einfach da*," as Husserl says of objects that are posited by the positivism of the natural attitude (Husserl 1982: section 27). Stripping away cultural or linguistic accretions, we shall never find a pure place lying underneath—and still less an even purer Space or Time. What we will find are continuous and changing qualifications of particular places: places qualified by their own contents, and qualified as well by the various ways these contents are articulated (denoted, described, discussed, narrated, and so forth) in a given culture. We designate particular places by the place terms of the culture to which we as place designators and place dwellers belong, but the places we designate are not bare substrates to which these terms are attached as if to an unadorned bedrock. They are named or nameable parts of the landscape of a region, its condensed and lived physiognomy.[24]

The power of place consists in its nontendentious ability to reflect the most diverse items that constitute its "midst." In many regards, a place *is* its midst, being in the midst of its own detailed contents; it is what lies most deeply amid its own constituents, gathering them together in the expressive landscape of that place. No mind could effect such gathering, and the body, though necessary to its attainment, requires the holding and keeping actions native to the place it is in.[25]

> Truths involve universals, and all knowledge of truths involves acquaintance with universals.
> — *Bertrand Russell*, The Problems of Philosophy

Thus we are led back to a question that was posed at the beginning of this essay: Is place a universal? Here we are inclined to ask in a skeptical vein, How can the epitome of the local be a matter of the general? What kind of generality can place possess? What sort of universal might it be? Indeed, how could it be a universal at all in face of the enormous diversity of places which anthropology, more than any other discipline, brings to our attention? Does not all this diversity make the search for sameness a futile and misguided effort?

In *Aspects of the Theory of Syntax,* Chomsky (1965) distinguishes between "formal" and "substantive" universals. Substantive universals are fixed in character and delimited in number: for example, Jakobson's list of the distinctive features whose various combinations determine the phonological component of given natural languages, or the Port-Royal syntactic categories of Noun, Verb, and so forth. Formal universals, in contrast, specify the abstract conditions of possibility for the pervasive structures of any and every natural language: for example, the condition that proper names must designate objects that are spatiotemporally contiguous or that color words have to divide up the color spectrum into continuous parts with no gaps (see Chomsky 1965:27–30).

The choice here proffered by Chomsky is pertinent to place, but only by dint of calling the choice itself into question. On the one hand, place is something like a formal universal in that it functions like a general feature, even a condition of possibility, of all human (and doubtless all animal and plant) experience—however expansive the term "experience" is taken to be. On the other hand, place is also a quite distinctive feature of such experience. Place is not a purely formal operator empty of content but is always contentful, always specifiable as this particular place or that one. And if *both* things are true of place, if it is both formally true of every experience and true to each particular experience, then any rigid distinction between formal and substantive universals will dissolve before our very eyes. The deconstruction of this distinction will already be effected by the character of place itself, by its inherent generative force. For in the end, place is neither formal (place is not a condition *of* but a force *for*) nor substantive (there is not a fixed number of places in the universe, or of particular features or kinds of places).

This allows us to ask: Is the *only* choice that between "bloodless universals" and "substantive identities" (Geertz 1973:43–44)? Is not the aim, in anthropology as in any philosophy that is sensitive to the differences different cultures make, to discover genuine concrete universals, that is, structures that are at once elastic enough to be exemplified in disparate cultures yet also taut enough to be discernibly different from each other in content or definition? An example would be funeral practices, which are observed by all known cultures yet which differ dramatically from culture to culture. The marking of death and the remarking of the life that preceded it is concretely universal, though the modes of marking and remarking are tangibly diverse. A concrete universal of this sort is neither so adamantine as to be indifferent to its instantiations nor so purely reflective as to be the indifferent mirroring of any and every cultural difference: neither form of indifference does justice to the actual difference which the embodiment of a concrete universal introduces. As Hegel insisted, a concrete universal is operative in contingent circumstances and has no life apart from those circumstances. Let us say that it is endoskeletal to what happens in a given time and place and yet sufficiently generic to be immanent to occurrences in other times and places (not just by homology but by actual ingredience).

Does this mean that the kind of universal at stake in place is nothing but an "empirical commonality," that which just happens to be the case in several or even many times and places?[26] No: the empirically common comes down to statistical frequency or contingent overlap and fails to capture what is shared by members of a class of things that all possess some genuinely generic trait (whether this be an action, a quality, a relation, or some other characteristic). While manifested in the "special world" (*idios kosmos*, as the ancient Greeks would say) of a particular place and time, the shared trait nevertheless belongs to the "common world" (*koinos kosmos*) of authentic concrete universals. Such a bivalent universal, belonging both to special worlds and to a common world, serves to relate items that would otherwise be a mere congeries of terms that, at most, resemble each other. It is thus a *relational* universal that consists in its very capacity to assemble things as well as kinds of things.

Thus we might well agree with Bertrand Russell (1912:152) that a relational universal is "neither in space nor in time, neither material nor mental," yet "it is [still] something." But what kind of something is it? If it manages not to be in space or time, can it nevertheless be in place? I would hazard that the kind of universal most relevant to a philosophically informed anthropology of place is at once concrete and relational—concrete *as* relational (and vice versa)—and serves to connect disparate data across cultures, yet not emptily and in name only. Such a universal proceeds *laterally*, by assimilating phenomena of the same level of abstraction, rather than vertically (by subsuming concrete phenomena under more abstract terms).[27] Lateral universals are especially pertinent to the anthropology and phenomenology of place. For in their very concreteness, particular places do not form hierarchies of increasing abstraction. Instead, they fall into various groupings of comparably concrete terms: home places, workplaces, way stations, and so forth. The constitution of such places is at once concrete-relational and lateral in scope and is effected *by places themselves* (much more so than by times, which serve to separate more than to connect). Minds may note the sameness shared by different places, but they do not make this sameness. The sameness is the work of places in interaction with bodies that find themselves engaged in them.

But what does sameness of place signify? Certainly not identity of *position*—a much more delimited concept. Places are significantly the same when they are members of the same material *region*. Places concatenate with each other to form regions of things. A region, as Husserl conceives it, holds together things that share the same "material essence" (*sachhaltiges Wesen*), which—unlike a formal essence—has its own positive content. This content affiliates things in such a way that we may consider them as belonging to the same overall region. Thus physical things qua physical belong to the region of Nature. Psychological phenomena—for example, memories and thoughts—belong to Soul, regarded as a distinctively different region (yet one that is commensurate with that of things).[28] Similarly, placial phenomena such as location and situation belong to the region Place. Within Place as a generic region, particular kinds of places abound: wild places and built places at one level, kitchens and bedrooms at another, and so on.

A given place, like anything else characterized by material essences, is inseparable from the concrete region in which it is found and instantiates qualities and relations found in that region. This is true not just of physical places but of other sorts of places as well: just as, say, the Grand Canyon is qualified by properties that are regional in a geological sense (e.g., the presence of arroyos, colored sandstone rock layering, certain effects of seasonal weather), so the place of the Grand Canyon in my *memory* of it occupies a region of my psyche (roughly, that of "memories-of-traveling-in-the-American-Southwest"). From this simple example it is evident, once again, that place is not one kind of thing: it can be psychical as well as physical, and doubtless also cultural and historical and social. But as a coherent region in Husserl's sense of the term, it holds these kinds—and much else besides—together.[29]

If place is indeed regional in any such sense as this, it cannot be universal in traditional Western acceptations of this term. In particular, it cannot be a substantive or a formal universal. The universality of place is too complex—or too loose—to be captured by these classical forms of universality, one of which reduces to sameness of content and the other to identity of form. Place is more complicated than this, and its universality is at once concrete, relational, lateral, and regional. Of these traits, "regional" is the most comprehensive and can be regarded as containing *in nuce* the other traits. For as a regional universal, place is defined by a material essence or set of such essences, each of which is concrete and relational and each of which also operates by lateral inclusion. In its regionality, a place cannot superintend objects *in general* (i.e., abstract objects such as numbers) in the manner of a formal domain. A given place such as the Grand Canyon bears only on its own actual occupants, which are structured by the same material essences by which the place itself is to be construed. The things and localities, the people and animals in the canyon, are held together not just by their literal location in the same piece of geography but, more significantly, by the fact that they are *part of the same place*—a place exhibiting various material-essential features possessed or reflected by everything in that place (aridity, verticality, rough textures, etc.).

As a regional universal, place cannot be tucked away in cross-cultural area files as just another "common-denominator of culture" (Murdock

same word goes back to Latin *colere,* "to inhabit, care for, till, worship." To be cultural, to have a culture, is to inhabit a place sufficiently intensely to cultivate it—to be responsible for it, to respond to it, to attend to it caringly. Where else but in particular places can culture take root? Certainly not in the thin air above these places, much less in the even thinner air of pure speculation about them.

To be located, culture also has to be *embodied.* Culture is carried into places by bodies. To be encultured is to be embodied to begin with. This is the common lesson of Merleau-Ponty and of Bourdieu, both of whom insist on the capital importance of the "customary body"—the body that has incorporated cultural patterns into its basic actions. These actions depend on *habitus,* "history turned into nature," a second nature that brings culture to bear in its very movements (Bourdieu 1977:78). Moreover, just as the body is basic to enculturation, so the body is itself always already encultured. No more than space is prior to place is the body prior to culture. Rather than being a passive recipient or mere vehicle of cultural enactments, the body is itself enactive of cultural practices by virtue of its considerable powers of incorporation, habituation, and expression. And as a creature of habitus, the same body necessarily *inhabits* places that are themselves culturally informed. (It also inhabits places by rising to the challenge of the novel circumstance.) Far from being dumb or diffuse, the lived body is as intelligent about the cultural specificities of a place as it is aesthesiologically sensitive to the perceptual particularities of that same place. Such a body is at once encultured and emplaced *and* enculturating and emplacing—while being massively sentient all the while.

Basic to local knowledge, therefore, is knowledge of place by means of the body: such knowledge is "knowledge by acquaintance" in Russell's memorable phrase (1912: ch. 5). Bodies not only perceive but *know* places. Perceiving bodies are *knowing bodies,* and inseparable from what they know is culture as it imbues and shapes particular places. It is by bodies that places become cultural in character. It is all too easy to suppose that what is cultural represents an articulated separate stratum laid down on a mute perceptual ground. In fact, even the most primordial level of perceiving is inlaid with cultural categories in the form of differential patterns of recognition, ways of organizing the perceptual field and acting in it, and manners of designating and naming items in this field. Thus culture pervades the way that places are perceived and the fact that they are perceived, as well as how we act in their midst. As Merleau-Ponty puts it, "the distinction between the two planes (natural and cultural) is abstract: everything is cultural in us (our *Lebenswelt* is "subjective") (our perception is cultural-historical) and everything is natural in us (even the cultural rests on the polymorphism of wild Being)" (Merleau-Ponty 1968:253).[31]

In other words, the endemic status of culture—pervading bodies and places and bodies-in-places—is matched by the equally endemic insinuation of "wild Being" into the body/place matrix. Even the most culturally saturated place retains a factor of wildness, that is, of the radically amorphous and unaccounted for, something that is not so much immune to culture as alien to it in its very midst, disparate from it from within. We sense this wildness explicitly in moments of absurdity—and of "surdity," sheer "thisness." But it is immanent in every perceptual experience and thus in every bodily insertion into the perceived places anchoring each such experience. This ontological wildness—not to be confused with literal wilderness, much less with mere lack of cultivation—ensures that cultural analysis never exhausts a given place. Just as we should not fall into a perceptualism that leaves no room for expressivity and language, so we ought not to espouse a culturalism that accords no autochthonous being to places, no alterity. In the very heart of the most sophisticated circumstance is a wildness that no culture can contain or explain, much less reduce. The wildness exceeds the scope of the most subtle set of signifiers, despite the efforts of painters to capture it in images and of storytellers to depict it in words.[32]

Precisely because of the ubiquity of such wildness in body, place, and culture, the temptation to espouse the idea of a primary "precultural" level of experience is difficult to overcome. Perhaps no serious Western thinker, including Husserl and Merleau-Ponty, has altogether resisted the charisma of the precultural—especially when it accompanies a preoccupation with uncovering the foundations of experience and knowledge. But the passion for epistemic (and other) origins is itself culturally specific and stems from an epistemophilic proclivity that is not ingrained or instinctual, Aristotle's and Freud's claims notwithstanding. All human beings may desire to know, but they do not always desire to know in the foundationalist manner that is an obsessive concern of European civilization. Moreover, whatever people may wish to know, they are already *doing* at the bilateral level of knowing bodies and known places. As knowing and known, bodies and places are not precultural—even if they are prediscursive as directly experienced. Their very wildness contains culture in their midst, but culture itself is wild in its intensity and force.

This is a lesson to be taken back into place. Despite the inherent wildness of all places (including urban places), there are no first-order places, no First Places that altogether withstand cultural pervasion and specification. But we can continue to endorse the Archytian Axiom of place's primacy—to be is still to be in place—provided only that we recognize that places are at once cultural and perceptual as well as tame and wild. And provided, too, that we realize that the place-world defies division into two distinct domains of Nature and Culture. If it is equally true that "everything is natural in us" and that "everything is cultural in us," this is so primarily within the concrete and complex arena of place, where the coadunation of the natural and the cultural arises in every experience and every event—and in every expression thereof.

> I can only say, there we have been: but I cannot say where. And I cannot say, how long, for that is to place it in time.
> —T. S. Eliot, "Burnt Norton"

Place is not only coadunative but also (as I have already hinted) deconstructive—deconstructive of oppositions that it brings and holds together within its own ambience. These oppositions include binary pairs of terms that have enjoyed hegemonic power in Western epistemology and metaphysics. I am thinking of such dichotomies as subject and object, self and other, formal and substantive, mind and body, inner and outer, perception and imagination (or memory), and nature and culture themselves. It is always from a particular place that a person, considered as a knowing "subject," seizes upon a world of things presumed to be "objects." The reduction of persons to subjects—and, still more extremely, to minds—and of things to objects could not occur anywhere other than in place. Yet to be fully in a place is to know—to *know* by direct acquaintance as well as by cultural habitus—that such a double reduction delivers only the shadowy simulacrum of the experiences we have in that place. (It is also to know that the mere representation of objects by minds, or of places by maps, is a further reduction.) Similarly, to be emplaced is to know the hollowness of any strict distinction between what is inside one's mind or body and what is outside, or between what is perceived and what is remembered or imagined, or between what is natural and what is cultural. When viewed from the stance of place, these various divisions enter into a deconstructive meltdown—or more exactly, they are seen to have been nondiscontinuous to begin with: at-one, "esemplastic" in Coleridge's word.

One very important dichotomy subject to the deconstructive power of place is that of space and time, which we have seen to be twin preoccupations of modern thinking in the West. But the phenomenological fact of the matter is that *space and time come together in place.* Indeed, they arise from the experience of place itself. Rather than being separate but equal cosmic parameters—as we believe when we say (with Leibniz) that space is "the order of co-existence" and time "the order of succession" (Leibniz 1956:1066)—space and time are themselves coordinated and co-specified in the common matrix provided by place. We realize the essential posteriority of space and time whenever we catch ourselves apprehending spatial relations or temporal occurrences *in a particular place*. Now I am in a room in Atlanta, and it is here that I am composing this essay. Not only the punctiform here and now, but also relations and occurrences of much more considerable scope collect around and in a single place. My quarters are an integral part of a house in a certain neighborhood and city, themselves set within an entire region called "the South," all of which have their own dense historicities as well as geographies. Even these extensive geo-histories I grasp from within my delimited room-place.[33]

Space and time, then, are found precisely in place—the very place that was declared by Newton to be merely "a part of space which a body takes up" (Newton 1687: Scholium to the Definitions, III). As we have seen, Newton considered space to be "absolute." But in a self-undermining aside, Newton himself wrote that "times and spaces are, as it were, the *places of themselves* as of all other things" (Newton 1687: section IV; my italics).[34] Not only do imperial space and time require recourse to lowly places in their very definition (rather than conversely), but also the status of space and time as equal but opposite terms is put into question by their common emplacement. The binarist dogma stretching from Newton and Leibniz to Kant and Schopenhauer is undone by the basic perception that we experience space and time *together* in place—in the locus of a continuous "space-time" that is proclaimed alike in twentieth-century physics, philosophy, and anthropology.

To speak of space-time is to speak once more of *event*. For an event is at once spatial and temporal, indeed indissolubly both: its spatial qualities and relations happen at a particular time. But the happening itself occurs in a place that is equally particular. Thus "event" can be considered the spatiotemporalization of a place, and the way it happens as spatio-temporally specified. It is revealing that we speak of an event as having "a date and a place," replacing "space" by "place." This is in keeping with Heidegger's observation that "spaces receive their essential being from particular localities and not from 'space' itself" (Heidegger 1971:154). Even if we cannot replace "date" by "place," we can observe that there is no such thing as a pure date, a sheer occurrence that occurs nowhere. Every date is an emplaced happening. And since every date, every *time,* is indissociably linked with space, it is ultimately, or rather first of all, situated in a "particular locality."

When we say that something "happens in space and time," this way of putting it not only reinforces the putative primacy (as well as the equally putative equiprimordiality) of space and time but also fosters the impression that for something to happen it must occur at a precise point or moment. Punctiformity is the very basis of specification by calendars, clocks, and maps and is thus a matter of "simple location," in Whitehead's term for isolated punctate positions in space and time. (For

Whitehead's treatment of simple location, see Whitehead 1925:50ff.) [35] The poet, along with the ordinary person, knows better: to say "*there* we have been" is not the same thing as to say precisely where we have been in geographical space, and if we are to express the duration of an event we "cannot say, how long, for that is to place it in time." In the modern Western era, to place in time or in space is ultimately to situate in site, that is, on a planiform surface of point-moments. A site is an exsanguinated place—precisely the sort of scene in which space and time seem to triumph over place. But what if matters are the other way around? What if time, space, and their projections and reductions as sites are non-simply located *in places?* Then place would no longer be the mere occasion for happenings positioned in an infinitely capacious space and time. Place itself would be the happening, and space and time what *it* occasions, what *it* specifies in determinate and measurable sites.

The "eventmental" character of places, their capacity for co-locating space and time (even as they deconstruct this very dyad), can be considered a final form of gathering. This form is not the gathering-out of particular persons and things in a configured place or region, or the in-gathering effected by the body as the crux of nature and culture, but a still more general and pervasive gathering-with that occurs by virtue of the very power of emplacement to bring space and time together in the event. Such comprehensive gathering is the turning point of space and time, the pivot where space and time conjoin in place. Just as this most inclusive and momentous gathering is the undermining of space and time construed as independent and preexisting dimensions, it is also the basis for any theory of space and time taken as absolute or relative, simultaneous or successive, intuitive or conceptual. The deconstruction of space and time by place clears the way for their conjoint reconstruction. But the two dimensions remain, first and last, dimensions of place, and they are experienced and expressed *in place by the event of place.*[36]

> As native concepts and beliefs find external purchase on specific features of the local topography, the entire landscape seems to acquire a crisp new dimension that moves it more surely into view. . . . In native discourse, the local landscape falls neatly and repeatedly into places.
> —Keith Basso, " 'Speaking with Names': Language and Landscape among the Western Apache"

The gathering power of place works in many ways and at many levels. At the mundane level of everyday life, we are continually confronted with circumstances in which places provide the scene for action and thought, feeling and expression. Think only of where you are as you read these words: the place you are in right now actively supports (or at least allows for) the act of reading this text. Just as I write these words in my Atlanta room, you read them in yours—somewhere. Of course, I could write in a different place and you could read in another place. But the loci you and I are in nevertheless influence, sometimes quite considerably, overt actions such as reading and writing, and they influence still more what Malinowski (1922:18) calls "the imponderabilia of actual life," such things as emotional tonality, degree of impatience, the understanding of a text, relations with consociates, and so forth.

If this is true of our immediate locus—of what Husserl called the "near sphere"—it is just as true of more generous placial units such as the house we inhabit or the building in which we work.[37] Both Bachelard and Heidegger insist that it is in dwellings that we are most acutely sensitive to the effects of places upon our lives. Their "intimate immensity" allows them to condense the duration and historicity of inhabitation in one architecturally structured place.[38] What happens in such "domestic space" is an event in the sense discussed in the last section. Equally eventful, however, are the journeys we take between the dwellings in which we reside, for we also dwell in the intermediate places, the *interplaces,* of travel—places which, even when briefly visited or merely traversed, are never uneventful, never not full of spatiotemporal specificities that reflect particular modes and moods of emplacement. Even on the hoof, we remain in place. We are never anywhere, anywhen, but in place.

Midway between staying at home and making a journey is the arena of *ceremonial action.* When ceremonial action concerns rites of passage (a term redolent with the idea of "the passing of time"), however, it is all too tempting to consider this action a matter of sheer diachronic development—"stages on life's way," in Kierkegaard's timely phrase. Thus it is all the more striking that van Gennep, whose *Rites of Passage* was first published in 1909 (the same year in which Hertz's "The Pre-Eminence of the Right Hand" appeared), refused this temptation and insisted on describing the three-fold process of separation, transition, and incorporation in resolutely spatial, or, more exactly, *placial,* terms. Van Gennep insisted, for example, that "territorial passage" provides the proper framework for an understanding of ritualized passage in the social sphere:

> The passage from one social position to another is identified with a *territorial passage,* such as the entrance into a village or a house, the movement from one room to another, or the crossing of streets and squares. This identification explains why the passage from one group to another is so often ritually expressed by passage under a portal, or by an 'opening of the doors'. (van Gennep 1960:192; his italics)

Under the heading of territorial passage itself, van Gennep discusses such notions as frontiers, borders, crossroads, and landmarks. Most important of all, however, is the concept of *threshold,* in which movement from one place to another is effected. A threshold is the concrete inter-place of an important transition. Van Gennep emphasizes the particu-larity of the threshold; only as *this* place can it serve as the support for a rite of passage:

> The door is the boundary between the foreign and domestic worlds in the case of an ordinary dwelling, between the profane and sacred worlds in the case of a temple. Therefore to cross the threshold is to unite oneself with a new world. It is thus an important act in marriage, adoption, ordination, and funeral ceremonies. (van Gennep 1960:20) [39]

The very "transition" effected by passing through a threshold is inextri-cably place-bound, and its description requires an entire paraphernalia of place predicates (e.g., "boundary" and "zone").

But precisely at this critical juncture, van Gennep disappoints us. Ignoring the manifest place-situatedness of his own descriptions, he as-serts that "the symbolic and *spatial area of transition* may be found in more or less pronounced form in all the ceremonies which accompany the passage from one social and magico-religious position to another," con-cluding that "the *spatial separation* of distinct groups is an aspect of social organization" (van Gennep 1960:18, 192; my italics). Here van Gennep, like Durkheim, relies on the language of space and spatiality as if it were the only alternative to talk of time and temporality. Van Gennep recog-nizes what Bourdieu calls a "theoretical space"—and this is a significant move beyond the temporocentrism implicit in the very idea of passage—but missing is an explicit acknowledgment of the concrete place-specific character of his own examples and primary terms of description. In company with so many other modern thinkers, van Gennep suffers from what Freud calls "the blindness of the seeing eye." [40] Place is there to be seen if only we have the vision to behold it.

A decisive step beyond van Gennep's is taken by Nancy Munn in her discerning analysis of *kula* exchange, a highly ritualistic action that, like a rite of passage, is subject to misconstrual from the start. In this case, however, the primary misprision has to do with space rather than with time: if "passage" leads us to think primarily of time, kula "exchange," especially in its inter-island form, tempts us to think mainly in terms of transactions across geographical space. As Munn demonstrates, nothing could be farther from the truth.

Although Munn's *The Fame of Gawa* opens with a cartographically accurate map of the Massim region of Papua New Guinea, her discus-sion of kula exchange soon posits a realm of intersubjective "spacetime" that is much closer to landscape than to geography. She shows that kula participants are indissolubly linked to local and extralocal places and to the pathways between them. Gawan acts of hospitality, for instance, "constitute a mode of spacetime formed through the dynamics of action (notably giving and traveling) *connecting persons and places*" (Munn 1986:9; my italics).[41] Gifts of food (as well as other items of hospitality) occur in particular places of exchange, either on one's home island or on an island to which one has traveled by canoe. These gifts precede kula exchange proper and are the "dynamic base" of such exchange by virtue of ushering in the event of exchange itself, which takes place in an extensive area all too easily conceived in terms of objective space. But Munn rightly refuses this temptation:

> Although kula shell transactions also entail dyadic exchange units [i.e., as in hospitality relations] . . . these transactions are not restricted exchanges or closed spacetimes. The shells that the two men transact travel beyond them. . . . The travels of kula shells create an emergent spacetime of their own that transcends that of specific, immediate transactions. This spacetime may be thought of as that of circulation. (Munn 1986:57–58)

Implicit here is a distinction between what I have called "place proper"—instanced in the concrete transactions of hospitality and shell exchange—and "region" (i.e., a collocation of internally related places), in which the defining unit is that of the kula shell in its circulatory journey. At every stage of this journey, the shell requires new transactions to relay it. Each such transaction can be said to constitute a spacetime and not merely to fit into an already existing framework of space and time. The framework is created and recreated with each successive transaction.[42]

Perhaps the most persuasive instance of such a constitution of spacetime is the construction and launching of the canoes that are requisite to kula exchange while also being objects of a special exchange themselves. To build canoes is both to engage in a specific spatiotemporal event of making—a bodily action calling for a particular place of construction—and to facilitate the reaching of other islands by a specific pathway (*keda*) between them. No wonder the launching of such canoes is a major event: "The canoe is finally launched," writes Malinowski (1922:147), "after the long series of mingled work and ceremony, technical effort and magical rite." This series of events is itself a rite of passage in which (as Munn observes) "transition takes place across spatiotemporal zones" as wood is located and bespelled above the beach, then made into finished vessels that are launched into the sea (Munn 1977:41.) The beach is a threshold and as such has many "medial qualities" (Munn 1977:41), above all its location as if between island and ocean.

Canoes thus connect one set of liminal rituals, intra-island (i.e., what happens *in* a place), with another set, specifically inter-island (kula and canoe exchange proper, i.e., what happens *between* places in a region).

In the end, both sorts of rituals are bound to place, whether to one and the same place or to different places connected by a sea route. In all these places, space and time combine forces. The sea voyage itself, adds Malinowski, "is not done on the spur of the moment, but happens periodically, at dates settled in advance, and it is carried on along definite trade routes, which must lead to fixed trysting places" (Malinowski 1922:85). Here space (in the form of "definite trade routes") and time (in terms of "periodical" journeys) *come together in place*—in places of exchange connected by regional pathways—just as space and time combine in the initial making of canoes. Place and region gather space and time in emergent events of construction and exchange.

For this gathering to happen, the place and region in which it occurs must possess a property alluded to earlier in this essay: *porosity of boundaries*. An important aspect of being in a place or region is that one is not limited altogether by determinate borders (i.e., legal limits) or perimeters (i.e., those established by geography). For a place or region to be an event, for it to involve the change and movement that are so characteristic of kula exchange, there must be permeable margins of transition. The permeability occurs in numerous forms. A beach, at the edge of the sea and subject to tidal encroachments, is certainly exemplary of a porous boundary, but even in a land-locked situation such as that of the Western Desert of Australia, places and regions can retain a remarkable permeability. As W. E. H. Stanner notes:

> The known facts of inter-group relations [in aboriginal Australia] simply do not sort with the idea of precise, rigid boundaries jealously upheld in all circumstances. And the idea that a region was cut up, as it were without remainder, into exclusive but contiguous descent-group estates, could not have sufficed for the dynamic aboriginal life we know to have existed. . . . The conception which most nearly accommodates the facts . . . is that of *spaced estates* with *overlapping ranges,* and, thus, *partially interpenetrative domains and life-spaces.* (Stanner 1965:11–12; his italics)

Distinct and impenetrable borders may belong to sites as legally and geographically controlled entities, and hence ultimately to "space," but they need not (and often do not) play a significant role in the experience and knowledge of places and regions—of "estates" and "ranges" in Stanner's nomenclature.[43]

Whether in the waters of the Massim region of Papua New Guinea or on the dry land of the Western Desert in Australia—or anywhere else place and region, rather than position and site, are of determinative import—we find that porousness of boundaries is essential to place. A place could not gather bodies in the diverse spatiotemporal ways it does without the permeability of its own limits. The sievelike character of places might well be regarded as another essential structure of place, one that could be called "elasticity." But I prefer to regard it as a corollary property of that perceptual structure earlier identified as "external horizon." For the very nature of such a horizon is to *open out* even as it encloses. It is intrinsic to perceptual fields to possess bleeding boundaries; the lack of such boundaries converts these fields to delimited and closed-off sites such as prison cells or jury boxes.

By returning to horizons we have come full circle, and we need only add that the horizons which form the perceptual basis of boundaries are themselves spatiotemporal in status. To be in a perceptual field is to be encompassed by edges that are neither strictly spatial—we cannot map a horizon (even if we can draw it)—nor strictly temporal: just when does a horizon happen? A given horizon is at once spatial and temporal, and it belongs to a field that is the perceptual scene of the place whose horizon it is. Once again, but now coming in from the margins, we discover that place includes space and time as part of its own generative power. Rather than being the minion of an absolute space and time, place is the master of their shared matrix.

> The old meaning of the word "end" means the same as place: "from one end to the other" means: from one place to the other. The end of philosophy is the place, that place in which the whole of philosophy's history is gathered in its most extreme possibility.
> —*Heidegger, "The End of Philosophy and the Task of Thinking"*

I started with an uneasiness occasioned by recent anthropological treatments of place as something supposedly made up from space—something factitious carved out of space or superimposed on space (in the end, it doesn't matter which, given the unquestioned premise of space's primacy). From there, a consideration of the perceptual basis of being-in-place revealed that human beings are emplaced *ab origine,* thanks to the presence of depths and horizons in the perceptual field and thanks also to the cores of sense that anchor this same field. The world comes bedecked in places; it is a place-world to begin with.

It was precisely the resonance of "to begin with" that led me later in this essay to reflect on the kind of universality possessed by place. Rejecting the standard choice between formal and substantive universals—as well as the related and equally standard choice between a priori and empirical universals—I explored the idea of a specifically regional universal that is concrete-cum-relational and that operates laterally, across cases and not above or under them. Such a universal, which could also be called a "general," is metaphysically neutral in that its instantiation is directly reflective of the particular entities in a given place and their mode of configuration. The instantiation itself occurs by means of essential structures that pervade places as we know them. I singled out two structures of special pertinence: the lived body's active ingredience in emplacement (i.e., getting into, staying in, and moving between places) and the gathering power of place itself. Gathering is an event, and an exploration of place-as-event allowed us to see how places, far from being inert and static sites, are themselves continually changing in accordance with their own proper dynamism. Places are at once elastic — for example, in regard to their outer edges and internal paths — and yet sufficiently coherent to be considered as the *same* (hence to be remembered, returned to, etc.) as well as to be classified as places of certain *types* (e.g., home-place, workplace, visiting place).

Moreover, the eventful potency of places includes their cultural specificity. Time and history, the diachronic media of culture, are so deeply inscribed in places as to be inseparable from them — as inseparable as the bodies that sustain these same places and carry the culture located in them. But inseparability and inscription are not tantamount to exhaustion; a factor of brute being, concealed within the locative phrase "this-here," always accrues to a given place, rendering it wild in its very idiolocality, and wild as well in its most highly cultured manifestations.

On this basis I was able to draw the heretical inference that space and time are contained in places rather than places in them. Whether we are concerned with dwelling places or places on a journey, with places in a landscape or in a story (or in a story itself indissociable from a landscape), we witness a concrete topo-logic, an experiential topology, in which time and space are operative *in places* and are not autonomous presences or spheres of their own. Proceeding in this direction, we arrive at the opposite side of the mountain of Western modernity, which had assumed (and often still assumes, at the level of "common sense") that time and space, in their impassive absoluteness, are prior to place. Instead, as Archytas had foretold, place is prior to all things — even if the very idea of *priority* needs to be bracketed along with the binary logic so effectively deconstructed by place itself.

Something else to be garnered from our considerations is that if we are to take the idea of local knowledge seriously, we have to rethink both "locality" and "knowledge." "Locality" must be rethought in terms of, first, the triple distinction between position, place, and region; second, the idea of porous boundaries; and third, the role of the lived body as the mediatrix between enculturation and emplacement — their localizing agent, as it were. Above all, what is local must be allowed to take the lead, in keeping with the Archytian Axiom: *place is in first place* with regard to its configurative arrangements, its landscape logic, its perceptual peculiarities, its regional universality, and its metaphysical neutrality. By the same token, "knowledge" needs to be reconstrued as specifically placial, as a matter of acquaintance with places, knowing them by means of our knowing bodies. Such knowledge—neither propositional nor systematic, and not classifiable as simply subjective or objective, natural or cultural—is knowledge appropriate to the particularities of places in keeping with their felt properties and cultural specificities. It entails an understanding of places, where "understanding" is taken literally as standing under the ample aegis of place (and pointedly not under the protective precision of concepts).

Merleau-Ponty (1964b:120) suggests that the anthropologist has "a new organ of understanding at his disposal." Is this organ not an understanding of *place*? After all, the ethnographer stands in the field and takes note of the places he or she is in, getting into what is going on in their midst. The ensuing understanding reflects the reciprocity of body and place—and of both with culture—that is as descriptive of the experience of the anthropologist as of the native. It also reflects both parties' grasp of a concrete universality, a generality immanent in place thanks to the lateral homologies and sidewise resemblances between things and peoples in places. The understanding of place activates universals that are as impure as they are singular.

Local knowledge, then, comes down to an intimate understanding of what is generally true in the locally obvious; it concerns what is true about place in general as manifested *in this place*. Standing in this place thanks to the absolute here of my body, I understand what is true of other places over *there* precisely because of what I comprehend to be the case for this place under and around me. This does not mean that I understand what is true of *all* places, but my grasp of one place does allow me to grasp what holds, for the most part, in other places of the same region. My ongoing understanding of surrounding and like places is characterized by essential structures manifested in my own local place and illuminating other places as well. That anything like this induction of place is possible exhibits place's special power to embrace and support even as it bounds and locates.

To insist thus on the considerable outreach of local knowledge in this manner is necessarily to argue against what might be called, modifying a celebrated phrase of Whitehead's, the Fallacy of Misplaced Abstractness. By this is meant the tendency to posit a plane of abstract perfection and purity onto which complexities and dirty details come crowding. The fallacy consists in believing the plane to be a priori and settled, the complications a posteriori and changing. The abstractness of this plane is misplaced in that its status as prior is the reverse of what actually obtains:

the plane is itself an abstraction from what is concrete, that is, from that which is supposedly only secondary and epiphenomenal and yet is in fact phenomenally given as primary.

A conspicuous instance of this fallacy is the presumption that space furnishes just such a perfected plane, in relation to which mere places are nothing but parts or constructs, decoration, or projection. Here the misplacement is of place itself, which is shoved into a minority position (or, which comes to the same thing, reduced to position per se). Time also exemplifies the fallacy, especially when it is conceived (as it was by Locke) as "the length of one straight line, extended *in infinitum*" (Locke 1690: Book Two, chapter 15). In both cases, it is a matter of showing that the true concreteness belongs to place—plain old place, the place under our feet and around our eyes and in our ears.

It is undeniable that the concreteness of place has its own mode of abstractness: that is, in its relationality (there is never a *single* place existing in utter isolation) and in its inherent regionality (whereby a plurality of places are grouped together). We can admit such relating and regioning and still avert the danger of a misplaced abstractness proper to place itself. This danger consists in making place, or its components, into a new plane of perfection, a new tabula rasa, onto which all that matters in human experience comes to be written. Spatiocentrism and temporocentrism would then give way to an equally spurious topocentrism!

In order to prevent this mere reversal of priority, I have maintained that place is no empty substratum to which cultural predicates come to be attached; it is an already plenary presence permeated with culturally constituted institutions and practices. As the basis of collective as well as individual habitus, these institutions and practices pervade the bodies of sensing subjects in a given place as well as the gathering power of the place itself: even when prediscursively given (and prereflectively experienced), neither body nor place is precultural. Just as place invades space from the bottom up, so culture penetrates place from the top down as it were. But only *as it were,* for the very directionalities of "up" and "down" are legacies of bodily orientation in places (as Kant reminds us) and are elicited by powers inherent in places themselves (as Aristotle affirms). It would be more accurate to say simply, and in conclusion, that as places gather bodies in their midst in deeply enculturated ways, so cultures conjoin bodies in concrete circumstances of emplacement.

NOTES

1. See Kant (1950 [1787]: A 426 B 454ff.). In an antinomy one has compelling reasons to assert the truth of both the thesis and the antithesis of a given proposi-

tion; here, the thesis is that "the world has a beginning in time, and is also limited as regards space."

2. We might as well say, whereby Nature becomes Culture, since the dominant assumption in Western thought of the last three centuries is that Nature presents itself primarily as Space. *Ngurra* itself is said, significantly, to be "the place where one belongs . . . and to which one returns" (Myers 1991:55). The idea of "geography" as plain starting-point is especially odd, since geography is itself a second- or even third-order accretion to the experience of place and, more particularly, of landscape. Even a geographer as sensitive as Yi-Fu Tuan embraces it: "All people undertake to change amorphous space into articulated geography" (Tuan 1977:83).

3. The full statement is: "Perhaps [place] is the first of all things, since all existing things are either in place or not without place" (cited from Simplicius, *Commentary on Aristotle's Categories,* and translated by S. Sambursky in Sambursky 1982:37n). The power of the Archytian Axiom pervades the ancient Greek world. Plato cryptically quotes it in the *Timaeus* when he writes that "anything that is must needs be in some place and occupy some room, and . . . what is not somewhere in earth or heaven is nothing" (*Timaeus* 52 B, in Cornford 1957). Aristotle similarly inscribes the axiom at the opening of his treatment of place in his *Physics,* Book IV, when, referring to Hesiod, he says that "he thinks as most people do that everything is somewhere and in place" (*Physics* 208 b 32–33).

4. Immanuel Kant, preface to *Anthropology from a Pragmatic Point of View* (1974 [1797]); my translation. In this lecture course, Kant distinguishes between "physiological" and "pragmatic" forms of anthropology, strikingly anticipating much later distinctions between "physical" and "cultural" anthropology. In physiological anthropology, one studies "what nature makes of man," while in pragmatic anthropology the aim is to grasp "what man, as possessing free activity, can or does or must make of himself." He also discusses the need for fieldwork, which he labels "voyages," and for avoiding an anthropological enterprise based on racial differences as such.

5. Aristotle discusses eight senses of "in" in his treatment of place, concluding that the most pertinent sense is "as a thing is in a vessel" (*Physics* 210 a 24).

6. The sentence cited is from Husserl (1973:32; in italics in text). Internal and external horizons are discussed in Husserl (1973: section 8, "The Horizon-Structure of Experience"). Merleau-Ponty discusses "primordial depth" in his *Phenomenology of Perception* (1962:254–67). The affinity of the notions of "horizon" and "depth" is close: just as every perceived thing is perceived in its *own* depth—that is, within the horizons provided by its own sides—so a collection of things in a given perceptual field has a depth as a whole that is limited only by the external horizon of this same field. The affinity of horizon-cum-depth to the phenomenon of "lift-up-over sounding" in Feld's descriptive term for the Kaluli experience of immersion in places of the Papua New Guinea rainforest calls for further exploration (see Feld, this volume).

7. See Descartes (1985 [1644]: Part Two, sections 10–20). In section 10, Descartes says that "there is no real distinction between space, or internal place, and the corporeal substance contained in it; the only difference lies in the way in which we are accustomed to conceive of them" (1985 [1644]:227). As equivalent to "space," "internal place" is tantamount to three-dimensional volumetric extendedness. "External place" refers to the surface surrounding a given body in a place. For a more complete treatment of Descartes—and of other early modern thinkers—see part three of my book *The Fate of Place* (1996).

8. "Almost," I say, since Kant did note in passing that motion is "alteration of

place" (1950 [1787]: A 32 B 48). On "position" (*Stelle*), see Kant (1950 [1787]: A 263 B 319ff.).

9. It is not widely known that before 1772 (often taken as the moment of the "critical turn"), Kant designated his philosophical project as that of "general phenomenology." The term "phenomenology" itself was borrowed from Lambert's physics, which Kant had read in the early 1760s. Similarly, though to much different effect, Wittgenstein sometimes described his philosophical work of the 1920s as "phenomenology," but under the influence of the early Vienna Circle he came to abjure the term.

10. On corporeal intentionality and intentional threads, see Merleau-Ponty (1962: Introduction, Part One). Merleau-Ponty rarely speaks of place as such, but on my reading it is entailed in everything he says about the lived body and its "setting" (*milieu*), "landscape" (*paysage*), or "world" (*monde*). Husserl had already singled out the voluntariness of bodily movement as a noncontingent character: "In virtue of its faculty of free mobility, the subject can now induce the flow of the system of its appearances. . . . With regard to all other things, I have the freedom to change at will my position in relation to them" (1958: Second Book, 166–67).

11. See Basso, this volume: "As places animate the ideas and feelings of persons who attend to them, these same ideas and feelings animate the places on which attention has been bestowed."

12. On the aesthesiological body, see Husserl (1989:297), along with p. 163 on the body as a "physical-aesthesiological unity." On sonesthesia, see Feld, this volume. Concerning the body as a "field of localization," see Husserl (1989: section 38, esp. p. 159). The term "operative intentionality," employed in the previous paragraph, is also Husserl's and is described by Merleau-Ponty as "that which produces the natural and antepredicative unity of the world and of our life, being apparent in our desires, our evaluations and *in the landscape we see,* more clearly than in objective knowledge" (Merleau-Ponty 1962:xviii; my italics).

13. See Kant (1928 [1768]:21–22). Aristotle had already recognized the relativity of the three dimensional dyads to bodily position: "Relatively to us, they— above, below, right, left [etc.]—are not always the same, but come to be in relation to our position [*thesis*], according as we turn ourselves about" (*Physics* 208 b 14–16). But this relativity to the body is for Aristotle a contingent fact, since in his view "in nature [*en te phusei*] each [dimension] is distinct and separate" (*Physics* 208 b 18). Husserl argues, on the contrary, that such bodily based dimensionality is a *necessary* structure: "All spatial being necessarily appears in such a way that it appears either nearer or farther, above or below, right or left. . . . The body (*Leib*) then has, for its particular ego, the unique distinction of bearing in itself the zero point of all these orientations" (Husserl 1989:166; he italicizes "zero point").

14. On the bi-gendered body, see Strathern (1988). Concerning bi-location, see Lévy-Bruhl (1978:5–17). In a striking instance of bi-location, a Chambri informant pointed to a rock in his back yard to which ancestors were believed to have moored a boat and said, "Here I am! There I am!" (Frederick Errington and Deborah Gewertz, personal communication, 1993).

15. On the flesh of the world, see Merleau-Ponty (1968:123, 267).

16. "Toynbee is profoundly right to suggest that the nomad is . . . *he who does not move.* . . . Of course, the nomad moves, but while seated, and he is only seated while moving (the Bedouin galloping, knees on the saddle, sitting on the soles of his upturned feet, 'a feat of balance')" (Deleuze and Guattari 1986:51, their italics, with reference to Toynbee 1947:164–86).

17. On a different but related sense of locus, see Husserl (1989:35); on changing place in space, see Husserl (1989:213): "I, the person, am in space at this place. Others are over there, where their bodies are. They go for a walk, they pay a visit, and so forth, whereby indeed their spirits, along with their bodies, change their place in space." The difficulty with this formulation, however, is that it subordinates place to space, conceived of as "the space of the one objective surrounding world" (Husserl 1989:213), and thus fails to acknowledge the priority of place.

18. In transportation, I am passively carried by an animal or machine whose purposes are independent of my own; in transition, I move in order to pursue my own purposes, purposes that can be attained only in the new place to which I move. Of course, I may choose to effect a transition *by means of transportation,* but then I bend the animal or mechanical purposes to suit the realization of my own aims. The difference, starkly put, is between letting the horse roam where it wants to go and steering it to my own destination. For further discussion of moving between places, see Casey (1993: ch. 9).

19. So say both Heidegger (1972:17) and Merleau-Ponty (1968:266), neither knowing the other had so spoken.

20. On the special aptitude of places for holding memories, see Casey (1987: ch. 9).

21. Such sameness of place contrasts strikingly with that posited by Leibniz in his Fifth Letter to Clarke (1716). For Leibniz, to be in the same place signifies merely to be in a *position* or "site" (*situs*) that can in principle be occupied by any other object and that stays unchanged by the fact of occupation. See Leibniz (1956:1145–48).

22. On "morphological concepts of vague configurational types," see Husserl (1982: section 74). Concerning "essentially occasional expressions," see Husserl (1970: section 36). In an essentially occasional expression, "it is essential to orient actual meaning to the occasion, the speaker and the situation" (1970:315). Husserl gives the example of "here," which "designates the speaker's vaguely bounded spatial environment. . . . The genuine meaning of the word is first constituted in the variable presentation of this place" (1970:317). For contemporary treatments of these same matters in analytical philosophy, see Matthews (1982), especially chapter 6, "Demonstrative Identification," which includes a discerning assessment of "here" (see pp. 151–69), and Kripke (1980), especially his brief discussion of demonstratives as "rigid designators" on pages 10n and 49n. Notice that the use of the definite article to refer to a place, though perfectly permissible in English, is often uninformative as to *location:* "the garage," "the grocery store," "the lake." In such cases, the location is presumed to be known in advance, as when we say, "Meet me at the library."

23. For a convincing critique of "stratigraphic" theories of meaning, see Geertz (1973:37–51).

24. I take landscape to be distinct from geography, which is a second-order representation of a physical place or region. Except for the two-handedness that is a condition of orientation in reading a map, in geography no body need be present; indeed, disembodiment is a geographical ideal. But we are in a landscape only by grace of being bodily there. On the distinction between landscape and geography, see Straus (1963:308).

25. It will be noticed that I have been attempting to speak of place — including landscape, construed as the face of place, its expressive facies or sensuous surface — without making any reference to *mind.* Even if it is true that "the mind is its own place" (Milton, *Paradise Lost*) or that "the mind is the place of forms" (Aristotle, *De Anima*), such statements do not establish that the mind, even the savage mind, is

essential to place. My emphasis on body is meant to dispute a mentalistic (if not overtly idealist) tendency that begins in Kant, continues with Cassirer, and is still present in contemporary speculation.

26. I borrow the term "empirical commonality" from Geertz (1973), who appears to employ it as equivalent to "substantive identity." Cultural anthropology, he writes, should seek "a definition of man stressing not so much the empirical commonalities in his behavior, from place to place and time to time, but rather the mechanisms by whose agency the breadth and indeterminateness of his inherent capacities are reduced to the narrowness and specificity of his actual accomplishments" (Geertz 1973:45). In the idea of shared "mechanisms," Geertz suggests something close to what Jerome Bruner has labeled "process universals," in contrast to "product universals." Speaking of the way in which languages distinguish between marked and unmarked features, Bruner observes that this is "a way in which *all* languages deal with the task of alerting the attention of the recipients of messages to what needs special processing. *That* is a process universal" (Bruner 1981:256; his italics). In contrast, a product universal is found in the fact that "*most* languages mark the plural form and not the singular" (Bruner 1981:257; his italics).

27. Merleau-Ponty (1964b:120) writes that in anthropology what is at issue is "no longer the overarching universal of a strictly objective method, but a sort of lateral universal which we acquire through ethnological experience and its incessant testing of the self through the other person and the other person through the self." I wish to thank Irene Klaver for drawing my attention to the importance of this passage.

28. Concerning regional ontology, see Husserl (1982: sections 9, 10, 16). Formal ontology is "the eidetic science of any object whatever" (1982: section 10). Notice that "material" in Husserl's usage signifies concrete content, *not* anything necessarily physical. On Nature versus Soul, see especially Husserl (1989: section 2, "The Constitution of Animal Nature").

29. For Husserl, "region is nothing other than the *total highest generic unity belonging to a concretum*" (1982: section 16, p. 31; his italics). The relation between a region and its concreta—whether entities or events—is not just relational but *reciprocally* relational. To its concreta (i.e., its inhabitants) a region lends "generic unity" in the form of an "essentially unitary nexus," but the concreta give to this unified nexus specific positions that are indicated by deictic markers, including both toponyms and choronyms: I remember myself as having been on the "north rim" of the Grand Canyon. (Husserl's phrases are from 1982: section 16, p. 31.) I resort to "choronym" as designating the name of a region proper (*chōrar*) in distinction to a toponym of a place (*topos*).

30. On eidetic singularities, which are tantamount to the lowest specific differences, see Husserl (1982: section 12, "Genus and Species"). The "object in general" is the proper content of formal ontology, while "this-here" is defined by Husserl as "a pure, syntactically formless, individual single particular" (1982: section 12, p. 29). To interpret place as an intermediate term as I have just done is to rejoin Lévi-Strauss's opening gambit in *The Savage Mind:* just as traditional peoples do not lack abstract categories ("concepts" such as "tree" or "animal"), so they are also not precluded from employing the most intensely concrete terms (on the contrary: they are remarkably adept in just this regard, for example, in the identification and naming of botanical or animal species). But even the most concrete terms are already abstract to some degree, already climbing the scale of forms: "Words like 'oak', 'beech', 'birch', etc., are no less entitled to be considered as abstract words than the word 'tree'; and a language possessing only the word 'tree' would be, from this point of view, less rich in

concepts than one which lacked this term but contained dozens or hundreds for the individual species and varieties" (Lévi-Strauss 1966:2).

31. See also his statement that "there is an informing of perception by culture which enables us to say that culture is perceived—there is a dilatation of perception" (Merleau-Ponty 1968:212).

32. Curiously but significantly, the wildness at stake here is precisely what makes cultural anthropology possible, in Merleau-Ponty's assessment. Once having lived in another culture, the anthropologist "has regained possession of that untamed region of himself, unincorporated in his own culture, through which he communicates with other cultures" (Merleau-Ponty 1964:120). The wildness within is the condition of possibility for grasping the wildness without. For further discussion of the relation of culture and nature in the context of wild places, see Casey (1993:229–40).

33. German *Raum,* "space," is the etymon of English *room.* Compare Merleau-Ponty's working note of June 1, 1960: "In fact it is a question of grasping the *nexus*— neither 'historical' nor 'geographic' of history and transcendental geology, this very time that is space, this very space that is time . . . the simultaneous *Urstiftung* of time and space which makes there be a historical landscape and a quasi-geographical inscription of history" (Merleau-Ponty 1968:259).

34. Newton adds: "All things are *placed in time* as to order of succession; and in space as to order of situation. It is from their essence or nature that they are places; and that the primary places of things should be movable, is absurd" (Newton 1687: section IV; my italics). Leibniz similarly claimed that "every change, spiritual as well as material, has its own place (*sedes*), so to speak, in the order of time, as well as its own location in the order of coexistents, or in space" (letter to De Volder of June 20, 1703, in *Philosophical Papers and Letters,* II, p. 865).

35. To be simply located is to be "*here* in space and *here* in time, or here in space-time, in a perfectly definite sense which does not require for its explanation any reference to other regions of space-time" (Whitehead 1925:50; his italics).

36. This is not to say that the status of space and time, once given a basis in place, becomes simply secure, or that their common reconstruction entails a creative, or even a productive, outcome. On many occasions, notably on many modern occasions, a thin temporality and a sheer spatiality derive from a placial matrix. Hospitals and penitentiaries of the sort analyzed by Foucault or shopping malls of the kind on which most Americans have come to depend are cases of deficient, or at the very least unaesthetic, modes of emplacement. They are architectural and institutional events whose spatiotemporality is literally superficial, a matter of surfaces rather than of depths. Yet even in these inauspicious instances space and time come paired in place, which continues to hold them together, however inauthentic or detrimental such holding may turn out to be. When emplacement enriches rather than deprives, as in imaginatively place-specific architecture, the space and time that result become the very basis of expansively expressive experiences.

37. On the near sphere (*Nähsphäre*), see Husserl (1981:249ff.) The idea is taken up by Patrick Heelan in the first chapter of his *Space-Time and the Philosophy of Science* (1979), where the specifically hyperbolic geometry of the near sphere is developed— with interesting implications for a mathematically precise study of place.

38. On "intimate immensity," see Bachelard (1964: ch. 8). The specifically social metaphoricity of the house is asserted by van Gennep (1960:26): "A society is similar to a house divided into rooms and corridors."

39. Concerning the particularity of the threshold, van Gennep says: "The neutral zone shrinks progressively till it ceases to exist except as a simple stone, a beam,

or a threshold" (1960:17). Concerning the complexities of the threshold in one particular culture, see Frake (1980:214–32).

40. Breuer and Freud (1955: ch. 4). Concerning "theoretical space," see Bourdieu's remark that "as long as mythic-ritual space is seen as an *opus operatum,* that is, as a timeless order of things coexisting, it is never more than a theoretical space" (1977:117). Durkheim's treatment of the collective basis of space (and time) is found in Durkheim (1915:23ff.).

41. Munn's definition of "intersubjective spacetime" is "a multidimensional, symbolic order and process—a spacetime of self-other relations constituted in terms of and by means of specific types of practice" (1986:10). The term "place" is rarely used by Munn. Exceptions include the following statements: a kula gift "will not disappear but will be retained as a potentiality within the ongoing present and at some later time (and place)" (1986:65); "each household and house is a relatively autonomous locus" (1986:69); gardens in Gawa "constitute an interior spacetime whose ancestral stones must be maintained in place" (1986:10). Munn also employs the locution "spatiotemporal locus" (1986:10).

42. Munn remarks that "sociocultural practices" of many sorts "do not simply go on *in* or *through* time and space, but [they also] . . . constitute (create) the spacetime . . . in which they 'go on'" (Munn 1986:11). She adds that kula transactors are "concretely producing their own spacetime" (1986:11). This, in my view, applies more appropriately to place.

43. Indeed, the distinction between *estate,* that is, the "country," as the locus of ritual ownership for patrilineal descent-groups, and *range,* that is, the circuit over which a given group hunts and forages, is by no means crisp. Sometimes quite distinct—for example, in times of drought—and sometimes coincident, as in times of good precipitation, their relationship is continually changing, which means that their common boundaries are always shifting. Hence Stanner proposes that the two notions, in their covariant vicissitudes, be considered a "domain": "estate and range together may be said to have constituted a *domain,* which was an ecological life-space" (1965:2; his italics). On the indefiniteness of aboriginal boundaries, see also Myers (1991:93): the "inseparability of people and place makes territorial boundaries highly flexible if not insignificant." Here Myers insists on a property of places that does *not* belong to "impersonal geography," that is, to sheer space regarded as preexisting the constitution of particular places. For an illuminating discussion of boundaries in general, see Lefebvre (1991:192–94). On *tok* as "path" in Kaluli culture, see Steven Feld's remark that "the concept . . . grounds the boundedness of places in the figure of their connectedness" (Feld, this volume).

2

Wisdom Sits in Places
Notes on a Western Apache Landscape
Keith H. Basso

Place is the first of all beings, since everything that exists is in a place and
cannot exist without a place.
—*Archytas,* Commentary on Aristotle's Categories

In this unsettled age, when large portions of the earth's surface are
being ravaged by industrialism, when on several continents indigenous
peoples are being forcibly uprooted by wanton encroachments upon
their homelands, when American Indian tribes are mounting major legal
efforts to secure permanent protection for sacred sites now controlled by
federal agencies, when philosophers and poets (and even the odd soci-
ologist or two) are asserting that attachments to geographical localities
contribute fundamentally to the formation of personal and social identities, when new forms of "environmental awareness" are being more
radically charted and urgently advocated than ever in the past — in these
disordered times, when contrasting ways of living on the planet are attracting unprecedented attention worldwide, it is unfortunate that cultural anthropologists seldom study what people make of places.[1]

Sensitive to the fact that human existence is irrevocably situated in
time and space, and keenly aware that social life is everywhere accomplished through an exchange of symbolic forms, anthropologists might
be expected to report routinely on the varieties of meaning conferred by
men and women on features of their natural surroundings. Yet ethnographic inquiry into cultural constructions of geographical realities is
at best weakly developed. Willing enough to investigate the material
and organizational means by which whole communities fashion work-
able adaptations to the physical environment, ethnographers have been
notably less inclined to examine the elaborate arrays of conceptual and

expressive instruments—ideas, beliefs, stories, songs—with which community members produce and display coherent understandings of it. Consequently, little is known of the ways in which culturally diverse peoples are alive to the world around them, of how they comprehend it, of the different modes of awareness with which they take it in and (in the words of Edmund Husserl) discover that it matters. Nor can much be said about the effects of such discoveries on the persons who make them, about why some localities matter more than others, or about why viewing a favored site (or merely recalling aspects of its appearance) may loosen strong emotions and kindle thoughts of a richly caring kind. In short, anthropologists have paid scant attention to one of the most basic dimensions of human experience—that close companion of heart and mind, often subdued, yet potentially overwhelming, that is known as *sense of place*. Missing from the discipline is a thematized concern with the ways in which citizens of the earth constitute their landscapes and take themselves to be connected to them. Missing is a desire to fathom the various and variable perspectives from which people *know* their landscapes, the self-invested viewpoints from which (to borrow Isak Dinesen's felicitous image [1979]) they embrace the countryside and find the embrace returned. Missing is an interest in how men and women dwell.[2]

As formulated by Martin Heidegger (1977), whose general lead I propose to follow here, the concept of *dwelling* assigns importance to the forms of consciousness with which individuals perceive and apprehend geographical space.[3] More precisely, dwelling is said to consist in the multiple "lived relationships" that people maintain with places, for it is solely by virtue of these relationships that space acquires meaning. (Thus, as Heidegger himself put it [1977:332], "Spaces receive their essential being from particular localities and not from 'space' itself.") As numerous as they are both singular and specific, and fully realizable across great distances, relationships with places are lived whenever a place becomes the object of awareness. In many instances, awareness of place is brief and unselfconscious, a fleeting moment (a flash of recognition, a trace of memory) that is swiftly replaced by awareness of something else. But now and again, and sometimes without apparent cause, awareness is seized—arrested—and the place on which it settles becomes an object of spontaneous reflection and resonating sentiment. It is at times such as these, when individuals step back from the flow of everyday experience and attend self-consciously to places—when, we may say, they pause to actively sense them—that their relationships to geographical space are most richly lived and surely felt. For it is on these occasions of focused thought and quickened emotion that places are encountered most directly, experienced most robustly, and (in Heidegger's view) most fully brought into being. Sensing places, men and women become sharply aware of the complex attachments that link them to features of the physical world. Sensing places, they dwell, as it were, on aspects of dwelling.

Persons thus involved may also dwell on aspects of themselves, on sides and corners of their own evolving identities. For the self-conscious experience of place is inevitably a product and expression of the self whose experience it is, and therefore, unavoidably, the nature of that experience (its intentional thrust, its substantive content, its affective tones and colorings) is shaped at every turn by the personal and social biography of the one who sustains it.[4] Hence, as numerous writers have noted, places possess a marked capacity for triggering acts of self-reflection, inspiring thoughts about who one presently is, or memories of who one used to be, or musings on who one might become. And that is not all. Place-based thoughts about the self lead commonly to thoughts of other things — other places, other people, other times, whole networks of associations that ramify unaccountably within the expanding spheres of awareness that they themselves engender. The experience of sensing places, then, is thus both roundly reciprocal and incorrigibly dynamic. As places animate the ideas and feelings of persons who attend to them, these same ideas and feelings animate the places on which attention has been bestowed, and the movements of this process — inward toward facets of the self, outward toward aspects of the external world, alternately both together — cannot be known in advance. When places are actively sensed, the physical landscape becomes wedded to the landscape of the mind, to the roving imagination, and where the mind may lead is anybody's guess.

This process of interanimation relates directly to the fact that familiar places are experienced as inherently meaningful, their significance and value being found to reside in (and, it may seem, to emanate from) the form and arrangement of their observable characteristics. A concise account of this phenomenon, couched in a broader discussion of how people interact with material things, appears in the philosophical writings of Jean-Paul Sartre (1965:87–91). Proceeding on the twin assumptions that "man can only mean what he knows," and that "things can reflect for individuals only their own knowledge of them," Sartre considers what happens when attention is directed toward physical objects.

> When knowledge and feeling are oriented toward something real, actually perceived, the thing, like a reflector, returns the light it has received from it. As a result of this continual interaction, meaning is continually enriched at the same time as the object soaks up affective qualities. The object thus obtains its own particular depth and richness. The affective state follows the progress of attention, developing with each new discovery of meaning . . . with the result that its development is unpredictable. At each moment perception overflows it and sustains it, and its density and depth come from its being confused with the perceived object. *Each quality is so deeply incorporated*

in the object that it is impossible to distinguish what is felt and what is perceived. (Sartre 1965:89; emphasis added)

Thus, through a vigorous conflation of attentive subject and geographical object, places come to generate their own fields of meaning.[5] So, too, they give rise to their own aesthetic immediacies, their shifting moods and relevancies, their character and spirit. Even in total stillness, places may seem to speak. But as Sartre makes clear, such voices as places possess should not be mistaken for their own. Animated by the thoughts and feelings of persons who attend to them, places express only what their animators enable them to say; like the thirsty sponges to which the philosopher alludes, they yield to consciousness only what consciousness has given them to absorb. Yet this may be quite considerable, and so it is, as everyone knows, that places actively sensed amount to substantially more than points in physical space. As natural "reflectors" that return awareness to the source from which it springs, places also provide points from which to look out on life, to grasp one's position in the order of things, to contemplate events from somewhere in particular. Human constructions par excellence, places consist in what gets made of them — in anything and everything they are taken to be — and their disembodied voices, immanent though inaudible, are merely those of people speaking silently to themselves.

And on numerous occasions, audibly enough, the voices of people speaking to each other. Although the self-conscious experience of place may at base be a private affair, tangible representations of it are commonly made available for public consumption. Indeed, as any seasoned traveler can readily attest, locally significant places get depicted and appraised by established local citizens almost as often as suspicious marital upheavals, bad weather, and the shortcomings of other people's children. Surrounded by places, and always in one place or another, men and women talk about them constantly, and it is from listening in on such exchanges and then trying to ascertain what has been said that interested outsiders can begin to appreciate what the encompassing landscape is really all about. Stated more exactly, the outsider must attempt to come to grips with the indigenous cultural forms with which the landscape is experienced, the shared symbolic vehicles that give shape to geographical experience and facilitate its communication — its re-creation and re-presentation — in interpersonal settings. For it is simply not the case, as some phenomenologists and growing numbers of nature writers would have us believe, that relationships to places are lived exclusively or predominantly in contemplative moments of social isolation. On the contrary, relationships to places are lived most often in the company of other people, and it is on these communal occasions—when places are sensed *together*—that native views of the physical world become accessible to strangers. And while attending to ordinary talk is always a useful strategy for uncovering such views, it is usually just a beginning. Relationships to places may also find expression through the agencies of myth, prayer, music, dance, art, architecture, and, in many communities, recurrent forms of religious and political ritual. Thus represented and enacted—daily, monthly, seasonally, annually—places and their meanings are continually woven into the fabric of social life, anchoring it to features of the landscape and blanketing it with layers of significance that few can fail to appreciate. Deliberately and otherwise, people are forever presenting each other with culturally mediated images of where and how they dwell. In large ways and small, they are forever performing acts that reproduce and express their own sense of place—and also, inextricably, their own understandings of who and what they are.

As I conceive of it, the ethnographer's task is to determine what these acts of expression purportedly involve (why they are performed, how they are accomplished, what they are intended to achieve) and to disclose their importance by relating them to larger ideas about the world and its inhabitants. In other words, naturally occurring depictions of places are treated as actualizations of the knowledge that informs them, as outward manifestations of underlying systems of thought, as native constructions wrought with native materials that embody and display a native cast of mind. And it is that cast of mind (or certain prominent aspects of it, anyway) that the ethnographer must work to grasp, intelligibly make out, and later set down in writing. Heaven, then, in a few grains of carefully inspected sand; instructive statements about places and their role in human affairs through the close contextualization of a handful of telling events.[6]

An assignment of this delicacy challenges the text-building pen as much as it does the insight-seeking mind. Mulling over imperfect field notes, sorting through conflicting intuitions, and beset by a host of unanswered questions, the ethnographer must somehow fashion a written account that adequately conveys his or her understanding of other people's understandings. As will shortly become apparent, my own preference is for chronological narratives that move from interpretations of experience raw to those of experience digested, from moments of anxious puzzlement ("What the devil is going on here?") to subsequent ones of cautious insight ("I think perhaps I see."). Because that, more often than not, is how ethnographic fieldwork actually unfolds. It is, to be sure, a discomfiting business in which loose ends abound and little is ever certain. But with ample time, a dollop of patience, and steady guidance from able native instructors, one does make measurable progress. To argue otherwise (and there is a bit of that around these days) is to dismiss ethnography as a valid source of cultural knowledge and turn it into a solipsistic sideshow, an ominous prospect only slightly less appealing than the self-engrossed meanderings of those who seek to promote it. As Isaiah Berlin remarked somewhere, it is better to write of things one believes one knows something about than to anguish in high despair over the manifold difficulties of knowing things at all. And better as well, having taken the plunge, to allow oneself to enjoy it. Doing ethnography can be a great deal of fun, and disguising the fact on paper, as though it were something to be ashamed of, is less than totally honest. It may also be less than effective. Current fashions notwithstanding, clenched teeth and furrowed brow are no guarantee of literary success. In crafting one's prose, as in going about one's fieldwork, it is always permissible—and sometimes highly informative—to smile and even to laugh.

It is permissible, too, to be pleased—and sometimes downright impressed—with things one happens to learn. From time to time, when luck is on their side, ethnographers stumble onto culturally given ideas whose striking novelty and evident scope seem to cry out for thoughtful consideration beyond their accustomed boundaries. Making these ideas available in perusable form is a worthy endeavor on general principles, but where places are concerned it is apt to prove especially illuminating. For where places are involved, attendant modes of dwelling are never far behind, and in this dimly lit region of the anthropological world—call it, if you like, the ethnography of lived topographies—much remains to be learned. Places and their sensings deserve our close attention. To continue to neglect them would be foolish and shortsighted. Intriguing discoveries await us, and the need to consider them thoughtfully grows stronger every day.

> American Indians hold their lands—places—as having the highest possible meaning, and all their statements are made with this reference point in mind.
> —*Vine Deloria, Jr.,* God Is Red

June 7, 1982. The foregoing thoughts would have mattered little to Dudley Patterson or the two other horsemen, Sam Endfield and Charles Cromwell, with whom he was speaking on a late spring day. Having spent nearly ten hours sorting steers and branding calves, the three were resting in a grove of juniper trees several miles from their homes at Cibecue, a settlement of eleven hundred Western Apache people located on the Fort Apache Indian Reservation in east-central Arizona.[7] The heat of the afternoon was still intense, and as the men waited for it to subside their talk was of their trade: the habits and foibles of horses and the dozens of things one needs to keep in mind when working excitable cattle in rough and rocky country. Veteran horsemen all, and intimately familiar with the rugged lands they had explored together for more than forty years, they spoke quietly of such matters, exchanging observations about Dudley's bay mare (strong and quick but reluctant to trot through heavy stands of brush), Sam's roan gelding (gentle and cooperative but apt to bite when hastily bridled), and the spotted maverick bull with curled horns and faulty vision in one eye who could be safely approached from the left side but not from the right. Western Apache shop talk: relaxed, confident, endlessly informative, rising and falling on the soft phonemic tones of the Athapaskan language the horsemen speak with total fluency. As an aspiring speaker of the language and a would-be horseman myself, I am completely absorbed.[8]

A few minutes later, the group beneath the trees is joined by another man on horseback, Talbert Paxton, who is highly regarded as an accomplished roper and a fearless rider in pursuit of bolting cattle. Considerably younger than Dudley Patterson and his companions, Talbert has worked with them many times before, but for the past three weeks, painfully upset over the collapse of a month-long love affair, he has thrown himself into other sorts of activities—such as drinking prodigious quantities of beer, spreading unfounded rumors about the woman who rejected him, and proposing sex to several other women who either laughed in his face or promised to damage his testicles if he took one more step in their direction. Normally restrained and unquestionably intelligent, Talbert had lost control of himself. He had become a nuisance of the first order, an unruly bother and an irritating bore, and the residents of Cibecue were more than a little annoyed.

Nothing is said of this or anything else as Talbert dismounts, tethers his horse to a tree, and seats himself on the ground at a respectable distance from his senior associates. Charles nods him a wordless greeting, Sam does the same, and Dudley announces to no one in particular that it certainly is hot. Talbert remains silent, his eyes fixed intently on the pointed toes of his high-heeled boots. Charles disposes of a well-chewed plug of tobacco, Sam attacks a hangnail with his pocketknife, and Dudley observes that the grass is certainly dry. A long moment passes before Talbert finally speaks. What he says deals neither with the elevated temperature nor with the parched condition of the Cibecue range. In a soft and halting voice he reports that he has been sober for three days and would like to return to work. He adds that he is eager to get away from the village because people there have been gossiping about him. Worse than that, he says, they have been laughing at him behind his back.

It is a candid and touching moment, and I expect from the smiles that appear on the faces of the senior horsemen that they will respond to Talbert's disclosures with accommodating expressions of empathy and approval. But what happens next—a short sequence of emphatically delivered assertions to which Talbert replies in kind—leaves me confused. My bewilderment stems not from a failure to understand the linguistic meanings of the utterances comprising the interchange; indeed, their manifest semantic content is simple and straightforward. What is perplexing is that the utterances arrive as total non sequiturs, as statements I cannot relate to anything that has previously been said or done. Verbal acts without apparent purpose or interactional design, they seem totally unconnected to the social context in which they are occurring, and whatever messages they are intended to convey elude me entirely.

> A grinning Dudley speaks first:
> Hela! Gizhyaa'itiné dį' nandzaa né. (So! You've returned from Trail Goes Down Between Two Hills!)
> Followed by a brightly animated Charles:
> Hela! 'Iłs'ą́ą́ nadaahi niłhiyeeg né. (So! You got tired walking back and forth!)
> Followed by Sam, on the verge of laughter:
> Hela! 'Ilizh diłtł'ii daho'higo bił 'óóhindzii né. (So! You've smelled enough burning piss!)
> Followed by Talbert, who is smiling now himself:
> Dit'įį dogosh'įįda. (For a while I couldn't see!)
> Followed once more by Dudley:
> Dá'andii! Gizhyaa'itiné goyą́ą́go 'anilą́ą́' doleeł. 'Iską́ą́ da łaa naiłdziig. (It's true. Trail Goes Down Between Two Hills will make you wise. We'll work together tomorrow.)

The sudden burst of talk ends as abruptly as it began, and silence again prevails in the shady grove of juniper trees. Nothing more will be said. Still chuckling, Sam Endfield rises from the ground, walks to his horse, and swings smoothly into his saddle. Moments later, the rest of us follow suit. Talbert departs on a trail leading north to the home of one of his sisters. Sam and Charles and Dudley head northwest to a small pasture where they keep their extra mounts. I ride alone toward the trading post at Cibecue, wondering what to have for supper and trying to make sense of the events I have just witnessed. But to no avail. What the place named Trail Goes Down Between Two Hills has to do with too much walking back and forth, burning urine, and making young men wise are things I do not know. And why mentioning them succeeded in lifting everyone's spirits, including those of the beleaguered Talbert Paxton, remains an unanswered question.

Arriving that evening at the outskirts of Cibecue, I was unaware that I had been exposed to a venerable set of verbal practices whereby Western Apaches evoke and manipulate the significance of local places to comment on the moral shortcomings of wayward individuals.[9] Neither did I suspect that I would soon develop an abiding interest in the system of ideas on which these practices rest. But that is how things turned out. During the past two decades, I have spent a fair amount of time exploring the physical and cultural territory from which these ideas derive their vitality and force, and it was Dudley Patterson, a man of generous intellect and unremitting kindness, who showed me how to begin.[10] For it was Dudley to whom I turned shortly after the incident with Talbert Paxton, and it was Dudley, sympathetic to my befuddlement and keen to supplement his income with some additional dollars, who explained what had happened and why.

June 12, 1982. Short of stature and trim of build, the 54-year-old horseman presents a handsome figure as he emerges from the small wooden house where he has lived by himself since the death of his wife in 1963. Dressed in freshly laundered Levis, a red-checked shirt, and a cream-colored straw hat, he moves with the grace of a natural athlete, and it strikes me as he approaches that nothing about him is extraneous. Just as his actions are instinctually measured and neatly precise, so is the manner in which he speaks, sings, and dances with friends and relatives at religious ceremonials. But he is also given to joking and laughter, and whenever he smiles, which is much of the time, his angular countenance lights up with an abundance of sheer good will that seems wholly irrepressible. Expert cattleman, possessor of horse power, dutiful kinsman without peer, no one in Cibecue is more thoroughly liked than Dudley Patterson. And few are more respected. For along with everything else, Dudley is known to be wise.

It was the merits of wisdom, Dudley informs me over a cup of boiled coffee, that Talbert Paxton needed to be reminded of earlier in the week. But before discussing that, Dudley inquires whether I have lately visited Trail Goes Down Between Two Hills, the place whose name is Gizh-yaa'itiné.[11] I tell him I have. Located a few miles north of Cibecue, its Apache name describes it well—two wooded knolls of similar size and shape with a footpath passing between them that descends to a grassy flat on the west bank of Cibecue Creek. And did I notice the big cottonwood tree that stands a few yards back from the stream? I did—a gigantic tree, gnarled and ancient, with one huge limb that dips to touch the ground before twisting upward and reaching toward the sky . And had anyone from Cibecue told me what happened long ago at Trail Goes Down Between Two Hills? No, only that the widow of a man named Blister Boy once planted corn nearby. Had I never heard the stories about Old Man Owl, the one named Mú hastiin? No, never. Well then, listen.

Figure 2.1. Keith H. Basso stands by the great cottonwood tree at Trail Goes Down Between Two Hills (Gizhyaa'itiné). Photograph © Gayle Potter-Basso.

Long ago, right there at that place, there were two beautiful girls. They were sisters. They were talking together.

Then they saw Old Man Owl walking toward them. They knew what he was like. He thought all the time about doing things with women. Then they said, "Let's do something to him."

Then one of those girls went to the top of one of the hills. Her sister went to the top of the other one. As Old Man Owl was walking between them, the first girl called out to him. "Old Man Owl, come here! I want you to rub me between my legs!" He stopped. He got excited! So he started to climb the hill where the girl was sitting.

Then, after Old Man Owl got halfway to the top, the second girl called out to him. "Old Man Owl, I want you to rub me gently between my legs!" He stopped! He got even more excited! So he turned around, walked down the hill, and began to climb the other one.

Then, after he got halfway to the top, the first girl called out to him again in the same way. He stopped! Now he was very excited! So Old Man Owl did the same thing again. He forgot about the second girl, walked down the hill, and began climbing the other one.

It happened that way four times. Old Man Owl went back and forth, back and forth, climbing up and down those hills.

Then those beautiful girls just laughed at him.

Fairly beaming with amusement and delight, Dudley wastes little time beginning a second story about Old Man Owl at Trail Goes Down Between Two Hills.

Those same two sisters were there again. I don't know why, maybe they went there often to get water.

Then Old Man Owl was walking toward them. They decided they would do something to him.

Then one of the girls climbed into the branches of a big cottonwood tree that was growing there. The other girl went to the top of one of those hills.

Then the girl in the tree lifted her skirt and spread her legs slightly apart. She remained motionless as Old Man Owl walked beneath her. Suddenly, he looked up! He had noticed something!

Now he got very excited! "Hmm," he thought, "that tree looks a lot like a woman. I really like the way it looks. I'd best bring it home. I think I'll burn it down." His eyesight was very poor. Old Man Owl was very nearly blind.

Then, having piled some grass at the base of the tree, Old Man Owl set fire to it. The girl in the tree pissed on it and quickly put it out. Old Man Owl looked all around. "Where's that rain coming from?" he said. "I don't see any clouds." So he started another fire at the base of the tree and the girl pissed on it again and quickly put it out. Now he was very confused. The other girl, the one on top of the hill, could hear all that Old Man Owl was saying to himself. She was really laughing!

Then Old Man Owl did the same thing again. He started another fire and the girl in the tree pissed on it and put it out. He was looking around again. "Where's that rain coming from? Where's that rain coming from? I don't see any clouds! There are no clouds anywhere! Something must be wrong!"

Then he tried one more time and the girl in the tree did the same thing again. Old Man Owl stood there shaking his head. "Something must be very wrong!" he said. "I'd better go home." He walked away with his head hanging down.

Then those two beautiful girls joined each other and laughed and laughed. They were really laughing at Old Man Owl.

As Dudley Patterson closes his narrative, he is laughing himself. It is obvious that he relishes the stories of Old Man Owl. Moments later, after pouring us another cup of coffee, he as much as says so—the stories are very old, he has heard them many times, and they always give him pleasure. Besides being humorous, he says, they make him think of the ancestors—the wise ones, he calls them—the people who first told the stories at a time when humans and animals communicated without difficulty. These are thoughts I have heard expressed before, by Dudley and other Apache people living at Cibecue, and I know they are strongly felt. But I have yet to learn how the tales of Old Man Owl played into the episode involving Talbert Paxton. If the point was to inform Talbert that beautiful women can be deceiving, or perhaps should not be trusted, or sometimes enjoy toying with the emotions of unsuspecting men, why hadn't the horsemen just come out and said so? Why had they beat around the bush?

Uncertain of how to ask this question in Apache, I attempt to convey it in English, which Dudley understands with more than fair success. He catches on quickly to the thrust of my query and proceeds to answer it with gratifying thoroughness. Speaking for Charles and Sam as well as himself, he explains that there were several reasons for dealing with Talbert as they did. To have criticized Talbert explicitly—to have told him in so many words that his recent behavior was foolish, offensive, and disruptive—would have been insulting and condescending. As judged from Talbert's apologetic demeanor, he had reached these conclusions himself, and to inform him openly of what he already knew would be to treat him like a child. In addition, because Talbert was unrelated by ties of kinship to either Dudley or Sam, and because he was related only distantly to Charles, none of them possessed the requisite authority to instruct him directly on matters pertaining to his personal life; this was the proper responsibility of his older matrilineal kin. Moreover, the horsemen were fond of Talbert. He was a friendly young man, quiet and congenial, whose undemanding company and propensity for hard work they very much appreciated. Last, and beyond all this, Dudley and his companions wanted Talbert to remember what they would urge upon him by attaching it to something concrete, something fixed and permanent, something he had seen and could go to see again—a place upon the land.

So the horsemen took a circuitous path—tactful, respectful, and fully in keeping with their status as nonrelatives—with Dudley leading the way. His opening statement to Talbert—"So! You've returned from Trail Goes Down Between Two Hills"—was intended to focus the young man's attention on the place where Old Man Owl encountered the two Apache sisters and to summon thoughts of what transpired there. Dudley's comment was also meant to suggest that Talbert, having acted in certain respects like Old Man Owl himself, would be well advised to alter his conduct. But in presupposing that Talbert was already aware of this— in announcing that he had *returned* from Trail Goes Down Between Two Hills—Dudley's comment also affirmed his friend's decision to refrain from drinking and resume a normal life. Thus, in a sidelong but deftly pointed way, Dudley was criticizing Talbert's misguided behavior while at the same time commending him for rejecting it as unacceptable.

The ensuing statements by Charles and Sam—"So! You got tired walking back and forth!" and "So! You've smelled enough burning piss!" —sharpened and consolidated these themes, further likening Talbert to

Old Man Owl by alluding to key events in the stories that recount his misadventures with the pair of beautiful girls. But these assertions, like Dudley's before them, were couched in the past tense, thereby implying that Talbert's resolve to behave differently in the future was a good and welcome development. The horsemen's strategy must have worked successfully because Talbert responded by tacitly admitting that his actions had indeed resembled those of Old Man Owl; simultaneously, however, he registered his belief that the resemblance had come to an end. In effect, his reply to the horsemen—"For a while I couldn't see!"—conveyed a veiled confession of improper conduct and an implicit declaration not to repeat it. But more was conveyed than this. At one level, Talbert's statement intimated a forcefully simple truth: he had been cold sober for three days and now, having recovered his physical senses, could once again see clearly. But at another level, and perhaps more forcefully still, the truth was allegorical. Unlike the myopic Old Man Owl, who never curbed his voracious sexual appetites and remained hopelessly at odds with everyone around him, Talbert was intimating that he had regained his social senses as well. Obliquely but sincerely, he was informing the horsemen that his moral vision had been restored.

Which was just what Dudley Patterson wanted to hear. As Dudley told Talbert before he left to go home, his imaginary visit to Trail Goes Down Between Two Hills would help make him wise. And maybe it would. With assistance from Old Man Owl and his two alluring tormentors, Talbert had been firmly chastised and generously pardoned, all in the space of a minute in which no one uttered a harsh or demeaning word. In a very real sense, involving at base a vividly animated sense of place, Talbert had been taken back into an important segment of the Cibecue community. He would return to work tomorrow, and that was why the horsemen, including Talbert himself, were still smiling broadly when they left the grove of juniper trees and went their separate ways.

Back at his house in Cibecue, Dudley Patterson drains his cup of coffee and leans forward in his chair. On the ground near his feet a band of red ants is dismantling the corpse of a large grasshopper, and within seconds the intricate patterns of their furious activity have riveted his attention. This does not surprise me. I have known Dudley for nine years and on other occasions have seen him withdraw from social encounters to keep counsel with himself. I also know that he is mightily interested in red ants and holds them in high esteem. I would like to ask him a few more questions, but unless he invites me to do so (and by now, I suspect, he may have had enough) it would be rude to disturb him. He has made it clear that he wants to be left alone.

We sit together for more than ten minutes, smoking cigarettes and enjoying the morning air, and I try to picture the cottonwood tree that towers beside the stream at Trail Goes Down Between Two Hills. I am acutely aware that my perception of the tree has changed. Having heard the stories of Old Man Owl, its impressive size seems decidedly less important, and what strikes me as never before is its standing in the Cibecue community as a visible embodiment of myth, a leafy monument to Apache ancestral wisdom. I am also aware that the placename identifying the tree's location—Gizhyaa'itiné—has taken on a vibrant new dimension. Formerly nothing more than a nicely descriptive toponym, it has acquired the stamp of human events, of consequential happenings, of memorable times in the life of a people. As a result, the name seems suddenly fuller, larger somehow, endowed with added force. Because now, besides evoking images of a piece of local countryside, it calls up thoughts of fabled deeds and the singular cast of actors who there had played them out. Gizhyaa'itiné. Repeating the name silently to myself, I decide that Dudley Patterson's narratives have transformed its referent from a geographical site into something resembling a theater, a natural stage upon the land (vacant now but with major props still fully intact) where significant moral dramas unfolded in the past. How many other places are there like it? Gizhyaa'itiné. In my mind's eye, I can almost see the beautiful Apache sisters, really laughing at Old Man Owl.

Still engrossed in his ants, Dudley remains oblivious to the sights and sounds around him—a pair of ravens perched on his tool shed, the distant wailing of a distressed child, a vicious dogfight that erupts without warning in the tall grass behind his house. It is only when his older sister arrives on foot with a dishpan filled with freshly made tortillas that he glances up and sets his thoughts aside. He explains to Ruth Patterson that he has been talking to me about the land and how it can make people wise. "Wisdom," Ruth says firmly in Apache. "It's difficult!" And then, after inviting me to stay and eat with them, she enters Dudley's house to prepare a simple meal. Prompting a surge of ethnographic gloom, Ruth's remark forces me to acknowledge that I know next to nothing about Apache conceptions of wisdom. In what is wisdom thought to consist? How does one detect its presence or absence? How is it acquired? Do persons receive instruction in wisdom or is it something they arrive at, or fail to arrive at, entirely on their own? And why is it, as Ruth said, that wisdom is "difficult"? If I am to understand something of how places work to make people wise, an idea I find instantly compelling, these are matters I must try to explore.

And who better to explore them with than Dudley Patterson? He is known to be wise—many people have said so—and I have to begin somewhere. So without further ado I put the question to him: "What is wisdom?" Dudley greets my query with a faintly startled look that recedes into a quizzical expression I have not seen before. "It's in these places," he says. "Wisdom sits in places." Hesitant but unenlightened, I ask again. "Yes, but what is it?" Now it is Dudley's turn to hesitate. Removing his hat, he rests it on his lap and gazes into the distance. As he continues to look away, the suspicion grows that I have offended him, that my question about wisdom (which now seems rash and impulsive) has exceeded the limits of propriety and taste. Increasingly apprehensive, I feel all thumbs, clumsy and embarrassed, a presumptuous dolt who acted without thinking. What Dudley is feeling I cannot tell, but in less than a minute he rescues the situation and I am much relieved. "Wisdom sits in places," he says again. And then, unbidden, he begins to tell me why.

Long ago, the people moved around all the time. They went everywhere looking for food and watching out for enemies. It was hard for them. They were poor. They were often hungry. The women went out with their daughters to gather acorns, maybe walnuts. They went in search of all kinds of plants. Some man with a rifle and bullets always went with them. He looked out for danger.

Then they got to a good place and camped there. All day they gathered acorns. The women showed their daughters how to do it. Now they stopped working for a little while to eat and drink.

Then one of the women talked to the girls. "Do you see that mountain over there? I want you to look at it. Its name is Dził ndeezé (Long Mountain). Remember it! Do you know what happened long ago close to that mountain? Well, now I'm going to tell you about it." Then she told them a story about what happened there. After she had finished she said, "Well, now you know what happened at Long Mountain. What I have told you is true. I didn't make it up. I learned it from my grandmother. Look at that mountain and think about it! It will help make you wise."

Then she pointed to another place and did the same way again. "Do you see that spring over there? Look at it! Its name is Dǫ' bigowané (Fly's Camp)." Now she told them a story about that place, too. "Think about it," she said. "Someday, after you have grown up, you will be wise," she said. Everywhere they went they did like that. They gave their daughters place-names and stories. "You should think about this," they said.

The same was done with boys. They went hunting for deer with their fathers and uncles. They didn't come home until they had killed many deer. Everyone was happy when they came back. Now they had meat to eat.

Then, when they were out hunting, one of the men would talk to the boys. "Do you see where the trail crosses the wash? Look at it! Its name is Ma' té hilizhé (Coyote Pisses In The Water). Something happened there long ago. I'm going to tell you about it." Now he told the story to them. "Don't forget it," he said. "I want you to think about it. Someday it's going to make you wise."

Then they would stop at some other place. "This place is named Tséé deeschii' ts'ǫsé (Slender Red Rock Ridge). Something happened here, also," he said. He told them that story. "Remember what I have told you," he said.

It was like that. The people who went many places were wise. They knew all about them. They thought about them. I've been all over this country. I went with my grandfather when I was a boy. I also traveled with my uncles. They taught me the names of all these places. They told me stories about all of them. I've thought about all of them for a long time. I still remember everything.

Sitting with my back to Dudley's house, I cannot see that Ruth Patterson has come to the door and is listening to her brother as he speaks of places and wisdom. I sense her presence, however, and when I turn around she is looking at me, her comely face arranged in what I interpret as a sympathetic smile. "It's true," she says in a bright tone of voice. "Everything he says is true. It happened that way to me."

One time—I was a young girl then—I went with my mother to Nadah nchii'é (Bitter Mescal). That was in 1931. We went there to roast mescal. There were other people with us, quite a few of them. They were all my relatives.

Then we made camp, right below that point at the north end of the mountain. We camped by the spring there. My mother was in charge of everything. She told us what to do.

Then we dug up a lot of mescal and brought it back to camp. It was hard work. It was hot. We were young girls then. We weren't yet strong and got tired easily. We really wanted to rest.

Then my mother talked to us. "You should only rest a little while. Don't be lazy. Don't think about getting tired. If you do, you'll get careless and something might happen to you."

Then she told a story. "Maybe you've heard this story before but I'm going to tell it to you anyway." She pointed to that mountain named Túzhį' yaahigaiyé (Whiteness Spreads Out Extending Down To Water). "It happened over there," she said to us.

"Long ago, on the east side of that mountain, there were lots of dead oak trees. There was a woman living with her family not far away. 'We're almost out of firewood,' she said to one of her daughters. 'Go up there and bring back some of that oak.'

"Then that girl went up there. She started to gather firewood. It was very hot and she got tired fast. 'I'm getting tired,' she thought. 'I've already got enough firewood. I'll go back home.'

"Then she picked up as much firewood as she could carry. She started walking down to her camp. She got careless. She stepped on a thin flat rock. It looked strong but she forgot she was carrying all that heavy oak. The rock broke when she stepped on it. She stumbled and fell down. She hit her head on the ground. For a while she was unconscious.

"Then she came to and noticed that she was bleeding from cuts on her cheek and chin. She walked unsteadily back to her camp. She told her mother what had happened.

"Then her mother talked to her. 'You acted foolishly but you're going to be all right. You failed to see danger before it happened. You could have fallen off the trail and gotten killed on those sharp rocks below it. You were thinking only of yourself. That's why this happened to you.'"

That's the end of the story. After my mother told it to us, she spoke to us again. "Well, now you know what happened over there at Whiteness Spreads Out Extending Down To Water. That careless girl almost lost her life. Each of you should try to remember this. Don't forget it. If you remember what happened over there, it will help make you wise."

Then we went back to work, digging up more mescal. I got tired again— it was still very hot—but this time I didn't think about it. I just tried not to be careless.

Nowadays, hardly anyone goes out to get mescal. Very few of us do that anymore. The younger ones are afraid of hard work. Even so, I've told that story to all my children. I've told them to remember it.

I thank Ruth for telling me her story. She tries to muster a smile but her eyes have filled with tears. Unable to stem the rush of her emotion, she turns away and goes back inside the house. Dudley is not visibly concerned. He explains that Ruth is recalling her youth. That was during the 1920s and 1930s when Ruth and her sisters were still unmarried and worked almost daily under the close supervision of their mother and two maternal aunts. Back then, Dudley says, Cibecue was different. There were fewer people and life was less centered on the village itself. Whole Apache families, including Dudley's own, spent weeks and months away upon the land—tending cornfields, roasting mescal, hunting deer, and journeying to remote cattle camps where they helped the horsemen build fences and corrals. The families traveled long distances— old people and children alike, on foot and horseback, through all kinds of weather, carrying their possessions in heavy canvas packs over narrow trails that now have all but vanished. It was a hard way to live— there were times when it got very hard—but the people were strong and hardly ever complained. They had able leaders who told them what to do, and despite the hardships involved they took pleasure in their journeys. And wherever they went they gave placenames and stories to their children. They wanted their children to know about the ancestors. They wanted their children to be wise. Ruth is remembering all of this, Dudley reports, and it makes her a little sad.

The aging horseman leans back in his chair, crossing a boot across his knee, and spins the rowel of his spur. *Vrnnnn!* He does this from time to time when thinking serious thoughts. He rolls a cigarette and lights it with a battered Zippo he has carried for years. *Vrnnnn!* Spinning and smoking at the same time—his thoughts must be serious indeed. Several minutes pass before he speaks. When he does, he tells me that he has not forgotten my question: "What is wisdom?" He now intends to address it. He will use his own language, and to help me understand he will try to keep things simple. He stubs out his cigarette, rolls and lights another one, and then goes to work. *Vrnnnn!* What follows is poetry and a great deal more about wisdom.

The trail of wisdom—that is what I'm going to talk about. I'm going to speak as the old people do, as my grandmother spoke to me when I was still a boy. We were living then at Ták'eh godzigé (Rotten Field).

"Do you want a long life?" she said. "Well, you will need to have wisdom. You will need to think about your own mind. You will need to work on it. You should start doing this now. You must make your mind smooth. You must make your mind steady. You must make your mind resilient.

"Your life is like a trail. You must be watchful as you go. Wherever you go there is some kind of danger waiting to happen. You must be able to see it before it happens. You must always be watchful and alert. You must see danger in your mind before it happens.

"If your mind is not smooth you will fail to see danger. You will trust your eyes but they will deceive you. You will be easily tricked and fooled. Then there will be nothing but trouble for you. You must make your mind smooth.

"If your mind is not resilient you will be easily startled. You will be easily frightened. You will try to think quickly but you won't think clearly. You yourself will stand in the way of your own mind. You yourself will block it. Then there will be trouble for you. You must make your mind resilient.

"If your mind is not steady you will be easily angered and upset. You will be arrogant and proud. You will look down on other people. You will envy them and desire their possessions. You will speak about them without thinking. You will complain about them, gossip about them, criticize them. You will lust after their women. People will come to despise you. They will pay someone to use his power on you. They will want to kill you. Then there will be nothing but trouble for you. You must make your mind steady. You must learn to forget about yourself.

"If you make your mind smooth, you will have a long life. Your trail will extend a long way. You will be prepared for danger wherever you go. You will see it in your mind before it happens.

"How will you walk along this trail of wisdom? Well, you will go to many places. You must look at them closely. You must remember all of them. Your relatives will talk to you about them. You must remember everything they tell you. You must think about it, and keep on thinking about it, and keep on thinking about it. You must do this because no one can help you but yourself. If you do this your mind will become smooth. It will become steady and resilient. You will stay away from trouble. You will walk a long way and live a long time.

"Wisdom sits in places. It's like water that never dries up. You need to drink water to stay alive, don't you? Well, you also need to drink from places. You must remember everything about them. You must learn their names. You must remember what happened at them long ago. You must think about it and keep on thinking about it. Then your mind will become smoother and smoother. Then you will see danger before it happens. You will walk a long way and live a long time. You will be wise. People will respect you."

Vrnnnn! Rising to his feet without another word, Dudley walks away in the direction of his outhouse. His suspicions were correct: I have had trouble grasping his statement on wisdom. No one from Cibecue has broached this subject with me before, and few have spoken with

such eloquence and grace. I am moved by what I have heard but uncertain what to make of it. And understandably so. Dudley delivered his
comments in a distinctive verbal register characterized by conspicuous
grammatical parallelism, marked lexical redundancy, and the measured
repetition of several dominant metaphors. All this resembles the language of Western Apache prayer, and therein lies one of my problems.
While the economy of Dudley's speech rendered portions of his statement readily accessible, the metaphors that anchored it—boldly figured,
densely compressed, and probably very old—stood far beyond my reach.
What, for example, is a "smooth mind"? A "resilient mind"? A "steady
mind"? There is another problem as well. I can safely assume that Dudley's
account was supported throughout by a covert cultural logic that imbued its claims with validity and truth. Yet it is quite unclear to me what
that logic is. What sort of reasoning supports the assertion that "wisdom
sits in places"? Or that "wisdom is like water"? Or that "drinking from
places," whatever that is, requires knowledge of placenames and stories
of past events? Maybe I have gotten in over my head. Dudley's statement
has caught me off guard and left me feeling unmoored. For a second I
imagine myself as a small uprooted plant bouncing crazily through the
air on a whirlwind made of ancient Apache tropes.

When Dudley returns he is smiling. "Did you understand?" I shake
my head. "No, not much." Ruth is also smiling. She is standing in the
doorway and looks fully recovered from her bout with nostalgia. She has
combed her hair and is sporting the triumphant look of one who knew
all along. "I told you!" she says sharply. "It's difficult! Now my brother
has made you think too much. Now your brain is really tired! Now you
look kind of sick!" Ruth's assessment of my mental and physical condition does little to improve it, and I look to Dudley for help. "I gave
you too much at once," he says. "You just need to think about it." Ruth
agrees. "That's right! You really need to think about it!" Then she flashes
her broadest smile and tells us our food is ready.

But before we go inside Ruth presents us with a suggestion. On the
coming weekend, when the horsemen will be off work, Dudley and I
will catch up our horses and go for a ride. It might last all day, so we will
need to take food. Ruth will provide the fresh tortillas. I will contribute
two cans of sardines, a box of Ritz crackers, a slab of longhorn cheese,
and four bottles of Barg's root beer. Dudley will take me to different
places, teach me their names, and tell me what happened at them long
ago. Then, maybe, I will understand something. When we get back home
Dudley will speak to me in English—"Boy Keez, I'll see you sometime."
Then he will leave me alone to think. In return for these services, he will
receive two sacks of flour, two cans of MJB coffee, one sack of sugar, a

pail of Crisco, and twenty dollars cash. Now, what about it? For all her endearing qualities—and she has them in abundance—Ruth Patterson is not a person to challenge when her mind is made up, and Dudley, who on prior occasions has pointed this out himself, wastes no time in endorsing her plan. Neither do I. "Good!" says Ruth, whose reputation also embraces an unswerving willingness to capitalize on promising business opportunities whenever they arise. "Good!" she says again. "My brother will help you out. I think you'll really like it."

> As soon as we have the thing before our eyes, and in our hearts an ear for the word, thinking prospers.
> —*Martin Heidegger, "Building Dwelling Thinking"*

June 15, 1982. Even the most experienced horsemen get hurt. That is what people say as news of Dudley's accident circulates through Cibecue. Yesterday, trailing the spotted maverick bull with poor eyesight at the base of a rocky sloped named Tséé deeschii'é (Long Red Ridge), Dudley's mare lost her footing, went down hard, and abandoned her rider to walk home with bruised ribs, a dislocated shoulder, and a badly swollen lip. Dudley's first concern was for the welfare of the mare, who returned to her pasture later in the day with nothing more than a few minor scrapes and a glassy look in her eye. This morning, wrapped in a homemade sling that keeps slipping off, Dudley is stiff and sore and in excellent spirits. We sit on the porch of his house as visitors come and go. Ruth has launched a get-well campaign whose main objectives are to accumulate gifts of thick beef broth and to surround her brother with as many children as possible. The children come in shifts to stand beside his chair. He tells them the story of his mishap, and their eyes grow wide with excitement and fear, and he smiles his warmest smile and tells them to be careful around horses and cattle. A little girl steps forward and gives him her orange Popsicle. As I stand to leave, Dudley tells me to come back tomorrow—things will be less busy and we can speak again of matters raised before. I accept his invitation. A small boy approaches his chair and hands him a piece of bubblegum. Dudley is delighted. Ruth's campaign is already a success. Dudley will rejoin the horsemen in less than a week. Our ride together has been postponed.

June 16–19, 1982. For the next four days—drinking coffee, watching ants, and pausing occasionally to speak of other things—Dudley and I engaged in a series of conversations about his earlier statement on wisdom and places. At my request, we began by examining some of the statement's linguistic features, focusing attention on the morphology and semantics of its several primary tropes. We then moved on to consider the internal logic of Dudley's account, exploring in some detail the culturally based assumptions that invested its claims with coherence and credible sense. Our discussions dealt with fairly abstract matters, and now and again, when Dudley sensed his pupil was getting muddled, he responded by telling stories that linked his generalizations to illustrative sets of particulars. It soon became apparent that Apache conceptions of wisdom differed markedly from those contained in Western ideologies. More interesting was the discovery that the Apache conceptions were grounded in an informal theory of mind which asserts that wisdom arises from a small set of antecedent conditions. Because these conditions are also qualities of mind, and because they vary from mind to mind, the theory explains why some people are wiser than others.

Stated in general terms, the Apache theory holds that "wisdom" —'igoyá'í—consists in a heightened mental capacity that facilitates the avoidance of harmful events by detecting threatening circumstances when none are apparent.[12] This capacity for prescient thinking is produced and sustained by three mental conditions, described in Apache as *bíni' godilkǫǫh* (smoothness of mind), *bíni' gontł'iz* (resilience of mind), and *bíni' gonłdzil* (steadiness of mind). Because none of these conditions is given at birth, each must be cultivated in a conscientious manner by acquiring relevant bodies of knowledge and applying them critically to the workings of one's mind. Knowledge of places and their cultural significance is crucial in this regard because it illustrates with numerous examples the mental conditions needed for wisdom as well as the practical advantages that wisdom confers on persons who possess it. Contained in stories attributed to the "ancestors" (*nowhizǫ'yé*), knowledge of places thus embodies an unformalized model of 'igoyá'í and an authoritative rationale for seeking to attain it. Although some Apache people embrace this knowledge eagerly and commit it to memory in exhaustive detail, others are less successful; and while some are able to apply it productively to their minds, many experience difficulty. Consequently, in any Apache community at any point in time, wisdom is present in varying degrees, and only a few persons are ever completely wise. By virtue of their unusual mental powers, wise men and women are able to foresee disaster, fend off misfortune, and avoid explosive conflicts with other persons. For these and other reasons, they are highly respected and often live to be very old. Likened to water because of its life-sustaining properties, wisdom is viewed first and foremost as an instrument of survival.

Although Western Apaches distinguish clearly between an individual's "mind" (*bíni'*) and his or her "brain" (*bitsighą́ą́*), both are described with a classificatory verb stem (*-áá*) that designates portable objects

whose shape is roundish and compact. However, only *bíni'* can be modified with adjectival constructions beginning with the prefix *go-* (space;
area), an instructive bit of morphology which indicates that the mind is
conceived as a region within the brain. This notion is illustrated by the
expression *bíni' godilkǫǫh* (smoothness of mind), which identifies the primary mental condition required for wisdom. When the adjective *dilkǫǫh*
is used without prefixes it serves to describe the texture of smooth and
even surfaces, such as the surface of a pane of glass or a piece of varnished
wood. But when *dilkǫǫh* is combined with *go-* it conveys the sense of
"cleared space" or "area free of obstructions," such as an agricultural field
from which all vegetation has been assiduously removed. This is the sense
in which *godilkǫǫh* is used in the Apache metaphor of the smooth mind.
Like cleared plots of ground, smooth minds are unobstructed—unclut-
tered and unfettered—a quality that permits them to observe and reason with penetrating clarity. Skeptical of outward appearances, smooth
minds are able to look through them and beyond them to detect obscured realities and hidden possibilities. Unencumbered by obstacles to
insightful thinking, smooth minds "see danger before it happens" and
"trouble before it comes." Thus does wisdom flourish.

Mental smoothness is believed by Apaches to be the product of two
subsidiary conditions—mental resilience and mental steadiness—which
ward off distractions that interfere with calm and focused thought. These
distractions are grouped into two broad classes according to whether
their sources are external or internal to the individual. "Resilience of
mind" (*bíni' gontł'iz*) combats those of the external variety, while "steadiness of mind" (*bíni' gonłdzil*) works to eliminate internal distractions.
Turning to the first of these expressions, it should be noted that the adjective *ntł'iz* is used alone in the familiar sense of "hard," thus describing
a wide array of objects whose rigid surfaces resist damage and destruction from outside forces. But when *ntł'iz* is combined with the spatial
prefix *go-* the resulting construction, *gontł'iz,* takes on a meaning equivalent to "an enclosed space that holds its shape." A tightly woven basket,
yielding but strong, is properly described as *gontł'iz,* as is an inflated
vinyl ball or a flexible cardboard box that withstands the weight of a
child. And so, too, is a resilient human mind. Resistant to the unnerv-
ing effects of jarring external events, resilient minds protect their interior spaces by shielding them against outside disruptions that threaten
quiescent thinking. Mental smoothness is thereby promoted and preserved. According to Dudley Patterson, fear and alarm present the greatest threats to maintaining mental resilience. Being aware of this, resilient
minds guard themselves against shock and consternation, keeping these
reactions at bay by centering themselves on what must be done to deal

with the problem at hand. Resilient minds do not give in to panic or fall prey to spasms of anxiety or succumb to spells of crippling worry. Largely immune to emotional turbulence, they do not become agitated or disoriented. Even in terrifying circumstances, resilient minds maintain their ability to reason clearly and thus neither "block themselves" nor "stand in their own way."

While resilience of mind contributes to mental smoothness by blunting the effects of external distractions, "steadiness of mind"—*bíni'gonłdzil* —accomplishes this objective by removing the sources of internal ones. The sense of "steady" conveyed by the adjective *nłdzil* is that which one associates with a post driven firmly into the ground. The post is stable, it does not wobble, and therefore it is reliable. But the post itself is not responsible for these desirable attributes. As interpreted by Apaches, the post's steadiness is imparted by the hole in which it is lodged, and this is the notion—a "supportive and accommodating space"—that is evoked by the form *gonłdzil*. Conceived and described in analogous terms, steady human minds maintain themselves in a manner that ensures their own stability and reliability. This is achieved by relinquishing all thoughts of personal superiority and by eliminating aggressive feelings toward fellow human beings. As a result, steady minds are unhampered by feelings of arrogance or pride, anger or vindictiveness, jealousy or lust—all of which present serious hindrances to calm and measured thinking. Because the essence of mental steadiness lies in a capacity to do away with self-serving emotions that exploit or degrade the worth of other people, wise men and women rarely encounter serious interpersonal problems. Free of conceit and hostile ambitions, steady minds "forget about themselves" and conduct their social affairs in harmony and peace.

Except for the mentally impaired, every Apache who enters the world can legitimately aspire to wisdom. Yet none is born with the three conditions of mind required for wisdom to flourish. Cultivating these conditions, a long and uneven process involving much introspection and many disheartening setbacks, has a private and a public aspect. On the one hand, it is the responsibility of individuals to critically assess their own minds and prepare them for wisdom by cultivating the qualities of smoothness, resilience, and steadiness. On the other hand, instruction is needed from persons sympathetic to the endeavor who have pursued it themselves with a measure of success. Although instruction may begin at any age, it usually commences when preadolescent children become aware that adult life entails an endless flow of demands that need to be met with special skills and abilities. Young people who have reached this level of understanding are told to be constantly alert to what goes on around them, to remember everything they observe, and to report on

anything out of the ordinary. They are also urged to pay close attention to the words and actions of older people whose general demeanor
is deemed worthy of emulation. And they are regularly invited to travel,
especially in the company of persons who will speak to them about the
places they see and visit. It is on these excursions that the relationship
between places and wisdom is first made explicit. "Drink from places,"
Apache boys and girls are told. "Then you can work on your mind."

This view of mental development rests on the premise that knowledge is useful to the extent that it can be swiftly recalled and turned
without effort to practical ends. A related premise is that objects whose
appearance is unique are more easily recalled than those that look alike.
It follows from these assumptions that because places are visually unique
(a fact both marked and affirmed by their possession of separate names),
they serve as excellent vehicles for recalling useful knowledge. And because the knowledge needed for wisdom is nothing if not useful, the
adage that "wisdom sits in places"—'igoyą́'í goz'ą́ą́ siką́ą́—is seen to make
perfect sense. But there is more to the adage than truth and logical consistency. The verb si- (it sits) incorporates a classificatory stem (-ką́ą́) which
applies exclusively to rigid containers and their contents. The prototype
of this category is a watertight vessel, and thus the adage creates an image
of places as durable receptacles, and of the knowledge required for wisdom as a lasting supply of water resting securely within them. This same
image supports the assertions that preparing one's mind for wisdom is
akin to a form of drinking, and that wisdom, like water, is basic to survival. As Dudley Patterson remarked during one of our conversations,
"You can't live long without water and you can't live a long time without wisdom. You need to drink both."

The knowledge on which wisdom depends is gained from observing
different places (thus to recall them quickly and clearly), learning their
Apache names (thus to identify them in spoken discourse and in song),
and reflecting on traditional narratives that underscore the virtues of
wisdom by showing what can happen when its facilitating conditions
are absent. Drawn from different story genres, these narratives juxtapose
a character whose mind is insightfully smooth with one or more characters whose minds are not. Distracted by troubling events or excited at
the prospect of achieving selfish gains, characters of the latter type fail
to understand the true nature of their situation and perform impulsive
acts that bring them and others to the brink of disaster. In sharp contrast, characters of the former type remain calm and undisturbed, grasp
the situation for what it really is, and avert misfortune by exercising the
clear and wary vision that is the hallmark of wisdom. The social group
survives, shaken but whole, and the qualities of mind responsible for its

continuation are made clear for all to see. Wisdom has triumphed over stupidity and foolishness, and the difference between them—a difference as large as life and death itself—cannot be ignored.

The two stories that follow were offered by Dudley Patterson to illustrate these themes. The first story deals with serious problems stemming from a lack of mental resilience; the second depicts a near catastrophe brought on by a lack of mental steadiness. In both stories, alarm and confusion run rampant until mental smoothness, accompanied by wisdom, comes to the rescue in the very nick of time.

> Long ago, some people went to gather acorns. They camped at Tséé názt'i'é (Line Of Rocks Circles Around). They gathered lots of acorns near Tséé ditł'igé naaditiné (Trail Goes Across Scorched Rocks). They almost had enough but they went on anyway. They were going to K'ai cho o'áhá (Big Willow Stands Alone). They stopped on their way where the trail crossed a shallow stream. They had been walking fast and were very thirsty. They wanted to drink. It was hot.
>
> Then their leader said to them, "Don't drink until I tell you to. I want to look around here first." He went off. Their leader was wise. He saw danger in his mind.
>
> Then, as soon as he was gone, a young woman said, "My children are very thirsty. They need to drink. This water looks safe to me. I'm going to drink it." The others agreed with her. "Yes," they said, "we must drink. This water looks good." So they started drinking.
>
> Then, pretty soon, they began to get sick. They got dizzy and began to vomit violently. All of them got sick, including the children. They got sicker. They vomited and vomited. They were scared that they were dying. They were crying out in pain, crying out in fear.
>
> Their leader was the only one who didn't drink. He walked upstream and looked on the ground. There were fresh tracks by the stream and he saw where Coyote had pissed on a flat rock that slanted into the water. Drops of Coyote's piss were still running off the rock into the water.
>
> Then he went back to the people. "Stop!" he told them. "Don't drink that water! It's no good! Coyote has pissed in it! That's why all of you are sick."
>
> Then one of those people said, "We didn't know. We were thirsty. The water looked safe. We were in a hurry and it didn't look dangerous." Those people trusted their eyes. They should have waited until their leader had finished looking around. One of those children nearly died.
>
> That's how that crossing got its name. After that, they called it Ma' tęhilizhé (Coyote Pisses In The Water).

And again:

> Long ago, here at Cibecue, just when the corn was coming up, an old man saw a black cloud in the sky. It was moving toward him. He watched the cloud come closer and closer. It was made up of grasshoppers, a huge swarm of grasshoppers. Soon they were eating the corn shoots. *Ch'iziid! Ch'iziid!* It sounded like that.
>
> Then that old man got worried. "If this is allowed to continue we will

have nothing to eat. All of our medicine men should work together on this for us." That old man was wise. He had seen danger in his mind. His mind was smooth. He knew what had to be done.

Then he spoke to some people and they went to the camp of a medicine man with strong power. The old man spoke to him. "Something terrible is happening to us. All of our medicine men should work together on this for us."

Then the medicine man said to them, "What you say is true but I will work alone. I will pray and sing. I will help you. I will bring a great rainstorm to kill these grasshoppers."

Then, that same evening, he started to sing. He sang throughout the night—but nothing happened! There was no rain. In the morning, there were no clouds in the sky. The grasshoppers were still eating the corn. *Ch'iziid! Ch'iziid!*

Then that medicine man sang alone again. He sang all night. "I will bring lots of heavy rain," he told the people. But still there was nothing! In the morning there were still no clouds in the sky. *Ch'iziid! Ch'iziid!*

Then another medicine man went to him and said, "We should work together on this. Something very bad is happening. If four of us sing together we can bring heavy rains and destroy these grasshoppers."

Then the first medicine man thought about it. "No," he said. "The people came first to me. I will bring heavy rain if I sing four times alone." So he started to sing again. He sang all night. It was the same as before—nothing happened. Those grasshoppers were still eating the corn. *Ch'iziid!*

Now the people were very frightened. Some were crying out in fear. They saw what was happening to their corn.

Then that medicine man sang one more time alone—and still there was no rain!

Then four medicine men got together. "That old man was right. We should have worked on this together. Let's get ready, we'll start tonight. That man who sings alone is far too proud. His mind is not smooth. He thinks only of himself."

Then those four medicine men started singing. They sang together throughout the night. They didn't stop to rest. They didn't stop to drink. They kept singing, singing, singing—all through the night.

Then, early in the morning, there was a loud clap of thunder! It started to rain. It rained hard. It rained harder and harder. It rained still harder! It rained for four days and four nights. The people were afraid. They thought their homes might be swept away.

Then it stopped raining. An old woman went outside and looked around. Everywhere there were dead grasshoppers. Their bodies covered the ground. The ground was dark with them. Then that old woman started to walk to her cornfield. To get there she had to cross a wide arroyo. When she got there she saw a long pile of dead grasshoppers reaching from one side to the other. "Grasshoppers piled up across," she said.

Then that old woman knew these four medicine men had worked together well.

Then that old woman went back and told the people what she had seen. "We have very little corn left," they said. "Most of it has been eaten. We will surely get weak from hunger. All of us will suffer because of one proud man."

Afterward, they called that place Naschagi naadeez'áhá (Grasshoppers Piled Up Across).

While cautionary narratives like these are appreciated by Apaches for their aesthetic merits (their hard-edged terseness, steady forward motion, and mounting suspense can be exploited by gifted storytellers to gripping effect), they are valued primarily as instruments of edification. For persons seeking wisdom, such stories provide time-honored standards for identifying mental flaws and weaknesses, thereby revealing where remedial work is needed and often instilling a desire to perform it. This kind of self-reflexive activity, which is described in Apache as *bíni' naayik'e'iziig* (working on one's mind), is understood to be a drawn-out affair that becomes less and less difficult as it becomes increasingly habitual. For it stands to reason that the more one scrutinizes one's mind — and the more one acts to improve it by reflecting on narratives that exemplify the conditions necessary for wisdom — the greater the likelihood that wisdom will develop. Disciplined mental effort, diligently sustained, will eventually give rise to a permanent state of mind.

Despite this encouraging premise, which for many Apaches is a source of early confidence, the trail of wisdom is known to be fraught with pitfalls. The human mind is a vulnerable space, and protecting it against obstacles that threaten incisive thinking is a formidable task. Life is full of alarming events — deaths, fights, illnesses, frightening dreams, the nefarious doings of ghosts and witches — and the forces of fear are hard to overcome. One tries to surmount them, and later one tries again, but repeated failures take their toll, and attaining the goal of mental resilience begins to look unlikely. Just as difficult is the challenge of ridding one's mind of self-centered thoughts that find expression in harsh and heated ways, antagonizing other people and causing them to retaliate with aggressions of their own. Again one makes determined efforts, and again they fall short, and again one must deal with uncertainty and doubt. Mental steadiness joins mental resilience in seeming out of reach. And then there is the never-ending problem of everything else. For someone caught up in the demanding swirl of daily life — caring for children, keeping peace with relatives, trying to get by on very little money — pursuing the trail of wisdom can become just another burden. There is enough to do already without thinking about places and working on one's mind! And so it happens, often with reluctance but also with a welcome sense of relief, that the work is abandoned. At different points on the trail of wisdom, Apache men and women decide to stop. They have traveled as far as they are able or willing to go. Wisdom, they have learned, is more easily imagined than achieved.

But a handful of persons resolve to persevere. Undaunted by the shortcomings of their minds, they keep striving to refine them—committing to memory more and more cautionary narratives, dwelling on their implications at deeper and deeper levels, and visiting the places with which they are associated as opportunities arise. Little is said of these activities, and progress reports are neither offered nor requested. But progress reports, as Dudley Patterson was quick to point out, are usually unnecessary. As people move forward on the trail of wisdom their behavior begins to change, and these alterations, which become steadily more apparent as time goes on, can be readily observed by relatives and friends. Most noticeably, inner strides toward mental smoothness are reflected in outer displays of poise and equanimity—signs of nervousness fade, irritability subsides, outbursts of temper decline. There is also to be detected a growing consistency among attitudes adopted, opinions expressed, and judgments proffered—personal points of view, built upon consonant themes, cohere and take definite shape. And there is increasing correspondence between spoken words and subsequent deeds—promises made are promises kept, pledges extended are pledges fulfilled, projects proposed are projects undertaken. As Apache men and women advance farther along the trail of wisdom, their composure continues to deepen. Increasingly quiet and self-possessed, they rarely show signs of fear or alarm. More and more magnanimous, they seldom get angry or upset. And more than ever they are watchful and observant. Their minds, resilient and steady at last, are very nearly smooth, and it shows in obvious ways.

And always these people are thinking—thinking of place-centered narratives, thinking of the ancestors who first gave them voice, and thinking of how to apply them to circumstances in their own lives. Having passed the point where cautionary narratives are useful mainly for disclosing mental weaknesses, they are consulted now as guides for what to do and what not to do in specific situations. As described by Dudley Patterson, what typically happens is this. Something unusual occurs—an event or a series of events—that is judged to be similar or analogous to incidents described in one of the stories. Unless these similarities can be dismissed as superficial, they stimulate further thought, leading the thinker to treat the story as a possible aid for planning his or her own course of action. This is accomplished by picturing in one's mind the exact location where the narrated events unfolded and imagining oneself as actually taking part in them, always in the role of a story character who is shown to be wise. If a powerful sense of identification with that character ensues—if, as some Apaches put it, thinker and character "flow swiftly together" (*ndǫhgo łeednlįį'*)—the experience is taken to confirm that the narrative in question will be helpful in dealing with the situation at hand.[13] If this sort of identification fails to occur, the narrative is discarded and other stories, potentially more instructive, are consulted in similar fashion. It is important to understand that wise men and women are able to consult dozens of cautionary narratives in very short periods of time. Such concentrated effort is not required of them under ordinary circumstances, but when a crisis appears to be looming they set about it immediately. Serene and undistracted, they start drinking from places (in times of emergency they are said to "gulp" from them), and soon enough, often within minutes, they have seen in their minds what needs to be done. Wisdom has finally shown its hand. And when it does, as Dudley Patterson remarked in English the day he cast off his sling and prepared to rejoin the horsemen, "It's sure pretty good all right." "Yes," he said thoughtfully. "That's sure pretty good all right."

These places are really very good!
—*Dudley Patterson*

August 10, 1982. But for a gate left carelessly open—and some thirty head of cattle that quickly passed through it to lose themselves in a tumbled maze of rock-strewn buttes, meandering arroyos, and dry box canyons— my instructional ride with Dudley Patterson might have proceeded as planned. The day began on a calm and peaceful note. We mounted our horses shortly after dawn, rode out of Cibecue on a trail leading north, and then turned east as the rising sun, a brilliant crimson ball, moved into view above a tree-covered ridge. The morning air was crisp and cool, and all one could hear was the comforting squeak of saddle leather and the hooves of the horses striking softly into the earth. A red-tailed hawk banked on the wind in a vast blue sky.

After lighting a cigarette with his antique Zippo, Dudley broke the silence.

> Do you see that ridge over there? We call it Tséé dotł'izhí deez'áhá (Turquoise Ridge). My grandmother took her family there when the smallpox came in 1922. So many people died—it was terrible. My grandmother was a medicine woman and knew what to do. She prayed each morning as the sun came up. Day after day she prayed. All of her children survived the sickness.
>
> And that ravine over there, the one with long white boulders on the far side? Its name is Naagosch'id tú hayigeedé (Badger Scoops Up Water). Badger lived there a long time ago, next to a spring where he went to drink. There was no daylight then and the people were having a hard time. Badger and Bear wanted to keep it that way—they liked the darkness—but Coyote outsmarted them. He gambled with them and won daylight for the people. They gambled up ahead where those four round hills sit in a row. Those hills are named Da'iłtąné (The Mounds).

And way over there, that little clump of trees? We call it T'iis sikaadé
(Cottonwood Stands Spreading Out). There's a spring there, too. It used to
give lots of water but now it's almost dry. Nick Thompson's mother camped
there with her parents when she was a young girl. One time an airplane went
shooting by. She didn't know what it was. She crawled under a bush and
covered her face with her hands. Her body was trembling all over. She stayed
under the bush for two days, trembling.

And that red bluff over there . . .

Dudley stops speaking. Two riders have appeared in the distance and
are moving toward us at a fast trot. Minutes later, Sam Endfield and
Charles Cromwell rein in their horses and deliver the troubling news.
Someone forgot to close the gate near the top of Hayaagokizhé (Spotted
Slope), and a large bunch of cattle—cows, calves, and the spotted maverick bull with one bad eye—has moved into the tortuous country behind
Kịh dotł'izhé (Blue House). Judging from their tracks, the cattle crossed
over yesterday afternoon. They should be rounded up without delay;
otherwise they will scatter over a wider area and make the job more difficult.

Dudley listens quietly, points once with his lips in the direction of
Blue House, and off we go to spend the next seven hours searching for
wily creatures sorely uninterested in ever being found. A day of quiet
learning turns into a punishing game of hide-and-go-seek, and no one
finds it the least bit enjoyable. But slowly the work gets done, the open
gate is wired shut, and by two o'clock in the afternoon most of the cattle
are back where they belong. Only the spotted maverick bull is missing.
His tracks disappear at the head of a narrow canyon. Dudley is uncon-
cerned. The bull is strong and smart. He will rejoin the herd when it
suits him. One day he will reappear. That is his way.

We have been working in land without water, and the heat of the
day is hard upon us. Horses and men are edgy with thirst, so instead of
returning directly to the village we ride southeast to the nearest accessible point of Cibecue Creek. As it happens, this is Trail Goes Down Between Two Hills, the place where Old Man Owl was shown to be a fool
by the two Apache sisters. It is wonderfully cool beside the stream, and
everyone drinks his fill. Sam Endfield, wearing his pants and hat, goes
for a dip. Charles Cromwell, whose tender modesties preclude displays
of unclad flesh, ambles off behind a thick stand of willows. And Dudley,
having twice bathed his face and neck with his handkerchief, sits down
beneath the cottonwood tree whose massive lower limb dips to touch
the ground. Joining him under the tree, I glance upward into its shade-
filled branches, a purely spontaneous act to which he responds by slap-
ping the ground and bursting into peals of high-pitched laughter. Sam

stops splashing in the water, and Charles, looking mildly alarmed, comes stumbling out of the willows trying to button his fly. *What* is going on?

"Our ancestors did that!" Dudley exclaims with undisguised glee. "We all do that, even the women and children. We all look up to see her with her legs spread slightly apart. These places are really very good! Now you've drunk from one! Now you can work on your mind." Still laughing, the weary horseman takes off his sweat-soaked hat and places it on the ground beside him. Then he lies down, cradles his head in the crook of his arm, and goes soundly to sleep. Beneath the ancient cottonwood tree the air is alive with humming insects.

> To know who you are, you have to have a place to come from.
> — *Carson McCullers,* The Heart Is a Lonely Hunter

If nothing else, this truncated tale of congenial Western Apaches, a distinctive brand of wisdom, and a slightly infamous cottonwood tree should lend substance to the claim that sense of place—or, as I would prefer to say, *sensing* of place—is a form of cultural activity. Though commonly viewed in different terms—as instinctual need by human ethologists, as beneficial personality component by developmental psychologists, as mechanism of social integration by theoretical sociologists—sense of place, as I have made it out, is neither biological imperative, aid to emotional stability, nor means to group cohesiveness. What it is, as N. Scott Momaday (1976) has suggested, is a kind of imaginative experience, a species of involvement with the natural and social environment, a way of *appropriating* portions of the earth. While this perspective renders sense of place no less challenging to fathom or describe, it demystifies the notion by assigning it to the familiar province of everyday events. Removed from the spectral realm of scholastic reifications—needs, attributes, mechanisms, and the like—sense of place can be seen as a commonplace occurrence, as an ordinary way of engaging one's surroundings and finding them significant. Albert Camus may have said it best. "Sense of place," he wrote, "is not just something that people know and feel, it is something people *do*" (Camus 1955:88; emphasis added). And that realization brings the whole idea rather firmly down to earth, which is, I think, where a sense of place properly belongs.

A variety of experience, sense of place also represents a culling of experience. It is what has accrued—and never stops accruing—from lives spent sensing places. Vaguely realized most of the time, and rarely brought forth for conscious scrutiny, it surfaces in an attitude of enduring affinity with known localities and the ways of life they sponsor. As

such, it is greeted as natural, normal, and, despite the ambivalent feelings it sometimes produces, entirely unremarkable. Experience delivered
neat (though not, as I say, always very neatly), sense of place is accepted
as a simple fact of life, as a regular aspect of how things are; and if one
were tempted to change it, which no one ever is, the effort would certainly fail. It is probable, of course, that your sense of place will center
on localities different from mine, just as ours together will center on
localities different from Ruth and Dudley Patterson's. But that each of
us should be drawn to particular pieces of territory, for reasons we take
to be relatively uncomplicated, is radically expectable. A sense of place,
everyone presumes, is everyone's possession.

But sense of place is not possessed by everyone in similar manner or
like configuration, and that pervasive fact is part of what makes it interesting. Like all the other "senses" we have invented for mankind (the
aesthetic sense, the erotic sense, common sense, etc.), sense of place is
inseparable from the ideas that inform it, and just for that reason, as Lawrence Durrell remarked in a letter to a friend, it is "everywhere parochial
and everywhere specific" (Durrell 1969:283). Locked within the mental
horizons of those who give it life, sense of place issues in a stream of symbolically drawn particulars—the visible particulars of local topographies,
the personal particulars of biographical associations, and the notional
particulars of socially given systems of thought. It is these last, of course,
that are least available to conscious awareness, and perhaps for this reason writers on place rarely see fit to examine them. Yet it is just these
systems of thought that mold and organize the experience itself, and to
casually ignore them, as so often happens, is to suppose that matters are
much simpler than in fact they really are. You can no more imagine an
Apache sense of place without some notion of Old Man Owl, smooth
minds, and what occurred at Grasshoppers Piled Up Across than you can
fancy a native New Yorker's sense of place without comparable ideas of
Woody Allen, subway rush hours, and strolling in Central Park on the
first warm day of spring. Everything, or almost everything, hinges on
the particulars, and because it does, ethnography is essential.[14]

For any sense of place, the pivotal question is not where it comes
from, or even how it gets formed, but what, so to speak, it is made with.
Like a good pot of stew or a complex musical chord, the character of the
thing emerges from the qualities of its ingredients. And while describing
that character may prove troublesome indeed (always, it seems, there is
something ineffable about it), the elements that compose it can be selec-
tively sampled and separately assessed. Which is what, in a roundabout
way, I have tried to do here. Transformative spatial prefixes, disquisitions
on wisdom, and cautionary stories of thirst-crazed women and puffed-

up medicine men do not "add up" to a Western Apache sense of place. But they can be used to construct one, and thus, taken together, they have something revealing to say about the quality of its tone and the substance of its style. They give us, in short, a sense of the Apache sense, an appreciation of what goes into it, an informed perspective on the angle of its thrust.

And also, I would add, a purchase of sorts on the wellsprings of its force. As vibrantly felt as it is vividly imagined, sense of place asserts itself at varying levels of mental and emotional intensity. Whether lived in memory or experienced on the spot, the strength of its impact is commensurate with the richness of its contents, with the range and diversity of symbolic associations that swim within its reach and move it on its course. In its more ordinary moments, as Seamus Heaney (1980) has observed, sense of place stays within the sphere of its own familiar attractions, prompting individuals to dwell on themselves in terms of themselves, as private persons with private lives to ponder. But in its fuller manifestations this separatist stance gives way to thoughts of membership in social groups, of participation in activities that transcend the concerns of particular people, of close involvements with whole communities and their enduring historical traditions. Experienced in this way—as what Heaney (1980:133) terms a "mode of communion with a total way of living"—sense of place may gather unto itself a potent religious force, especially if one considers the root of the word in *religare,* which is "to bind or fasten fast." Fueled by sentiments of inclusion, belonging, and connectedness to the past, sense of place roots individuals in the social and cultural soils from which they have sprung together, holding them there in the grip of a shared identity, a localized version of selfhood.

"Self and mind," Baruch Spinoza (1949:84) wrote, "are essentially one and the same." If we assume this claim to be true, it is hard to conceive of a cultural construct whose bearing on place is more intimately related to ideas of selfhood than the Western Apache theory of wisdom and its sources. Incorporating places and their meanings into a compact model of mental and social development, the theory of *'igoyą́'i* proposes that the most estimable qualities of human minds—keen and unhurried reasoning, resistance to fear and anxiety, and suppression of emotions born of hostility and pride—come into being through extended reflection on symbolic dimensions of the physical environment. Accordingly, features of the Apache landscape, their richly evocative names, and the many tribal narratives that recall their mythical importance are viewed as resources with which determined men and women can modify aspects of themselves, including, most basically, their own ways of thinking. And because changes in ways of thinking are mirrored by changes in patterns of conduct, these same individuals actually can be seen to alter who they are. As Apache men and women set about drinking from places—as they acquire knowledge of their natural surroundings, commit it to permanent memory, and apply it productively to the workings of their minds—they show by their actions that their surroundings live in them. Like their ancestors before them, they display by word and deed that beyond the visible reality of place lies a moral reality which they themselves have come to embody. And whether or not they finally succeed in becoming fully wise, it is this interior landscape—this landscape of the moral imagination—that most deeply influences their vital sense of place and also, I believe, their unshakable sense of self. For where the likes of Dudley Patterson are concerned—and Sam Endfield and Charles Cromwell and the stalwart Talbert Paxton—selfhood and placehood are completely intertwined. Having developed apace together, they are positive expressions of each other, opposite sides of the same rare coin, and their power to "bind and fasten fast" is nothing short of enormous.

At no time, I suspect, is this power more surely felt by Western Apache people than during those sudden flashes of acute intuitive insight that mark the presence of wisdom. In these clairvoyant moments, when wise men and women consult traditional stories and seek to identify with sagacious story characters, their sense of place (and with it, perhaps, their sense of self as well) may reach a kind of zenith. Yet such culminations of mind seem destined to occur with decreasing frequency in times that lie ahead. In communities throughout the Fort Apache Reservation—and Cibecue is prominent among them—fewer and fewer young people are currently embarking on the ancestral trail of wisdom. Caught up with other concerns and reluctant to appear old-fashioned before their watchful peers, they travel less extensively, learn smaller bodies of cautionary narratives, and subscribe with mounting conviction to the imported belief that useful knowledge comes mainly from formal schooling. This is not to imply that young Apaches fail to develop a robust sense of place—on the contrary, they do—but it is fashioned from new and different materials, and it points in fresh directions. And that may be all to the good, for as modern tribal leaders point out repeatedly, surviving in the contemporary world requires the acquisition of contemporary skills. It is doubtful, however, that future generations of Apache people will ever devise a more striking way to think about places—and by means of places to think about thinking itself—than the one made known to me by the horseman Dudley Patterson. To him, of course, the Apache theory of wisdom was as familiar as the land he knew so well, as familiar to him as himself. But to me, a peripheral outsider, the model of 'igoyą́'i was a wonderful discovery, an absorbing cultural form of large and subtle dimensions. And so it has remained, as moving in its way and somehow just as gripping as the largely unspoiled countryside from which it draws its strength. My own sense of place, which at times grows fairly fierce, rests in part upon it.

Time will tell what other cultural constructions await the ethnographer bent on an interest in place. But that such constructions are everywhere to be found—in deserts and savannas, mountains and rainforests, cities and rural towns—is altogether certain. We should begin to explore them with all deliberate speed, and not, I would emphasize, solely for the purpose of enlarging our knowledge of particular social groups. For as surely as place is an elemental existential fact, sense of place is a universal experiential genre, and therefore, as more and more work gets done, it may be found to exhibit transcultural qualities. In this connection, I have already touched on a few possibilities. Ubiquitously accepted as natural, normal, and unexceptional, sense of place is variously trained, variably intense, and, having grown to mature proportions, stoutly resistant to change. Its complex affinities are more an expression of community involvement than they are of pure geography, and its social and moral force may reach sacramental proportions, especially when fused with prominent elements of personal and ethnic identity. Requiring neither extended analysis nor rational justification, sense of place rests its case on the unexamined premise that being from *somewhere* is always preferable to being from *nowhere*. All of us, it asserts, are generally better off with a place to call our own. Places, it reminds us, are really very good.

> That was his way.
> —*Ruth Patterson*

November 7, 1992. Dudley Patterson joined the ancestors in the spring of 1983. His wake and funeral were attended by hundreds of people, some of whom came to Cibecue from many miles away. Sam Endfield, who no longer speaks of his absent friend and comrade, continues to work as a horseman. Charles Cromwell, hampered by arthritis and tired of herding cattle, recently called it quits at the age of sixty-six. After two or three more drinking sprees, Talbert Paxton settled down and became a model of sobriety. He later married a distant cousin and now is the father of three exuberant children. Ruth Patterson, invincible as ever, remains firmly and fully in charge.

On the evening Dudley was buried, not far from a place named Sǫǫ ch'íhi'oołé (Flakes Of Mica Float Out), the spotted maverick bull appeared on the point of a sandstone bluff overlooking the cemetery. He stayed there, an imposing silhouette drawn against the sky, for the next two days and nights. Then he went away. He has not been seen again. Most people from Cibecue think the bull is dead. Ruth Patterson is not so sure. "No one found his bones," she told me not long ago over a cup of boiled coffee. "The horsemen looked all over and no one found his bones. I think that spotted bull could still be alive. There are many places he could be, many places." A gentle smile crossed her face. "He knew them all, you know. That was his way." [15]

NOTES

In thinking through some of the ideas presented in this essay, I have profited from suggestions offered by Sue Allen-Mills, Gayle Potter-Basso, Vine Deloria, Jr., Jerry Flute, Alfonso Ortiz, and Vincent Randall; it is a pleasure to thank them all. For other kinds of useful advice, I thank everyone who participated in the advanced seminar from which this volume grew, especially Steven Feld, Karen Blu, Edward Casey, Charles Frake, and Nancy Munn. Once again, as so often in the past thirty years, I express my gratitude to the Apache people of Cibecue and that remarkable group of horsemen who, at home and on the range, spoke to me of places and their lasting social importance: Dudley Patterson, Sam Endfield, Charles Cromwell, Joe Case, Morley Cromwell, Francis Dehose, Charles Henry, Robert Machuse, Nick Thompson, Emerson Patterson, and the man to whom I have given the name "Talbert Paxton." I am grateful as well to Nashley Tessay, Sr., who helped me prepare English translations of all the Apache placenames and narratives appearing in these pages. When Ruth Patterson gave me permission to write this essay, she asked if I was planning to put her in it. I said that I was. She then requested a two-pound can of MJB coffee, a sack of flour, one dozen eggs, and a slab of bacon. When Ruth's request was granted, she cheerfully announced that others like it would be forthcoming. And so they have been, which pleases me no end.

1. For information on battles now being waged by indigenous peoples to control ancestral territories, see any recent issue of *Cultural Survival Quarterly.* On efforts by American Indian groups to protect and preserve traditional religious sites, see Vine Deloria's essay, "Sacred Lands and Religious Freedom" (1991). On the importance of place as formulated by contemporary poets, sociologists, and philosophers, see, respectively, the writings of Seamus Heaney (1980) and N. Scott Momaday (1974, 1976); Edward Shils (1981) and Peter Berger, Brigitte Berger, and Hansfried Kellner (1983); and Edward Casey (1987, 1993).

2. I would not wish to imply by these remarks that all modern anthropologists are uninterested in cultural constructions of place. On the contrary, exemplary works by Nancy Munn (1973), Clifford Geertz (1980), Steven Feld (1982), Renato Rosaldo (1980), James Weiner (1991), Fred Myers (1991), and others have demonstrated that some ethnographers consider the topic worthy of close attention. The fact remains, however, that place is usually treated as an ancillary phenomenon, as something to deal with descriptively and analytically only when other concerns make this unavoidable. My own point of view, which owes much to the philosophy of Heidegger (1977), Sartre (1965), and Casey (1987), is that place is a crucial element in many forms of social experience and warrants careful ethnographic study in its own right. And the sooner the better, for reasons I take to be obvious.

3. Heidegger's conception of dwelling proceeds from the fundamental premise, articulated first by Husserl (1958), that all consciousness is consciousness of something.

4. Any doubt that this is so is dispelled when one considers that the same locality may be perceived and apprehended in very different ways according to the immediate intentions of those who observe it. Described by some writers as the individual's "current project," these situated aims and purposes guide awareness in specific directions, determining as they do what sorts of knowledge are relevant and applicable, and also, though perhaps less directly, what kinds of sentiments are suitable and appropriate. Thus, a professional oceanographer engrossed in a study of wave mechanics will make of the same secluded cove something quite different than will a rejected suitor who recalls it as the site of a farewell walk on the beach, and this will be true even if oceanographer and suitor are one and the same person.

5. A vivid account of this kind of subject-object conflation is given by Sartre (1965:59–67), who describes in moving detail his encounter with a chestnut tree.

6. This approach to ethnographic research is discussed and illustrated at greater length in Basso (1991).

7. Consistent with the definition proposed by Grenville Goodwin (1942:15), the term *Western Apache* is used here to designate "those Apachean peoples living within the present boundaries of the state of Arizona during historic times, with the exception of the Chiricahua Apache and a small band of Apaches, known as the Apache Mansos, who lived in the vicinity of Tucson." Goodwin's *The Social Organization of the Western Apache* (1942), together with his *Myths and Tales of the White Mountain Apache* (1939), provide definitive statements on these people during prereservation times. Studies by myself—on the girls' puberty ceremonial (1966), on witchcraft (1969), and on a revealing form of joking (1979)—address aspects of modern Apache life, as does a short ethnography of the community of Cibecue (1970a) and a collection of essays on Apache language categories and patterns of speech (1991).

8. Most of the empirical materials on which this essay is based were recorded on tape, with the prior consent of all Apache parties. Events described under the headings "June 7, 1982" and "August 10, 1982" were documented in writing and later checked for accuracy with Dudley Patterson, Sam Endfield, and Charles Cromwell.

9. Descriptions and analyses of some of these verbal practices are presented in Basso (1984b) and Basso (1988), both reprinted in Basso (1991). Other aspects of the Western Apache placename system are treated in Basso (1984a).

10. For any cultural system, what counts as a "place" is an empirical question that must be answered ethnographically. In this essay, I have restricted the notion of place to "localities on the surface of the earth," or what Apaches term *goz'ą́ą́ ni'gost'án biká' yó*. A fuller treatment of Apache conceptions of place would explore the fact that places are known to exist in the sky (*goz'ą́ą́ yáá biyi' yó*), under large bodies of water (*goz'ą́ą́ tú bitł'áh yó*), and deep within the earth (*goz'ą́ą́ ni'gost'án bitł'áh yó*). The fact that places in these categories are seldom seen by human beings makes them no less real, and certainly no less important, than places on the earth's surface. And in this, of course, the Apache are not alone. How many of us can volunteer eyewitness accounts of the North Pole, or the thirteenth meridian, or heaven and hell?

11. Western Apache placenames are distinguished from otherwise identical expressions by the presence of a phrase-final nominalizing enclitic. The enclitic takes different shapes according to the phonological environments preceding it: *é* following consonants; *'é* following all unnasalized vowels except *a;* *'há* following *a;* and *'né* following all nasalized vowels.

12. Students of Apachean cultures will recognize that conceptions of "wisdom" (*'igoyą́'i*) bear some resemblance to those of "supernatural power" (*diiyi'*). According to some consultants from Cibecue, the resemblance is only apparent. Whereas wisdom is within the reach of everyone and results from mental discipline, supernatural

power is given to very few people and comes mainly from dreams and visions. It should also be noted that possession of supernatural power does not necessarily imply the presence of wisdom. As Dudley Patterson's story of the grasshopper plague at Cibecue illustrates clearly, persons with supernatural power sometimes act unwisely.

13. The idea that smooth-minded thinker and wise story character "flow swiftly together" is nicely consistent with other dimensions of the water imagery that pervades the Apache model of wisdom. The fact that wisdom is likened by Apaches to water—and that using wisdom, or drinking it, is considered basic to survival—seems more than appropriate for a people who have lived for centuries in a demanding desert climate.

14. It is just for this reason, I believe, that novelists and journalists are often more successful than academic writers in conveying to readers an unfamiliar sense of place. Rather than trying to describe sense of place, or somehow attempting to characterize it, the former seek to *evoke* it by presenting a host of local details and taking note of their own and others' reactions to them. An implicit aim of this essay is to suggest that similar strategies, suitably modified, can be usefully employed by cultural anthropologists and other social scientists interested in the problem.

15. For several years after Dudley Patterson's untimely death, I sought without success to discuss the subject of wisdom with other members of the Cibecue community. Everyone I approached gave the same reason for resisting my overtures, namely that he or she could add nothing to what Dudley had already taught me. "But how can you be so sure?" I asked one of my Apache friends in the summer of 1985. "I'm sure," Nick Thompson replied. "You had a good teacher. You know what you're supposed to know. Don't get greedy. It's not wise." On that unequivocal note, I let the matter drop and found other things to do.

3

Waterfalls of Song

An Acoustemology of Place Resounding in Bosavi, Papua New Guinea
Steven Feld

The sense of place: the idiom is so pervasive that the word "sense" is almost completely transparent. But how is place actually sensed? How are the perceptual engagements we call sensing critical to conceptual constructions of place? And how does this feelingful sensuality participate in naturalizing one's sense of place? These questions guide my inquiry into the sensing and sensuality underlying how places are named and poetically evoked by Kaluli people of Bosavi, Papua New Guinea. My desire is to illuminate a doubly reciprocal motion: as place is sensed, senses are placed; as places make sense, senses make place. Because sound and an ear- and voice-centered sensorium are central to Kaluli experience and expression in the tropical rainforest, the goal of this exploration is to interpret what I call an acoustemology, by which I mean local conditions of acoustic sensation, knowledge, and imagination embodied in the culturally particular sense of place resounding in Bosavi.

The chapter opens with brief notes on sensation, sound, synesthesia, and soundscapes that provide context for the general framework of my inquiry, that of a social phenomenology and hermeneutics of senses of place. I outline ways in which research on acoustic experience and expression of place has remained relatively underdeveloped and then introduce the sound world of the Kaluli. Next I offer two ethnographic sections on the acoustemology of flow. The first treats Kaluli naming practices to show how the inseparability of rainforest waters and lands is encountered and imagined to be like the flow of voice through the body's contours. This trope of flow is then examined as it appears in poetic song texts, where singing a sequence of named places takes listeners on a journey that flows along local waterways and through local lands. The flow of these poetic song paths is emotionally and physically linked to the sensual flow of the singing voice. Connecting these flowing paths reveals a Kaluli acoustemology of place relations, a fusion of space and time that joins lives and events as embodied memories. The evocative powers of this acoustemology reach an aesthetic apex in poetic performance, where the expressive flow of the voice merges with the experiential flow of sung placenames to create waterfalls of song, a sense of place resounding.

SENSE, EMBODIMENT, SYNESTHESIA

"Perception does not give me truth like geometry but presences" (Merleau-Ponty 1964:14). What are these "presences" that are given in perception? Merleau-Ponty insisted that they were first the presences of feeling and perceiving bodies, bodies whose sensory experience was never fully sublimated to abstract cognition. Sensations, he urged, were always experienced presences, presences of what later cognitive psychologists and philosophers called an "embodied mind" (Varela, Thompson, and Rosch 1991) or a "body in the mind" (Johnson 1987).

But the senses, the body's "sensorimotor surfaces," are not limited to embodied presences, and they constitute more than experiential sites for establishing points and places of physical and social contact (Straus 1963). Drew Leder's *The Absent Body* (1990) develops this line of critique to ask why, if the body is so central to sensory experience, if it so actively situates the subject, might it also be so experientially absent or out-of-focus. Why is the body not the direct thematic object of one's attention and experience, and why does it recede from direct experience? Leder develops these questions by addressing Merleau-Ponty's observation, made in *The Structure of Behavior* (1963), that "to be situated within a certain point of view necessarily involves not seeing that point of view" (Leder 1990:12). He elaborates: "This constitutes the necessary supplement to the Gestaltist figure-background description of perception. As Merleau-Ponty writes [in *The Phenomenology of Perception,* 1962]: 'one's own body is always the third term, always tacitly understood in the figure-background structure, and every figure stands out against the double horizon of external and bodily space'" (Leder 1990:13).

Leder's conjecture as to why some bodily dimensions are always experientially foregrounded while others are backgrounded relies on the same "figure-ground gestalt to characterize not only the body's field of experience but the structure of the experiencing body itself" (Leder 1990:24). He claims that "these modes of absence arise directly out of the fundamental structure of embodiment," further characterizing "the lived body as an ecstatic/recessive being, engaged both in a leaping out and a falling back. Through its sensorimotor surface it projects outward to the world. At the same time it recedes from its own apprehension into anonymous visceral depths. The body is never a simple presence, but that which is away from itself, a being of difference and absence" (Leder 1990:103; see also Levin 1985; Schilder 1950)

Establishing this complex and multiple presence and absence of the body clearly implicates another interactive figure-and-background, that of the senses. Lived experience involves constant shifts in sensory figures and grounds, constant potentials for multi- or cross-sensory interactions or correspondences. Figure-ground interplays, in which one sense surfaces in the midst of another that recedes, in which positions of dominance and subordination switch or commingle, blur into synesthesia, "the transposition of sensory images or sensory attributes from one modality to another" (Marks 1978:8). Synesthesia points to the complexity of sensory ratios, the rich connections inherent in multiple sensation sources, the tingling resonances and bodily reverberations that emerge from simultaneous joint perceptions (Cytowic 1989). This "medley of the senses bleeding into each other's zone of expectations" (Taussig 1993:57) reveals how "the synesthetic, like the metaphoric in general, expands the horizon of knowledge by making actual what were before only potential meanings" (Marks 1978:254). Taussig's *Mimesis and Alterity* argues that this metaphoric and synesthetic potential recalls mimesis, "the magical power of replication . . . wherein the representation shares in or takes power from the represented" (1993:2). This same metaphoric and synesthetic potential also recalls iconicity, or the ways in which perceiver and perceived blur and merge through sensuous contact, experiencing inner resemblances that echo, vibrate, and linger as traces from one sensory modality to another, present at one level while absent at others, continually linking bodily experience to thought and to action (Feld 1988; Jackson 1989:119–55; Ohnuki-Tierney 1991).

But sensation, sensual presence, is still more than embodiment, more than perceptual figure-grounds, more than the potential for synesthesia. It was Henri Bergson's insight, long ago in *Matter and Memory,* that "there is no perception which is not full of memories. With the immediate and present data of our senses, we mingle a thousand details out of our past experience" (1988 [1908]:33). Hence, "what you have to explain . . . is not how perception arises, but how it is limited, since it should be the image of the whole, and is in fact reduced to the image of that which interests you" (1988 [1908]:40). Bergson's problem—linking the active body as a place of passage to processes of making memory—is developed in Edward Casey's *Remembering* (1987). He writes:

> Moving in or through a given place, the body imports its own emplaced past into its present experience: its local history is literally a history of locales. This very importation of past places occurs simultaneously with the body's ongoing establishment of directionality, level and distance, and indeed influences these latter in myriad ways. Orientation in place (which is what is established by these three factors) cannot be continually effected *de novo* but arises within the ever-lengthening shadow of our bodily past. (1987:194)

Because motion can draw upon the kinesthetic interplay of tactile, sonic, and visual senses, emplacement always implicates the intertwined nature of sensual bodily presence and perceptual engagement.

LANDSCAPE, ACOUSTIC SPACE, SOUNDSCAPE

The overwhelmingly multisensory character of perceptual experience should lead to some expectation for a multisensory conceptualization of place. But by and large, ethnographic and cultural-geographic work on senses of place has been dominated by the visualism deeply rooted in the European concept of landscape. Denis Cosgrove has analyzed how two distinct notions of landscape, both sharing a pervasive visualism, have merged in the West. In the first instance, over some four hundred years,

> the idea of landscape came to denote the artistic and literary representation of the visible world, the scenery (literally that which is seen) which is viewed by a spectator. It implied a particular sensibility . . . closely connected to a growing dependency on the faculty of sight as the medium through which truth was to be attained: 'seeing is believing.' Significant technical innovations for representing this truth included single-point perspective and the invention of aids to sight like the microscope, telescope, and camera." (1984:9)

In the second case, that of landscape as a notion incorporated into the analytical concerns of academic geography, the concept "denotes the integration of natural and human phenomena which can be empirically verified and analyzed by the methods of scientific enquiry over a delimited portion of the earth's surface" (1984:9). Cosgrove argues that these two senses of landscape "are intimately connected both historically and in terms of a common way of appropriating the world through the objectivity accorded to the faculty of sight and its related technique of pictorial representation" (1984:9).

But what of place as heard and felt? Place as sounding or resounding? In contrast to the long history of the landscape idea in both artistic and scientific inquiry and representation, approaches to ways in which worlds are sonically apprehended have shallower histories. Arguing this point, that the "hearsay" of aural-oral experience was never accorded the same evidential or representational primacy as visual "insight," Edmund Carpenter and Marshall McLuhan introduced the notion of "acoustic space" in their journal *Explorations* (1953–59). The term derived from their projects at the University of Toronto Center for Culture and Technology concerning media transformations, specifically the ways the history of orality and literacy could be reinterpreted from the vantage point of electronic communications in the twentieth century. In this context, Carpenter's article on acoustic space was the first statement describing the cultural implications of a directionally simultaneous and diffuse "ear-point," his alternative to "viewpoint" (1960). His later studies (1971, 1973, 1980) went on to relate acoustic space to visual-auditory interplays, as in the way the Inuit experience of spherical dynamic space in the Arctic related to local artistic imagination and process, especially visual puns and depictions of motion, depth, and noncontainment.

The notion of "auditory space" also emerged in the mid-1950s, in an entirely different context. The music philosopher Victor Zuckerkandl (1956), drawing substantially on the philosophy of Henri Bergson and Martin Heidegger and on the psychophysics and the Gestalt and perceptual psychology of William James, Géza Révész, and Erwin Straus, argued vigorously against the notion that music was purely an experience of tone as time. He did so by detailing ways in which space is audibly fused with time in the progression and motion of tones (1956:267–348). While this interpenetration of auditory space and time has not had a general impact on theorizations of space and place, *Music and the External World,* the first volume of Zuckerkandl's *Sound and Symbol* (1956), has certainly had a critical impact elsewhere, as in Kathleen Higgins's vigorous philosophical critique of musical Platonism (Higgins 1991), in anthropological explorations of ritual, music, and sound symbolism in the work of Ellen Basso (1985) and Paul Stoller (1989:101–22), and in Roy Wagner's theoretical essays on symbol and metaphor (1986).

Just as Zuckerkandl the musician influenced anthropologists, Carpenter the anthropologist principally influenced musicians. When composer Murray Schafer organized the World Soundscape Project at Simon Fraser University in 1970, the Carpenter and McLuhan ideas, marginal both in the anthropology of the arts and in cultural geography in the 1950s and 1960s, were introduced to composers and acousticians in a new framework, the study of the sound environment and acoustic communication. Schafer's group began recording, observing, and acoustically analyzing the sonic experience of space and place, especially in Canada and Europe, and developed an analytical vocabulary, a notation system, and a comparative framework for the study of acoustic space and its human interpretation and feedback. This work went under the general rubrics of two terms coined by Schafer, "acoustic ecology" and "soundscape design."

Schafer and his colleagues disseminated their ideas in media ranging from music compositions to radio collages and from technical reports to print and cassette travel journals, all of which led to a general synthesis, Schafer's *The Tuning of the World* (1977). This book has drawn substantial attention to the acoustic complexities of environments, especially northern ones, but its impact has largely been felt among musicians, acousticians, architectural designers, and audio and radio artist-composer-recordists (for example, see Schafer 1993; Truax 1984; Werner 1992). Acoustic ecology and soundscape studies have had rather less impact on ethnographers, who might study how people hear, respond to, and imagine places as sensually sonic. On the other hand, humanistic geography, deeply impacted by perspectives from phenomenology in the 1970s and 1980s, began to notice the acoustic dimensions of place somewhat less cautiously (for example, Buttimer and Seamon 1980; Seamon 1979; Seamon and Mugerauer 1985; Tuan 1977) but rarely explored them, and never in the fully grounded way that would draw anthropological attention.

The work of the Carpenter-McLuhan-Schafer lineage was not taken up seriously by anthropologists; indeed, it was criticized by those most interested in its consequences for analyzing both the senses and orality-literacy issues (Feld 1986; Finnegan 1988:139–74). Despite its stated concern with sensory ratios, this line of thinking often reified a visual-auditory great divide, one that reproduced some variant of the notion that "seeing is analytical and reflective. Sound is active and generative" (Schafer 1985:96). Such oversimplified rhetoric led most ethnographers to turn their ears and sparked the critical tack taken by Don Idhe, whose phenomenological essay *Listening and Voice* pointed out the futility of countering the historical centrality of visualism in Western analytical discourses by simply erecting an antivisualism (1976:21).

What Idhe called for instead—a call recently echoed by anthropologist David Howes in *The Varieties of Sensory Experience* (1991:3–21, 167–91)—was a reevaluation of all the senses from the standpoint of their interplay. Only then, Idhe and Howes both claimed, could a serious analysis of sound emerge in an adequately experiential or ethnographic way. Given recurring tendencies to essentialize vision as a characteristic of the West (e.g., Ong 1982), in polar opposition to a presumed centrality of sound, smell, and taste that is essentialized to non-Western cultural "others," a reevaluation of sensory ratios must scrutinize how tendencies for sensory dominance always change contextually with bodily emplacement. That perspective informs my position on sound in sensory experience, specifically its implications for interpreting life-worlds of Kaluli people in Papua New Guinea.

TOWARD AN ACOUSTEMOLOGY

If, in perceiving, "our whole body vibrates in unison with the stimulus . . . [then] hearing is, like all sense perception, a way of seizing reality with all our body, including our bones and viscera" (Gonzalez-Crussi 1989:45; compare Idhe 1976:81 and Ackerman 1990:186–90 on ways sound penetrates the body). Sound, hearing, and voice mark a special bodily nexus for sensation and emotion because of their coordination of brain, nervous system, head, ear, chest, muscles, respiration, and breathing. "The vocal mechanism involves the coordinated action of many muscles, organs and other structures in the abdomen, chest, throat and head. Indeed, virtually the entire body influences the sound of the voice either directly or indirectly" (Sataloff 1992:108). Moreover, hearing and voice are connected by auditory feedback and by physical resonance, the immediate experience of one's presence through the echo-chamber of the chest and head, the reverberant sensation of sound, principally one's own voice. By bringing a durative, motional world of time and space simultaneously to front and back, top and bottom, and left and right, an alignment suffuses the entire fixed or moving body. This is why hearing and voicing link the felt sensations of sound and balance to those of physical and emotional presence.

This position problematizes Abu-Lughod and Lutz's argument that "emotion can be studied as embodied only after its social and cultural—its discursive—character has been fully accepted" (1990:13). Although they assert that "as cultural products [emotions] are reproduced in individuals in the form of embodied experience" (1990:12), it seems unwise to abstract discourse, or the production and circulation of topics through speech styles and genres, from the embodied voice, the site of verbal articulation, the resounding place of discourse as fully feelingful habits. Emotions may be created in discourse, but this social creation is contingent on performance, which is always emergent through embodied voices (see Urban 1991:148–71).

Acoustemology, acousteme: I am adding to the vocabulary of sensorial-sonic studies to argue the potential of acoustic knowing, of sounding as a condition of and for knowing, of sonic presence and awareness as potent shaping forces in how people make sense of experiences. Acoustemology means an exploration of sonic sensibilities, specifically of ways in which sound is central to making sense, to knowing, to experiential truth. This seems particularly relevant to understanding the interplay of sound and felt balance in the sense and sensuality of emplacement, of making place. For places are as potentially reverberant as they are reflective, and one's embodied experiences and memories of them may draw significantly on the interplay of that resoundingness and reflectiveness.

Acoustemology means that as a sensual space-time, the experience of place potentially can always be grounded in an acoustic dimension. This is so because space indexes the distribution of sounds, and time indexes the motion of sounds. Yet acoustic time is always spatialized; sounds are sensed as connecting points up and down, in and out, echo and reverb, point-source and diffuse. And acoustic space is likewise temporalized; sounds are heard moving, locating, placing points in time. The placing of auditory time is the sonic envelope created from the layered attack, sustain, decay, and resonance of sounds. The placing of auditory space is the dispersion of sonic height, depth, and directionality. Space-time inevitably sounds in and as figure and ground, as comingness and going-ness. Its presence is forward, backward, side to side, and is heard in tra-jectories of ascent, descent, arch, level, or undulation. What these rather abstract formulations suggest, in simple terms, is that experiencing and knowing place — the idea of place as sensed, place as sensation — can pro-ceed through a complex interplay of the auditory and the visual, as well as through other intersensory perceptual processes.

BOSAVI ACOUSTEMOLOGY:
BODILY UNITY OF ENVIRONMENT, SENSES, AND ARTS

In common with their rainforest neighbors on the Great Papuan Plateau and in the surrounding rainforest region of Papua New Guinea, Kaluli people hear much that they do not see. The diffuseness of sound is sig-nificant in the tropical forest, and the bodily orientation of its inhabi-tants through hearing, listening, and voicing has strongly impressed itself on ethnographers who have worked in the area (e.g., Feld 1990; E. L. Schieffelin 1976; Sørum 1989; Weiner 1991). Kaluli commonly develop acute hearing for locational orientation. Whether it is used in marked forest activities such as hunting by sound or in mundane ones such as walking along forest trails or attending to the details of the surrounding bush from inside a village longhouse, the locational information avail-able from sound in this environment often greatly exceeds that available from vision, in both variety and salience. Even though one quickly real-izes that hearing is the most culturally attuned sense in Bosavi, audition is always in interplay with other senses, particularly in a tense dialectic with vision. This is because much of the forest is visually hidden, whereas sound cannot be hidden. A Kaluli man named Jubi once impressed this on me by analogy. He said that just as the identities of costumed cere-monial dancers, or those of spirit mediums performing in total darkness, are revealed only by the presence of a singing or speaking voice, so the presences of forest places are sonically announced even when visually hidden away.

Acoustic revelatory presence is thus always in tension with visual hidden presence in primal experiences of the forest. Linking experience and expression, this same tension adheres in Kaluli poetic concepts — for example, the intersensory desire to interpret songs, conversations, arguments, or stories by "turning over" (*balema*) their surfaces to reveal their *heg,* "underneath," or *sa,* "inside." Turned over insides and underneaths reveal the resonant depths, meanings, subtleties, and implications of sounds, song poetics, stories, allegorical speeches, or dance costumes, just as they reveal the hidden presences of forest locales—the significance of the way places are physically shaped, such as the way rocks, waterfalls, mountains, or creeks emerge as presences with meaningful "inside" and "underneath" pasts. Thus the commonplace notion that objects and events are always more than they appear to be takes on a particularly sensual and poetic character when it comes to Kaluli modes of interpreting the depths and dimensions of local experience.

Another way the Kaluli dialectic between what is hidden and what is revealed emerges is powerfully signaled by the intersensory iconic *mama,* "reflection" or "reverberation." *Mama* is one's image in water or in the mirror; it is the close-up reflection of oneself in the eyeball of another, the visual presence of the self apart from the self. It is also the lingering audio fragment of a decaying sound, its projection outward as it resounds by vanishing upward in the forest. Like the fading sharpness of a mirror image, *mama* is the trace of audio memory, fragmentary sonic remembrances as they reverberate. And *ane mama,* a "gone reflection-reverberation," is a spirit, a human absence returning in imagined (often avian) presence. Announced by flashes of sight or, more typically, by conspicuous sounds experienced without the accompaniment of a corresponding visual image, an *ane mama* presence instantly stimulates feelingful memories.

These Kaluli vision-sound interplays are also locationally intersensual to smell. Any number of everyday examples could be cited. It is hard to imagine the trickling of a shallow creek at a stand of sago palms without smelling the aroma of fresh or rotting sago pith; the experience and memory of sago-place presence is deeply multisensory. Similarly, the dense sensuality of evening darkness, with voices overlapping the misting light rains and insects and frogs of the nearby bush, is sensually continuous with smoky aromas that fires or resin torches release into the longhouse and diffuse out into the ever-moist night air. Evoking the diffuseness of this motional sensorium, the processes of sound and smell are incorporated into the same Bosavi verb, *dabuma,* or absorption by ear and nose. Hearing is the unmarked form, the major kind of sensory absorption or taking in; smelling requires marking the odor's name before the verb, such that the action of smelling carries the linguistic feel of "hearing the odor." The metaphoric potential here inversely plays on the familiar Western synesthetic notion that the pleasures of music have long been absorbed as the "perfume of hearing" (Ackerman 1990:202).

At its broadest, the multisensory character of Bosavi acoustemology is suggested by the complexities of everyday practices linking sensory experience of the rainforest to artistic processes in visual, verbal, musical, and choreographic media. These practices are encompassed in discourse by two synesthetic metaphors: *dulugu ganalan,* "lift-up-over sounding," and *a:ba:lan,* "flow." Both are important to Kaluli experience and expression of emplacement. Because I have discussed *dulugu ganalan* in some detail before (Feld 1988), I will here review its importance to the interplay of the senses only briefly and then concentrate on flow. Flow concerns the interrelated sense and sensuality of water flowing through and connecting landforms, as well as the voice flowing through and connecting the thinking, moving, feeling body. It also concerns the hold, the lingering grip, of sound and poetic song, the resoundingness of voice in silent memory. These notions of flow all merge in the performance of the path maps that are a central feature of poetic song texts.

"Lift-up-over sounding" is the metaphoric construct that prescribes and describes natural sonic form for Kaluli people. Calling attention to both the spatial ("lift-up-over") and temporal ("sounding") axes of experience, the term evokes the way all sounds necessarily coexist in fields of prior and contiguous sounds. When applied to the sound world of the rainforest, "lift-up-over sounding" highlights the observation that there are no single discrete sounds to be heard. Everything is mixed into an interlocking soundscape. Forest sounds constantly shift figure and ground to create staggered alternations and overlaps, a sense of sound that is completely interlocked and seamless. One hears no unison in nature. Presence and absence of sound or changes in its direction and dimension coordinate space as intersecting upward and outward. Sounds constantly interact to produce the sensation that one sound is momentarily about to stand out from the others, while at the same time conveying the sense that any primacy is fluid, as quickly lost as it is gained.

In the tropical rainforest, height and depth of sound are easily confused. Lack of visual depth cues couples with the ambiguities of different vegetation densities and with ever-present sounds such as the hiss of water to make depth often sensed as the diffuseness of height moving outward, dissipating as it moves. "Lift-up-over sounding" precisely yet suggestively codes the ambiguous sensation that auditorally, kinesthetically, and sensually projects a space-time: upward *feels* like outward. This placing of sound is at once a sounding of place. One knows the time of day, season of year, and placement in physical space through the sensual wraparound of sound in the forest. This way of hearing and sensing the world is internalized as bodily knowledge, part of the everyday "body hexis" (Bourdieu 1977:87), the naturalized regime of "body techniques" (Mauss 1979 [1935]) basic to routine Kaluli encounters in their world.

Kaluli transform these everyday encounters with acoustic figure-grounds, extending their naturalness from the experience of the rainforest soundscape to their own vocal and instrumental music. Voices and rattles are made to "lift-up-over" like the trees of the forest canopy; sounds of drums and work tools are made to "lift-up-over" like tumbling waterfalls into swirling waterpools. These ideas are elaborated by Kaluli in musical practices favoring dense and layered cooperative singing or sounding that always avoids unison. To create a "lift-up-over sounding," voices or instruments or both must be in synchrony while out of phase. To be in synchrony means that the overall feeling is one of togetherness, of consistently cohesive part coordination in sonic motion and participatory experience. Yet the parts are also out of phase, that is, at distinctly different and shifting points of the same cycle or phrase structure at any moment, with each of the parts continually changing, even competing, in degree of displacement from a hypothetical unison.

Additionally, "lift-up-over sounding" is created in timbre, by textural densification through a layering of attacks, decays, and fades, of playful accelerations, lengthenings, and shortenings, of the fission and fusion of sound shapes and phrases. Musical parts that interlock, alternate, or overlap create a form of participation that blurs competition and cooperation, mirroring the larger Kaluli tendency toward tense egalitarianism in social activities ranging from speech and work to negotiation, transaction, and exchange.

In concert with these dimensions of musical creativity, face-painting styles visually mirror sonic "lift-up-over sounding" through a parallel figure and ground principle in the texture contrast between shiny and dull and the color contrast between black and red. Ceremonial costumes further exploit textural densification by mixing many types of materials, blending and layering fur, bird feathers, red, black, and white paints, shells, woven bands, bamboo, rattles, palm streamers, and colorful leaves. As the ceremonial dancer bobs up and down in this paraphernalia, layers of "in synchrony and out of phase" sound emanate from his shells and streamers in motion, "lifted-up-over" by his drum, rattle, or voice.

Taking in nature, music, body painting, costume, and choreography, "lift-up over sounding" metaphorically unites Kaluli environment, senses, and arts. In complementary ways, the notion of *a:ba:lan,* "flow," similarly pervades and unites experiential realities of place to its expressive evocation. To illustrate how this happens, I turn first to the routine ways in which Kaluli people encounter, sense, and name places in their world, and then to the ways this flow of world sensing turns into a sensual poesis of place.

FROM SENSATION TO NAMING:
PLACING PATHS OF FLOW IN KALULI EVERYDAY EXPERIENCE

The importance of place and placenames to Kaluli everyday experience, discourse, and ritual expression has been a long-standing issue in the ethnographic and linguistic research that my colleagues and I have undertaken in Bosavi since 1966. Edward L. Schieffelin's first work recognized the primacy of Kaluli identification with locality:

> The identity of each longhouse community is not primarily associated with the clan membership of the people who inhabit the *a* [longhouse]. Rather, over a period of time the community becomes bound up with the area it moves about in and comes to be referred to by the name of the locality. Thus for example, lineages of Gasumisi and Wabisi whose communities' successive longhouses have been located in the vicinity of Bagolo Ridge are called Bagolo people. (1976:41)

Moreover,

> place names, including that of the longhouse vicinity, refer to familiar forested ridges, streams that are full of fish, house sites and sago stands where a person has lived most of his life. . . . These places are meaningful because they mark the contexts of one's past experience. Kaluli identify themselves with place names because they see themselves reflected in their lands. (E. L. Schieffelin 1976:44–45)

Bambi B. Schieffelin's discourse-centered ethnography of Kaluli socialization (1979, 1986, 1990; Ochs and Schieffelin 1983, 1984) has not focused thematically on place, but her transcripts of everyday Kaluli family interactions indicate the prominence of place and travel as conversation topics in the circulation of talk about family history, movement, and work activity. Of particular interest is her discovery of how everyday family discourse involves a report citation form in which placenames are preceded by the third-person possessive marker and followed by a verb of staying—for example, *ene Bolekini sab,* "s/he's at her/his Bolekini" (B. B. Schieffelin, personal communication 1990). This form routinely ties place to person, identity to locality, and heightens the affective resonance of placenames. Its prominence in caregiver-child interactions underscores the biographical sense of place Kaluli children are socialized to assume.

My own work on Kaluli poetics (Feld 1990) has concentrated on the ways sequential citation of placenames in texts of song and lament construct improvised or composed maps that evoke memories of events, times, and social relations. The idea of a *tok,* or "path," emerged as one of the key devices of song composition and performance, and my Kaluli teachers made me well aware of how much the emotional and memorial power of songs depended on their placename sequences. Continuing research reveals how invocation of the notion of *tok* signals a generic set of assumptions about the connectedness of Bosavi places, and with that connectedness, a connectedness of people, experiences, and memories. *Tok* signifies path, passage, canal, a nondirectional entry and exit, an opening in the sense of road, trail, or track. Connection as *tok* involves multiple images: a string of localities, contiguities and continuities of marked space, temporal progression from one place to another. The concept thus grounds the boundedness of places in the figure of their connectedness.

Tok are regularly placed in everyday experiences as Kaluli people travel to and from their home longhouse area, going to gardens, sago places, or other longhouse communities. Time traveling always means time walking on trails, time traversing places both familiar and new, time with others and time alone, time crossing the numerous brooks, streams, creeks, and rivers that section all lands in the Bosavi rainforest region. But Kaluli life also involves daily activities in the immediate longhouse community and its surroundings: socializing at the longhouse, gathering and cutting firewood, gathering water for drinking and cooking, making and repairing net bags, sharpening knives and axes, making and repairing clothing, tending pigs, making fences, hunting and fishing, cutting, planting, weeding, and tending banana, pandanus, vegetable, fruit, and sweet potato gardens, and cooking, distributing and sharing food. All these activities bring Kaluli people together to share and exchange, especially food and talk.

Indeed, one could say that almost every Kaluli social activity is co-constituted in action and talk, and one certainly doesn't get far listening to Kaluli talk without hearing about places. More formal discourse modes, including stories, arguments, negotiations, laments, and songs, equally participate in this pattern, validating the centrality of place to experiential exchange and memory. Central to all this talk is place-naming practices. At the most basic lexical and semantic levels, these practices indicate the perceptual salience of demarcating an exceptionally varied geography, one experienced by engaging with sensual continuities and discontinuities in the surrounding rainforest environment.

Whether a descriptive recounting or a prescriptive instruction, whether talk of home, of the world within reach, of a journey, or of travel, every naming practice involves path making through a co-referencing of specific placenames (henceforth PN) with a generic terminology of place forms. The most basic place form distinction is between *hen,* "land," and *ho:n,* "water." These are named and cited with *hena: wi,* "land names," and *ho:na: wi,* "water names." But the distinction fuses as much as it distinguishes dimensions of place, because everyday experience in Bosavi always involves a coordinated intermeshing of named lands and waters.

This coordination is well indicated by the subtleties of the most generic names for place forms. For instance, the two most significant types of land formations are *fele* and *do:m*. The term *fele* is related to the word *fe*, "thigh," and refers to a relatively wide, flat expanse of land that rolls off and downward to either side—what Australian bushwalkers, in an instructive metaphoric contrast, refer to as a "saddle" of land. *Fele*, which can also refer to the relatively level area along a ridgetop, are reached from an ascent and lead to a descent at either end. Those conjoined segments of ascent, descent, and roll-off in the land are its "sides," or *do:m*. *Do:m* segments always imply the existence of *fele* above, below, and/or to the sides. *Do:m* has the same phonological shape as the word for "body" in Kaluli, and although this might be accidental, other lexical-semantic and discourse-in-context evidence leads me to believe that the image of the body as "hills" or "sides" connected by "thighs" is quite a primal one for Kaluli speakers.

In any case, *fele* and *do:m* are hardly experienced autonomously as interconnected land formations. They are inseparable from the equally prevalent but far more sensuous presence of waterways. Walking a *do:m* implies a body of water below; once it is crossed, there is another *do:m* to climb on the other side. And *fele* implies one and usually more water *eleb* lying off and below to either of its sides. *Eleb* refers to the place in an ascending or arching elevation where creek water stops. Kaluli paraphrase this as the "head" of the water and say that water "sleeps going down from its head." In other words, water reclines, moves along a body lying down, typically flowing downstream from its slightly elevated "head." Another local paraphrase says that like a person standing upright, water stops and orients up to its "head."

In fact, water stops by moving along the *do:m*, up toward the *fele*. Following the local idiom, Kaluli guides are apt to point out that the *eleb* is not on the *fele* but in the *do:m*. This is another way of saying that the body is like the curves of land between, around, and over which water flows. But this embodied imagination goes farther still, for as these primal landforms are connected like thighs to the body, so the passage of water through them flows like the motion of voice. Voice flows by resounding through the human body, feelingfully connecting its spatially contiguous physical segments, resonating so as to sensually link and stress the whole. Likewise, when water flows through land, it is always multiply connected, always multiply present across and along a variety of relatively distinct, contiguous landforms, linking them and revealing their wholeness.

It is worth inserting here that aside from the obvious correspondences between the forms designated *hen,* "land," and *ho:n,* "water," in Kaluli and English, there are considerable difficulties both in linguistically glossing and in paraphrastically evoking much sense of the distinctness and inter-connectedness of *do:m, fele,* and *eleb* as either bodily or landscape images. Names like these three inevitably seem far more abstract when one reads about them in English than they must feel to Kaluli people, who experience them directly as signs of the sensual obviousness of place. Part of the difficulty of grasping them comes from the clear lack of visual correspondence between these Bosavi rainforest forms and ones more experientially familiar to Westerners. For while *do:m* are relatively hilly and chestlike, and *fele* relatively flatter and thighlike, these terms do not really mean "hill" and "flatland" in the sense of the English terms, any more than *eleb* exactly signifies the "head" or the "end" of a small creek.

An additional part the problem here is that *do:m, fele,* and *eleb* are experienced and distinguished less as purely visual forms and more in a multisensual way by the coordination of walking, seeing, and hearing—the kinesthesia and sonesthesia of shaped place, encountered and learned by the moving, sensing, experiencing body. Surrounded by dense forest, Kaluli acutely attend to the heights, depths, and densities around their tracks through foot- and ear-felt indicators as much if not more than through visual ones. That is, they principally feel and hear whether the land ahead is relatively flatter or hillier than the land behind or to the sides. The land is virtually always wet from rain, so the presence of wetness in the air and the slick, slippery feel of different thicknesses of mud on the feet are central to orienting onself in visually dense places. Additionally, one simultaneously hears what kinds of water presences are above, below, ahead, behind, or to the sides and whether these waterways are diminishing or augmenting in and out of presence. This sensuality of locating and placing, along with its kinesthetic-sonesthetic bodily basis of knowing, is critical to a Kaluli acoustemology, a sonic epistemology of emplacement.

GENERIC PLACES AND PLACING

To continue with generic processes, land and water names often take the form of a specific placename plus a descriptive modifier that specifies the place form (henceforth PN + ___). Although the specific placename can stand alone, as can the descriptive modifier (as an abstract noun), they usually are combined. To take the most generic instances, one often hears places cited as PN + *do:m,* or PN + *fele,* or PN + *eleb.* In the larger sentential discourse setting, these combinatorial sets may be further enhanced and illuminated by immediately conjoined locative and deictic particles, some of which encode directionality as specifically up, down, above, below, behind, or across. These and additional emphatic and paralinguistic markers all indicate aspects of the direction, elevation, density, and depth of land or water, as well as its experiential and evidential obviousness—for example, whether it is in or out of sight or audition.

Other terms that distinguish significant patterns in land formations are cited as PN + *dugu,* for the foothill area or the lower part of a hill or mountain; PN + *misiyo:,* for a high place rising from a *do:m;* PN + *dagon,* for a visually distinct mountain site or peak; PN + *kugun,* for a valleylike area of uncut forest flattening off by the side of a hill or mountain; PN + *bulo,* an obviously flat segment of land on a *fele.* Additionally, the same placename can be attached to several different descriptive modifiers to indicate ways in which a large stretch of land connects to a diversity of specific forms. Several discontinuous places on the same land can have the same PN + form designation, further emphasizing the complexity of abstractly reckoning land strictly through naming.

Other familiar anchors in place terminology indicate lands cleared for living spaces. These include PN + *ba* or *ba-daido:,* a clearing or degrassed clearing, implying the presence of a main longhouse opening onto a cleared yard. This clearing would be connected outward to forest, gardens, and sago areas by customary trails of several different sizes and use patterns, ranging from the ten-foot-wide intervillage tracks (*gamane tok* or *dalaka,* from English "track," for government road) that signal intensified contact and government presence in the area since the 1960s to the small forest clearing or mud-and-vine trail openings into the forest whose pig or human footprints indicate customary daily travels. These types of tracks lead beyond living, gardening, or familial arenas to forest places progressively *usa,* "within," or *heno: usa,* "within the land." They lead away from villages and larger trails toward *ilabode,* "bush," deep in the forests.

Places are explicitly connected as paths by PN + *tok,* or by attaching a specific placename to a path descriptive like *soso:go:f,* the point where two trails come together, thus locating a place by means of its entry or exit point. Talk about paths also indicates qualities such as how "straight" (*digalo:*), "bending" (*koagelo:*), or completely "meandering" or bending back on itself (*sisiali*) a trail might be, as well as how it might be distinguished by characteristics of forest vegetation or density.

Similarly, land names are made more distinct by markers indicating human impacts. Names attach to swidden garden sites as PN + *ikuwo:* or

PN + *egelo:* (literally "tree-cut" or "plant-planted"), as well as to garden qualities. For example, PN + *asak* indicates a garden edge with planted ridge on the top. PN + *ikuwo:sak* ("tree-cut" + *asak*) indicates the appearance of a double ridge with some trees cut and some left above; hence the appearance of two canopy layers, the lower layer regrown on a hill and the upper layer including original growth on a ridge.

Places where sago palms grow, are felled, and are processed into the staple starch of the Kaluli diet further link human impacts to land tracks and to waterways, particularly small creeks and streams. Sago places are noted as PN + *ma:n kuwo:* ("sago-cut"), and the placename can equally mark the adjacent land or waterway. Like the centrality of longhouse site names in creating the merged time and space of a community, human presence is always relational to named gardens and sago places and thus central to the identity of those who work and live nearby. Memories— of food, work, labor assistance—are magnetized to those names, making place a fused locus of time and space.

WATER

Always heard even when it cannot be seen, water has dramatic visual presence as well, a depth and dimensionality of presence as it travels through places, linking and demarcating them throughout the forest. The acoustic presence of water changes constantly through the seasonal weather patterns, swelling and resounding with every day's rains. At first a seemingly constant hiss, water's ever-present varieties of sonic volume and immediacy comprise a multiplicity of subtly differentiated presences. These are instantly felt and interpreted by Kaluli as indexes of the progressive space-time of day and season. In addition to the terms *ho:n* and *eleb,* numerous other descriptives indicate the variety of waterway dimensions and segments encountered every day. These include PN + *kini,* "downstream"; PN + *mogan,* "deep waterpool"; PN + *bese,* a "recess," a depression or minor pool where water slows; and PN + *sa:,* the "bank" of a creek or river, the edge of water. Waterways are further demarcated as *sisiali,* curved, crooked, or meandering, with constant bends, or *tili,* with no pool, just water flowing downstream. There are specific water forms as well, like *ho:n-si,* a little spring hole where one draws drinking water.

The two most significant waterway forms besides *eleb* are those that link waterways together and mark significant boundaries or land elevation changes. Water PN + *so:k* marks a "conjunction," a place where two waters come together, and water PN + *sa* indicates a "waterfall." Because water conjunctions and waterfalls mark boundaries that coordinate land and water forms, they are additionally important for demarcating fishing areas, boundaries, and rights. Waterfall segments themselves are further marked for both their contour in the surrounding land and their impact on shaping the water below—for instance, water PN + *sa-wel*, "waterfall crest" or ledge; water PN + *sa-mi*, a "waterfall drop-off" or break point; water PN + *sa-mogan*, a "deep waterpool" at the base of a waterfall; water PN + *sa-ko:f*, where water breaks off a *mogan* beneath the fall; and water PN + *sa-ga*, where water rejoins after a split below the fall.

Other ways in which downstream waterways are co-referenced with landforms include water PN + *da:l*, where a water section opens up to flow from a cleared gap; PN + *du*, marking a land or rock bank between two segments of the same waterway; and PN + *min*, where one water breaks into two to rejoin later. When two creeks run roughly parallel over a long stretch of land, thus coordinating land and water features, they are termed *ida:ni galiali*, "two of them lying/staying together."

But the sensual primacy of water emerges in Kaluli naming practices in another way, namely, through the descriptive prominence of onomatopoeic ideophones for water sound and motion. While these ideophones are common in talk about waterways, they only rarely substitute for either specific water names or for water descriptives. Six iconic patterns convey the sound sensations of the basic water motions:

"falling"	*bu, bulu, gu, gulu, gulugulu, gululu*
"spraying"	*fu, fuga, fuwa:n*
"flowing hard/fast"	*fo, foo, oo*
"flowing light/slow"	*tin, tintin, tiya, tiyatiya*
"swirling"	*go, gogo, golo, gologolo, gololo*
"splashing/plunging"	*kubu, kubukubu, tubu, tubutubu*

Further extensions of these terms use lengthened vowels to iconically mark durative intensity, or syllabic reduplication to iconically mark durative continuity. Additionally, ideophones can attach to regular verbal morphology in talk, as well as attach to special poetically marked aspectual morphology in songs. In a few cases, placenames actually incorporate these sonic ideophones. The waterfall named Gulusa (the *sa* of an iconically named creek, the Gulu) is formed from *gulu* + *sa*, "downward falling water sound" + "waterfall." Bulusami, the place where the Bulu creek (again, the name is ideophonic) joins the Gamo river below a large waterfall and waterpool, is formed from Bulu + *sa-mi*, Bulu creek + "waterfall-drop edge," literally, "sound of loud, downward rolling water sound" + "drop place." In these examples the evocative powers of ideophonic expression emplace the direct relationship of sound to sense in the voice, forcefully linking everyday sensual experience to the aesthetic depths of poesis.

LAND AS WATER AS LAND

In *The Sorrow of the Lonely and the Burning of the Dancers,* Edward L. Schieffelin notes the connectedness of Bosavi lands and waters:

> Most places in the forest are named after the stream that gives the land its contours in that vicinity. . . . The waters, as they turn and fall, generate new localities for every new configuration of the land. The name of a locality carries, in effect, its own geographical coordinates, which place it in determinate relation to the brooks and streams that flow through the forest. (1976:30)

Hence, the experience and naming of Bosavi lands and waters is always interpenetrated. This is most forcefully indicated by the flexibility of attaching landform descriptive modifiers to specific water names and water-form modifiers to specific land names.

Primary examples of this process derive from the many small creeks running along large stretches of land. In the community I know best, a creek named Sulu is not just an abstract watercourse but one whose path connects to lands named Sulu *do:mo:* and Sulu *fele.* Moreover, even though Sululeb (Sulu + *eleb*) marks where the Sulu creek comes to a head, it is equally a name for the arch of land where the Sulu stream ends. And because the hill just beyond this particular place is where members of Bono: cleared land and built their longhouses in the 1960s, 1970s, and early 1980s, Sululeb is also a longhouse site name and, by extension, the primary referent for people who live there (Sululeb *kalu,* Sululeb people). At the same time, everyone knows that Sulu is quite explicitly a creek, with named places along its banks where there are varieties of sago palms and named waterpools (Sulu *mogan*) and dips (Sulu *bese*), as well as a downstream (Sulu *kini*), a waterfall (Sulu *sa,* Sulu *sa-wel*), and a junction (Sulu *so:k*). What this example indicates is the constant play between specific and general, personal and social, momentary and historical resonances for these names, along with the time-space connections they consummate in place.

PLACENAMES, LINGUISTIC REFERENCE, AND MEMORIAL INDETERMINACY

The formula "PN + form descriptive" names and thereby implements everyday emplacement, anchoring everyday talk descriptions of where one is, has been, or is going. Additionally, tendencies in the formation of placenames hold important potentials related to memory and biography. For the Kaluli, as for the neighboring Foi, "place names act as mnemonics for the historical actions of humans that make places singular and significant" (Weiner 1991:45). Some placenames serve forcefully as shorthands, encapsulating stories about historical or mythical events whose magnitudes vary from mundane to cosmic. Some Bosavi places, for example, are named in relation to mythic origins or events responsible for establishing taboos. Others are directly constructed as primal sources of spiritual or supernatural power, and stories are attached to these place-names to indicate why the place is avoided in sight or visitation or why certain actions, words, or motions are avoided there, sometimes lest they create resentments or offend mythocosmic beings. Some of these matters are revealed in stories that are variably well known or quite esoteric; others are exposed through the kinds of talk and revelation specific to spirit-medium seances (E. L. Schieffelin 1976:29–45, 1977, 1984, 1985; Schieffelin and Crittenden 1991:58–87; Schieffelin and Kurita 1988).

At the simplest level, name structure itself points toward layers of referential possibilities. An example of the most explicit variety would follow the pattern seen in the placename Hinibululo:wo:, which is formed from *hini* + *bulu* + *lo:wo:,* literally, "earthquake" + "broke open" + nominal, meaning "place where earthquake broke open the ground there." The place referred to is a dramatically visual and unusual landform, and the event that created this depression is historically rare and at the edge of current historical memory. Because the place in question now follows alongside a major government road outside the longhouse community of Suguniga, there is a clear linkage between the referential semantics of the placename, an event, a placed landform, and stories that are important to the history of a specific community and its members.

Yet semantically bundled placename packages like this one are relatively rare in the Bosavi language. Far more prevalent among names with some overt referential distinctiveness are ones taken to be related to an event or act without specifying a land or water formation itself. These are quite important in local community history. For example, while walking Bono: lands in 1992, I came across places named Baoamisa:n and Baoho:mo:no:. The first is formed from *bao* + *a* + *misa:n,* signifying "ceremonial hunting lodge" + main longhouse ("house" + "head"), that is, "longhouse site where people lived during a *bao a.*" The second, Baoho:mo:no:, is formed from *bao* + *ho:n* + *mo:no:,* signifying "ceremonial hunting lodge" + "water" + "drink," indicating "drinking place during time of holding a *bao a.*"

The *bao a* was a male ceremonial lodge and a period of seclusion, hunting, esoteric instruction, and homosexual liaisons between men and boys (E. L. Schieffelin 1982). The institution ended in 1964 because of the simultaneous threat to secrecy and call for labor when missionaries arrived to construct the Bosavi airstrip. The lands named Baoamisa:n and Baoho:mo:no: are close to a place named Wogole, the site of the last Bono: *bao a.* As time now (as I write in 1995) approaches thirty years since the last *bao a* was held in Bosavi and thirty-five years since the last one held on Bono: lands, meanings and stories connected with this institution shift considerably in the living population. Names like Baoamisa:n and Baoho:mo:no: are thus explicit reminders of past presences and activities to which members of Bono: or other communities have varying degrees of linkage or distance according to age, gender, and knowledge of esoteric cultural practices. The names thus ring variably transparent or deep, and lead to stories variably shallow or dense.

More typical yet are names whose referential potential opens out to biographical or historical stories that have complexly varied personal or regional resonances. For example, one morning in July 1992, Ayasilo and I were walking on the government track past the former Bono: longhouse site of Sululeb. As we crossed the Yolo creek I asked him the land name of the hill arching above along the left side of the track. He replied, with a sweeping, nose-pointing deixis (another bodily placing-spacing convention), that the place was called Gasoamisa:n. This was instantly recognizable as a name formed from Gaso + a + misa:n, that is, Gaso, a man's name, plus "main village longhouse," or the "place where Gaso built a large village longhouse." I then asked if there was an "underneath," a heg or "reason" for the name, and as I switched on my cassette recorder Ayasilo remarked (in Kaluli, rather literally translated), "A man named Gaso, Wasoba's father's father, a man of clan Wabisi, well, long ago, having left Muluma, staying here by the Yolo he built a big house, later he quit it, left to stay at Nageba:da:n, that's all."

Despite the contextual artificiality (i.e., a direct question elicitation), it is striking to notice how quickly and thoroughly a person and a memorable feature of his life are narratively located in a placed space-time. Gaso is generationally linked to an elder man of Ayasilo's father's generation from their longhouse community; he is also linked to a specific clan, to a land name of central historical and contemporary importance to that clan and the surrounding community, to the creek we were just then crossing, to a defining act marking significance and boldness around a man's personal memory, to the people of the former longhouse community of Sululeb, and to another longhouse community involved in a history of fission and fusion with Ayasilo's own. Biographical, geographical, historical, and regional memories are thus encapsulated in and unleashed by the name Gasoamisa:n, reciprocally indicating how personal identity is emplaced and how places are central to personal identities. As with the neighboring Bedamini described by Sørum (1989:4), "temporality is usually concretized by location, and phenomena of time may be seen as objectivated through this practice. The landscape is also history. Time is located as an immanent part of the topography. . . . time and space must be seen as dimensions of a unified space-time percept."

Sometimes name structures are referentially descriptive of a land formation alone. In these cases the significance of the name is transparent at one level but in no way obvious at others. For example, Walaheg is formed from *wala* + *heg,* meaning "rock cliff" + "under." Nothing hints that the place so named is a historically significant cliff overhang in the Sulu *do:mo:,* just to the side of the place where Sulu *sa-wel,* the Sulu waterfall ledge, has its junction with the Sago river. But in fact many stories go with the name, at least for members of Bono: who know that the bones of some of their relatives are scattered under the cliff there. When I went to photograph the Sulu waterfall—one of the most spectacular on Bolekini's lands—Deina and Hasele took me up to Walaheg. There they told me of the times when bones of Bono: dead were deposited in rock cliffs like this one so that pigs and dogs could not get to them. And our co-presence at the site brought out other contexting stories, like ones about the time when Bono: lived at a longhouse site named Diwailo, and how between that time and the time they moved to Balasawel (recounted backward by longhouse names from the present ones), bones were deposited at Walaheg. This was Hasele's way of placing a space-time, explaining that we might be looking at the remains of his father's father, a man named Gulabia, as well as of Gulubia's peers, perhaps Tulunei, Hewabi, Sowiya:, Kogowa:, Diba:, and Mayowa.

Some placenames have etymological structures hinting that a referential dimension or story of significance might be attached to them, but then further examination indicates that they are largely transparent. A creek called Haidokini could certainly refer to a place downstream (*-kini*) from a *haido* palm tree, but no one presently seems to attach any particular significance to that. And Momayo turns out to be just a creek name, *ba madale,* "for no reason," with no referential or associative linkage to a place where *moma* flowers are found. Stories or significances might have been associated with these names in the past but have now been lost. Similarly, names referentially formed as PN + *di ko:lo:,* signifying PN + "made" + anaphora, can mean a "place of X's making" or a "place where X was made." But questioning the possibility for stories in three or four terms of this type evoked shrugged shoulders more often than not.

The obvious point here is that place significance neither starts nor ends with the linguistic referentiality of placenames. The experiential core of names and naming practices is irreducible to the linguistic structure of toponyms or to the range of modifiers or grammatical markers that can attach to them. While some terms might seem to mark publicly accessible meanings, even those meanings are in no way predictably fixed, not to mention evenly or broadly shared. Whether once held or long held, storied meanings can be equally packed into any name. That is, every place and placename, regardless of linguistic formation and markedness, can and does peg some sort of story for someone, and a broad spectrum of possibilities surrounds the extent to which those stories are shared, significant, meaningful, or memorable through time for particular individuals or social groups. The meanings of these stories far overshadow whatever meanings may be directly linked to the lexical semantics of the "PN + ___ " structure and its overt content. While it might be possible to suggest something of a hierarchy of placename types, say, in terms of the amount of affect loading they could potentially carry—longhouse site names, garden and sago site names, main creeks crossed leading to and from these three kinds of sites, places marking important connections to relatives and friends—in fact there is considerable variation in how names hold and unleash significance. Ultimately, it is processes of experienced activity, including the activity of talk, rather than linguistic structure, physical type, or function, that invests places with memorable depths, laminating living to language.

The semantics of placenames and their attachable descriptive modifiers are thus much more referentially indeterminate than are other nominal lexical domains. Because they are fundamental to the description and expression of experiential realities, these names are deeply linked to the embodied sensation of places. Yet over and beyond reference, placenames and their modifiers are central to implementing sensation through the ways in which verbal invocation brings place into heightened conceptual presence, whether or not a place named is simultaneously experienced in physical proximity. Naming strengthens the naturalness of place, the tacitness of its sensately felt dimensions in thought and action. In the language of Heidegger: "The naming calls. Calling brings close what it calls. . . . Thus it brings the presence of what was previously uncalled into a nearness. . . . But even so the call does not wrest what it calls away from the remoteness, in which it is kept by the calling there. The calling calls into itself and therefore always here and there—here into presence, there into absence" (1971:198–99).

Kaluli naming and storying are highly salient and sociable everyday practices, forms of social participation thoroughly related to other everyday practices such as traveling, working, and visiting. Social identities, indeed, all imagination of relatedness, are enacted in Bosavi through the coordination of talk, work, stories, and other everyday activities, activities that give both sedimented and emergent structure and feeling to the sense of sharing and belonging. Experiential layerings from one's birthplace to other places lived and traveled actively map place into identity, conjoining temporal motion and spatial projection, reinscribing past in present, creating biography as itinerary.

SINGING PATHS OF FLOW:
THE POETIC INTENSIFICATION OF PLACE MEMORIES

Writing about place-naming practices among the Foi, neighbors of the Kaluli along Lake Kutubu, forty-five kilometers northeast of Bosavi, James Weiner urges that "language and place are a unity. The manner in which human action and purposive appropriation inscribes itself upon the earth is an iconography of human intentions. Its mirror image is speech itself, which in the act of naming, memorializes these intentions, makes of them a history-in-dialogue" (1991:50). The thorough natural-ness of those memorialized intentions likewise grounds a Kaluli poetics of place. This is essentially to argue that the experiential dimensions we call "mundane" and "aesthetic" are mutually interdependent, that they always involve reframings and emergent sensations. The poetic is an emergent figure that reframes an everyday ground, both strengthening that ground and contributing to its solidity and fluidity. Likewise, the everyday ground stands ready to be reframed, to take on new heights or depths, to evoke more than to signify, to move more forcefully into the realm of feeling and sensation. This figure-and-ground is the central motion of Kaluli song poetics, and the transformation from speaking names to singing them thoroughly heightens the sensuousness of their evocation.

The aesthetic power and pleasure of Kaluli songs emerges in good part through their textual poesis of placename paths. Composed and per-formed by guests in ritual contexts to evoke tears from their hosts over memories of persons and places left behind, these songs can also be sung during work, leisure, and everyday activities by women and men as they move through and pass time in forest locales. In both ritual and everyday contexts, the songs are always reflective and contemplative, qualities en-hanced in each instance by construction of a poetic cartography whose paradigmatic parallelism of path making and naming reveals how places are laminated to memories, biographies, and feelings. To indicate some of the cartographies imagined and realized in Kaluli poetics and song performance practices, I provide a brief account of the three songs sung by Ulahi of Bolekini at the nearby Wo:lu creek that are recorded on the "Relaxing at the Creek" segment of *Voices of the Rainforest*, a compact disk and audiocassette soundscape recording of a day in the life of a Kaluli community (Feld 1991).

WATERFALLS OF SONG

Ulahi's three songs are all short versions of the most important Kaluli song genres, *gisalo, ko:luba,* and *heyalo.* These three genres are melodically,

Figure 3.1. Ulahi sings at the Wo:lu creek. Photograph © Steven Feld.

structurally, and historically distinct, but their poetic strategies share the four Kaluli conventional textual and narrative practices called *sa-salan,* "inside speaking," *bale to,* "turned-over words," *go:no: to,* "sound words," and *tok,* "paths." *Sa-salan,* "inside speaking," involves strategies for reframing ordinary discourse so that it can implicate only contexts and situations of sadness, loss, and abandonment. *Bale to,* "turned over words," compliments *sa-salan* through techniques of metaphor, allegory, and obfuscatory veiling. *Go:no: to,* "sound words," involves a broad range of phonesthemes, of sonic ideophones. And *tok,* "paths," involves narrativizing the space-time of song as a journey through a progression of named lands and waters, linking quotative and affective imagery with a specific set of places (on Kaluli poetics, see Feld 1990:130–62; on Kaluli ceremonial and song performance genres, see E. L. Schieffelin 1976:225–29.)

Ulahi's *gisalo* song follows the five-part structure typical of the genre. The song begins with a section called the *mo:,* or "trunk," and *talun,* or

"lines." This section consists of paired sets of segments. The first segment
is a refrain, that is, a text and melody that repeats identically and regularly in alternation with a verse, that is, a segment consisting of slightly
changing text sung to a second, unchanging melody. With each repetition of the verse, small portions of the text change; these portions
(transcribed in what follows in boldface) highlight the way variation
dynamically plays on repetition. After several phrases of development,
the entire "trunk + lines" section is poetically and melodically divided
off from the remainder of the song. This is signaled by the *sa-gulab,* the
"waterfall *gu* sounding," that begins with the paired lines "o" and "e" in-
toned at length on the pitches that will be the song's tonal center.

After a brief textual development of the *sa-gulab,* the song's next
major section is the *dun,* "branches," and *talun,* "lines." It consists of
another refrain-and-verse structure, parallel to the one found in the
song's "trunk" section. Again, paired sets of segments combine a repeated
refrain image with shifting verses. The end of the song's "branches" section is called the *sa-sundab,* the "waterfall knotting" or tying up. It consists of a paired and repeated set of formulaic poetic and musical phrases
leading to the final *sa-gulu,* or "waterfall *gulu* droning," completing the
song, carrying it off on its tonal center with an elongated voicing of "o"
or "e" or both.

The following schematic structure shows the conjuncture of poetic
and musical organization in Ulahi's *gisalo* song. The column on the right
lists the pitches sung, corresponding to section. Notice the way the song's
pitch inventory tapers as it progresses, producing an image of a waterfall.

mo: + *talun*	[(A + B1) + (A + B2) + (A + B3)]	$\mathbf{9}$:	**e–g–a–c–d**
sa-gulab	[C]	$\mathbf{9}$:	**e–g–a–c**
dun + *talun*	[(D + E1) + (D + E2) + (D + E3)]	$\mathbf{9}$:	**e–g–a–c**
sa-sundab	[F + G]	$\mathbf{9}$:	**e–g–a**
sa-gulu	[H]	$\mathbf{9}$:	**g**

Women usually sing only short *heyalo* or *ko:luba* when working or
relaxing. Ulahi, having recently moved back to Bolekini after a long
stay elsewhere, told me that the longer process of thinking about a *gisalo*
came to mind while she and her husband, Tulunei, were building a new
house just above Wa:feyo: hill. Her *gisalo* song was still in the process of
composition when she sang it informally at Wo:lu creek. Because of its
relatively short length, Ulahi's song is a musical and poetic simplification
of the fully elaborated ceremonial *gisalo* model in three ways. First, the
song omits a *mo: moso* or "just trunk" section before the *mo:* + *talun.* A
mo: moso would typically consist of three to six poetic segments before
introducing the actual refrain. Next, the song is simplified by the shortening of the *mo:* + *talun* to three pairs from the usual five to seven. Finally,

the shortening of the *dun* + *talun* to three pairs from the usual eight to ten additionally simplifies the structure. One poetic consequence of the song's brevity is that there are relatively fewer places named than one typically hears in a ceremonial *gisalo* song. Moreover, Ulahi's sung places tend, particularly in the *dun* + *talun,* to be much farther apart than is usual in a *gisalo* song *tok,* which often sings a set of names progressively closer together on the land, or else alternates distant and very close places as the *dun* + *talun* develops.

A
seyago	*seyak* Hooded butcherbird (calling)
Wa:feyo:-sana selega siliki	perching in the large *sal* tree at Wa:feyo hill
we kidafi ganalabo-	calling in the *uf* [another big hardwood tree]
weo:ba:mo: ganalabo-	calling from the close-by *haido* [a lone palm]
we kidafi ganalabo-	calling in the *uf* there

B1
aowo: *nilo: siyo:makaka:mi*	brother, I didn't say anything back to you
o-o	(calling in sadness to brother's anger)
Wa:feyo:-sana *gola mesa:siyolo*	I'm coming to stay at Wa:feyo: hill waterpool
wo:funa: *dok mesa:siyolo-*	coming to stay over the creekside leaves
Wa:feyo:-sana *gola mesa:siyolo*	I'm coming to stay at Wa:feyo: hill waterpool

A
seyago	*seyak* Hooded butcherbird (calling)
Wa:feyo:-sana selega siliki	perching in the large *sal* tree at Wa:feyo hill
we kidafi ganalabo-	calling in the *uf*
weo:ba:mo: ganalabo-	calling from the close-by *haido*
we kidafi ganalabo-	calling in the *uf* there

B2
ada:yo: *nilo: siyo:makaka:mi*	*ada:* I didn't say anything back to you
o-o	(calling in sadness to *ada:* 's anger)
Diyo:so *gola mesa:siyolo-*	I'm coming to stay at the Diyo:so: waterpool
ka:la:na: *dok mesa:siyolo-*	coming to stay as a *ka:la:n* fish
Diyo:so *gola mesa:siyolo-*	I'm coming to stay at Diyo:so: waterpool

A
seyago	*seyak* Hooded butcherbird
Wa:feyo:-sana selega siliki	perching in the large *sal* tree at Wa:feyo hill
we kidafi ganalabo-	calling in the *uf*
weo:ba:mo: ganalabo-	calling from the close-by *haido*
we kidafi ganalabo-	calling in the *uf*

B3
aowo: *nilo: siyo:makaka:mi*	brother, I didn't say anything back to you
o-o	(calling in sadness to brother's anger)
Elade *gola mesa:siyolo-*	I'm coming to stay at the Elade waterpool
wo:funa: *dok mesa:siyolo-*	coming to stay over the creekside leaves
Elade *gola mesa:siyolo-*	I'm coming to stay at Elade waterpool
wo:funa: *dok mesa:siyolo-*	coming to stay over the creekside leaves

C

o-o	(waterfalling, sounding outward from source)
e-	(waterfalling, reverberating back to source)
Kida:n-sagu "A:bo:lo:-"	Kida:n waterfall (calling out) "A:bo:lo" [pig name]
Kida:n-sagu "A:bo:lo:-"	Kida:n waterfall (calling out) "A:bo:lo"

D

ni ka: wela:ligo:lo:	I keep calling out for my pig
Kida:n-besewela:ligo:lo:	keep calling out where the Kida:n creek dips
"Gayo" wela:ligo:lo:-e	keep calling out "Gayo" [pig name]

E1

ne dogo misiyo: *nela-ba:ba:no:-*	I want to see the hilltop
A:ba:lebo: *nela-ba:ba:no:-*	hilltop over the head of A:ba: creek
A:ba:leb a:ba:l *kosa dowabi(ki) ba:ba:-miyo:wo*	I came to see the lone black palm swaying above A:b:aleb
e-	(reverberant sound coming back)

D

ni ka: wela:ligo:lo:-	I keep calling out for my pig
Kida:n-bese wela:ligo:lo:-	keep calling out where the Kida:n creek sinks
"Gayo" wela:ligo:lo:-e	keep calling out "Gayo"

E2

dogo misiyo: *nela-ba:ba:no:-*	I want to see the hilltop
So:lo:-sawa:lo: *nela-ba:ba:no:-*	I want to see So:lo: waterfall ledge
waya *kosa dowabi(ki) ba:ba:-miyo:wo*	I came to see the lone swaying palm

D

ni ka: wela:ligo:lo:-	I keep calling out for my pig
Kida:n-bese wela:ligo:lo:-	keep calling out where the Kida:n dips
"Gayo" wela:ligo:lo:-e	keep calling out "Gayo"

E3

kuguno: *nela-ba:ba:no:-*	I want to see the creek valley
Yagafo: *nela-ba:ba:no:-*	I want to see Yagaf
akol *kosa dowabi(ki) ba:ba:-miyo:wo*	I came to see the lone *akol* spirit tree

F

gululu-lebe	(continuous waterfalling sounds) *"gululu"*
So:lo:-sawa:l folebe	So:lo: waterfall ledge (surges, sounding) *"fo-"*
gululu-lebe	(continuous waterfalling sounds) *"gululu"*
So:lo: sawa:l folebe	So:lo: waterfall ledge (surges sounding) *"fo-"*

G

mo fuwa:n-ibo	water (continuous spray sounds) *"fuwa:n"*
Kida:n sawa:l fuwa:n-ibe	sounding *"fu:wa:n"* off Kida:n waterfall ledge
mo fuwa:n-ibo	water (continuous spray sounds) *"fuwa:n"*
Kida:n sawa:l fuwa:n-ibe	sounding *"fu:wa:n"* spraying at Kida:n-*sawa:l*

H

o	(sound of waterfall droning out and on)

MO: + TALUN

In each A segment of the *mo: + talun,* the first word, *seyago,* announces the presence of a *seyak* or *sagelon* bird, the Hooded butcherbird, *Cracticus cassicus.* This is a highly social bird of village edges whose presence is constant in Bosavi and whose loud, melodious, multipart calls are heard throughout the early morning and late afternoon. Beginning by singing this bird's name invokes its presence; the song's words are thus understood as "bird sound words" or *o:ba: go:no: to,* framing what follows as voiced from a bird's point of view. While this reference is direct and obvious here, it later alternates between background and foreground, when the poetics switch from narratively positioning the song as a bird's voice to positioning it as a text about a bird, a story of a spirit presence.

The bird's initial place image is Wa:feyo:-*sana.* In Ulahi's home region in eastern Bosavi, *sana* is the Ologo dialect variant of the word *do:mo:,* so Wa:feyo: *sana* is a hillside above the Wa:feyo: waterpool on the Wo:lu creek. Lines about staying in a *seleg* tree, calling from a *kidaf* tree, and calling from a *weo:b* tree embellish the depth of Wa:feyo: *sana,* creating a sense of space and movement there. These lines simultaneously mystify the listener and draw his or her attention and anticipation by using Ologo variants for trees more commonly known in the local Kaluli dialect as *sal, uf,* and *haido.* The cumulative images of two lone hardwood trees standing on a hill that has been cleared above Wo:lu creek and, across the way, one palm left to stand alone while a garden area is cut around it together triangulate ridge, hill, and garden around a creek's bends. The lines simultaneously give a sense of space, movement, area, volume, depth, and the connectedness of places, suggesting ways lives and stories might be written onto the lands there. Places a bird can go and places it calls from are all markers of human living, motion, centering, and leaving.

The B segments of the *mo: + talun* begin with the kin term "brother" + *nilo: siyo:makaka:mi,* which means "I didn't say anything back to provoke or anger you." This is a stock poetic phrase. It implies a self-righteous sense of innocence, as if to say, "I didn't start or fuel your anger." The sense is that it suits the other party to be unjustly angry and unwilling to bury that anger. Kaluli usually paraphrase this line as, "You said something to me but I didn't say anything back to you." Or, "I'm thinking that I didn't say anything to you but you're just cross (*kulufeyab*) with me." The phrase is meant to intensify the feeling states central to song as evocation: states of loss, abandonment, or feeling sorrow, particularly that caused by unjust refusal, anger, or agitation. The use of the pure vocalic sound "o" for a whole poetic and melodic line following this initial phrase serves as a connective, an evocative sigh, a calling out. This both transforms the words to more purely vocal "bird sound words" and also creates contemplative time and space for the listener, with the effect of underlining the words that were just said, making them reverberate in memory.

The following three lines link the Wa:feyo: hill to the same named waterpool, Wa:feyo: *mogan* (for the Kaluli term *mogan*, Ulahi uses the Ologo dialect variant *gola*, from the swirling sound ideophone *golo* or *gololo*). *Wo:fun* is a kind of weedy, scrubby tree growing to a height of just a few feet alongside the creek at its pool. *Wo:funa: dok* indicates the point just over the top of these dwarf creekside trees. The bird says that it is coming to stay at the waterpool below the hill, coming to stay in these short-tree leaves by the creekside. But this is not a place where a bird can really stay, and so this is instantly a pathetic image, that of a bird who can't find a home, a bird lost in the lower depths of a watercourse rather than homing in the treetops above. Following on the previous image, where a bird cannot stay with its angry brother, these lines make it clear that the bird has no home.

In the boldface alternations of the B verse phrases (B1, B2, and B3), there are three kinds of progressive changes. First, there is a change in the initial word of the phrase, the opening kin/relationship term, from *aowo:*, "brother," to *ada:*, "older sister/younger brother," and then back to *aowo:*. This progression marks a switch to, and then a return from, an intensified form. *Ada:*, a reciprocal relationship term for older sister and younger brother, invokes begging and appeal, carrying the sense that one is calling out sadly; the one called to should feel a deep sense of obligation to respond. Use of this term implies strategic provocation, expectation of action. The switch back to *aowo:*, "brother," implies that this expectation has not been met, that calling for *ada:* didn't get any response, didn't bring the sister any closer to comfort or recognition (on *ada:*, see B. B. Schieffelin 1990:112–35; Feld 1990:24–27).

Second, there is a progression from Wa:feyo: *mogan* to two other waterpools farther down the Wo:lu creek, Diyo:so *gola* (= *mogan*) in B2, and Elade *gola* (= *mogan*) in B3. This progression takes the song along a watercourse that moves out of the living area of Bolekini village. There are a number of waterpools in the Wo:lu creek, but citing these three is particularly effective. Wa:feyo: *mogan* is right beneath the hill where the bird starts out. Diyo:so *mogan* is the last pool of the Wo:lu directly below houses where Bolekini people live. And Elade *mogan* is right above the place on the Wo:lu where it is crossed by the big government track, clearly signifying the crossroads to lands beyond.

Finally, corresponding to these changes in kin/relationship and watercourse terms, there is a progression from the image of the creekside leaves (*wo:fun*) at the waterpool to the image of a tiny scaly fish there

(*ka:la:n* is another Ologo dialect variant, for a fish similar to the kind
Kaluli call *yan*), and then back to the image of the *wo:fun* creekside leaves.
Understanding this final progression relates more to the imagery of the
spirit world, where waterpools and fish signal the presence of *ane mama,*
"gone reflections," spirits of the dead. The imagery makes the cumulative and interactive pattern of the three B segments quite explicit: the
bird can stay only with fish in waterpools, can stop only by dwarf scrub
at creekside; through abandonment, someone has been reduced to the
state of a bird, in effect reduced to a "gone reflection," a living absence
transformed into a spirit presence.

Taken together, the *mo:* + *talun* segments construct a narrative image
of departure and rupture. In the morning, a bird is flying around in
Bolekini lands, but someone is angry about the bird's being there. Like
moving water, the bird is leaving the village, following Bolekini's main
watercourse, with no place to stay on the way, finally arriving at the village edge. Land, water, tree, and place features are joined together with
images of loss, indicated as family, bird spirits, places left, places to go
toward. All of these are forcefully united through sound and the presence of a bird's voice calling in a progression of verbs linking reported
to quoted speech.

SA-GULAB

The *sa-gulab* breaks this narrative and reframes it, first through the sensual
pure musicality of its "waterfalling" sound, a drone tonal center incorporating the phonesthesia of outward reaching "o" and returning reverberant "e." This is followed by a major thematic development in the text,
expressed by the repeated line *Kida:n sagu, A:bo:lo:-.* This line conjoins
visual and sonic images juxtaposing a water name with a phonesthemic
descriptive and then a calling voice. The first part of the line, the words
Kida:n sagu, direct the hearer to imagine a place, a small waterfall of the
Kida:n stream where the fall sounds *gu.* This is relatively far from the
places just sung in the *mo:* + *talun,* but all Kaluli listeners would know
that the "junction," or *so:k,* of the Kida:n is where its waterfall empties
into the Wo:lu creek, considerably downstream from Elade *mogan.* So
the song now takes a large step outward, creating the expectation that
the narrative "branches" to follow will fill in the story of the places linking back to the "trunk."

The second part of the line is just "A:bo:lo:," a pig name. No linguistic marking indicates how to read the juxtaposition of the water name
and the pig name; nothing pinpoints whether the pig is at that place,
calling from that place, or staying at that place. Nor is there any linguistic marking to indicate that a voice is calling this name out by that place.

The options for interpreting the juxtaposition come not from linguistic semantics but from the poetic juxtaposition of the water placename and the pig name, particularly from interplay of their melodic and performative dimensions.

The melodic contour of the whole line is the key to this interpretation. The rhythmic and melodic structure here is syllabic, that is, one melody tone to one rhythmic pulse per syllable. The tones ascend for the two syllables of the word Kida:n (pitches a, c), then descend and hold for the next two syllables, the word *sagu* (pitches a, a). The two words are thus conjoined melodically in an up-over-holding arch (pitches a-c-a-a) that sonically imitates the visual structure of the waterfall in the upper range of the song's melody. Then, after a rest pulse, the melody goes to its lowest tone and from it bounces up a minor third to hold at length on the tonal center for the last two syllables of the pig name A:bo:lo: (pitches e-g-g—). These low tones are a sonic icon of the lower-toned human voice; that it is a voice calling out to the pig is performatively keyed by the elongated last syllable. This textual and sonic juxtaposition of two kinds of continuous calling out, that of rushing waterfalls (higher pitches a, c) and that of a yearning voice (lower pitches e, g), is thus iconically marked in the internal ordering and combinatorial patterning of musical material. This relationship remains intact for the remainder of the song, until the calling of water and that of the yearning voice finally merge to become the same.

DUN + TALUN

The *dun + talun* includes three paired refrain (D) and verse (E1, E2, E3) sets. The refrain (an exact-repeating text and melody) is set in a plaintive first-person voice. The voice is calling to a pig, and the phrase is aspectually marked to give the sense of "I keep calling." Time and continuity are thus fused to the motion and space signaled by the directional connection of the placename Kida:n *bese* to the prior places named. Finally, the name of another pig being called is added in the last line. When women take to the trails late in the afternoon to call their piglets, they usually walk along watercourses. The twist here is that now the pigs are being called by a bird making its way along the Wo:lu and Kida:n. Combining this content with the previous switch from "brother" to *ada:* and back to "brother," it is now evident that the bird voice of the song is a female one.

The three verse alternations E1, E2, and E3 (same melody but changing text; paradigmatic variations indicated in boldface) name, in successive lines, a landform, a corresponding placename, and a tree found there. The first lines progress by naming a mountaintop (E1), another mountaintop (E2), and a valley (E3). The second lines fill in actual placenames but not precisely the kinds of landforms noted in the first lines, thus supplying surprise and intensifying the poetic impact. A:ba:leb (A:ba: + *eleb*) is not a mountaintop but a creek head, So:lo:-*sawel* is not a mountaintop but a waterfall crest, and Yagaf is not exactly a valley but a steep downhill slope. Citing the place form before the specific place named creates the space-time of moving toward that place. In the first two instances this is done by evoking the flight path of a bird coming toward the actual places from higher ridges; in the last instance it involves the bird's descending through more of a valley to enter the Yagaf slope. The third lines all name trees located by the place indicated in the previous line: first, two different lone palms, *a:ba:l* and *waya,* then a huge, buttressed *akol* spirit tree.

The spatial and temporal coordination of the bird's flight progression moves along the path indicated by these three sets of parallel verse segments. This space-time immersion is further heightened by the verb constructions. The first two lines of each verse end with the first-person future verb form "I'll see," often paraphrased by Kaluli as "I want to see." The third line of each verse deepens the sense of temporal passage, ending with the conjoined full past form *ba:ba:miyo:wo:,* "came and saw." This is further complicated by the immediately preceding *kosa dowabi(ki),* a processual aspect indicating that the tree is continuously blowing in the wind. So these verses temporally progress from "coming to see" to "came and saw" images of the bird visiting trees along its path.

The pathos of this imagery is heightened by the fact that the trees in the first two verses (E1, E2) are tall, lone palms, not trees that can be home. Only the *akol* named in the last line of E3—which is also the last line of the whole *dun + talun*—is a spirit tree home, a tree with fruit that is food for a spirit bird. In this section the poesis relies on the sense of listening to the bird's quoted speech. This speech is, of course, metaphoric *bale to,* "turned over words," because trees are the bird's brother. The "want/will see" and "came and saw" indicate that, parallel to the song's trunk, its branches continue the story of loss, of the brother's scorn and the singer's sadness. This is heightened by the final place image, that of the descent down to Yagaf and the presence of a lone and very rare *akol* spirit tree there.

SA-SUNDAB + SA-GULU

The imagery of the *sa-sundab* dramatically reframes these branches (as the earlier waterfalling did for the song's trunk) by switching completely to non-narrative poetic resources. The *sa-sundab* evokes three kinds of water sounding: the *gululu* falling and droning sounds of the huge falls of the So:lo: and Kida:n; the *fo* sounds of their waters pulsing and flowing outward and hard over rocks; and the *fuwa:n* sounds of waters spraying

Figure 3.2. Gulu creek; water flows through land as voice flows through the body. Photograph © Steven Feld.

and anchoring in place. These ideophones fuse the sensation of water falling from above to below, pulsing outward from the pool at the bottom, flowing off and away, and spraying off both rocks and the water's own surfaces. Directly creating the spatial feel of waterfall presence, this phonesthesia of flow equally evokes time, through the sensation of water connection and movement. In addition to fusing this sensate space-time, the *sa-sundab* section draws the song to a close with a placed parallelism, linking together the two main creeks, the So:lo: and the Kida:n, which run parallel, *ida:ni galiali,* to join the Wo:lu, substantially defining important connections for Bono: people living at Bolekini. The song then ends with a single droning of the *sa-gulu,* the flowing open "o" that carries the song off with the water as Ulahi's voice fades.

POETICS OF PLACE

Ulahi's song coordinates named places with trees, with light and wind qualities, with sounds, and with affecting acts and quotes. She builds images of a bird following a watercourse, images of departure, of familial rupture. The song's *tok,* its place path, evidences an interpenetration of land and water names, all connected to the poetic resources of "inner speaking," "turned over words," and "sound words." Yet compared with most *gisalo* songs, particularly ones performed during a *gisalo* ceremony, Ulahi's song does not name many places. Its evocative power depends not on the quantity or detail of places named but on their connectedness, on the extent to which they map a place narrative that emotionally resonates with personal, biographical, and historical self-consciousness for Bolekini listeners. Through song, a Kaluli listener is suspended into places, passes along and through them, makes an interiorized macro-tour in the internalized micro-space-time of listening. Path naming creates a context for imaging prior, contiguous, and continuous, though not necessarily linear, sets of placed connections. Ulahi's song, emerging in the making, might end up with almost twice the places and details. But the narrative strategy leads Kaluli listeners to imagine a path of significant connections, creating a rich and coherent *tok,* a path evoking the interplay of presence and absence at Bolekini.

These poetic practices articulate strongly with Keith Basso's general proposal that

> placenames are arguably among the most highly charged and richly evocative of all linguistic symbols. Because of their inseparable connection to specific localities, placenames may be used to summon forth an enormous range of mental and emotional associations—associations of time and space, of history and events, of persons and social activities, of oneself and stages in one's life. . . . Poets and songwriters have long understood that economy of expression may enhance the quality and force of aesthetic discourse, and that placenames stand ready to be exploited for this purpose. (Basso 1988:103)

ULAHI

Understanding the personal and social evocation of Ulahi's song requires some greater sense of her life at Bolekini and of how her biography colors what typical listeners might feel when they hear her sing. The most salient feature of Ulahi's social position at Bolekini is that she is an outsider who comes from a distant area where people speak the eastern, or Ologo, dialect of the Bosavi language. Married into the central Kaluli dialect area as the second wife of a clan Bono: man named Tulunei, her linguistic outsiderness is overtly marked by the fact that she pronounces his name Sulunei.

heyalo and *ko:luba* songs; only recently has she felt an interest in composing *gisalo*. This interest is clearly unusual, indeed, extraordinary, and the moment Ulahi began her song at the Wo:lu creek my jaw dropped. My response was hardly unique. The most astonished "ah!" reactions Kaluli men and women made and still make when listening to *Voices of the Rainforest* universally come just as they hear Ulahi sing the first few phrases of this *gisalo* song.

Typically and predictably, women at Bolekini were very positive about the song, usually responding to first hearings with a highly enthusiastic "*mada ko:le sele*" ("really very different!"). But men at Bolekini were suspicious of the song and were made somewhat anxious by it. They all reminded me that *gisalo* are sung by men, and some asked me either privately or publicly why I included a woman singing *gisalo* on the tape. I replied that no men were composing *gisalo*. They shrugged and said things like "*hede ko:sega . . .*" ("true, but . . ."), trailing off into silence. Hasele conceded that the *bale to*, the "turned over words" of Ulahi's *gisalo*, were *halaido*, "hard," in other words, forcefully evocative. But since the song was not sung by a man for a ceremony with the aim of provoking another to tears, or by a spirit medium for a seance where it would announce a specific spirit presence, he concluded that this was *defe sa:lan*, roughly, "illustrative talk," implying that it was just an example, something to indicate the nature of *gisalo* without being a real one. Essentially this is to recognize that Ulahi's song was a new and different kind of *gisalo*, one of self-expression rather than for social provocation. The story Hasele constructed for himself and other men was that this song was composed to explain to Americans what a *gisalo* was. Some found this a perfectly suitable explanation and adopted it as their own.

Whether or not Ulahi is explicitly talking back oppositionally to her problems of living with Tulunei and finding a place to live, her song is a powerful female intrusion into momentarily unoccupied male expressive space. Yet even though Ulahi is composing and singing in a markedly male genre, the song and its poetic materials are quite continuous with her *heyalo* and *ko:luba* compositional practices of the preceding twenty years. When I asked her about the song, Ulahi herself returned often to a familiar phrase. She said it was a *gisalo ba madale*, a *gisalo* "for no reason" or "to no purpose." This is a complicated phrase to understand, but one that I have heard Ulahi and other singers use before when referring to reflective compositions. While *ba madale* can mean "with no basis" and be a negative characterization, particularly when it modifies a verb of speaking, it also can mean "just by itself" or "just for itself." And this is what Ulahi emphasized to me—that her *gisalo* was just for herself: "*nina:li asula:sa:ga: ka sa-molan*," "Having thought about it alone, I could compose it." A *ba madale gisalo* means the song didn't spring from an agenda to provoke a specific person to tears, as a ceremonial song might. Instead of having a specific evocative purpose directed outward toward another, Ulahi's song was composed in reflection, for herself only. Rather than being a means of persuasion, her song emerged as something to sing alone, to explore her feelings about coming back to Bono: lands after a considerable time away.

WHAT ARE YOUR NAMES?

Moments after finishing her *gisalo,* Ulahi continued with a second song, a short tag, in the *ko:luba* genre:

wo: wo:	(calling out)
ni America kalu-o-e	my American men
gi wi o:ba-e	what are your names?
ni Australia gayo-o-e	my Australian women
gi wi o:ba-e	what are your names?
ni America kalu-o-e	my American men
wo: wo:	(calling out)
ni America kalu-o- wo: wo:	my American men (calling out)
gi wi o:ba-e	what are your names?
ni Australia gayo-e	my Australian women
gi wi o:ba-e	what are your names?
ni America kalu-o-wo:	my American men
o wo:—wo: wo:	(calling out)
gi wi o:ba-e	what are your names?
ni Australia gayo-e	my Australian women
ni America kalu-o-e	my American men
a:-ye- wo: wo:	(calling out)

As my tape recorder kept running, Ulahi paused, then continued in a singing-quoting voice: "My American men . . . *wo: wo:*" And then she switched to full speaking voice, continuing (rather literally translated):

Well, myself, thinking about it, speaking sadly, I won't see your place but you see mine, I don't know your names, who you are? I'm wondering, I'm think- ing like that, you people living in faraway lands, listening to me, I haven't heard your land names, so who are you? That's what I'm saying. Steve, you, having come before, you can say, "My name is Steve, American man," but all the others, what are your names? "Many people will hear your Bosavi songs," you said like that to me before, but thinking about it, singing by myself I'm thinking, what are your names? That's what I was thinking. I don't really know the land names, just America, Australia, so I'm sadly singing like that so that they can hear it.

The background and context for these remarks was a conversation Ulahi and I had had as we walked together from Bolekini to the spot on Wo:lu creek where she sang her songs that day. Ulahi asked why I wanted to record her songs again. I replied that this time many new people would hear the recordings. I couldn't really explain in a Kaluli framework how *Voices of the Rainforest* was to be a serious departure from the limited academic LP releases I had published before (Feld 1981, 1985). It would mean nothing to tell Ulahi that the recording would be published by Ryko-disc, a major independent company, or that Mickey Hart, percussionist of Grateful Dead fame, was its producer, or that it would have worldwide publicity, distribution, and sales. And there was no way I could explain how this was going to be the first compact disk, an object no Kaluli had even seen, entirely devoted to music from Papua New Guinea, or that it would be sold at hundreds of stores and played over hundreds of radio networks. These topics, people, companies, and issues, as significant as they might be to academics or general consumers, are entirely alien to the Kaluli everyday experiential world. So I just kept telling Ulahi that many, many people in America and Australia, the two large places that Kaluli have heard about through contact with outsiders, would hear her voice and be very happy about it (on the aesthetics of the recording, as well as the ethical issues about its royalty and ownership politics, see Feld 1992).

Obviously, the sense of both wonder and strangeness promoted by this conversation lingered with Ulahi as she sang her *gisalo*. Her way of continuing the dialogue emerged in her short, improvised *ko:luba* song. Singing in a low, fluid, quizzical, semispoken register, Ulahi contrasted the explicitness of placenames with the mystery of personal names as an essential identity juncture. But her voice, calling out from the side of Wo:lu creek to American men and Australian women, might resound elsewhere as an overwhelming example of the ethnoscapes of "schizophonia" (Schafer 1977), a local noise from the global boombox of "banished difference" (Attali 1985). However the song satisfies a postmodern narcissism that can see only a world of fragmentary reflections off mirrors of its own shattering, there is something exquisitely local and deeply rooted here. Outsider placenames stress what Kaluli poetics always stress, that song paths connect lives and memories near and far, that they acknowledge the simultaneous sense of closeness and rupture that is central to emotionally confronting human loss.

Use of outside placenames is not an oppositional practice here, not a move to subvert or to gain power over others who now dominate. Rather, like all Kaluli songs, this one animates a dialectic of emplacement and displacement and resolves it in a poetics of replacement. Kaluli practitioners of this song path aesthetic, singers whose best songs make their listeners weep, are matter-of-fact about drawing on distant placenames to enhance their own powers of evocation. For at the heart of all Kaluli song is the creation of a dialogic space-time where imagining others by singing their lands takes in their humanity and presence as well as their otherness and absence. This is why Ulahi's song and her spontaneous commentary so poignantly articulate that wondering, that questioning whether, when we hear her voice, we can possibly feel both her sense of recognition and her sense of loss.

PLACES ARE LIKE FAMILY CALLING OUT

The third of Ulahi's Wo:lu creekside songs is in the *heyalo* genre, a form structured as alternating *mo:,* "trunk," or refrain, and *dun,* "branches," or verses.

mo: 1	2	3	4
nimo sa:iyalena: imolobo:			
Wafulo: *sa:iyalena: imolobo:*	*Weane*	*Ho:iyo:*	*Wafulo:*
nimo sa:iyalena: imolobo:			

dun 1	2	3	4
kuguno: ge aowo: a:la:lubiyo:			
Ho:iyo:wo: *ge aowo: a:la:lubiyo:*	*Ho:bi*	*Imano:*	*Ho:bi*
bolo: *ge aowo: a:la:lubiyo:*	*a:ba:lo:*	*bolo:*	*bolo:*

"trunk" 1	2	3	4
my water cicada is hungry			
at **Wafulo:** ridge cicada is alone	**Weane**	**Ho:iyo:**	**Wafulo:**
my water cicada is abandoned			

"branches" 1	2	3	4
the valley is like your brother calling			
at **Ho:iyo:** your brother calling you	**Ho:bi**	**Imano:**	**Ho:bi**
at the **bol** tree there, your brother calling	**a:ba:lo:**	**bolo:**	**bolo:**

The song alternates four paired sets of "trunks" and "branches." Each repeat of the "trunk" changes the placename of a ridge, repeating the initial image the final time. Each alternating repeat of the "branches" changes the placename of a mountain and a tree there, using the same placename the second and fourth times through and the same tree name the third and fourth times through. Notice the lack of regularity in the repeating names of places and trees, such that the repetition is not too predictable.

The places in this song are situated by the Dibano river, far southeast of the area Kaluli people inhabit. Wafulo:, Weane, Ho:iyo, and Imane are all *hen dagon,* "mountain ridges" over the Dibano river, on lands of Wo:siso: people. Ho:bi is a mountain toward the village of Walagu in Onabasulu country, farther north. The trees mentioned are *bol,* a tall fruiting hardwood, and *a:ba:l,* a thin palm; both always stand alone. Against these places the song juxtaposes visual and sonic images of aloneness, hunger, emptiness, and familial connection. Ulahi says that the "turned over words" or metaphoric potency here is that hunger, emptiness, is like a voice calling out to you, or like a noisy cicada by the stream. Like the high hiss of water or the churning of an empty stomach, it is a constant, grinding, chilling sound that won't go away. Staying in the valleys beneath these mountain ridges is like your brother calling to you. This is because *kugun,* "uncut forest valley," is like a brother to *dagon,* "mountain." Closely linked places are like family to each other, so landforms that tower over others call out to one another, yearning to be connected, like brothers.

"Like a Waterfall in Your Head"

Taken as a group, Ulahi's three songs in the "Relaxing at the Creek" segment illustrate contrastive ways in which paths of placenames hold and express biography, memory, and feeling. Her *gisalo* song ranges over relatively nearby local places that define part of how a specific person's life connects to an awkward sense of community and its margins. Like the *gisalo* song, Ulahi's *ko:luba* illustrates the centrality of placenames to the poesis of evocation and loss. But it goes farther, linking the power of placenames to the power of personal names to create a sense of identity, near or far, familiar or other. And her *heyalo* song sings a fragment of long-ago and faraway images, evoking the memory of a time and an event, thoughts of others who were moved by it, and thoughts of how living far away, one is deeply reminded of places as kin; path connections are like familiar places calling back to you.

Something important has so far been left out in this account of the evocative powers of place naming and of path memory circulation, namely, Ulahi's performance itself. As she sang, Ulahi sat on the bank of Wo:lu *du,* a rocky segment of land in the middle of the creek, with her son Wano, one of her pigs, and me. But she was not singing just to and for us. She was singing with the Wo:lu, singing with water, singing like water, singing about water. This was not a gimmick for the recording. Kaluli men and women often compose songs by creeks and waterfalls; women often sing songs at sago-place creeks or other waterways.

Singing like water is an idea that reverberates throughout Bosavi language and expressive practices. For example, the verb for "composing" in Kaluli, *sa-molab,* concerns hearing and singing inside, "like a waterfall in your head" as Jubi once put it. In this and other cases, the metaphoric potency of water is indicated by the polysemy of all water terminology to the semantic field of song. Composing a song is said to be like the way a waterfall flows into a waterpool. When the words come to your mind and fit the melody, it is like the way a waterfall flows into a pool, holding, bonding, then flowing away. Recall also that the central portion of the *gisalo* song, where its tonal center is established, is called the "waterfalling." This is where it echoes to establish an "o" calling out and

Figure 3.3. The surging foo— *of So:lo: waterfall that climaxes Ulahi's* gisalo *song. Photograph © Steven Feld.*

"e" reverberating back rhyme, and when it pauses before reaching out to its "branches." Likewise, the final one or two lines of *gisalo* are the "waterfalling droning," where the song is carried off by droning "o" and "e," again on the tonal center. And in addition to these ways in which melodies flow like water, the timing and rhythmicity of singing are also forms of flow; the terminology of musical rhythm and meter are polysemic to the pulsing, splashing, and motional qualities of water.

Water flowing through land, experientially embodied as the pulsating flow of the voice through the resonating body, animates the imagination and practice of song, from its melodic and rhythmic structure to its timbral and textural qualities and its evocative power to remain in mind. This is how the performative flow of singing with water and the musicality of singing like water connect deeply with the emplacing textuality of singing about water, following creek paths, evoking their sonic presence through phonesthetic ideophones. Ulahi once told me that every one of her songs was like a *mogan* on a creek. I take her to mean that every song is a pool, a swirl, something that centers and circles in place for some moments, then turns and flows downstream to mingle and merge in other pools. In this sense, Ulahi's songs, like the Wo:lu creek where she sang them, meander and flow through Bosavi communities, reverberating through Kaluli lives and our own by linking places together and suggesting that these paths always connect stories about people's memories and feelings.

PLACE, EXPERIENCE, EXPRESSION

"While perception measures the reflecting power of the body, affection measures its power to absorb" (Bergson 1988 [1908]:56). Places may come into presence through the experience of bodily sensation, but it is through expression that they reach heightened emotional and aesthetic dimensions of sensual inspiration. Kaluli emplacement involves sensory naturalization of ways water courses flow by moving in and through land, ways land is always in and around water. This emplacement is implemented by bodily analog: voice moves in and *through* the body, but the physical and emotional presence of the entire body is always *in* the voice. Linking what Bergson calls the "reflecting" and "absorbing" powers of the body, Kaluli sing about waterways, sing with water, imagine song as water flowing like an embodied voice. Here the poetics of place merge with the sensuousness of place as soundscape and with the sensuality of the singing voice.

But there is more: flow, water's perpetual record of resounding images, carries and lingers in embodied memory beyond the perceptual immediacy of an actual voicing in performance. So, when standing by a forest waterway and then walking on in the forest, one hears how the water carries on and thus knows that it can flow back into perceptual immediacy as easily as it flowed out of it. This concretely reprises one of Edward Casey's themes in his essay for this volume: "Perceiving bodies are knowing bodies, and inseparable from what they know is culture as it imbues and shapes particular places. It is by bodies that places become cultural entities" (Casey, this volume; see also Casey 1987:146–80, 1993: 43–105). Which is to say, places make sense in good part because of how they are made sensual and how they are sensually voiced. Poetic and performative practices centralize the place of sense in making a local sense of place. This is how a poetics flows from everyday experience, and how Kaluli imagination and practice make water an acoustemology of embodied place resounding.

NOTES

Kaluli words are spelled according to the orthography in Feld (1990:17–19). For simplicity in reading here, *o:* signifies phonetic open *o,* pronounced like the vowel in b*ou*ght, and *a:* signifies phonetic epsilon, pronounced like the vowel in b*e*t. Other vowels are spelled to approximate close phonetic English equivalents: *i* as in b*ee*t, *u* as in b*oo*t, *e* as in b*ai*t, *o* as in b*oa*t, *a* as in b*o*b. Consonants likewise are spelled to approximate close phonetic English equivalents.

The research on which this essay is based was undertaken in 1976–77, 1982, 1984, 1990, and 1992 and further checked in 1994–95 in the Kaluli communities of Sululeb and Bolekini in Bosavi, Southern Highlands Province, Papua New Guinea. I thank all of my hosts, especially Jubi, Kulu, Ayasilo, Ho:nowo:, Hobole, Hasele, Gigio, Ha:gulu, Deina, Seyaka, and Ulahi for their years of friendship and their efforts to make their world of places understandable to me. I am equally indebted to Bambi B. Schieffelin and Edward L. Schieffelin for years of polyphonic linguistics and ethnography. My interpretation of placename paths in Ulahi's three songs is drawn in good part from discussions during and following tape playback and transcription-translation sessions at Bolekini in August 1990 and July and August 1992. On these occasions I worked closely with Ulahi and Ayasilo and was also assisted by Deina, Hobole, and Hasele.

Research support has been generously provided by the Cultural Studies Division of the National Research Institute of Papua New Guinea, and in the United States by the National Science Foundation, the National Endowment for the Arts, the National Endowment for the Humanities, the Wenner-Gren Foundation for Anthropological Research, Rykodisc, 360° Productions, and the John D. and Catherine T. MacArthur Foundation.

For comments and criticism on this essay I thank Keith Basso, Edward Casey, Alison Leitch, Bambi B. Schieffelin, Edward L. Schieffelin, Alan Rumsey, Lowell Lewis, Andrew Lattas, and Jadran Mimica. For additional critiques during lectures at the University of Oslo in May 1993, I am grateful to Odd Are Berkaak, Vigdis Broch-Due, Arve Sørum, and Graham Townsley. I also thank participants in the Tuning of the World Conference on Acoustic Ecology at Banff, Canada, in August 1993 for responding so musically to a lecture on Bosavi "echomusecology" and acoustemology.

4

An Occupied Place

Kathleen C. Stewart

This chapter evokes the "senses of place" emergent in the doubly occupied landscape of the hills and *hollers* of southern West Virginia. At the end of a long century of occupation by the coal industry—through the economic and cultural destabilizations of cycles of boom and bust, the mass migrations to the cities and returns to the hills, and the final mine closings in the eighties—the hills find themselves reeling in the dizzying, diacritical sensibilities of the local and the transnational, the past and the present, the all-too-real effects of history and an alternate way of life embodied in the very look of *thangs got down*. The impossible dream of a stable home place proliferates within the shock of a threatening surround that has penetrated it to the core. The detritus of history piled high on the local landscape has become central to a sense of place emergent in re-membered ruins and pieced-together fragments.

Far from being a timeless or out-of-the-way place, the local finds itself reeling in the wake of every move and maneuver of the center of things. It continually reconstitutes itself through a ruminative re-entrenchment in local forms and epistemologies. *Things that happen* are re-membered in an incessant, daily narrativization of the accidental, contingent, and phantasmic effects of the industrial and postindustrial order of things. Local *ways of talkin'* and *ways of doin' people* become meta-cultural markers of a local way of life in distinction to the demonized ways of the cities. As they say in the hills, *thangs are not what they seem,* and everything depends on the prolific creativity of *makin' somethin' of thangs* that happen. The sense of place grows dense with a social imaginary—a fabulation of place contingent on precise modes of sociality and on tense, shifting social deployments of local discourses that give place a tactile, sensate force.[1]

The problem for the ethnography of such a sense of place is how to track its densely textured poetics through its own tense diacritics of

Figure 4.1. Amigo, West Virginia. Photograph © Em Herzstein.

center and margin, local and global, past and present without reducing it to the "gist" of things or to the abstract schemas of distant "cause" and encapsulating "explanation." This is a poetics emergent in the daily practices of textualizing *thangs that happen* in precise, mimetic detail that dramatizes rhythms of life, artful turns of phrase, and palpable tensions and desires. It resides in the labored breathing of all the old men slowly smothering from black lung disease and in all the nervous, restless action of people *runnin' the roads* and *runnin' their mouths* all day. It depends on the dialogic provisionality of things remembered and retold; it begins with things overheard or seen out of the corner of the eye and ends in "truths" lodged in the concrete yet shifting life of signs. *Thangs are not what they seem,* and yet people search for signs of palpable if ephemeral meaning. The sense of place grows more, not less, present and pressing as a social imaginary emerges in talk and signifying action—a network of signs that are scanned and *studied on* and collected like the dense layers of trashed objects that demarcate people's *places* in the hills.

The problem of considering "senses of place," then, is a problem of tracking the force of cultural practices subject to social use and thus filled with moments of tension, digression, displacement, excess, deferral, arrest, contradiction, immanence, and desire. Theorists such as Barthes (1957, 1974, 1975), Bakhtin (1981, 1984, 1986), and Benjamin (1969, 1978) have each in their own way pointed to this excessive and hard-to-grasp quality of cultural productions. For Barthes, there is the relentless "texting" of things coupled with the indeterminacy of "meaning" in the text, the inevitable gaps or slippages in the working of signs coupled with the uncontained excesses of reading. For Bakhtin, there is the radical dialogics of cultural production, the genealogical "meaning" of signs and forms discoverable only in their social and historical usage, and the ungraspable "something more" of genre and voice. Benjamin makes a claim for the redemptive potentiality of images and objects whose meaning is inherently dialectical and politically double-edged.

In such accounts, culture is not an end point or a blueprint for thinking and acting but an order of effects glimpsed in gaps or pauses in the sign where epistemological certainty is arrested by the hard-to-grasp sense of something "more" and "other." The very effort to imagine culture, then, is itself a continuous effort to reopen a space attentive to the forms and moves of cultural production. It takes more than the safe distance of a relativist chant or the effort to debunk stereotypes or to "disprove" myths. It takes more than an artful re-presentation of local voices as if they could "speak for themselves." It takes not less theorizing on the part of ethnography but more, in order to expose the complicity of our own cultural critique-as-usual in obscuring or enclosing the force, tension, and density of cultural imaginations in practice and use.

"Sense of place" in the account that follows refers to the effects of contingency, signifying density, and social location glimpsed at moments of tension, displacement, and deferral. It is written into the West Virginia landscape not as a smooth story that follows the lines of its own progress from beginning to end as a master narrative would but as a collection of fits and starts in the moves of master narrative itself. It is made up of narrativized moments of encounter, shock, description, digression, and lyrical, ruminative aporias that give pause. It dwells in and on the formed particularity of things and the spaces of desire (and dread) they incite in the imagination.

In the effort to re-present, or translate, in an academic context something of the force of the sense of place in the hills, my account finds itself sharply divided between evocation and theoretical exegesis. It performs, rather than obscures, the inescapable problematics of subject and object, power and powerlessness, distance and closeness, form and meaning that are not only central to ethnographic efforts at intercultural speculation but also key to the everyday machinations of cultural poetics and senses of place in the "modern" world. My claim is that it is only in holding open the gaps and tensions in cultural representation itself that we can glimpse an "other" mode of cultural critique that speaks from a "place" of contingency, vulnerability, and felt impact. This, it seems to me, is the significance for "us" of the sense of place and the point of holding open an interpretive space in which to consider it.

In the hills, the sense of place is lodged in precise ways of attending to things. It begins and ends in an incessant compulsion to story things that happen to interrupt the progress of events. It tracks along through an endless process of remembering, retelling, and imagining things. It fixes on a tactile mimesis of decomposing objects and launches itself again and again as a continuous search for redemptive, luminous signs that speak to people and point to the possibility of the "something more" in a culture and a place. In the effort to evoke something of this sensibility, I have used every trick I could imagine to catch the reader up in the dialogic provisionality of its "truths," including dense descriptions with amassed details, direct polemics, re-presented stories, and direct appeals to the reader to "picture" this and "imagine" that.

My story, like the stories I heard in the hills, begins and ends in a process of re-membering, retelling, and re-placing. It began with two years of fieldwork between 1980 and 1982 and continued through a dozen return visits in the years that followed and through the twists and turns of fieldnotes, tape recordings, memories, photographs, phone calls, postcards, letters, telegrams, and professional papers. Over time, it has become a process of long dwelling on things remembered and retold, forgotten and imagined.

In the account that follows, I re-present stories with ethnopoetic notations meant to evoke something of the intensely elaborated cultural poetics of the placed, local speech in the hills (see Derrida 1978; Hymes 1975, 1981, 1985; Tedlock 1972, 1983) and to mimic the effects of poetics in performance (see Bauman 1977, 1986; Bauman and Briggs 1990). I use boldface lettering to indicate emphasis, line breaks to indicate rhythm and pause, and occasional representations of spoken pronunciations to evoke the differences between Appalachian dialect and "Standard English." My interpretive strategy here, of course, is a process of translation both of the oral to the written and of a local (and stigmatized) language to a particular audience for desired effects. It is not in any way an effort to achieve an objective representation of a linguistic reality but is an ideological strategy, informed by Bakhtin's translinguistics (1981; see also Vološinov 1986), that traces forms in their social and political use. It is an effort to evoke some of the density and texture of expressive forms that voice a cultural poetic embedded in a way of life and the politics of its constant subversion and reproduction in the face of national and transnational forces.

To the same end, I use italics to indicate culturally marked local terms or terms that have some marked cultural relevance in their social use. For the sake of textual fluency, most terms are italicized only the first time they appear; for the sake of the critical difference that emerges at moments of interruption and arrested progress, some terms are italicized repeatedly to mark and remember the space of the local sense of place. The sense of place in the hills, as I imagine it, stands as an allegory of an interpretive space or a mode of cultural critique that often finds itself crowded into the margins of the American imaginary and yet haunts the center of things and reminds it of something it cannot quite grasp.

DIGGING IN

Picture hills so dense, so tightly packed in an overwhelming wildness of green that they are cut only by these cramped, intimate hollers tucked into the steep hillsides like the hollow of a cheek and these winding, dizzying roads that seem somehow tentative, as if always threatening to break off on the edges or collapse and fall to ruins among the weeds and the boulders as so many others have done before them. Picture hillsides so steep that the sun shines down on them for only a few hours a day before passing over the next ridge. Picture hills slashed round and round with the deep gashes of strip mining like a roughly peeled apple, and hilltops literally lopped off by machines the size of ten-story buildings. And these creeks—this ever-audible soundscape to the everyday—that in the spring swell and rage at the bridges and overhanging shacks and leave behind a wake of mud and trash that reaches high into the trees. Picture mountainous heaps of coal slag that catch fire from internal combustion under all the thousands of tons of their own weight and burn for months or years at a time, letting off a black stench of oily smoke. Picture the hills bursting into red and orange flames at all hours of the night— flames likened to the pits of hell. Picture sagging creek banks shored up with tires, rusted trucks, and refrigerators, and picture treacherous slag "dams" holding back lakes of black oily water from the mines. Picture how, when it rains, the men go on watch through the night, climbing the steep hills to peer into the blackness and wonder if the dam will hold.

Picture the tattered remnants of the old coal-mining camps crowded

Figure 4.2. Devil's Fork Creek, Amigo. Photograph © Em Herzstein.

into the hollers, and the way people's places perch precariously on the sides of hills or line the roads with the hills pressed hard against their backs. Some stand freshly painted in yards filled with kitsch figurines and plastic swimming pools. Others bear the faded pastel blues, greens, and yellows they have worn for many years, the paint worn through in places to weathered boards, their porches starkly swept and lined with chairs. Others still are deeply decayed, with broken porches, partially caved-in roofs, broken water pipes gushing out the underside, and relatives' trailers packed tight into their yards for lack of land to rent or buy.[2]

Picture the places way up the hollers in a wilder, more dangerous zone away from the hardtop and neighbors. Here whole compounds may be pieced together with the remains of the old places now long fallen into ruin. A main house may be surrounded by tiny shacks made out of scrap metal and no bigger than a bed, where grown sons or crazy relations stay. There may be an outhouse, a cold cellar, a pump house, chicken coops, a pigsty, and several small gardens. Or there may be only a grassless yard heaped with metals and woods, bits of toys, and dismembered machines. There will be chairs stuck out in the middle of it all—the place where Fred or Jake or Sissy sits—and farther out, encircling the compound, a ring of rusted, disemboweled trucks and cars, a pen filled with baying hounds and, beyond that, the hills themselves where you will come across the graveyards, the orchards, the ruins, the named places, the strip mines, the trucks belly-up, the damp, decayed mattresses, some scattered items of clothing, some·campfire sites, some piles of beer cans, some bags of trash . . .

I could tell you how sometimes clumps of coal mud explode into the sink and then the water runs black, or there is no water at all, for the rest of the day. Or how sometimes, when a house falls vacant, it disappears overnight and later reappears as an addition to someone else's place. I could say that houses, like people and things, circulate until they become abstracted into moving forms, that it is their movements and re-memberings that seem to matter most.

If I had fifty thousand words in which to describe the life of watched and remembered things in these hills, I would use them, as James Agee did in *Let Us Now Praise Famous Men* (Agee and Evans 1941), to heap detail upon detail so that we might at least imagine an escape from the "you are there" realism of ethnographic description into a surreal space of intensification. Like Agee, I could describe the rooms and rafters, the cracks in the walls, the damp underneaths of the houses where dogs and fleas and other creatures lie, the furniture, the contents of drawers, the smell of coal soot ground into the floors over years and covering the walls with a thin greasy layer, a second-story bedroom ceiling open to the sky where the roof has fallen in, the way gauzy curtains are drawn across the windows so that everything outside can be seen without knowing it is being watched, a poor family of six huddled together on mattresses on the living room floor because that is the only room that gives shelter in the winter.

For Agee, every "thing" he encountered became a sign communicating exploitation, injustice, disappointment, and desire. Writing during the Great Depression, he railed against existing forms of documentary writing in an effort "to open up a passionately ambiguous new space" (Reed 1988:160) beyond any claims to be able to represent such "things" as tenant farmers (or "hillbillies" or "white trash"). He turned his book into a political allegory about relations between "Us" who represent "Them" and Them represented in an attempt to destabilize not just a particular representation of "them" but the very claim to know the "meaning" of such "things" at all. The inevitable failure of representation to capture an absolute "real" meant only a further commitment to the political act of poesis—the continuous effort to imagine what might be called a "cultural real." Escape, he said, is impossible: ruin is our only hope—a complete abandonment to the currents of existence.

In the effort to clear a space in which to imagine a cultural poesis, Agee's writing grew hypergraphic, pushing minutely described things into a space of "mimetic excess" (Taussig 1993) where they were at once naturalized as the real and marked in their very textualization as a cultural construction. Reality and writing seemed to transpose themselves in cultural objects (Reed 1988:161); a cultural poesis seemed to have somehow scripted itself right into the matter of things. The texture of wood on a country church wall appeared "as if it were an earnest description" (Agee and Evans 1941:38). "A chain of truths did actually weave itself and run through: it is their texture that I want to represent, not betray or pretty up into art" (1941:240). He wished he could put bits of wood, fabric, and excrement on the page rather than words. He wished the book could be printed on newsprint so that it would fade and fall apart with use, mimicking the ephemerality of everyday life and cultural meaning.

Picture, then, a place that has given itself over to such "abandonment to the currents of existence." A place, as people would say, "caught between a rock and a hard place"—a home place hardened into a protective cocoon from the threatening life beyond the hills and yet always emptying out as people leave in search of work. A place mired in the abject decay of things left behind, yet vibrant with re-membered presence. A place grown at once tactile and imaginary, at once real and as insubstantial as ghostly traces. A place where place is everything, and yet a family's place is not where they "live" but where they *stay at,* as if the staying has to be marked, like a temporary respite requiring constant vigilance. Imagine how "place" and even "culture" itself could become a space of desire— "a thousand plateaus of intensification" (Deleuze and Guattari 1991).

Imagine the desire to amass such a "place" around you, to dig yourself into it, to occupy it. The porches piled high with couches, chairs, plastic water jugs. The yards filled with broken toys, washing machines, scrap metal and salvaged wood, cars and trucks on blocks or belly-up, being dismembered piece by piece. All the living room walls crowded with pictures of kin who have left and the dead in their coffins, the paintings of the bleeding Sacred Heart of Jesus with the beautiful longing eyes. All the mantels and tabletops covered with *whatnots* and shrines. The newspaper clippings of deaths and strikes. The children's drawings and trophies. The heart-shaped Valentine's Day chocolate boxes saved every

Figure 4.3. Sylvie Hess's place, Odd. Photograph © Harriette Hartigan, Artemis.

year for twenty years and mounted on bedroom walls. All the velveteen tapestries of John L. Lewis, John F. Kennedy, and Elvis.[3]

THE SHOCK OF HISTORY

Imagine life in a place that was encompassed by the weight of an industry, that was subject to a century of cultural displacements, and that now faces the final collapse of mining and the slow, inexorable emigration of the young. Imagine a history remembered not as the straight line of progress but as a flash of unforgettable images. Remember the *old timey* cabins in the hills, the fires, the women dead in childbirth, the slick company representatives who dropped by the cabins of unsuspecting farmers, stayed for dinner, and casually produced a bag of coins in exchange for parcels of "unused ridgeland" (Eller 1982:54). Remember the company camps that sprang up around mines like someone else's mirage, complete with company scrip, company stores, company doctors, company thugs, company railroads, company schools, company churches, and company baseball teams. Company thugs carried sawed-off shotguns, **po**licing who came and went on the trains. They say the thugs stood sentry in the hills over a camp in the night. You could see their lanterns and that's how you knew they were there. Then the lights would go out and you didn't know. Imagine all the arresting images of strikes, lockouts, house evictions, people put out in the alleys with their stuff all around them and the snow coming down.

> They was a settin' in chairs
> like they was in their own **livin' room.**
> And that's the **truth.**
> They had nowhere to go and the snow comin' down right on top of 'm.
> People lived in tents and the babies lay upon the quilts on the ground.

Armed miners holed up on a mountain and the federal government was called in to drop bombs on them from airplanes.

There were the dizzying swings of boom and bust, the mechanization of the mines, the mass migrations of the fifties and sixties, the final boom during the oil crisis of the 1970s, the final mine closings in the eighties, the collapse of the place, the painful hanging on, the unthinkable leavings. Imagine how the place became a migrational space that caught people in the repetition of drifting back and forth from the hills to the cities looking for work (Ardery 1983; Coles 1971; Cunningham 1987; Gitlin and Hollander 1970). How country songs of heartache and displacement became their theme songs. How ecstatic fundamentalism boomed in a performative excess of *signs* of the spirit and dreams of another world beyond. How the place itself drew them back to dig themselves in—"so far in I ain't never comin' out." How the place grew palpable to the remembered senses: the smell of snakes in the air, the sound of slow voices chatting in the yard, the breeze striking the tin pie plates in a garden, the taste of ramps and dandelion greens.

Imagine a place grown intensely local in the face of loss, displacement, exile, and a perpetually deferred desire to return to what was always already lost or still ahead, just beyond reach. Picture how a home place long threatening to dissolve into the sheer shiftiness of history might grow filled with an intense synesthesia of person, sociality, and landscape, how a haunted cultural landscape becomes a dizzying, overcrowded presence. Imagine how people say they *smother* and are hit by

Figure 4.4. Lance Smith on porch, Amigo. Photograph © Em Herzstein.

waves of *the dizzy* and *the nerves,* how they say they wouldn't "never want to leave." Imagine how they find themselves "caught between a rock and a hard place," re-membering a home place that is always emptying out and backing away from the cold impossibility of the foreign land of the cities "beyond" that remains their only option.

Imagine the need to remember through the constant repetition of images fixed, condensed, studied on, and made visceral, the need to watch, to chronicle, to make something **of** thangs, the attachment to things that matter, the fascination with objects on which the mind can stare itself out.[4] Remember all the named places in the hills that mark the space of accidents and tragedies. Imagine how people *just set* and talk at the old gas stations and stands—the beat-up old stores on the side of the road that sell daily necessities with long shelf lives like cigarettes, soda pop, candy, cakes, and the canned milk for the endless pots of coffee.[5] Picture how people watch for things that happen and scan for signs. Picture the endless proliferation of stories throughout the day and over the years.

Imagine how an encompassed and contested way of life can grow immanent, how it might be scripted right into the matter of things, how objects and bodies marked by events could become images that twist and turn in the strands of history and sociality and then rise like moons on the horizon—sudden caesuras in which the mind could collect itself by staring itself out on things. Imagine the desire to amass such a place around you, to dig yourself into it, to occupy it . . .

RE-MEMBERING PLACE

Imagine the past and the present as sensed, tactile places that remember and haunt, how the past *just comes* to people out roaming the hills in body or mind. Picture a "real" embodied in the particularity of precise effects—how identity, social history, and a sense of place can all be recounted together in a litany of *places* in the hills, social places, and places on the body. There is the constant recounting of places on the body where life has left its impact—the scars, the locations of pain, the disfigurements, the amputations, the muscles and joints and bones that remember. There are the constant social rituals of placing people—Who are your kin, where do you work, who do you know, where do you stay at, what has happened to you? There is the constant remembering of named places in the hills: the remains of the big white houses of the *operators* (managers) looming over the camps, the worked-out mouths of mines lying dark and gaping on the sides of the hills and, farther in, the chimneys and aging orchards that *remember* a family farm, the graveyards and rusted train tracks and mining tipples that *remember* accidents, strikes, and other "striking" scenes like the prayer services held underground at the start of a shift, when hundreds of miners would crouch in the water under the low ceilings listening to the preaching of death and salvation, the place where the union organizer was shot dead and his blood ran out in the coal dirt and was lost, the strip-mined hill that collapsed in on itself and slid down to cover the Graham family graves, the places of hunts, suicides, murders, and car accidents, of children electrocuted on old mining wires, of fires when the people trapped inside cried out for help while the others stood outside and listened, helpless.

Imagine the watchfulness, the effort to track the workings of a "system" that is "located," if anywhere, in the nervous, shifting, hard-to-follow trajectories of desire. Picture the restlessness, the need to get out and go: all the coming and going, the *running the roads,* the *running their mouths,* the *roaming,* the *trading*—how people literally "keep moving" as if to occupy this place and to fill somehow its overfilled yet emptying space. Then picture all the places where people *just set*—a chair left out in the middle of the kitchen floor or on the porch or in the yard or out in the hills, a favorite stump or rock.

Picture the constant working on things, the dismembering and re-membering of things, the strange agency of fashioning aesthetic effects out of things that are always falling apart or are already fallen into decay. Picture how people are always *foolin' with* their places—someone is tearing off his back porch, someone else is building on a bedroom or jacking up a sag, another is building an arbor for her grape vines, and another leaves her coal stove out in the front yard for weeks "for spring cleaning." Bud Caulley had his house half repainted for longer than anyone could remember: "Hit's where he cain't tell whether he likes the old or the new. And tell you the truth, buddy, I cain't either. Can you?"

Picture the proliferation of signs of a local life written tentatively yet persistently onto the landscape. The tiny wooden or cinder-block post offices that bear the names Amigo, Red Jacket, Ruin, Helen, Black Eagle, Viper, Iroquois, Hard Shell, Winding Gulf, Odd, East Gulf, Coal City, Cook Town, Persistence, Lillybrook. The tiny particleboard entrepreneurial shacks with signs that read "BEeR CiGArETs PoP" in huge irregular lettering. The trucks perched on the side of the road selling watermelons or made-in-Mexico velveteen wall hangings of the Last Supper, the Sacred Heart, the rebel flag. Hand-painted road signs—"Please Don't Throw Your Trash Here," "Anteeks," "Eggs For Sale," "WATCH IT: Road Washed Out Up Aways Ahead." Church signs advertising a welcome and a warning: "Sinners Welcome," "Sinners Apply Within," "Repent, For The Day Is Near." The massive coal trucks rushing around steep curves, their names mounted in bold letters on the grill—"Heaven's Highway," "Good

Time Buddy," "Let the Good Times Roll." At one curve, two hand-painted billboards crammed with biblical quotations face each other in a heated debate over how literally to interpret the signs of the "End Times." At another, a hand-painted road sign perched at the top of a treacherous hill offers only the starkly haunting warning: "ETERNITY AHEAD."

Picture people sitting on porches, standing beside fences, clumps of men gathered around benches at the gas station or the stand, how they stare as you pass, keeping track.

GETTING CAUGHT

Imagine yourself always already caught in the tense fabulation of story and sociality and surrounded by events you *cain't hep but notice*. Imagine tracking a day in the camps by a constant watching out of the corner of the eye . . .

> June 24, 1982. Kitty passes my place to see Sissy about the girls' fighting. Sissy goes to see about Miss Banks, who has had an operation on her knee. Kitty comes to see if I think Sissy's mad at her "for saying anything **to** her;" Sissy, she says, has been acting funny with her. Anna Mae, out hanging her rugs, yells to Lilly to come out "if you want to" and they stand talking over the fence that joins their places. Kitty, still with me, wonders what they are talking about, "not that it's any a my business." She says they say Anna Mae's daughter has cancer and this leads to stories of the grotesque — cancers, bizarre accidents of mothers rolling over on their sleeping babies, bloody childbirth in the truck on the way to the hospital, babies born with the mark of the beet or the hamburger or the apple that the pregnant mother craved — "looks just like it." We say it's a shame that Kitty's daughter Julie had to find out from the other kids on the school bus that she was adopted, that Kitty should have told her herself. This leads us to talk about the danger of things left unsaid; Mr. Walker in Rhodell shot himself to death because he kept things to himself. I recall the look in his eyes the last time I saw him — at the public auction of his store which he had neglected more and more over the years as his drinking got worse until finally people got tired of sour milk and bugs in their rice and "quit tradin' with him." I bring Sissy her cuttings and we sit out on her porch in the late afternoon sun, dangling our legs over the edge. Sissy says Kitty thinks she was the one who told about Julie being adopted, but she never would — "Ain't nobody's business." We watch the men on evening shift leave out, the men on day shift come in. We can smell Miss Murdock's greens cooking ("She's sa hateful she won't tell nobody where she got em"), Dreama's pork frying ("You reckon Bud's back workin?").

Imagine a vigilant scanning become automatic, relentless, compulsive; people cain't hep but notice. Imagine that passing trucks can be recognized by their distinctive sounds, that their comings and goings are automatically tracked and timed to figure where they have been and how long they have lingered there. Imagine the scanning for signs . . . how everything depends on things overheard, overseen, on the effort to make somethin' **of** thangs. Imagine how when someone falls sick or dies the others quite literally miss seein' 'm.

Imagine the *aggravation* that builds when the responsibility to bear witness is drawn to the task of tracking those who run the roads all day or those who stay holed up out of sight. How the constant necessity for fluid, relational engagement seizes up into the sensation of smothering in the face of too much stuff, too much talk, the ever-present excesses of action and expression, the smothering intensity of being left to study on thangs. Picture how people, holed up and studyin' on thangs, get *squirrelly* and have to git out and go.

. . . Picture the restlessness of the young men runnin' the roads day and night until they run out of gas and money or until they are stopped by the force of accident. Then picture them, still restless, roaming up and down the holler in their wheelchairs. Picture Riley Meadows's neighbors, who watched him when he stayed "holed up in there" after his wife died. "And they say he's got a calendar in there on his wall and every morning when he gets up he marks an *X* through another day gone by without her. He counts the days she's gone." He's gone "mean." He won't talk to anyone. He won't get out and go. "He'll aggra**vate** you to death." Picture those who watch for Miss Graham when she drops out of sight for a while. They "figure she's in there a drankin'. Hit's just a matter a time 'fore somethin' happens."

Picture how the hills grow infilled with the excesses of a place re-acting to the threat of a world *got down*. Picture the shifting satisfactions and aggra**va**tions of those who sit on their porches in the gathering dusk to re-collect a barrage of images that have an impact and leave a trace as the hills come in to darken the sky at the end of the day. Picture, too, all the old men, slowly smothering with black lung, who dream of going back up into the hills once more—to a place "far in" where they could just set. More than once I have been persuaded to take them, pushing their wheelchairs over roots and wet leaves to a clearing and propping spare oxygen tanks around them.

A SOCIAL IMAGINARY

Picture the place as an intense social imaginary born in the nervous oscillation of loss and the dream of return and raised in the tense fabulation of a ghostly insubstantiality that is also a tactile attachment. Picture the enchantments and investments in these hills as a lost and possible world. Here, sociality is not an afterthought or a "context" that adds a dimension to meaning after the fact, but a force field that pulls meaning along in its wake on a twisted path through dread and desire, loyalty and betrayal.

Imagine those moments when the hills abandon themselves to a social imaginary, when the place becomes a phantasmagoric dream space —a wild zone beyond the pale filled with things dangerous, tragic, surprising, spectacular, and eccentric. Imagine the "real" at such moments as a resistant surface scanned by wishes and regrets and disclosed by desire— a collection of fantastic fragments and effects through which things appear obliquely yet powerfully as what they are and what they can be.[6]

. . . They say there are snakes up there and wild young men who lie in wait or come in the night to rob and maim. Once there were hippies— demon worshippers—who lived out there under a rock. There are eccentric hermits living on nothing and white trash families filled with incest; there are criminals in stolen car rings drifting back and forth to Chicago and hiding out from the **po**lice.

. . . There was the night that Frankie, a Vietnam vet who was rumored to be living under rocks, went on a burning spree that took out five barns and shacks in the hour before dawn while volunteer firefighters raced from one call to the next, unable to keep up with him or to find a trace of him.

. . . There is Eva Mae. Poor, black, and "crazy," she walks the road between Amigo and Rhodell all day long, waving a gun or a butcher knife at any car that tries to stop and give her a ride.

. . . They say people are crazy and there's no telling what they might do. They keep guns loaded by the bed and at the door and shoot at the sound of noises in the night. They say the smell of snakes in the dog days of August is strong enough to make you sick.

Yet the wildness and danger only fan the flames of desire. There are the graveyards to visit, the old orchards to be harvested, the berries and greens to gather if you dare. Old women venture out in packs, salivating over dandelion greens, ramps, and a dozen named varieties of weeds as if they embodied desire itself. Lacy Smith talks of a place up in the hills where a tiny hole opens into a great big room full of Indian things. He and Bud have looked for it but they never could find it again "where the hole is so small."

Danger and promise mark the space of a dream world born of the tense union of contingency and desire, or what is and what could have been. Caught between a rock and a hard place, people cling to the hills as a place of impossible possibility. They say people shouldn't get above their raisin'. They say they would never want to leave. They scavenge and loot. They hunt. They fish. They scavenge wood, they loot coal from the slag heaps at the worked-out mines. They scavenge checks as they scavenge meat—food stamps, social security, black lung, disability, welfare. They carry away booty under cover of darkness.

. . . There was the night that a group of striking miners sitting in the waiting room of the health clinic spun a collective fantasy of how they would scale the big brick walls of Governor Rockefeller's mansion and loot it for all it was worth.

. . . Or the night, like so many others, that some of the young men, caught in the trap of alcoholic roaming, made the trip to Chicago as a bold, spontaneous adventure, drinking all the way. They woke up in the city, in the noise, the traffic; they got lost; there was trouble with the police. Then again a drunken, dreamy night and they found themselves back in the hills, dreaming of losing themselves in a place "way back in" where they could never find their way out again.

There are all the stories of those who have found themselves adrift out in the world beyond the hills and dreamed of return. There was Ray Meadows, stationed in Germany in the seventies, who caught himself staring out the kitchen window at a lone dandelion in the yard and, hillbilly that he was, it was all he could do to keep from *showin' hisself* by running out and plucking it to eat. There was Bobby Lilly, who was too *backward* to get anything to eat on the train coming home from the Korean War and who arrived home so weak from starvation that he fell sick and had to be nursed back to health on a diet of beans and corn pone. There was the day Jimmy Cunningham started back from Baltimore but was stopped by a feeling and turned back. He started out again the next day and made it back all right. "I ain't superstitious. I don't believe in black cats and all that. But a feelin' is somethin' different. A feelin' ain't somethin' you ignore." And one night Helen James had a dream. She dreamed that she was driving away in a big slow luxury car, drifting past beautiful pastoral mountain scenes filled with color and sound. She was coming up over the top of a big hill and she felt something "big" was going to happen. But then there was nothing—the terrifying annihilation of free fall. She woke up smothering. "It makes you not want to go nowhere."

PLACED ITINERARIES

Imagine yourself, then, not in a cleared ethnographic space of explanatory contexts and structures but in a distracted space, moving as if in body from one place to the next and drawn along by digressions that lead into the social imaginary.[7]

> **All** right now, you know where Miss **Banks** stays at up there, don't you?
> All right, now, go on down Miss Banks's place past that **big ol' bridge** where that **McKinney** boy went over and hit looks like you might go in **after** 'm if you ain't careful, buddy.
> **Yeah BUDDY.**

All right, now, you'll see a **bridge** what's got one side **down** and the other side 'bout covered up in **briars.**

Keep on 'til you see the **Black Eagle** post office.

That's where the **snake** handlers **stay** at and Bud says **he's** skeered to deliver the **mail** down there where he might put his hand in a mailbox and there's a **snake** in there.

I don't guess they get much **mail** down there, do you?

All right, now, **keep** on, **keep** on, pretty soon you come to that place where they shot up that **boy. What** was that boy's name?

You know that one **kilt** his **wife.**

Well, really, I don't believe it **was** his **wife,** but they was a **livin'** together and **I** don't know **what** all.

Well they was **in** to it and he **kilt** her right **there.**

They said there was blood all over the walls and never could get it out of the carpet because Sissy went down there right after it happened and **she** told **me** it was **bad.**

All right, now, you know where that old **woman** stays, there's a **washin'** machine out front, well it's just past the sign for "free coffee."

. . . and perty soon you come to a big ol' **red** colored house up on the hill . . .

Imagine a place constantly rewritten and re-membered, a place where sociality emerges in digressions and culls itself into *big meanings* at moments of shock. Imagine the force of social imagination at work in the desire to mime, to re-member, to participate in the matter of things. To matter. To follow distraction into something like "the heart of things"—if only as a temporary resting place, a place to just set.

Picture how people out roaming in the hills come up against places, and how a memory of inescapable impact just comes. Every time Tammy goes to the river now she "cain't hep but recall that pore man drownded." A young, strong man was swimming out in the river with his friends,

where it's just over your head even way out.

And he started to go **down.**

Well they tried to **hep** him and they was all around him but they said hit was **just like** somethin' was **pullin'** him **down.**

And finally he told em, he said, "you better let me **go** and y'all get back to the **shallow.**"

He said "I'm a **goin down.**"

And they said they could **feel** him go down their **legs,** and they felt his **hands** slide down their **legs** like he wanted to **hold on** and then he was **gone.**

Honey, that **haunts** me.

And it **does,** too.

Picture how events actively imagined in this way and weighted with social use reverberate beyond the particularities of any account, how "the image contains its own remainder, in the act of the imagination" (Strathern 1991:xxiii). Imagine how meaning, memory, and motive adhere to storied things to become an encountered force that stops people dead in their tracks, effects a gap in understanding, and motivates a search for meaningfulness.

June 4, 1982. Sissy and I walked up Devil's Fork holler. As we passed Amigo 2, stories just came to her of the people and events that once surrounded the now-deserted shacks.[8] The farther we went up the holler, the more our talk drifted into a lyrical, melancholic rumination. At a bridge Sissy recalled the old swimming hole there when the creek was still clean:

> But that was back before they got the **commodes** in and the **gover**mint come in, told us a septic tank had to be so many feet **apart** and that's the **law.**
>
> **Well, all right,** now, in **'Migo** most a them lots ain't **big** enough for the **law** and we **tried** to **tell** 'm but you just cain't **talk** to them people. They said, "You have to have 'm so far **apart.**"
>
> So people started dumpin' in the **creek.**
>
> Honey, I hated to **see** it where that water was as **blue!** an' **used to** we'd swim here, the sun shined down on it, an all us comin' up then, we'd spend all **day.**

I noticed an overgrown stand of *ramblin' roses* in the middle of an empty field. Sissy said:

> Well, you cain't **see** it but there's a **chimbley** other side them **blooms,** runs right up the far side of 'm, the grass is about covered it now.
>
> **Jake Catlitt,** he built that house, **big** house and it had a stone front to it and them **old timey** beams and big ol' windas.
>
> Well, Jake lived in it and then his baby **Pete, he** lived there **too.**
>
> An he'd just got **married** and they was livin' there and there was another young couple stayin' there with 'em to help pay the **bills.** There wasn't much **work** at that time but **Jake,** he was workin' down at that Joe's service station down **Black** Eagle and he was off at **work.**
>
> And the two **women** were home **alone** and it was where they didn't know how to make the **fire** in the **stove** and reckon they got it too **hot** and they said it musta **caught** on one of them old beams.
>
> Well they run out with the **baby,** cause one of em had a **baby,** an pore old **Petey,** he was a comin' back from work, an he **seen** it and come a **run**nin' and a **holler**in', **buddy.**
>
> And the **Reeds,** they stayed right down here, **they** come on and them other people down **'Migo 2,** they seen the smoke and **they** come on. **Ever'**body come a **run**nin' but there weren't nothin' they **could** do.
>
> The fire bust out a them windas and burned them old timey beams and it tuk that whole house, burned it right down to the **ground,** buddy.
>
> **Petey** an them went down **Viper** to stay, and I never **did** hear what happened to them other people.
>
> But that's where them **roses** bloom 'round that old **chimbley.** It's a **perty** place, but it's been **lonely** too long. They oughta get somebody **in,** come **stay** out here.

A rambling rose vine entwined around a crumbling chimney "remembers" an old family farm, the dramatic fire in which the place was lost, and the utopic potential still clinging to the traces of history. Concrete objects that have decayed into fragments and traces embody absence and the process of remembering itself; they haunt people. The deserted place "remembers" and grows lonely.

Imagine how "meaning" can coalesce in the tactility of a cryptic object. How representation occurs as a kind of re-presenting that stimulates and provokes rather than provides the closure of information, explanation, or code decoded. How people search for a profundity lurking in appearances. How they find excesses that encode not "a meaning" per se but the very surplus of meaningfulness vibrating in a remembered cultural landscape filled with contingency and accident, dread and depression, trauma and loss, and all those dreams of escape and return.

Imagine a place reverberating with countless accounts like Bud Graham's hunting story—accounts in which a distracted, everyday chronicling of events is repeatedly interrupted by "striking" images of places where things have happened. Imagine how simple itineraries suddenly give themselves over to a striking image, as if arrested by a space of intensification, and then recover—shifting back to an everyday sensibility but one that has become infused with the promise of shocking interruption.

Yeah, buddy, I been all **over** these here **heels.**

Used to, we'd go up **huntin'** and them **dogs**'d run all up **Devil's Fork** clear up to the old **Graham** place, crost **Tommy Creek** and way over yonder to **Madeline,** and them **dogs** a **mine** was as good coon dogs as you'd ever wanna **see** and couldn't nobody else's dogs **catch** em and buddy they'd **try,** too. [laughing]

I remember the **time,** that Bud **Henson** fella useta stay down here at **'Miga,** awful bad to **drank.**

And one night he was out here a layin' out **drunk.**

And his **dogs** got after them dogs a **mine,** and I said **buddy,** I said, you better **git** them **dogs** 'fore they run **their**selves t' **death.**

Well, he said, **my** dogs can outrun **any**thang and I said well all **right** then, I guess you know your own **dogs** and them dogs run all night.

And in the mornin' they was ever' one of em **dead.**

Well he was **tore up.**

We hadda go pick up them **dogs** and brang em on **back** to 'm and he jest **set** there an watched em **come.**

Well we **buried** em for 'm, right there by that big ol' overhangin' **rock** looks out over nothin' where that old feller **jumped off** that time after his **boy** got kilt in the **mines** and there was people **skeered** a that place.

Claimed the old man's **h'aint** was still up there.

Well I can't say nothin' about **that,** but we buried them **dogs** up there.

Yeah boy! them days we hunted **coon** and **rabbit, possum,** and just **ever'**thang, **buddy,** and we'd brang it on back and **skin** it, cook it **up** and we'd **eat** it.

Anymore, people's got to where they won't **eat** wild thangs but they're good t' **eat.**

You have to know how to **cook** it, is **all.**
First you let it **cool,** you have to cool the **wild**ness out of it and then **par**boil
  it, and cook it and **eat** it.
People don't know t' **par**boil it.
People don't know thangs like **'at** anymore.
But I been **all** over these here **heels.**

Imagine, once again, the problematics of trying to "picture" such a place in an overview or to name it "in a word" (see Clifford 1983, 1986) — whether as a colonized space (settled, shaped, and finally abandoned by King Coal), an exotic space (filled with alterity), or a dying and degraded space (filled with decay). Picture me as the ethnographer trying to get the story straight.

Picture me, in the length of an afternoon, grilling Riley Hess for an accurate outline of his work history in the mines so that I could help him document his eligibility for black lung benefits. Sifting through a suitcase full of old pay stubs and papers, I tried to reconstruct the requisite twenty years of mining out of his fragmented documentation of a work history of fits and starts and migrations back and forth from one camp to another and from the hills to Detroit and Arizona and back. Riley, sitting with me, grew nervous and digressed from my futile attempts at chronology into stories of dramatic encounters, hilarious failures, and bitterly hard times. I remember the baffled look on his face. And I remember that his stories grew progressively more graphic and imaginary until they had wrenched us (or at least him) into narrative space that was at once more situated and contingent and yet opened an interpretive, expressive space in which there was more room to maneuver (Chambers 1991).

I bet you didn't know there's hills underground, same as above, a hill's got a
  inside same way its got a **out**side.
They're **two sided.**
And this **one** time, buddy, I started out and I was a pullin' two hundred and
  ten cars and ever' one of em loaded up over the **top.**
I always checked my brakes but I reckon they were **wet** because they weren't
  no good a' **tall** and I didn't know a thang **about** it.
And at the **bottom** of one a them **hills** there's a right smart **twist,** where the
  track takes a **turn.**
And its a low **ceilin'** and no room on the **sides** but just for the **train** to git
  through.
You have to **feel** your way through.
You kin loose your **head** if you stick it out like that Reed boy got **kilt.**
You gotta keep your **head** and **feel** your way **through.**
Well we started down and we was a goin' perty **good,** y' know.
And I tried the **brakes** and honey they weren't nothin' **there.**
Well I told the **brake**man, **buddy,** we're a **runnin'** away.
I said **find** yourself a **place** and **jump off** if you **can** because I knowed we
  was gonna come **off.**

Well the **brake**man, he was on t'other **side** and he found hisself a **place** and
   he **jumped.** There wasn't no place on **my** side and I **knowed** it.
Well I called the **dis**patcher and I **told** him, I said, **buddy** I'm a **run**nin' a**way**
   and I got down inside the engine and let it **go.**
We hit that **ceil**in', and **bu**ddy, there's **coal** and **steel** a **fly**in'.
We went right **into** that **hill** and twenty-eight cars come in after us and they
   hadda **time** of it. They hadda take that thang **out** a there **piece** by **piece**
   where they said it done melted together.
They hadda tear that engine **apart** to git me outta that **thang.**
Well they wanted me to go to the **hos**pital and they had the **am**bulance a
   waitin' at the mouth and the lights a flashin' but I said **huh uh, NO-**
   OOO, now I've had **enough,** and I got up and **went home.**
But I never did work no more **motor**man job no more after that.

Imagine yourself, then, not in the space of the "you are there" realism of flat ethnographic description but in an intensely occupied and
imagined space, watching to see what will happen. Imagine the sense of
being at home in a place caught between a rock and a hard place—at
once protected from a threatening outside world and smothering. The
sense of groping along in the midst of a mine field of forces, tracking
the traces of earlier impacts. Imagine a subjectivity located not in the
power to name and evaluate but in the memory/imagination of events
and images that just come and stand as reminders of things uncaptured
by any sense of an overarching "order of things." Imagine the desire to relate an impact, the sudden move "to incarnate oneself, to become more
determined . . . (the) sudden narrowing of horizon" (Bakhtin 1979:357,
as quoted in Todorov 1984:106). Imagine yourself surrounded.

Picture Sissy, who sits on the stoop with her coffee in the early morning watching the blanket of mountain fog rise in floating, ghostly shapes.
Picture all the neighbors as they sit on the porches in the evening to
watch the hills darken in a ring around the camp.

THE SPECTACLE OF IMPACTS

Imagine the kind of place where, when something happens, people make
sense of it not by constructing an explanation of what happened but by
offering accounts of its impacts, traces, and signs.

   . . . Once there was an underground explosion that shook camps in a
radius as wide as thirty miles. No one (but me) was interested in identifying what it "was"—what had "happened" to cause the ground to shake.
Instead there was a flurry of talk about its placed effects—in Winding
Gulf they said it knocked all the plates off Kitty's shelves; in East Gulf
it knocked old man Graham out of his chair and he's got a place on
his arm to show for it; in Helen, it knocked a bucket of coal out of

Julie's mommie's hands and spread a blanket of greasy coal soot over her kitchen floor—"seems like she never could git that flo' clean agin' after that." In the end, we have the graphic, culled images of the plates being knocked off the shelves, the "place" on the old man's arm, the spooky, ever-greasy floor.

Another time, in the spring of 1981, a forest fire burned in the hills surrounding Amigo, slowly working its way down to the camp. For days the air was so thick with smoke that all you could see beyond the alleys of the camp were bursts of blue and orange flame. At night the sight was spectacular and people would sit on their porches and comment on its beauty and force and its chilling resemblance to the pits of hell—a world on fire. During the day there was a feeling of aggra**va**tion. There were dramatic stories of people going up into the hills to fight the fire and contentious/nostalgic claims of how *used to* a forest fire meant **everyone** worked day and night to save the farms. Finally, the fire threatened to jump the creek. Its presence grew more pressing and the houses closest to the creek began to steam. The atmosphere in the camp grew more watchful and calm—more satisfied—as the threat of fire grew palpable. All afternoon we carried buckets of water from the creek to throw on the threatened houses and people noticed everything that happened as if out of the corners of their eyes. Later, there were hilarious comments. They were *tickled* by the look of old Miss Henson running back and forth from the creek with a rusty bucket full of holes. They noticed that Bud Smith would walk right by the Graham's place to dump his buckets on some other place where he was still speaking to the people. They noticed how the smoke just seemed to gather round that *no account* hypocritical Preacher Cole, the flames licking at his heels.

In Agee's words, these are moments of "abandonment to the currents of existence." They are moments of what Taussig (1993) calls "mimetic excess," in which an image flashes uncontained, objects and events become spectacles, subjects become spectators and performers in the spectacle, and the act of mimesis, given over to its own excesses, comes into its own as a local mode of interpretation and an epistemological principle. They are moments that enact the cultural poetics of being in place in a place that actively surrounds, impacts, and remembers. They are moments of occupying an always already occupied place.

A VISIT(ATION)

February 1985—a visit back. Dreama sat in the living room with picture albums, coffee, cigarettes, and ashtrays spread around her. The TV was on, the beans were on the cookstove, there was a cake in the oven, her rugs were soaking in the ringer washer, she had just washed the floor, and she was on the phone with her sister. There was an awkwardness between us—a space made by my long absence and our inability to *just talk* about neighbors and the camp. She asked if I was still in Michigan and if I liked it there. She said she herself could never leave West Virginia and never would. Then we began with talk about bodies: Opal was eight now and still weighed only forty-two pounds; Gary Lee and Opal got glasses but they broke them right away; it was almost a year before they got them fixed and now the eye doctor said Gary would have to wear them for years instead of for just six months if he had worn them when he first needed them. Dreama had had a hysterectomy after years of hemorrhaging and her organs hanging out down there. Then the endometriosis got so bad that she finally consented to another operation. But they "still didn't git all of it," and now the pain was getting bad again and her stomach was distended as if she were pregnant.

> But I won't have another one, I figure they tried **twicet** and they didn't get it.
> Bud's doctor says he'll be dead in a year if he don't quit **drankin'.** There ain't nothin' wrong with his **liver** but they say the **likker,** hit's poisonin' his system.
> Ever' day when I come home I look for him to be **dead.**

The statement is surrounded by smaller statements about livers and modes of death and the places Dreama is coming back from when she "looks for" him to be dead and how "good he is with the kids and don't take nothin **from** us for his likker" and how

> he never has been **mean** but for the one time when I was big with Sissy and he got **into** it with me and tuk off with that **Birdsong** woman.
> But he **come back.**
> They fuss at me to throw him out where he **dranks** s' **bad** but I couldn't never leave him now, not and leave him all alone.
> We get along good. He says he don't **wanna die** but he says he cain't **hep** hisself. And you can see how his belly's got. That ain't **fat** on him, he don't **weigh** but a hundred twenty pounds. He don't **eat** nothin'. It's bloat where he's poisoned hisself and he cain't **hep** it.

Then the talk moved to people leaving the area to find work—talk of displacement and opportunities and broken hearts and broken homes and broken links of communication.

> **Ricky** and **Ellen, they** went **off,** and they went down North C'raliny I b'lieve they went to work and they weren't down there **no** time and she **found** herself **some**body and **Ricky,** he come on **home.**
> I seen him go up the road yesterday but they say he tuk it **awful** hard.
> But she **found** herself **some**body and **Ricky,** he come on **home.**
> They say **Buster Reed,** from up over Graham's store, he's kin to Miss **Reed** and them, he went down North C'raliny.

Had him a job waitin' for him when he got **down** there.
And he went to work for that R. J. Reynolds company they got down there.
But he come back when he got him a job on one a them **tree** farms.
Now **he** had him a job set up for him to come **back** to.
I seen him goin' up the **road** little while back.
Then them **Lacy** boys and **Grahams,** they been goin' **in and out.** But they's
  just **boys,** you know, they hitchhike down and back all the time but
  I ain't heared if they ever found **work** yet. Seen some of 'm yesterday
  runnin' up and down the road.
Then there was one a Miss **Taylor's** daughters, left out for North C'raliny,
  tuk the **kids** and **all.**
But I ain't heared nothin' **'bout** her.
Miss Taylor closed up the **stand,** said nobody wasn't comin' **in** no more and
  she had to give it up for a while and I hate to see it **go.**
Well, way it is, you got to go all the way down the **Dairy Queen** to git your
  cigarettes.
Buddy, I'm lookin' for the stand to git back **up.**

In between stories there was the continuous action of noticing the
dogs, the beans, the washing, the creek, and the constant phone calls
back and forth tracking people's whereabouts—"Has Bud got up there
to take mommy?" . . . "Well. Ewolt said he seen him down Iroquois
while back . . ."

Mickey Heath from down at **Wyco,** he went out to some place in **Ohi**a.
They said the rent's **$350 a month** and that's just **rent.**
Then you got your **lights,** and you know that's gotta be high in the city, and
  you got your **cookin' gas.**
All right. Then there's your **phone,** there's your **cable.**
And nothin' left for **groceries** I don't **guess.**
Mickey and them, **they** come on **back.**
But they already done **sold** their house, **now** they ain't **got** no place.

Her nephew Wes called to give Dreama the plot of the "story" (soap
opera) she missed seeing yesterday.

I didn't git to **see** it where Bud was a layin' **home** and he tuk to wantin' to
  watch the **cartoons.**
Oh! I was s' **mad!**
Well it's been up over a year and a half he's out a work this time and he's got
  s' bad to lay home and I can't get none a my **work** done where he tries
  to get me to set and **talk,** you know.
. . . **Well all right.**

Dreama's sister called to say Bud got there and left to take their
mother to the doctor's.

Mom's been down **awful** bad, well she never did get over **Hollie.**

Bud came in with stories of the parking lot at the doctor's office:
". . . an' I seen Miss Lavender down at the **tracks.** Somebody oughtta go

see about her." Bud and Dreama's nephew Dewayne sat at the kitchen table drinking beer and staring at me out of the corners of their eyes. From time to time one of them would quietly add something to the talk.

I told them some stories I had heard the day before. One was of a woman who went to Ohio and had to take an apartment that had no bathroom (even in the city they have places without bathrooms) and they had to "rig up somethin'" in the kitchen. Another was of a woman who had been gone for years and came back to show off her big fancy car and diamond rings. Then I remembered Jerry Graham's story of how *thangs had got down* in Iroquois and the people were being shipped by bus to the tobacco fields in No'th C'raliny and how those people out there wouldn't even give them water to drink and how the wind came and blew away their trailers and all their stuff and how they lost everything and had to come home and were livin' all piled up like cats and dogs.

Dreama repeated the images after me, and then, after a silence, she launched into a litany of her dead whose pictures hung on the walls — some in coffins, some in uniforms, the ancestors in ancient photographs that she had had colorized. Some were mounted on small wooden shrines. She pointed them out one by one where they hung amid her collection of vibrant, heartrending things — the letters from her people in Michigan and Ohio who had "left **out** of here," the Sacred Heart of Jesus, pierced and dripping blood. I said how beautiful his eyes were. She said she just loved hearts.

> I don't know **why,** I just always have **tuk** to 'm.
> That there is **Liam,** he got kilt in the **war.**
> Then **Peanut,** he drank hisself to **death.**
> He was up **Cook Town** one day, wasn't even drunk they said and they said
>   he just **laid** his head **down,** well, they didn't even know he was **dead,**
>   just thought he kindly seemed to go to **sleep,** you know.
> Peanut just put his **head** down and **died.**
> Then **Sissy,** that's the one that hurts the **most** cause she was **special, buddy.**
> She'd **stand up** for us, you know, **talk up** for us if somethin' **happened.**
> She left her inspiration on ever'thang she come near.
> Well, **Lenny,** that's her **husband,** he'd go cut down **trees,** you know, and
>   sell the wood where he was outta **work.**
> This time she begged him "Lenny, don't you **do** it" where it was **Sunday.**
> Sissy told **Mommy,** she said she had a bad **feelin'** like somethin' was gonna
>   **happen, you** know.
> But he went and he made her to come **with** him, he made 'm **all** to go.
> **Well first tree** he **cut,** and it started to come down on Sissy's **baby** where
>   she was a **playin'** and Sissy jumped to push the baby free and the **tree** hit
>   come right down **on** her
> bust her head all to **pieces** on the ground.
> They said they had to cut her out from **under** it.
> I just **never could** get over that. . . .

*Figure 4.5. Bridge at Dreama's place on the 'Migo-Rhodell road.
Photograph © Harriette Hartigan, Artemis.*

Course you **know** 'bout **Hollie,** he was the **sweetest thang** there ever **was**
    and never did hurt nobody.
Thought he was gonna get to go **fishin'** and Jesus tuk him **on.**

Bud and Dewayne went out and sat in the truck. The room was nearly
dark and the air was heavy with heat and smoke. The next time the
phone rang Dreama told Ellen, "Bud and Dewayne are back drankin'."
We could hear them playing Waylon Jennings in the driveway.

The kids came in from school and climbed up on us. Dreama said the
house was haunted. Bud saw a beautiful woman standing in the doorway staring at him ("like ta **skeered** him to **death**"), and once the lid to
the washing machine lifted itself all the way up and then slowly lowered
itself down.

We **all** seen it.

Several times they heard people moving around in the rooms upstairs, and there was often a tapping on the back window up there.

Not like they was tryna **git in** or **git out** but just **tappin',** fast.

I ain't seen nothin' since I got **saved** again but **Bud, he** sees thangs.

Opal whimpered: "Mommy, you **skeered** me, you **skeered** me bad." Dreama explained:

She means **that night.**

I was a layin' in the bed and I seen Sissy [her dead sister] kindly **slide** around the corner of the **stairs** like she'd just come down from up**stairs,** I could see her like a shadow out the corner of my eye, and she come and **stood** right **there** at the foot of the bed and beckoned me to **come on, come on,** just like **that.**

Honey, that like to **skeered** me near to **death** an' I set up in that **bed** and screamed and **I mean screamed.**

I thought she meant come on **right then** out of this **world,** you know.

So I made 'm to turn on all the lights and we had t' sleep with all the lights on for the **longest time** after that happened.

Well, I'd been a **dreamin'** on her ever' night when she **come to** me like that. But this **here,** this weren't no **dream** b'cause it **skeered** me too **bad** to be no **dream.**

But what skeers me **worst** is **people.**

Any**more,** it's got to where you don't know **what** they might try and that **glass** out in the **door,** well anybody could just reach in and git the handle and come on **in** on us.

And the **bridge** worries me **awful** bad.

Last week 'nother one a them **ties** come out and went in the creek an' Opal says **she's** skeered to try and make it **acrost,** small as **she** is, if we lose another one.

Lenny, he won't fix it.

After **Sissy,** he married **Corlee,** that's **Liam's** widda, and they bought **this** place.

Somethin' happen to that **bridge,** and we'd be here with no way to git the **truck** out.

But I just **love** it out here and I wouldn't **never** want to leave.

Well, this place is **home** to **me.**

NOTES

I would like to thank the School of American Research for its gracious hospitality in hosting the advanced seminar, and Keith Basso and Steven Feld for organizing the seminar, for their endless encouragement, and for their painstaking editing.

1. The term "social imaginary" as I am using it necessitates extending Anderson's (1983) concept of "imagined communities" beyond metacultural, ideological claims to community into the micropoetics of the density, texture, and force of everyday modes of discourse and sociality.

2. Thirty percent of the people in the counties of southwestern West Virginia live in trailers, because eighty percent of the land is still owned by coal, oil, and gas companies.

3. John L. Lewis was the powerful leader of the United Mine Workers of America in its heyday. JFK visited West Virginia in 1960, focusing national attention on the problems of Appalachia as a "depressed area."

4. In *The Origin of German Tragic Drama* (1977), Walter Benjamin articulates a theory of allegorical thought as a process in which the mind stares itself out on luminous images. In *Mimesis and Alterity* (1993), Michael Taussig traces the politics of this phenomenon in "primitive" mimesis and "magical thought" and its resurgence in contemporary life.

5. The term *stand* derives from the farming days when local merchants would establish stockades or "stands" alongside the road where animals being driven to or from market could be fed and watered and travelers could stay the night. They developed into local trade centers where farmers traded corn and other products for retail goods (Eller 1982:14) and finally became the local version of the urban corner store and the suburban convenience store.

6. See Zizek (1991) for an extensive discussion of relations between desire and a Lacanian sense of "the real."

7. In his article "Tactility and Distraction" (1991), Taussig articulates the need for alternative models of cultural meaning to displace the still dominant inclination to see meaning as mental thought and clearly modeled symbolic code. He introduces what he calls the tactility of meaning and the distractedness of everyday life in contemporary advanced capitalist culture.

8. Amigo was once a collection of four camps stretching up the holler—'Migo 1, 'Migo 2, 'Migo 3, and "the colored camp."

5

Your Place and Mine

Sharing Emotional Landscapes in Wamira, Papua New Guinea
Miriam Kahn

The experience of traveling to and living in different places provides the methodological anchor and theoretical springboard for anthropology. Indeed, the discipline developed in response to European exploration and the resultant awareness of other places (Hallowell 1965). Yet until recently, the topic of place has been neglected in contemporary anthropological theory. "The problem of place arises, paradoxically, because the meaning of place too often seems to go without saying" (Rodman 1992:640). In general, "there is little recognition that place is more than locale, the setting for action, the stage on which things happen" (Rodman 1992:643).

While anthropological descriptions of place have remained relatively monological, places themselves are fertilized into being through a confluence of voices. Places are complex constructions of social histories, personal and interpersonal experiences, and selective memory. Curiously, it is while anthropologists themselves are most out of place that they attempt to gain an understanding of the place and placement of others. Here I choose to examine concepts of place by focusing specifically on the process of finding one's own place while struggling to understand that of others, for I believe it is in the dialogical dimensions that the tangled threads of perspective unfold most insightfully. I focus on place through the shifting vistas and dimensions of the anthropological encounter, through the ways in which "my" view and "their" view meet at points of inclusion, exclusion, and overlap to create a sense of "our" place.

I examine ideas about place in relation to the people of Wamira, a village of some 450 people on the northern shore of the southeastern tip of Papua New Guinea.[1] The Wamiran landscape resounds for Wamirans with narratives of collective history and personal experience. It provides tangible forms for the mooring of memory. What looks like a river, a hill, or a group of stones may, in fact, resonate meaningfully to Wamirans as a type of moral landscape conveying messages about human frailties, foibles, and responsibilities. Meaning attached to the landscape unfolds in language, names, stories, myths, and rituals. These meanings crystallize into shared symbols and ultimately link people to a sense of common history and individual identity. Place becomes "something both fixed and fleeting, something you can walk on and something you can speak, a curious and uneasy product of experience and symbol" (Richardson 1984:1).

Places capture the complex emotional, behavioral, and moral relationships between people and their territory. They represent people, their actions, and their interactions and as such become malleable memorials for negotiating and renegotiating human relationships. Places and their stories also become metaphors that are heavily relied upon during social discourse about relationships. They serve as a kind of "veiled speech" (Strathern 1975) through which harsh realities can be softened by oblique reference in order to preserve harmonious social relations. Talking about place becomes a euphemistic way of communicating important messages, such as reminders of social obligations that have gone unfulfilled or of moral responsibilities to feed and care for kin.

It is impossible to talk about place, or to talk about how people talk about place, without encompassing biography, including one's own at the points of social interaction. My understanding of Wamiran place lies most profoundly at the juncture of Wamiran biography and my autobiography. Places blossom, along with my understanding of them, where Wamirans and I connect. Writing about "our" place is to write both intimately and descriptively about differences and commonalities. My approach intentionally combines my feelings and perspectives with those of Wamiran individuals in order to highlight the sense of place as meaningful shared experience. I combine the two perspectives in order to illustrate how much of my growing understanding occurred precisely when our perspectives merged and mingled or diverged and clashed.

Because place is many things and speaks in many voices—individual biography, shared history, meaningful memory, and moral lesson, as well as euphemism—it is constantly shifting, emerging or receding, being accentuated or veiled. But ultimately, places are, for Wamirans as they are for me, profoundly emotional territories.

TWO PERSPECTIVES ON ONE "PLACE"

My anthropological journey began one day in 1976, when I left home and all that was familiar and comforting. I had decided to work in Papua New Guinea precisely because it was the last place in the world in which

I could imagine myself being. Soon after arriving, I found myself one afternoon sitting on the floor of my room at the mission station of Dogura, tossing a coin to decide where to do my fieldwork. After three weeks of visiting various coastal and mountain villages on the eastern end of Papua New Guinea, explaining my presence and my interest in horticultural ritual to people I met and trying to imagine myself in the villages I saw, I had narrowed the choice down to two places: a damp, isolated mountain village and a sunny, expansive coastal village. As I wondered about what seemed to be the arbitrariness of choosing a place to do fieldwork, I realized that I had kept tossing the coin over and over until Wamira—the sunny village by the sea—won.

Obviously, choice of an anthropological field site follows matters of the heart as much as those of the mind. On the one hand, I rationalized that Wamira was the perfect place for academic research. It was large; the irrigation system I wanted to study included the only aqueduct in the Papuan part of New Guinea; the language was the lingua franca of a larger region and knowing it would enable me to do comparative research in neighboring villages—and so on. Yet what continually tugged me in its direction was the fact that the emotional "fit" felt right. Physically, it seemed spacious, breezy, and sunny. The sea was in constant view. Moreover, it was only an hour's walk from Dogura with its ties to the world beyond in the form of an airstrip, a wharf, a post office, and a trade store. And most important, the Wamirans I had met appeared welcoming, emotionally open, and good-humored. I felt embraced by their animated personalities. Thus, opportunistic moments, my personal leanings, and chance elements all came together to produce a fieldwork location.

Soon thereafter, loaded down with possessions that filled a small outboard motorboat, I moved into the village. Although I wanted to stay in the seemingly neutral village rest house, I was ushered away and encouraged to move into the home of Alice Dobunaba and her family. Alice's daughter, then a student at the University of Papua New Guinea, with whom I had talked while I visited the capital city of Port Moresby, had written a letter of introduction for me to use when I toured the region. As a result, Alice felt responsible for my well-being. "You need someone to take care of you," I was told, "to cook your food and to help you with your work." I later learned that in Wamirans' eyes, the rest house was not an option if I was to be integrated into village life by entering a web of social exchanges and relations. The social act of Alice's feeding, caring for, and helping me and my reciprocal obligation to provide her family with trade-store goods were what created my place—not the physical existence of an abandoned government rest house.

Before long, the space that had been cleared for me in the back of her family's small house took on more definition as Alice and her brother, Aidan Gadiona, assembled what they thought I needed.[2] One day, upon returning from washing at the river, I found Aidan nailing slabs of sago spathe into a wooden frame to construct a wall around my space. He had also cut a window into the woven coconut-frond wall so I would have some light. Young children from the hamlet carried baskets of small, sea-washed pebbles up from the beach and smoothed them into a new, clean, thicker layer of floor under my sleeping mat. Nestled into Alice's family with a space of my own, I felt very much at home.

The final thoughtful gesture that clinched my feeling at home was Alice's decision to write a letter to my mother in New York so she "would not worry about me." In the letter Alice reassured my mother that I was fine because "Wamira was a good place" and there were "plenty of mangoes." Alice's expression of parental concern comforted my mother immediately, although it was only later that I understood the full implication of Alice's message about the quality of the place in relation to food and feeding me.

My feeling at home, however, was countered by Wamirans' expressions of concern. Each day, as I accompanied Wamirans in their daily tasks—washing pots or clothes at the river, gathering food from the garden, going to the market at Dogura, visiting friends—they kept shaking their heads, clucking their tongues in dismay, and mumbling, "Kapore," a word I came to understand as an expression of sympathy and pity. These feelings were always, as they explained, because I was "so far away from my place." They kept explaining (in contrast to what Alice had written to my mother) that "Wamira is a bad place . . . there is no food." Their reaction was most intense when I showed them pictures of my home, family, and friends. I was perplexed by the depth of their concern and why it applied to my settling into Wamira. After all, from my perspective, I had chosen to be there.

No matter how much I tried to assuage their concern, their compassionate laments continued. Even people I passed casually on the path looked regretfully at me and exclaimed, "You are very sad." I adamantly protested, "No, I'm not. Why do you say I'm sad?" Again, they explained, "Because you are so far away from where you belong, far from your family and your home. Someone like you should be in your own place with your family and friends, not so far away all alone." Only much later was I to begin to comprehend the emotional sense of loss and sorrow that being away from one's place triggered for Wamirans.

One day, while accompanying several women who were making a new communal garden, I was serenaded with a song. I listened and watched as tears rolled down their cheeks. When I asked what the song

Figure 5.1. Sybil Gisewa (Alice's mother) and Hilarion Watiwati examining a picture postcard of "my place" (New York). Photograph © Miriam Kahn.

was about, they mournfully explained that it was about being away from home and needing to travel back to the place where one belongs. Later, I recorded and translated the words:

Travel home, your father is calling you
Get up now and go back
Listen to your father's voice
Hear his voice calling you

Your father did not hate you
You walked out of your house all alone
You traveled a long way and you are hungry
Get up and go back to your home

Your father has built a nice house for you
And he is waiting for you
He is watching your road
Get up and go back to your home

Your father is not angry
He is thinking of you
Think about it now
And go back to your father's house

Chorus:
He is calling you to travel home
He is calling you to come to him

I gradually grew accustomed to their constant mutterings of
"Kapore," their tears and sentimental songs, and their nostalgia about
places, but I continued to be puzzled about what it all meant. Why did
they pity me just because I was far from home? In my mind, I was embarking on the adventure of my life. I had visited as many places as
my around-the-world ticket would allow while on my way to Wamira.
Although hardly settled into Wamira, I was already planning a future
field break to the highlands of Papua New Guinea to see still more places.
After all, wasn't this what my profession prescribed? Weren't we supposed to go on a kind of pilgrimage on which to find "a sense of the extraordinary that comes when one is temporarily out of place" (Richardson 1984:1)? More than a professional mandate, the desire to experience
other places was one of my personal goals. Indeed, the professional re-
quirement of sporadic uprootedness was one of the main reasons I had
chosen anthropology as a profession. I was in agreement with its emphasis on the importance of getting at "the comprehension of the self by
the detour of the comprehension of the other" (Ricoeur 1969:20). But
after having come half-way around the world to be in a particular place,
Wamirans were telling me that I wasn't "there." How was I to make sense
of this?

The same landscape that surrounded Wamirans with a comforting
and meaningful context seemed to present me with a void. Our lack of
agreement was obviously due to clashing perspectives. Wamirans and I
did not share the same image of their place. I saw it as sunny, sea swept,
and inviting. They told me it was a "bad place" because there was "no
food." Nor did we share the same sense of the relevance of their place
for me as a displaced person. I wanted to be removed from my roots so
I could learn to make sense of a different place. They thought I should
go back to my family and friends where I belonged. Nor did we even
share the same understanding of the personal value of traveling to distant
places. For me, travel to foreign places was a necessary, circuitous path

to knowing life and self. For them, the idea of purposefully uprooting oneself was simply beyond comprehension.

Thus, emotionally uplifted by the newness of the place and intellectually puzzled by the reaction I was getting, I settled in, calmed by the sea and mountains, comforted by the walls around me, and energized by the people, to learn about Wamirans and their place. It was their empathy, however, focused on me and filtered through places, that resonated most deeply in our growing interconnectedness.

PLACE AS METAPHOR FOR SOCIAL RELATIONS AND OBLIGATIONS

While I mused about my place in Wamira I was also gaining an understanding of what place meant for Wamirans, an understanding that continued to mature over the next two years. After a month or two of fieldwork, instead of triggering tears and feelings of pity, I became the brunt of their jokes. "*Io!* You are becoming a Wamiran girl," they chuckled. At this point, whenever Wamirans saw me they bombarded me with the very questions they knew I was learning to answer: "Where are you from?" ("Inibuena hamlet," I'd respond); "To which clan do you belong?" ("I'm from Manibolanai clan"); "Who is your mother?" ("Alice"); and so on. My appropriate answers were greeted with fits of laughter that conveyed both amusement and disbelief, comfort and awkwardness. When the laughter died down, they would nod with approval and say, "*Ata dobu,*" meaning "our [inclusive] place." They were acknowledging my efforts to adapt to their customs yet were still puzzled by my desire to do so.

In spite of the raucous encounters that made me feel more accepted, included, and connected, the laments continued, although less persistently than before. "*Kapore,* why did you come? Wamirans are kind, respectful, and friendly. But it is a dry place with too much sun and no water. There is no food. Our land is like stone." For the entire time I lived in the village, Wamirans described their situation as one of famine (*gomara*). Indeed, *gomara* appeared to be the normal condition. Each time I inquired about the perpetual state of "no food" I was emphatically told it was "because of Tamodukorokoro." They explained that Tamodukorokoro, a hairy, ugly ogre, was "their monster" who would have brought them a life of bountiful food, but in their ambivalence between desiring and fearing him, they chased him away. They attribute their fate of having no food to their unfriendly actions toward him. They now have to suffer, destined to what they perceive to be a life of persistent and unalterable "famine." I soon learned that Tamodukorokoro's presence was felt everywhere in the landscape—in tangible features such as rocks and hills and in intangibles such as the dry climate that bestows insufficient rain.[3] The Tamodukorokoro myth gives credence to the way Wamirans view and experience their place. An abridged version of the myth follows.[4]

Two Wamiran sisters decide to go visiting inland from the village. Along the way, they meet an old, mouthless woman and her "pet," who is both a snake and a handsome young man. The girls stay and marry the young man. The younger sister eventually gives birth to a child. One day the sisters decide to visit Wamira with their child. On the way back to Wamira they encounter the monster Tamodukorokoro (who some say is the same as the snake-husband from the mountain village). They are both enticed and repelled, and try to rid themselves of him. Each time they attempt to do so, however, he uses magic that draws them back to him. Finally, as they approach Wamira, they run to their brothers' house and ask to be hidden from the monster. But, once again, the monster entices them to find him.

Back in Wamira, the girls' brothers try to kill Tamodukorokoro, under the guise of inviting him to make a garden with them. At each step in the horticultural process, they try to destroy him. They stab his legs with sharpened digging sticks while turning the sod. They surround him with fire when burning off the grass. When the garden is ready to be harvested and they search for fish to accompany the taro (the Wamirans' main food), they try to drown him in the sea. Each time, however, he miraculously escapes as he chants a spell about abundant, festively prepared taro. The Wamiran men feign joy at his return, all the while plotting more ways to annihilate him. Finally, they decide on a plan which entails picking and roasting a fruit called *kumika*.

The next day they all set out, picking *kumika* and collecting stones along the way. They build a stone oven to roast the fruit and coax Tamodukorokoro into sitting down for a communal feast. They call out to the monster using the term *egubeda* (which indicates a trusting relationship based on people having shared food together), and ask him to open his mouth so they can toss in some fruit. They do this twice, but on the third turn toss in a hot stone instead. At that point Tamodukorokoro rises in anger. He snatches his pouch, grabs his two wives, and leaves Wamira. He tries settling in a number of places, but is always tormented by the visibility of Wamira. He decides to cross the bay and settle on Iriwavo (Fergusson Island). There he sits down with one wife on either side of him, all three turning their backs to Wamira. They all turn into stone and are now the three peaks one can see across the bay.

According to Wamirans, the myth explains why their land is hot and dry and produces "no food." They say that if the monster had stayed in Wamira, food would be plentiful. But they were both attracted to and repelled by him and, in their ambivalence, chased him away. They explain that in the act of throwing a hot stone into his mouth, they tossed famine out onto their land. They compare the roasted stone to the parched land where it is hard to grow food, calling their land *latana,* which is the name given to the heated stones of an earth oven—like the oven they built when plotting the destruction of Tamodukorokoro.

Although Tamodukorokoro abandoned Wamira, Wamirans' memory of him and of their failed relationship with him is profoundly felt throughout the landscape. Today Wamirans point to the named places in the environment where various events in the myth took place: where the sisters rested on their journey inland, where they sat down to chew areca nut on their trip back to Wamira, where Tamodukorokoro laid down his bag of areca chewing paraphernalia, the spot on the beach where he was washed ashore after diving for clams, the place where he sat down to sharpen his adze before crossing the bay to Iriwavo, the mountainous peaks on Iriwavo that are Tamodukorokoro and his two wives, and many more. Indeed, the large, fertile garden area behind the village is called Tamodukorokoro. It is fed by an aqueduct, the use of which is surrounded by great controversy and fear precisely because it presents the potential for producing "too much food" (see Kahn 1984, 1985, 1992). As Wamirans cultivate the parched earth under a searing sun, the very name of the ground is a shared symbol of their place and a constant reminder of their unsociable behavior and the permanent predicament in which it put them. Their land and its name link them to "their myth," which maps out and explains the very history and nature of their social relationships.

Not only are events in the myth linked to places, but both mythical events and placenames also revolve around food and feeding. Food is the Wamiran idiom par excellence for talking about social relationships (see Kahn 1986, 1988). As is common in Melanesia, a person's passage through life is traced "in terms of the social and cultural values of food giving/food taking, production/reproduction, and reciprocity" (Fajans 1985:373). "Being hungry" usually expresses both a physical state and an emotional sentiment. For example, in writing about nearby Goodenough Island, Young says that "it is shameful . . . to admit to hunger, for it carries the implication not only that one is a poor gardener, a man of no worth in oneself, but also that one's kin are neglecting their obligations to feed, and one's fathers their obligations to teach" (Young 1971:159).

Likewise, for a Wamiran, "hunger" indicates need and neglect. To feed someone indicates that one cares for them; to fail to do so is a sign of antagonism. In explaining his love for his mother, a man once commented to me, "Of course, I love her. If I didn't she would be hungry all the time." People left alone feel and express their loneliness as hunger. Thus, geographical distance from kin translates into feelings of neglect, loneliness, and hunger. Seen in this light, the words that Wamirans sang to me—"You traveled a long way and you are hungry"—are more than a literal description of the distance I had come or the potential rumblings in my stomach. They imply a profound kind of social deprivation brought about by being bereft of place and context. In sum, places in

Figure 5.2. Tamodukorokoro, the large fertile plain behind the village of Wamira, with the Dogura cathedral appearing as a white dot on the distant plateau. Photograph © Miriam Kahn.

the Wamiran landscape are more than constant reminders of the Tamo-dukorokoro myth. They resonate more deeply about the importance of social relations and obligations based on feeding, sharing, and caring for one another. They serve as both mnemonic devices and moral authority.

Other myths provide further illustration of the way in which moral lessons are written into a landscape that rings out emotionally as a constant reminder about sharing food and all that feeding implies. One myth is about two Wamiran sisters, Maradiudiva and Marakwadiveta, who live together. Each time Maradiudiva goes down to the sea to fetch saltwater for cooking, her sister, Marakwadiveta, gobbles up all the food and later tells lies about relatives who, she claims, came and ate it. Feeling hungry and rejected, Maradiudiva walks into the sea and turns into stone. Now, with her stony countenance, she stands all alone in the bay. As the

Figure 5.3. The stony figure of Marakwadiveta, amidst the grassy hills high above the village. Photograph © Miriam Kahn.

tide rolls in and out, Wamirans see Maradiudiva rising and descending. She is a constant reminder to all that social life depends on the sharing of food. Her sister, Marakwadiveta, later turns to stone also and today is seen high above the village amidst the grassy hills. She looks out over the sea at the sister she did not feed.

Another myth, from the nearby village of Boianai, describes the origins of the villagers and their ancestral connections to the cassowary. Again, the plot revolves around withholding food. A young woman lives with her husband and child. Her husband goes to the garden every day but returns with only firewood and no food. Being hungry, she boils stones so she and her child can drink the broth from the cooked stones. One day, having endured enough maltreatment, she decides to turn herself into a cassowary and leave. She makes wings from coconut fronds, knee caps from coconut husks, and legs from black palm sticks. When her husband comes home that evening she spreads her wings and flees. Trying to call his wife back, he hurls stones after her, but to no avail. Today one can still see the stones in the village. There is a massive pile of stones, a full meter high, that is said to have accumulated as each day the hungry woman boiled them and tossed them aside. The rocks that her husband threw at her lie scattered along the path that leads from the village into the mountains.

In these two myths and the Tamodukorokoro myth, stones and other features in the landscape mark the spots where mythical events "took place." But each stone, or each spot, does more than recall the myth. The landscape surrounds the people with a sense of shared history rooted in the past and memorialized in the present through shared symbols. It provides a focus for feelings of common identity as well as a charter for moral action. As villagers walk along paths and look upon the landscape where significant mythical events took place, they are reminded of the importance of social obligations to feed and care for one another—the very thing they failed to do with Tamodukorokoro.

This idea of the landscape as moral lesson is similar to what Keith Basso (1984b) has described for the Western Apaches, for whom features of the landscape take over and perpetuate stories. "Mountains and arroyos step in symbolically for grandmothers and uncles. Just as the latter have 'stalked' delinquent individuals in the past, so too particular locations continue to 'stalk' them in the present" (Basso 1984b:43). It is also reminiscent of what he describes as interior landscapes of the moral imagination:

> Like their ancestors before them, they display by word and deed that beyond the visible reality of place lies a moral reality which they themselves have come to embody. And whether or not they finally succeed in becoming fully wise, it is this interior landscape—this landscape of the moral imagination—that most deeply influences their vital sense of place, and also, I believe, their unshakable sense of self. (Basso 1984b:43)

The Wamiran landscape, as provider of food as well as sense of self, furnishes a tangible trope for talking about social relations, a topic of paramount importance which, because of its potential volatility, can be addressed most effectively if addressed obliquely. To talk about Wamira as "a good place" but a place with "no food" is to communicate the conflicting emotions involved in engaging in social exchanges. "No food," as I learned much later, is a euphemism for not wanting to engage in the tangled web of sociality. Taken to its extreme, as we have seen, social disengagement becomes "hunger."

The desire for social distance can arise at various levels and is phrased in appropriate euphemisms at each level. No food in the landscape, on the communal level, may be reproduced on the group level as no food on the store shelf or on the family level as no food in the house. Thus, when a hamlet leader once admonished his group for lacking cohesive work habits, he did not say they were acting like lazy, thoughtless, self-ish people but instead discussed at great length the lack of food on the shelves in the hamlet store. Or, when individual Wamirans arrived at Alice's house asking for sugar for their tea, they were told that there was none (as the bag of sugar was quickly whisked out of sight). "We have sugar," Alice privately explained to me, "but just enough for ourselves, not enough to give."

When Wamirans say their land is like stone, they are communicating more than a casual metaphor. They are recalling "their monster," and in doing so they are conveying messages about the thin line between social cooperation and conflict, sharing and hoarding, caring and neglecting, communal life and loneliness. In asking me time and again, "Why did you come? . . . there is no food," or in oscillating between saying that Wamira is "a good place" and "a bad place," they were telling me, and re-minding one another, about the moral dilemmas they faced when I (far from home and "hungry") arrived in their midst. How would they care for me? What would they feed me? And equally importantly, what would they get in return? No wonder Alice wrote to my mother that there were "plenty of mangoes." The letter, while couched in terms of food, was meant to convey information about my physical condition and my emotional well-being. That the ground was covered with fallen, rotting mangoes indicated that Alice was going to fulfill her parental responsi-bility. I had settled in a land that was "like stone," but, in contrast to their treatment of Tamodukorokoro, Wamirans were, or at least Alice was, going to behave morally. She would feed me — and mangoes, not *kumika!*

ANCHORING GROUP IDENTITY AND RIGHTS THROUGH STONES

As I progressed with my work, I turned to what seemed a standard anthropological task, namely, the drawing of maps. I enlisted the help of Wamirans to tell me about places as I jotted their names and locations on my sketches. But what I thought would be a relatively straightfor-ward exercise took forever because each stone, each tree, each dip in the ground had a name and a story.

In addition to communal landscapes such as those shared through the Tamodukorokoro story, there are also places that provide clans, lin-eages, and families with sources of identity and proof of their rights. As Margaret Rodman (1987:40) has described it, the greatest insult for the people of Longana, Vanuatu, is to demand, "Where is your place?" So, too, in Wamira, to be without a place is to exist humiliatingly outside the bounds of sociality. Every time arguments arose among people, the conversation turned to land. "This is my land, my father lived here, you can't throw me out" was an expression commonly heard. To call someone an orphan (*kedakeda*) expressed pity and sadness because it indicated that the individual lacked land and kin, and consequently, food and care.

Connections to one's land are marked tangibly by such things as houses, trees, and stones. Stones and their stories, in particular, are important anchors to the land. Bishop Henry Newton, who visited Wamira in the beginning of the century, noted the importance of stones:

> We were shown various things that had virtues, stones . . . that had an influence on the life and health and prosperity of the people. . . . In all the villages there are stones which are reverenced, and which may not be moved. . . . There are others, short stunted obelisks stuck in the ground with rude markings. All these are really tabu; they may not be interfered with or trouble will follow. Whence they came no one knows, they were here in the time of our ancestors, they remain forever. (Newton 1914:170–71)

The story of Tauribariba, the ancestral founder of the Maibouni clan who is now a stone, provides an example of how clans may be associated with named stones. Tauribariba is by far the most remarkable and spirited ancestral stone in Wamira (see Kahn 1990). Tauribariba turned from a human being to a stone when he first came ashore to settle in Wamira. The story describes the original settling of Wamira by various clans and the establishment of the relationships among them. The leader of the Maibouni clan was Tauribariba, who arrived with his sister, Tauanana. When they were coming ashore, waves thrashed at the canoe and Tauanana fell into the sea. Everyone rushed to get Tauribariba and carry him onto land before he, too, fell into the water. They set him in the center of the hamlet of Irere where he was until 1936. He "lived there and walked around at night." He watched over the taro gardens to protect the food. As I was told the story, Osborne Kaimou, the narrator, said, "But, look, today he is not there! Several years ago my mother's brother was approached by Father John Bodger from the mission station at Dogura. Father Bodger said, 'My friend, are you the chief of these stones?' My mother's brother answered, 'Yes, I am.' Father Bodger said, 'Give us that stone so I can cement it in the cathedral wall.'" When Osborne finished narrating the story to me he wistfully added, "When Father Bodger took Tauribariba he did not just take a stone. He took away our entire identity and spirit."

Tauribariba is a small stone, no bigger than a person's outstretched hand. Before being placed in the cathedral wall, he formed part of a large circle of stones, about five meters in diameter, in the center of the Wami-

Figure 5.4. The assemblage of stones consisting of Tauanana in the center, surrounded by her children. Photograph © Miriam Kahn.

ran seaside hamlet of Irere. His sister is a large boulder, about four times the size of Tauribariba. She sits in the middle of the circle, surrounded by their "children," who are numerous small stones. All of them are believed to have the ability to walk around, and their favorite time to do this is at night. Wamirans say that occasionally new children appear at the shore in the morning. When Wamirans see new children on the beach, they add them to the circle of stones, which thus continually changes in number.

In 1936, when the Cathedral of St. Peter and St. Paul was completed at Dogura, Father Bodger decided to cement Tauribariba into the pulpit wall alongside other stones from cathedrals in England. The missionaries saw this move as symbolizing the transference of the Wamirans' "worship of stone" to that of God. The following mission record describes the transportation of the stone to the cathedral:

Two native men from the villages of Wedau and Wamira . . . came up to the Sanctuary, each bearing a large piece of stone or rock in his hands, and presented them to the priest, who took them, blessed them, and offered them at the Altar.

One of the stones was a curiously striped slab of rock resembling nothing so much as a slice of chocolate cake with layers of icing. These two stones were treasured memorials of the old heathen days, one belonging to a special family in Wedau and the other, the striped one, to Wamira. Their present owners or guardians, being Christians, had voluntarily removed them from their places and brought them to God's House. They are set in the walls of the new Cathedral together with stones sent from Abbeys and Cathedrals in England, there to be silent witnesses to the Faith which has proclaimed that God alone is Giver of all good things.

The Wamiran stone is known by the name of Tauribariba. . . . It has been an object of veneration to its owners of many generations, who believed that on its presence in the village depended the prosperity of their gardens and good and plentiful food crops. Those who have inherited the care of the stone are all Christians and have brought Tauribariba also to his resting place. It is safely embedded in concrete and its wandering days are over. Even so have the children of darkness and superstition become living stones in the House of God's building—His Church. (Anglican Archives 1936)

Although the mission account ends with the stone's being "safely embedded in concrete," the Wamiran version of the story is more complex and indicates how the stone, as an important marker of Maibouni identity and a link to the clan's history and land, could not be whisked away so easily. According to Wamirans, that night, after being taken to Dogura but not yet cemented into the wall, Tauribariba "walked back to Wamira."[5] The following day Father Bodger again fetched the stone. This time, he cemented it into the wall upside down with Tauribariba's face turned toward the wall. It was "turned upside down as a symbol that the magic had been emptied out of it, and that it was now fitted to occupy a place in the Christian Church" (Papuan Annual Report 1936–37:5). Ever since, upside down and shackled by cement, Tauribariba has remained firmly and faithfully within the pulpit wall (Kahn 1990:58).

The tug-of-war between the missionaries and the villagers about the placement of Tauribariba indicates the two groups' different perspectives on, and the different values they attached to, markers of place and identity. What to the missionaries was a striped rock resembling a slice of chocolate cake was to members of the Maibouni clan tangible proof of their rootedness and connection to others. It recalled their past, gave them rights to their land, and assured them that their gardens would yield abundant food, which, as we have seen, was needed to nurture social bonds.

Farther down the coast, in Boianai, the Meiakurana clan has rights to an arrangement of stones called Dararugu that, like the Maibouni stone

Figure 5.5. Tauribariba (the dark stone) cemented into the base of the pulpit in the Dogura cathedral. Photograph © Miriam Kahn.

circle in Wamira, is also believed to anchor taro in their garden. They explain that the stones assure abundance "by tugging at the roots of the taro to hold it down." After some clan members narrated the story to me, they allowed me to map and photograph the stones if I would do them a favor in return. They wanted me, once I was back in the United States, to have the floor plan of the stone arrangement printed on two dozen rugby shirts. They gave specific instructions. On the front should be my drawing of the stone arrangement, including one of the trees that was near the stones, the name of the stones (Dararugu), and the name of the place where the stones are located (Worewore). On the back should be the name of the clan (Meiakurana) that owned them. The shirts, printed in assorted sizes and colors, should be made in America, a place of "power" in the minds of the owners of the stones.

I learned that they wanted their sacred stones emblazoned on the shirts to ward off jealousy. They told me that many people envied them because they had built a store, which brought in a fair amount of income. Like the Wamiran men who, motivated by jealousy, tried to destroy Tamodukorokoro, some people in Boianai tried to ruin the store. If members of the clan wore images of their stones on their chests, they said, it would be "proof" for all to see that they had the right to act as *gulau* (chiefs). "Our stones are our power," they told me, believing that portable proof of the physical anchor to their land might even allow them to win rugby games.

I returned home, had the shirts made, and mailed them, musing about the ironic twist to the layers of inscription. The clan's "power," originally inscribed upon the land, could be transcribed onto an anthropologist's map and then further reproduced on shirts. Like the wanderings of Tauribariba, Tauanana, and their children, the numerous movements and permutations seemed to enhance, not lessen, the sense of power embedded in place. As the rugby players aggressively skirmished with printed reproductions on their chests, they felt empowered through their association with the original stone markers and the place to which it tied them, all of which was intensified by the stones' brief journey to America.

In both of the examples just given, clans claim identity and gain rights through their association with specific places in the landscape that are marked by stones. In both examples, the markers of place, or images of them, are also transported to new places, with either disastrous or victorious results. Tauribariba was painfully transferred to the cathedral in Dogura. Trying to return home to Wamira, he was removed again, this time forever. Sadness prevailed, as exemplified by Tauanana's retreat into the sea. The map of the Dararugu stones, on the other hand, was taken, by request, to America in order to provide the stones with increased

Figure 5.6. The Dararugu stones in Worewore that anchor taro in the gardens in the village of Boianai. Photograph © Miriam Kahn.

power—to ward off jealous rivals of other clans and allow the stones' rightful owners to succeed with their store and to win rugby games.

In almost every region of Melanesia where stones are markers of past events, they are described as being capable of movement. Andrew Strathern (1979:50) discusses the "itinerant quality" of the stones in the western highlands of Papua New Guinea. Near Buka, in the Solomon Islands, stones are known not only to walk about at night but also to fish, swim, dance, and even grow (Blackwood 1935). As I have suggested elsewhere (Kahn 1990), stones move because mythology and history are negotiable and subject to revision. Wamiran history, like all history, is not static but represents a dynamic, ongoing relationship between past events and the present. Events that are recorded in stone can most easily be brought up to date by the movement of the stones. A past recorded and enlivened by stones that walk up from the sea, wander in the night, disappear from cathedral walls, or jump from boats bound for Australia is effectively and energetically receptive to alterations and additions. Because a stone can fix events in time, it must, like time, be able to move.

CREATING PERSONAL PLACES THROUGH HOUSES, HEARTH STONES, FRONT STOOPS, AND PIGS

After several months, because a friend was coming to visit and planned to stay a while, members of my hamlet decided to build me a house. The experience allowed me to deepen my social obligations and emotional ties. Unbeknownst to me at the time, it also allowed me to construct magnets for my own stories.

Alice gave me some land for my house next to hers. A house, itself capable of shifting locations (see Rodman 1985), is a locus of social cohesion. A Wamiran house, the posts of which are categorized as male and female and the end wall of which is called the heart, symbolizes the unification of maternal and paternal kin, of clan (matrilineal) and residence (patrilocal) groups, both of whom assist in building it. Like food, a house represents the social ties that nurture. As I watched people build the house, I often recalled the song in which Wamirans sang, "Your father has built a nice house for you," and the way in which houses embody symbols of the nourishment and comfort one acquires through social connections and cooperation. Long before the walls were in place, the hearth was arranged. Three hearth stones were carefully set in place, and food was cooked to feed the workers. As the hearth stones were inserted into the ground, people pointed to another, similar stone, named Kiori, that stood in solitude several feet away in front of Alice's house. It was all that remained of the group of cooking stones—intentionally left as a reminder—from the communal men's house that existed in the hamlet long ago.

Each day, as my house was being built, I fed the workers as payment for their help. When the house was completed I purchased a pig, the meat of which was distributed to all those who had helped. As I was told on numerous occasions, "You now own the land. You killed a pig and fed the workers. Your memory has been made strong." Because I paid for the land according to village custom, Wamirans said, "The house and land are now yours. You can do what you want in your house. You can play your radio very loudly and nobody can complain. We could issue you citizenship papers for Papua New Guinea. If you go away for a while, you have the right to put a fence around your house and put a lock on it and it would stay like that until you returned. If someone else moved in, you could charge them rent!"

The final anchor for the house, however, was the large, flat, gray stone my friend laboriously carried from the riverbed and placed at the doorstep. Wamirans immediately explained that it would be my *buderi*, a material object that represents emotional events and triggers memories. Eventually I was also given a pig, another *buderi,* that would be kept in my memory after I was no longer in Wamira. Because a pig is usually given the name of the place from which its owner comes, the name chosen for my pig was "America."

Thus, places gradually evolved that had my own stories attached to them. Some places, such as my house, gave me rights — I could blast my radio, I could charge people rent. Landmarks within and around places, such as my hearth stones and front stoop, were moorings for the many memories of my connection to Wamirans. Even my wandering pig became an anchor for emotional meaning. A few years later, in a letter, Alice asked permission to kill my pig for a feast. After the feast she wrote again, describing how they had all wept for me when "America," my *buderi,* was slaughtered. Their tears were emotional outpourings as they thought of me.

A PERSONAL LANDSCAPE ENDOWED WITH EMOTION

The evening before I left Wamira to return to the United States, numerous friends gathered outside to join Alice and me as we sat in the moonlight reminiscing about my stay and contemplating my departure. Anticipating my journey home, Alice said,

> When you are busy traveling, you will have a lot to think and worry about, getting your ticket and catching your plane. But when you are home again sitting in your room all alone, you will think about Wamira and cry. You will tell stories about our place to your friends and play our tapes for them. They will hear everything, but only you will really know. You will cry for Wamira. You will be homesick for Wamira. Only you have been to our place. Only you will really know.

The next morning Alice helped me get my luggage ready. After we had moved my suitcases outside, she went back into the house. I assumed it was to check whether I had left anything behind. Once inside, she turned her back to the doorway and me, facing the place where my possessions had been. As she fondled things I had intentionally left behind, she wailed in a very controlled, melodic voice:

Kapore, my child, who will take care of me now? You stayed here and took care of us. You helped us and now you are leaving. Everywhere I go I will think of you, the places where we walked, the places where we sat, *kapore* my child. This is the house you built. These are your things. We will live in it and think of you. *Kapore.*

As I listened, my mind flashed back to my arrival two years earlier. People cried for me because I was so far away from where I belonged, from family and friends who cared for me. Now they cried for me because I was leaving a place where I finally belonged. "You stayed in Wamira a long time and left your mark in many places," they said, "now you belong here and we are sad because you have to go." The places in which I had done things became bittersweet memorials. Wamirans recalled each place, each event.

Under that breadfruit tree you first gave Emmaline some tobacco . . . on that hill you helped the Watiwati family turn the sod in their garden . . . at that rock on the riverbank you washed your clothes . . . at that tree stump you rested to eat mangoes on the way home from market . . . there is the garden at Aibodaboda where you sat on top of the fence, causing it to come tumbling down.

The places were not preexisting empty stages to be filled with activity; they took on meaning only when activity gave them form. They blossomed into places of significance through my actions and interactions with others. They reverberated with profoundly emotional shared experiences. The tears Emmaline shed when I compassionately helped her, the pity they felt when they saw me, an inexperienced laundress, pounding my clothes on the rocks, the laughter we all shared when I clumsily broke the garden fence—all these were emotions that infused and created the landscape. A meaningful landscape resulted where my actions had taken place and my memory lingered. I had become Wamiran by literally becoming part of Wamira, not in the communal sense of sharing the Tamodukorokoro myth or in the clan sense of having rights to certain clan land, but in an individual way, when landmarks of my experiences shaped the Wamirans' landscape and triggered their thoughts and feelings. History, biography, memory, and emotion all merged with and settled in the landscape. These places would trigger strong emotions for Wamirans after I had left, because they would be all that Wamirans had as reminders of me. In discussing how places with strong emotional content often evoke loss, Steven Feld (this volume) says that "living far away, one is deeply reminded of places as kin; path connections are like familiar places calling back to you."

It was ironic that after two years, just as I was beginning to blend into the Wamiran landscape, I felt the desire to return to my own cultural place. No matter how content, comfortable, and included I had felt in Wamira, it was not the place that resonated most richly for me. Instead, I began to long for the landscape that connected me to my own roots. From my perspective, I had gone from being in a place I could previously only vaguely imagine to being in a place I somewhat knew. For me, Wamira was an experience that had seeped inside and reshaped me. For Wamirans, much of me and their connection to me became permanently inscribed in their landscape.

GROUNDING MEMORIES AND ESTABLISHING SOCIAL OBLIGATIONS

I went home and thought, talked, and wrote about Wamira. As people had predicted, I cried about it, too. I was, as Alice had warned, "homesick." Thus, a few years later I traveled to Wamira again.

When I arrived back in the village I was startled. I saw that I was already "there." As I walked into my house (now inhabited by Alice and her family), I saw that not only was Wamira inside me but also that I, or bits of me, were in Wamira. My possessions were purposefully kept everywhere as *buderi*. In almost the exact spots where I had left them, I found my kerosene lamp, my dishes and cups, my sleeping mat, my radio, my blue plastic bucket, my old water jug, my pillow, and my metal storage trunk. Even an old tube of toothpaste, squeezed flat and stiff, was stuck in the wall where I used to keep it. The Christmas card my mother had sent Alice three years earlier was on the wall, as was an old calendar she had sent them while I was living there. It was an eerie feeling. Some old people had died. Some children had been born. But my toothpaste tube had remained as untouched on the wall as I had in their memory. I had fixed Wamira in my mind. Wamirans had fixed me in their place.

Wamirans, rather than seeming happy to see me, once again greeted me with tearful faces and exclamations of *"Kapore."* This time it was because my mother had died back home in the interval between my two trips, and they mourned the fact that I was now an "orphan" *(kedakeda)*. Trying to make sense of my leaving home this time, they explained to themselves that I had to come to do my work. Knowing that my financial resources were from the government, they rationalized that my government had made me come. "Why did you leave your father all alone? You should have stayed to take care of him," they reprimanded. When I jokingly commented about how he didn't like to cook for himself, they became somber and concerned. I thought of Marakwadiveta, the stone-faced woman who did not feed her sister and became a rock in the bay. I had not learned my lesson from the landscape.

Several months before I was to leave Wamira on this second visit, some of the men from my hamlet asked whether my government could "pay" them for having taken care of me. "You have lived in Wamira for a total of almost three years. You helped us and we helped you. Surely there should be something big to remember you by." Ideas were bandied about among the men: a boat, a truck, a tractor—no, something more permanent. Finally there was agreement on a community hall. They had hopes of using it not only as a place where people could gather but also as a place where women could bake bread and where overnight guests could be housed. They fantasized about its being a kind of hotel that might even attract tourists. They discussed how they could earn money and get rich. When I explained that my budget could probably accommodate a small building, they cleverly asked, "Will you come back again in a few years?" "I hope so," I said. "Well, then the community hall will have to be built out of permanent materials that will last forever, not bush materials that will rot." We all agreed. A Wamiran who had done some carpentry in town prepared a list of needed supplies, and Alice and I planned a boat trip to the port town of Lae to purchase what was needed: timber, corrugated iron, bags of cement, Masonite, ridge capping, gutter pieces, nails, hinges, and paint.

We arrived back in Wamira with all the supplies about a month before my planned departure. Disagreements immediately arose about the location of the community hall. I soon understood that the arguments had to do with the symbolic nature of the politics of place and with conflicting emotions of desire and fear that accompanied the specter of prosperity. Once again, I thought of Tamodukorokoro.

In order to follow the gist of the Wamirans' arguments, it is necessary to understand that Wamira is divided into two named wards: Damaladona and Rumaruma. Each is further subdivided into many named hamlets. I lived in Rumaruma, in the hamlet of Inibuena. I wanted the community hall to be for all of Rumaruma, whereas the people of Inibuena had conflicting feelings about whether it should be only for their hamlet or for all of Rumaruma. If it were to be for Inibuena, it would be built within the hamlet. If it were for Rumaruma, it would be placed at Werau, the communal grounds for Rumaruma. Whereas I saw Inibuena as included within Rumaruma, the Wamirans saw it as opposed to Rumaruma. Their conflicting emotions had to do with the idea of wanting abundance but fearing the consequences for individuals should they become prosperous. As is common in Melanesia, prosperity on the part of some leads to jealousy on the part of others. And jealousy, it is thought, leads to sorcery, destruction, and death.

Discussions about the location of the community hall were animated and frequent, lasting for many days.

King: We will build the house. Mimi spent all her money on it. Now it is up to us to build it. Others won't laugh at us. We are now *gulau* [chiefs, rich people]. Mimi did this for us.

Brian: You should pick the location of the house carefully. Cement will be poured. It will be permanent.

The meaning of these comments was later explained to me. Even though Brian talked about the location of the house, the "inner meaning" of the talk was about money and jealousy. If money was earned from the bread baking or the overnight guests, people would argue about who had the right to it, Rumaruma or Inibuena.

Nigel: We should speak about the location. Later the people of Inibuena may complain, saying that they took care of Mimi and that the house should have been in Inibuena. If we put it in Werau, will the people of Inibuena later complain?

Jeremiah: Mimi wants the house to be for all of Rumaruma, not just for Inibuena. Her insides are going to Werau. It is her wish. The communal ground will be the chief, no one person will be chief.

Malcolm: Mimi wants the house for all of Rumaruma. It will be put in Werau. Our ancestors were here.

Manson: We have finished discussing the location of the house.

In the same way that people often reconstruct myth through lived experience (see Gillison 1993; Young 1983a), Wamirans seemed to be playing out a contemporary version of Tamodukorokoro when deciding where to place the building. As I soon learned, the community hall, with its potential for producing income from overnight guests or the sale of bread, symbolized wealth and prosperity—all that Tamodukorokoro had forbidden them or, one might say, all that they had forbidden themselves. The dilemma they faced over where to place the building produced mixed emotions like those they had felt about Tamodukorokoro. On the one hand, as the Inibuena people explained, they had taken care of me, and so the community hall should be in their hamlet. Yet if they gained too much prestige from having cared for me and having erected the building, others would be jealous.

Although the community hall seemed to represent what Tamodukorokoro had denied them, there was a major difference. Unlike Tamodukorokoro, whom Wamirans had "chased away," the community hall was to be a permanent edifice—literally cemented into the landscape—that would remain long after my departure. The introduction of permanent materials, cement, and money added new dimensions to their quandary. Job, the most respected elder of Rumaruma, arrived at my house one day to discuss his concern. He was old, he explained, and understood only about taro, jealousy, famine, and death. But he felt ignorant about money. The younger men wanted the house to bring in money, he said, but he was anxious about the consequences if it did.

I thought that, as Malcolm had announced several days previously, the Wamirans had "finished discussing the location of the house." But when I went one day to watch what I thought would be the pegging of the house site, I witnessed more arguments instead. Some men warned about putting the house too close to the path for fear that people, motivated by jealousy, would slash the walls and ruin the house. Again, I had visions of Tamodukorokoro and how Wamirans had tried to slash his legs. In response, the suggestion was made to move the house slightly farther from the main path. At that point, Henry, whose house was near the proposed site, complained that he didn't want it near his house. Finally, about a week later, a compromise was reached and the house was pegged in a spot neither too close to the path nor too close to anyone's house—a spot that belonged to Manibolanai clan, the clan into which I had been adopted.

Once the decision about its location was reached, the house was erected relatively quickly. When it was finished and my farewell feast was held, several men spoke.

> Jeremiah: Thank you, Mimi, for putting the house up at Werau in the name of Inibuena. When all the people have a good time at Werau, the name of Inibuena will be lifted up as well.

> King: You are a very brave woman to put the house at Werau. Thank you for not putting it at Inibuena. If you had put it in Inibuena, then when you returned to Wamira one day you would not find us here. We would all be dead—in the cemetery. That is the custom here. If we make ourselves rich, others will be jealous and kill us.

As the cement was drying on the front stoop of the community hall, I was asked to inscribe my initials in the sticky surface. Henceforth, it was to be called the Mimi Community Hall in my honor. It now became a place with a name and a permanent "mark," all of which were associated with me and my social obligations in Wamira. It was a memorial to the relationships I had already established in the village, as well as a conscious reminder that they be continued even after I left. I was asked to promise that I wouldn't forget Wamirans once I was back in the United States. I was to send money from time to time "for the community hall." And to this day I continue to receive letters with requests and to honor my promise. My anthropological activity had created lasting social obligations, the evidence for which was literally cemented upon the land. As one man remarked, "You poured cement so your power will stay here forever." In pouring the foundation for a permanent structure, I had also cemented my relationships and obligations. I recalled how the Wamirans had cleverly asked, "Will you come back again? Then the community hall will have to be built out of permanent materials that will last forever, not bush materials that will rot." They were talking about more than building supplies. They were indicating that my relationship with them was permanent, not ephemeral. Our connectedness, and my social obligations to them, will last forever.

CONCLUSION

Although, in the past, place has been neglected in the anthropological literature, it has recently received more careful and creative exploration (Aihoshi and Rodman 1992; Augé 1995; Basso 1984a, 1984b, 1988; Hirsch and O'Hanlon 1995; Kahn 1990; Munn 1990; Myers 1991; Pandya 1990; Parmentier 1987; Rodman 1992; Stewart 1988; Wassman 1991; Weiner 1991). Geographers, too, who have long held place as their central concern, have expressed a renewed interest in the topic by developing a more person-oriented approach to place as landscape constructed through human activity (Berdoulay 1989; Entrikin 1989, 1991; Nir 1990; Shields 1991; Tuan 1991; Yoon 1986). Their approaches take into account the cultural significance of daily interactions between people and environments, or what Berdoulay (1989:130) calls "lived space." There is an attempt to "redirect geographical research toward a concern for the richness of human experience and an understanding of human action" (Entrikin 1989:40).

Anthropologists, in their recent discussions of place, have advanced our understanding of the culturally constructed nature of places. Much of the research in the Pacific Islands that analyzes place from the local perspective rings true for Wamiran points of view. For example, the Maori of New Zealand connect knowledge to specific landmarks, and their attitudes toward the environment are reflected in their proverbs, legends, and myths (Salmond 1982). In Belau, cultural history is interpreted through the naming of places, houses, stones, valuables, and so forth. Social relationships are inscribed in named places, connecting people and things in placed events. The result is a historical topography that gives landscape a human meaning (Parmentier 1987). In Vanuatu and Papua New Guinea, anthropologists have also discussed the idea that life activity is punctuated and recalled by places where people have been (Rodman 1987; Weiner 1991; Young 1983b). In Papua New Guinea, history, in general, is described in terms of relationships between migrations, myths, names, and localities that are recalled in songs, stories, and ritual (Jorgensen 1990). History is most precise when it is geography, organized spatially rather than temporally. Temporal order is given as the sequence of localities associated with events (Wassmann 1991). Even genealogies are enhanced by the association of persons with events in designated places (Schuster 1991).

For Wamirans, we have seen that the concept of place emerges from social interactions and relationships, whether at the village, the group, or the individual level. Features in the landscape and other markers such as stones, community halls, cement stoops, and even toothpaste tubes, while looking like everyday objects to outsiders, resonate deeply as they link people to ancient myths and current history. They represent connections between people and their common past, links between individuals and their group, or sources of individual identity. They are outer tangible projections of inner emotional landscapes. Both concrete evidence and continual reminder, they can be anchored in stone, printed on rugby shirts, or poured in cement. They can be meaningful to the whole village, one group, or one individual.

Village (or communal) places are uniquely Wamiran and unite people by surrounding them with reminders of connected pasts and common values. These are deeply rooted in mythology and serve as mnemonic devices to recall shared history and to act as moral guides for current behavior. For example, Wamirans all share knowledge of places from the myths about Tamodukorokoro or about Marakwadiveta and Maradiudiva. Communal places are similar to those Basso describes for the Western Apaches, where the meanings of some places are shared by everyone. Even after living in Wamira for three years, drawing its maps and writing its stories, I did not share village places with Wamirans.

Group places, too, remained their own, specific to the clan or hamlet that created and nurtured them. Clan places such as those referred to in the Tauribariba story are also shared, but by a smaller group. Even people who do not belong to the Maibouni clan are at least vaguely aware of the Tauribariba story and its associated places and markers. Places specific to select groups are reminiscent of those described by Karen Blu (this volume): each of three different groups in North Carolina experiences the same place in its own very different way.

Personal places, on the other hand, are continually created whenever meaningful social interactions take place. My personal places, for example, resulted when I engaged in social exchanges with Wamirans. For both of us, personal places were embodied in physical markers that recalled shared stories, acts of compassion, or experiences of loss. Every individual has a number of such places, which occasionally overlap with those of others. They are endowed with strong emotional meaning and correspond most closely to the places Steven Feld (this volume) discusses for the Kaluli or those Kathleen Stewart (this volume) describes for the people of Appalachia. My own personal places emerged on the Wamiran landscape only when I interacted in meaningful ways with Wamirans, and they have become marked points in a larger journey.

As an anthropologist, I move among places that I imagine, explore, construct, and reconstruct. Unlike most Wamirans, whose territory is more circumscribed, I journey widely in search of places that speak to me. I take my places with me, for places are "tools for the imagination . . . eminently portable possessions" (Basso 1988:102). As Chateaubriand (1803) said, "Every man carries within him a world which is composed of all that he has seen and loved, and to which he constantly returns, even when he is traveling through, and seems to be living in, some different world." Places to which I travel remind me of other places I have known. Each validates my sense of self, articulating with narratives of either personal history or professional identity. In moving among places, I try to capture something of their essence. I recreate them in museum exhibits, lectures, books and articles—as I have done here. But ultimately, places are emotional landscapes, and the most intimate, personal ones are shared with only a few. I think Alice understood this when she told me, "Only you have been to our place. Only you will really know."

NOTES

1. I conducted fieldwork in Wamira in 1976–78 and 1981–82. The research trips were made possible by generous support from the National Science Foundation, the National Institute of Mental Health, the Wenner-Gren Foundation for Anthropological Research, and the Institute for Intercultural Studies. Throughout my work on this chapter, my husband, Richard Taylor, provided support and helpful commentary. I especially thank my many friends in Wamira, who walked the landscape with me and recounted the stories attached to the places. My deepest gratitude goes to Alice Dobunaba, Aidan Gadiona, and the late Sybil Gisewa, who created my home away from home. I alone accept responsibility for any misinterpretation of the data.

2. At the time of my first visit, the family members living in the house were Alice Dobunaba, her brother, Aidan Gadiona, and their elderly mother, Sybil Gisewa. Alice's husband was living in the town of Lae. Their daughter, Felicia Dobunaba, lived in Port Moresby, where she attended the University of Papua New Guinea.

3. Wamira lies in a dry belt that extends from Boianai to Cape Frère, a coastal strip some thirty kilometers in length. Within that region, average annual rainfall is only 1,400 millimeters. For this reason Wamirans and other villagers within the region must irrigate their taro, a crop which needs much water.

4. For a complete version of the myth and a structural-symbolic analysis of it, see Kahn (1986:60–73).

5. There are several versions of this event. According to Father Bodger, the stone had not yet been cemented into the wall but was lying on a table in the cathedral (Bodger, personal communication 1978). According to a Wamiran, it had been

cemented into the wall with its face looking out toward Wamira. As I was told, "Tauribariba saw the village and was drawn back to his home." Yet another, more embellished Wamiran version claims that the stone was carried to England and Australia. When it arrived in Australia, it jumped from the side of the boat and swam back to Wamira because "that is where it belonged."

6

"Where Do You Stay At?"
Home Place and Community among the Lumbee
Karen I. Blu

Making comparisons is what anthropologists do. So when I first heard Keith Basso deliver a prepublication version of "'Stalking with Stories': Names, Places, and Moral Narratives among the Western Apache" (1984b), I drew comparisons between the Apaches Basso described and the Lumbees with whom I had worked. On the face of it, the differences seemed stronger than the similarities. Western Apaches have well-established federal reservations and a reputation for conserving their old ways, whereas Lumbees have never had a reservation and have gained only limited federal recognition of their Indianness. Lumbees, like Apaches, have a certain reputation for toughness, but unlike Apaches, they do not maintain highly visible traditions that outsiders can easily identify as ancient and "Indian."

Having heard Basso explain, however, some of the ways in which places are important and are used by Apaches, I began to see that places are important to Lumbees as well, in ways that I had insufficiently appreciated in my earlier work (Blu 1980). This feeling sent me back to rural North Carolina during the very hot summer of 1984 to learn more about how Lumbees talk about places, so that I might better understand their sense of place.[1]

Ultimately, the quest for understanding in one highly particular southern setting led me to ponder larger questions about home places. At first, I considered how Native Americans' relationships to their home places, past and present, get shaped. That consideration, in turn, provoked thoughts about the political ramifications of ideas of home place in national and international arenas. In this way, moving back and forth between local particulars and broader issues in grander settings, I sought illumination as anthropologists so often do. What emerged was my version of what a number of Lumbees told me about their home places, a suggestion that a Lumbee-like model of conceptualizing places might

help us comprehend early colonial and precolonial population movements in North America, and some ruminations on both the allure and
the dangers of devotion to home places anywhere in the world.

Regarding the particulars of Lumbees' lives in North Carolina, three
points are worth making at the outset. One is that the way socially
significant Lumbee places get construed turned out to confound my
assumptions that they would be presented primarily as visual images.
Instead, they were visually vague—vital centers with blurry borders. I
came to see that this indistinctness in boundaries of community could
be a way of resisting or evading attempts by those with greater economic
and political power to locate and control Indian people and their lands.

The second point is that "community" itself has multiple referents
for Lumbees. It refers to named local areas that I discuss in greater detail
later. At times it is also used more encompassingly for Lumbee people
as a whole, as in the phrase "the Indian community." By the same token,
Black and White neighbors of the Lumbees also use the term "community," sometimes in similar ways, sometimes in discordant ones.[2] This
needs to be borne in mind throughout.

The third point is that today, spaces inhabited by Native Americans
encompass non-Indians as well. Too many studies of American Indians have assumed that neatly bounded, geographically distinct peoples
with similarly distinctive cultures inhabit clearly definable territories.
Appadurai (1988), Gupta and Ferguson (1992), and Lawrence and Low
(1990) have called for the disarticulation of these increasingly ill-fitting
categories. They question the appropriateness of such categories in the
postmodern world with its global economy, hegemonic politics, and
roving transnationals with multiple identities. Despite such calls, it is all
too easy to imagine Native American conceptions of place as timeless
givens, constructions made by homogeneous peoples, each with a culture and social order all its own, in splendid isolation from others. Federal
and state legal systems, of course, encourage these formulations.

Such a view is counterproductive at a time when Indians all over the
country are insisting that they be accorded recognition as Native Americans and as men, women, and children who live and work in a fully modern world, for it leaves out that world. Even on reservations, how the land
is to be construed, interpreted, and used is very much a matter for negotiation and often contestation. Native American cultural constructions
of space and place have rarely been accomplished in complete isolation,
are subject to change, and can most fruitfully be discussed as products of
interactions, competing views, negotiations, and struggles, current and
past, not only within and between tribal bodies but also between native

and non-native peoples. This is as true for the Navajos amidst their huge reservation as it is for Lumbees who have never had one.

In puzzling over Lumbees' apparent rejection of visual imagery in their talk of the communities that heavily define their moral universe, I needed to consider some of the ways their Black and White neighbors view communities. Like so many other matters of vital importance (ethnicity, race, and gender, for example), the community places and their significance are socially and culturally constructed, contested, and reconstructed over time. They appear and disappear from human consciousness and alter in meaning for those who mark them.

OF RURAL PLACES AND MULTICULTURAL SPACES

Recently, while driving through the gently rolling, densely farmed countryside of southern Ohio, I was struck by the very different look, the very different arrangement of space to be seen in the flatter but equally farmed, equally rural former swampland of southeastern North Carolina, where I have worked on and off for more than twenty-five years. In Ohio, one can drive for a good many miles without seeing anything except farmed land, larger and smaller clumps of trees, and mostly neat, painted farmhouses, barns, silos, and other outbuildings that are spaced at relatively great distances from one another.

In the similarly rural coastal plain of North Carolina, houses, tobacco barns, and sheds vary far more in their outward appearance and relative tidiness—surface suggestions of a broader range of economic conditions. Houses often are built in small clusters. In addition, one can drive only a short distance in North Carolina before encountering a crossroads that hosts a small store, usually with gasoline pumps (these days, sometimes in service and sometimes not), or a roadside café. Both kinds of commercial places are scattered over the countryside and act as magnets, drawing people, mostly men, throughout the day for companionship, storytelling, exchanges of news, and the passing on of vital community information. In Ohio, community socializing seems to go on in places like small restaurants in town, either at breakfast or at the midday meal.

In pondering these differences, I was reminded that the Midwesterners among whom I grew up negotiated their way through their landscape by using the cardinal directions. One drove a mile and a half down the road and turned north at the first intersection, west at the second. During my numerous stays in Robeson County, North Carolina, it seemed that I was always asking directions to someone's house or store or workplace, and the responses I got from Indians were usually couched in terms of places I already knew how to get to ("You know the Union Chapel road, well, you go to the second crossroads and turn left to the first paved road to the right . . ."). The instructions were always oriented in terms of the individual making the trip. That is, one turned to the right or left, not to the "universal" north, south, east, or west. Sometimes, in my confusion, imagining to myself a roadmap, I asked, "Is that on the north side?" In answer, I would generally receive a puzzled look and very often an "I don't know." Cardinal directions were not significant for orienting travelers, however significant they might prove for burials and other matters.

What do these at-a-glance differences in the spatial relations of two rural, still-farmed areas suggest? To me, they are a vivid reminder that the social uses and cultural meanings attached to space, which are at once creative and expressive, both products and producers of history, can sometimes be seen "on the ground," but that such concrete patternings nevertheless need very close "readings" if we are to understand what people who live and work in the spaces make of them.

Discussions of space and place often overlook aspects of the landscape that are not expressed in visual imagery, that are taken for granted, or that are unmarked in linguistic terms.[3] When, in 1984, I asked a young Lumbee Indian man in his twenties what he considered to be "landmarks" in Robeson County, he mentioned some physical features such as swamps and branches (creeks), some built features such as churches, and finally "areas": "Like Black Ankle. You know it when you hit it, but you can't see it. It's like courage, you can't see it but you know what it is." This was truly perplexing, a "landmark" that was not visually distinct, a contradiction in my terms but clearly not in his.

Other Indians used the terms "community" or "settlement" for "area," but in each case, the territory covered was vaguely defined, lacking the sort of firm boundaries that result in lines on a map or the clearly visible density and ordering of a town plan. These visually unmarked, indistinct "areas" turned out to be among the most important features of Robeson County to its Indian population and, perhaps not surprisingly, the least marked and remarked upon by Robesonian Whites. It is vitally important to know that the landscape is inhabited principally by three different, strongly socially demarcated sets of people — Native Americans, African Americans, and White Americans — all of whom make something different of the spaces they share as near neighbors and as county, state, and national citizens.

Such a setting is a good one in which to challenge more standard notions of neatly bounded, geographically distinct peoples, cultures, and territories. Space and place, who constructs them and for what purposes, how they are used in storytelling and in discourse, and what power implications can be drawn from their construction and from negotiations over them have become significant issues in anthropology since about 1980. Although earlier anthropologists — Boas (1934) on Kwakiutl placenames being perhaps the type case — considered placenames and naming important issues, concerns about these matters languished for many years until fresher impressions and newer perspectives from interpretive anthropology and cultural studies were brought to bear on them, renewing our interest.

Renato Rosaldo (1980) called our attention to what seemed at first a boring recitation of a series of places through which Ilongot individuals had moved. Such recitations consumed much of their storytelling and ultimately turned out to be crucial keys to Rosaldo's (and consequently our) understanding of Ilongot history. Basso (1984b:21) remarked on Apaches' initially puzzling insistence that the land they know helps Apache people to "live right" but that it doesn't "go to work on [some people] anymore." He then went on to show the implicit connection the speakers were making between the land and the properly moral way to be Apache. Both of these writers called attention to the difficulty of "reading" the meanings speakers assume when they inject placenames into their conversations, stories, and not-so-offhand remarks.

With Rosaldo and Basso in mind, I realized with a jolt that during my stays in Robeson County, placenames had abounded in Lumbee conversation.[4] But they were bits of stories or news or reports of political activities that I usually skipped over or read "through" in my eagerness for what I imagined were the "meatier" parts. This led me to ignore the fact that "being placed" in the landscape communicated much about social identity and social life, about assumptions concerning local "character," about likely political clout, about stories commonly told of events in a locality, and about a number of other things to listeners better attuned than I.

The Lumbee Indians have a "homeland" that has never had even a semblance of protection by treaty or reservation. As far back as documentary evidence takes us, Lumbees have had to share this homeland with non–Native Americans. The look of the land and the uses to which it has been put have changed dramatically during the long period for which we have documentation. The flat land, cut by rivers, swamps, branches, and bays, was at first heavily forested, part of an area of pine woods bordering the Cape Fear River that made Wilmington, North Carolina, at the base of the river, "the world's greatest market" for "naval stores" of tar, rosin, and turpentine by the time of the Civil War (Evans 1966:14; see also Silver 1990:121–29). Many Indians found work in the pine woods gathering and preparing these products and in lumbering, activities that supplemented the mostly subsistence agriculture practiced in the swampy areas.

During Reconstruction and the Jim Crow period that followed it, the look of the land gradually altered. Swamps began to be drained, expanding the amount of land that could be placed under cultivation. The woods were gradually cut, shrinking their extent greatly. What had been tracks and even corduroy roads were replaced by more formal and better maintained roads. And from the middle of the nineteenth century, railroads began to crisscross the county (Thomas 1982:178–85). Today, although the look of the land still marks it as rural, and farmed acres are much in evidence, there are numerous scattered factories and much larger towns, complete with suburban-style "developments," that provide the bulk of the population with employment in manufacturing industries. The driving forces behind these changes — those who provided the capital, the plans, the determination, and the political clout to put them into effect — were White, although the occasional Indian entrepreneur participated.

For Indians and Blacks, who fought or adapted to but rarely instigated the changes, more often merely taking advantage of them where they could, the end of the Civil War and the formal emancipation of slaves meant steadily growing participation in a national and international market economy (Wright 1986). This economy gradually eroded their ability to hold onto their land if they already owned it, or to buy it if they did not. Since 1880, farmed holdings have tended to grow larger and the numbers of farm owners have lessened, fitting a pattern of changing landownership throughout the cotton and tobacco regions of the South (P. Daniel 1985). These changes came about with a move into cotton growing in Robeson County after the Civil War and a subsequent switch to tobacco in the early years of the twentieth century (P. Daniel 1985: 18–21, 31–37; Lawrence 1939:122–23). Since the middle of the twentieth century, there has been a steady shift into manufacturing as the major source of livelihood. Meanwhile, the railroad boom of the late 1800s and early 1900s came and went, rearranging the placement of towns, infusing new life into some places and leaving only ghostly reminders of old station stops in others. Now the railroads have been superseded by interstate highways and by increasingly paved county and state road systems.

COMMUNITIES WITH BLURRY BOUNDARIES

Throughout these sometimes dramatic changes in the landscape, Indians, with strong senses of family attachment, placed themselves in mostly rural settlements, or communities, with indeterminate boundaries that operated as sturdy anchors to their homeland while it was transformed around them. The indefiniteness of borders was clearly useful in an earlier

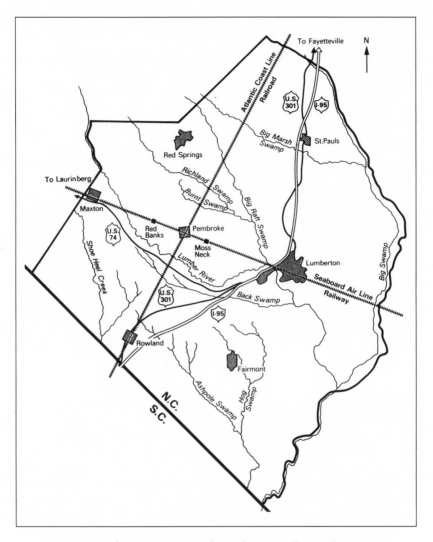

Figure 6.1. Robeson County, North Carolina. Map by Carol Cooperrider.

period when prying White men with guns posed a problem of survival, particularly for a band of outlawed men led by culture-hero Henry Berry Lowry during the close of the Civil War and the early days of Reconstruction (see G. Barton 1992; Blu 1980; Dial 1993; Dial and Eliades 1975; Evans 1971). By 1973, when I heard what follows, the vagueness was more a matter of fooling White people in less serious contexts. A venerable Indian man was telling me about the history of the Lumbees. He mentioned that the area we were then in, Pembroke town,

> used to be named Scuffletown. It was a fictitious name. When tourists come through they'd ask the Indians, "Where is Scuffletown?" And the Indians would say, "Fifteen miles down the road." They'd go fifteen miles down the road and run into some White people, and they'd ask them, "Where is Scuffletown?" And they'd say, "Turn around and go back down that road fifteen miles." And they never could find it. Black Ankle is a fictitious name like that.

The names of places, then, provide openings to multiple interpretations, entries into a variety of imaginings. In using the term "fictitious," this elder sardonically called attention to the sometimes denigrating use by Whites of the names "Scuffletown" and "Black Ankle." The unsavory reputations attributed to these places by Whites were widely viewed by Indians as "lies," so that when Whites spoke these names, Indians heard denigration. When Indians spoke the names, they seemed to use unspoken quotation marks to set their usage apart from that of Whites.

Just before the United States entered World War II, Joseph Mitchell, who was born into a White family and grew up in Fairmont, a town in the southern part of Robeson County near Black Ankle, wrote some stories for the *New Yorker* set in a fictitious "Black Ankle County," named after "the sticky [black] mud of the bottom fields and the sloblands" (1992:349–50). A more recent suggestion of White tone, albeit a somewhat sanitized one, is reflected in a county history written by a knowledgeable local White woman who mentions that in the nineteenth century, Black Ankle had a reputation for isolation, whiskey, and violence, for being a place where people did not farm much and hid in the swamps because they were outlawed (Thomas 1982:187). She also provides an explanation for the name:

> Black Ankle was not a community, but supposedly the area has had that name for some time. One story of its name origin is: In 1820, when it was a custom for men and boys to take off their shoes to walk to church, Colin Evans was at church with a group of his neighbors. Since it had rained and the men had walked barefooted, their feet were muddy. After church someone asked Evans to his home, but Evans reputedly said that he had better go back home "with his black-ankled crowd." Others say that the name came from the fact that "a plowman's ankles would be black after plowing his soil." (Thomas 1982:58–59)

What is unstated in this folk etymology is the widespread use in this general part of North and South Carolina of combinations with "ankle," such as "Brass Ankle," to designate people of mixed ancestry, with the implication that the mixture includes Black. The Indian elder I spoke to thus disavowed support for the White meanings of "Scuffletown" and "Black Ankle" by calling them fictitious, and at the same time referred to their indefiniteness, their indistinctness in White eyes (Thomas bears this out when she says Black Ankle "was not a community"). Indians have communities where Whites sometimes do not recognize them, and they may make humorous play or serious business over the discrepancy.

When Lumbees meet one another for the first time, one of the early questions they ask is, "Where do you stay at?" By this they mean, "Where, especially in the homeland region, are you living? Where do you come from?" If the answer seems ambiguous, perhaps because the speaker's accent does not seem to be the right one for the area named, further questioning can ensue. "Where do your people stay at?" "Who are your people?" In this context, "your people" means family and is not considered insulting. An inquiry in a different context may suggest that "your people" is a gloss for "your race," in which case the question might be considered impolite or demeaning because direct inquiries about one's race are deemed rude.

When questioned about why he had asked an Indian waitress in an Indian-owned restaurant who her people were, an Indian friend responded in the "because-my-ancestors-did-it" vein that is all too familiar to anthropologists: "My daddy, he was like me. Just like the girl at the restaurant I asked who her people was. He'd always ask, 'Who are his people?'" My friend had asked and found out not only what the young woman's name was, who her family were, and where they were from, but also who owned the restaurant now and who his people were. Although this man perhaps asks such questions more often and more persistently than other people do, the connections he assumes between family name, kinship group, and geographic locale are commonly accepted ones. They are generally considered to be important pieces of information about someone with whom one has dealings.

Other people reinforced this set of connections quite explicitly. After an Indian woman mentioned the special accent associated with one community, I asked whether she could tell from people's accents what part of the county they came from. She said, "Yes, that together with their name." Surprised, I said, "Their name?" Her husband responded, "Different names are associated with different areas. Prospect has a lot of Bullards. And the Brooks settlement has a lot of Brookses." (This last, no doubt, for the benefit of a slow-witted anthropologist.)

These connections were made even clearer when I asked a particularly thoughtful Indian man why people seemed to "have to" know what community a person was from. He thought for a minute, at first denying the necessity. He said the question "Where do you stay at?" was just a kind of conventional question, like "How are you?" But, I said, people keep coming back to it until it's answered. So he thought some more and then said that the answer might tell you something about a person's family. "If someone comes from Saddletree and his name is Hammonds, he might be from a very influential family. The Hammondses have been well-to-do, important people in that area for a long time." He said the answer might also tell you something about a person's economic or social status, but not as much as it used to. The area where Rex-Rennert (a school) is, for example, used to be extremely poor. But by the time we spoke, in 1984, many people there were doing very well, according to this man. Families, then, are at the core of localized communities.

To an extent, the family nexus is visible, plotted onto the land in the clusters of houses nestled close to one another. A young man contemplating marriage was showing me the farm he planned to buy just down the road and around the corner from his fiancée's parents' house. Driving past her house, we passed several others close by, and as we did, he told me who lived in each one and how they were related to her—her grandmother, her uncle, and so on. He jokingly said, "If anything were to happen and things don't work out, her relatives would have to go past [my house and farm] every day, because that's the main road out. I don't think they'd like that." Proximity to so much family can cause a bit of uneasiness for the in-marrying spouse. This countryside pattern, although not universal, is quite common where space and resources are sufficient. When family finances do not permit so much house building, trailers are sometimes substituted. In towns, space is less flexible and the clustering of families less common and more difficult to achieve.

Although Indians, African Americans, and Whites all talk about "communities," what they mean by them and their respective senses of rootedness in them differ. In 1984, I spoke with a man who had been a leader in one of the Black town communities during the civil rights activities of the late 1960s. He was still a respected leader, still politically active, but the scale of political movement in the county had generally diminished. When I asked him about Black communities in the county, he looked at me blankly. Perhaps too promptingly, I asked, "Which ones would you say are the most active?" He said, "Lumberton. [pause] Fairmont. Those are the most active. Then on down the line Maxton. Red Springs is beginning to be active again, beginning to get organized. And Rowland has a Black mayor, you can't leave Rowland out." Notably, these are all towns, and they were all major loci of political activity twenty years earlier. A number of the same leaders, like him, were still in place.

When the conversation moved on to the subject of out-migration, this man, in contrast to the Indians I talked to, was not particularly upset about it. He said that what children do "depends on what training they have. If they have a Ph.D., they're not going to live in Robeson County. There's nowhere they can use it." He noted that many young people were moving to jobs then available in Greensboro and Charlotte, North Caro-lina, each a little over one hundred miles away. When I asked whether people would prefer it if their children returned to where their parents lived, he said the children should go where they could do well. "Younger people are attaching to where they can make the best economy, do the best. Right now that is in a city or adjoining a city." He did not seem to have the great feelings of anger or sadness that Indians so often express over the "loss" of their children when they leave the homeland.

It is not that Indians do not migrate, but rather that they tend to do it reluctantly, and parents who are left behind are often torn and angry at a system that does not provide jobs for their ambitious children. For them, in the best of all possible worlds, the local situation would allow all the Indian children who wanted good, secure jobs and adequate housing to have them so that the community could be whole. For Indi-ans, unless some children "stayed home" in the homeland, there would be no localized community, no focus, no peopled homeland. Lumbee identity, like the particular identities of other Native American peoples, depends heavily upon connection to a particular place, a home place. Lacking a home place, a home people, their identity would be a more generalized pan-Indian one, a free-floating kind of ethnicity with a very different emotional and conceptual construction. I never had the sense from either Blacks or Whites in Robeson of the same kind of connec-tion between place and people-as-a-whole, however attached particular parents were to their children or their land, however much they feared or mourned their children's leaving or the loss of privately owned land. Familial bonds might be strong for Whites or Blacks, but not the sense of localized, community-identifying bonds, a sense Indians possess acutely. To convey some sense of how Lumbees characterize and use their com-munities in discourse, I have selected a few to elaborate upon—some central, others quite peripheral.

Pembroke Town and Community
While the bonds of family and locality are woven tightly in all the com-munities or settlements, each one is deemed to have its own character and to reflect something about the way life is conducted there. The com-munities are also sources of rivalry that mainly takes the form of good-natured teasing but sometimes becomes real hostility—particularly, it would seem, in the political arena. Because the communities are rooted in family ties, the rivalries, too, often have familial overtones.

These days—although, as people repeatedly assured me, it was not always so—Pembroke is the community with which others tend to compare themselves, the dominant town "other" among the countryside Indian communities. Partly this not-always-flattering dominance may come from the growth of all the county towns, Pembroke among them, in population and in importance for the economic and social life of everyone. As the only Indian-run town, Pembroke figures largely for Indians all over the county. It is the home of several institutions vital to the Indian community as a whole: "the college" (now Pembroke State University, a branch of the North Carolina University system), "LRDA" (Lumbee Regional Development Association), Lumbee River Legal Services (LRLS), and the offices of a number of Indian professionals—doctors, lawyers, veterinarians. What happens in Pembroke often has powerful effects elsewhere in the county, and that is sometimes a matter of resentment in the countryside. It is good to keep that tension in mind as the qualities of the communities are unfolded, largely in the words of people who talked about them in 1984.

Pembroke town was a relatively late creation in the heavily Indian area of the county. It owed its birth to the railroads.[5] When the main east-west railroad was built across the county in 1860, it passed through the area later to become Pembroke, stopping nearby (Thomas 1982:179). But it was not until 1892, when a north-south railroad crossed the east-west line, that the station and town of Pembroke were laid out. At that time "streets, blocks, and subdivided lots were laid off by the Atlantic Land and Improvement Company" (Thomas 1982:181; see also Dial and Eliades 1975:142–43). The grid plan established then largely remains today. This development was conceived and executed by Whites in an area of dense Indian population. Struggles over the formal political control of the town have been resolved in favor of the Indians, who, as voters and officeholders, have dominated the town since at least the 1950s.

But signs of the earlier domination by Whites remain and continue to be resisted. Street names, for example, are often posted one way on street signs but spoken of in other terms by Indian residents—just as New Yorkers persist in using "Sixth Avenue" to designate the formally renamed "Avenue of the Americas." When I moved into an apartment on the edge of town for a summer of work in 1984, my Indian landlord assured me that the correct address was simply "Number 3" of the apartments named after him and that such a designation would tell the telephone and power companies everything they needed to know. But for these White-run companies, a label on the street and a number on the building were essential. What the street sign said was irrelevant to Indian life as lived in Pembroke, but it was of primary relevance to outsider-run service companies.

Since the creation of the town, although business life and government were at first largely in the hands of White residents, the Indian presence has been overwhelming. And when "the college," which opened in 1887 to train teachers for segregated Indian schools, moved to Pembroke in 1909, the town unquestionably became the educational center for Indian people. Teachers were trained there for Indian schools in Robeson County and a number of other counties in the state. The town has also had a number of Indian-run newspapers, such as the *Indian Observer,* which began its short life in 1911 (Thomas 1982:254). Since 1973, the *Carolina Indian Voice* has been Pembroke's newspaper of record. It is important to note that the official boundaries of the town, those used to determine eligible voters in town elections, do not circumscribe "the community" of Pembroke, which is somewhat amorphous but encompasses a much larger area.

One Indian friend, who was born and grew up in Pembroke and who lives there now, suggested in the mid-1980s that it once was the social and cultural center for Indian people from Robeson and neighboring counties. But that has grown less so, he thinks. One of the indications is that there are Indian-organized chapters of voluntary organizations such as Jaycees and Kiwanis in many other Indian parts of the county besides Pembroke. He said, "It used to be if you [an Indian] wanted to belong to one [of the organizations], Pembroke was the only place to come. . . . Pembroke has always been a center, and people came here. They still come, but they don't admit it. . . . I guess the business of its being a center goes back to the days of segregation, when it was the only place [for Indians] to come and be welcome." Then he remarked that it wasn't always as it is today. "It used to be known as a rough town—violent." To illustrate what he meant, he told me about a relative who had been shot and killed not far from town, and about an incident he had witnessed right there in Pembroke:

> Yes, I was standing there in town one day, and I started to hear sirens in the distance. And they got closer and closer, and pretty soon I could see a black Chevrolet coming down the road, with a big cloud of dust behind it, and several police cars right after it. As it went by, I could see that it was D. N. [a man who later settled down to become a prominent and highly respected figure in the town]. I never did know what happened, whether he lost them or not. . . . When I was a boy [during the 1930s], it wasn't uncommon at all to see bodies in the street in Pembroke.

But even then, he said, when you heard about violence in Pembroke, most often it was somebody from outside the community who had come in and made trouble.

Such is one of the views from the center, a view full of the recognition of changes and of tensions between center and erstwhile peripheries. Views from other communities put the matter somewhat differently and further reflect long-standing rivalries. In a conversation I had at about the same time as the preceding one, an impassioned young man from the southern part of the county saw Pembroke in another light.

Pembroke, he said, was "generally disliked by the other communities. Pembroke people think everyone else is green with envy, that Pembroke is disliked because it has everything going for it." Part of the "everything" is "the fact that Indians run everything." He continued:

> In the old days, there were only three things you [an Indian] could do. You could farm, or you could teach, or you could go in the army.. . . . The center of Indian education was in Pembroke, and the educated people moved to Pembroke. Their attitude is, "We are better educated, and better and smarter than the rest of the people." . . . Pembroke people are not exposed to people of other races. They boast about being exposed, but with the exception of Prospect, they are the least exposed. They have egocentric ideas: "We got this and we must be better because we got this." C. C. [who comes from Pembroke] once said to me, "You're just envious because you weren't born and raised here." . . . I resent Pembroke for thinking it's better.

In these ways, older rivalries are perpetuated.

PROSPECT COMMUNITY

If Pembroke town is a relatively recent "center" for Indian people in Robeson County, its main rival today, Prospect, which still is not a town, is generally acknowledged as the former cultural center. It is an older, rural community not more than a couple of miles from Pembroke, an area with fine farmland and few non-Indians. In 1950, Lumbee writer Lew Barton described it as a "rich agricultural section" containing "about 1,500 people." He called Prospect High School the "civic center," noting that there were also a grammar school, two churches, and several businesses:

> Here, too, one will find a civic pride in the small community that is unequaled by citizens of most small towns in Robeson. There has always been a strong spirit of friendly rivalry between Prospect and other communities, and most especially between Prospect and Pembroke. In athletics the two communities are bitter rivals; each considers the other its major opponent. (L. Barton 1950:6)

Significantly, Prospect and Pembroke high schools no longer exist; they were consolidated, together with a few other schools, into West Robeson High School in 1983. Although some Indians maintained that distinctions between communities, which the local high schools surely helped to maintain, had decreased and that rivalries were more muted, I still heard grumbling from adults, principally about Pembroke. A young Pembroke woman who was at the time a student at West Robeson said that some of the students from other parts of the county thought Pembroke students were "stuck up," that Pembroke students thought they were "better than everybody else. But we don't [think that]." When she indicated that she had friends from outside Pembroke, I asked her whether she knew what communities they were from, and she said she did. And when I asked what people from Prospect were like, she said, "They're nice." And then, with a shy smile, "They talk funny. They have a real funny accent." At the consolidated West Robeson High School, the major divisions among students are, apparently, less between Indians from different communities than between Indian and Black students.

The view of a man reared in Prospect of his "home" community reflected a civic pride of the sort mentioned by Lew Barton in 1950. He said, in the mid-1980s, that whenever he got ready to write his autobiography, he already had the first sentence for it: "I was born on [month] [day], 1922, right in the very *heart* of the Lumbee Indian community." Knowing him for a long time, I said, "By that you mean Prospect?" and he said, "Yes, Prospect." He went on to elaborate the ways in which Prospect was and continues to be the heart of the Lumbee homeland:

> The first Indian doctor came from there, and the first county commissioner, and the first Indian school was out in that direction, by New Hope. It has the densest Indian population, and in a five-mile radius there are only two parcels of land not owned by Indians. . . . And you know there are a large number of Locklears among the Lumbee. Well, there are a larger number of them concentrated in Prospect than elsewhere.

But Prospect still lacks the "Main Street" and commercial focus of a town, making it difficult for the uninitiated to recognize it as an important community.

Views of Prospect from elsewhere are, not surprisingly, less boosterish. Prospect is often chosen as a point of contrast by Pembroke people. One Pembroke man said, "Prospect people are said to be *country* people, who speak nowhere near proper English, or at least this is how Pembroke people tell it." He also remarked that the image other people have of someone from Pembroke is that he or she is "a know-it-all and holier than thou."

Many people from Prospect and from elsewhere alluded to its rootedness in older ways, to a depth of in-placeness manifested in respect for family life and the views of elders and in the continued use of older forms of English, which some called "Elizabethan" and others "funny" talk or "that Prospect accent." A man from one of the southern communities contrasted Pembroke and Prospect. "Prospect is different. There things are run by the 'patriarchs.' The patriarch is the old man or old lady of the family." He expanded on what he meant by retelling the story of the emperor

> who had no clothes on when he walked past the people, but all the people bowed before him and told him what lovely clothes he had, except for one little boy who said, "He's naked." When the old man walks past the family, and he says "we talk this way and we do that way," you talk that way and do that way. He whips everybody—he whips his daughters-in-law's butts, his sons', his grandsons', everybody's.

He traced the heavy dialect there to the fact that it was the old people who ran everything and told the younger ones how to talk. "That old Elizabethan talk—that's why you get it there. It's there and nowhere else." Of Pembroke he said, "Prospect people say, 'They don't like anybody but themselves.'" Of Magnolia and Fair Grove: "They say, 'Me, I don't know any of them.'" He said they feel that "Prospect is the center of the Indian community and that it always has been. It *is* old."

In my experience, these two rival centers, Pembroke and Prospect, are those communities whose images and erstwhile characters are the most highly elaborated and frequently discussed. People born there or residing there often spontaneously discuss the places as centers. Other communities' characters and images emerge more cursorily, as thumbnail sketches rather than as full-blown essays.

UNION CHAPEL COMMUNITY

From the beginning of my time in Robeson County in 1966, one such rural community, Union Chapel, frequently shortened to "Chapel," emerged again and again as one associated with danger and violence, especially for outsiders. Although I was often warned away from it by people from elsewhere, I never encountered anything there but hospitality. One night in the late 1960s, however, at a meeting held to discuss politics and voter registration, I began to see how the community might impress others with its fierceness. I had been to many such meetings in different parts of the county and would go to many more. This one was distinctive because when the men, who had been standing around talking and joking with one another, sat down on the wooden benches of the meeting room, there was a series of loud "thunks." I learned later that this was the sound of handguns tucked into their belts and back pockets hitting the hard wood of the benches.

In 1984, when a middle-aged Pembroke man wanted to explain what he meant by saying that too many young Indian men grew up with a "perverse" sense of manhood, he cited what used to happen when he was young. "A bunch of us would get into a car and drive up to Union Chapel. Even to drive through there was asking for trouble in those days. But we *had* to do it." It was unstated but understood that once the young men in the car arrived at Union Chapel, a fight with youths from Chapel was likely to ensue. Young men from Chapel were considered to be more prone than youths from anywhere else to fight fiercely and with little provocation. Thus, they provided the toughest test for young men from elsewhere who wanted to demonstrate their manhood. This practice of looking for fights, of proving one's manhood through violence, was what the speaker considered "perverse."[6]

Although many people not from Union Chapel would have agreed with its characterization by one younger man as "a violent, strange community," to another Indian outsider, one who had actually worked there for a number of years, its main characteristic was that many people were tenant farmers and that only a few small farmers owned their own land, making it one of the poorer communities.

People from Union Chapel know their reputation among outsiders and sometimes play upon it either to intimidate or, more often, to tease. In 1968, I met an Indian nurse in a local doctor's office, and when she found out I was living in Pembroke, she said banteringly, "You know, I'm one of those bad Indians."[7] She was from Union Chapel. Later, in a barbershop there, a three-year-old girl was being teased by her grandfather, who asked her if she was a "bad Indian." For residents, the community provides intimacy, friendship, and support — it is a place for their families, a place that is "really" Indian, unlike, say, Pembroke, which has "too much of a White orientation."

MAGNOLIA COMMUNITY

A much larger rural community is Magnolia, which lies near Lumberton, the largest Robeson town and its multiethnic county seat. Magnolia has long been one of the more important Indian communities. According to one Indian man from elsewhere, "It's the biggest Indian community [in the area]. I don't know how many people there are. It's hard to get around, easy to get lost." He remarks that there are two special physical features people talk about in Magnolia. One is "the Burnt Islands," which he says he doesn't understand very well. They've been pointed out to him, and they look like a bunch of trees thickly clustered and close together. The other is "the Desert, a real sandy area, with some pines, but mostly clear fields." He says of the community that it is "more civic minded and more exposed [to Whites and Blacks]" than most other communities. "They have a different perception of urban life" because of their proximity to Lumberton, where Indian people have to deal with outsiders all the time.

One of the main national north-south highways, Route 301, has long run through Magnolia, even before the coming of Interstate 95, and one woman friend who grew up in Magnolia recalled in the late 1960s that her family had been tenants on a farm by the side of the old highway. Tourists on their way north or south constantly stopped to take pictures and ask for souvenirs of cotton and tobacco. Her family had earned a small but steady flow of cash from such encounters, which also became subjects for sometimes humorous storytelling.

So, it seems, which community an Indian person is "from" or "staying at," a phrase that does not necessarily suggest temporariness, reveals much to those with local knowledge. It reveals something about likely economic and social status, about possible kinship ties, about interconnections with the non-Indian world, about the community's role in the history of the Indian people, and about probable political positions.[8] Each area has at least one informal political leader. These leaders make alliances and compete with each other for prominence within their area and, if they are particularly ambitious, among Indian people more generally. The human and financial support available to a leader very much depends on the character of his local community. Thus, leaders from Prospect and Pembroke tend to achieve wider visibility both among Indians and among Whites and Blacks, in part because of the numbers of people involved but also because of the relatively greater wealth and education in these communities. This leadership is often resented and contested. One could argue that the political movement of the 1950s to rename the people "Lumbee," which was Pembroke based, wrested primary leadership away from the Prospect community at about the same time Pembroke Indians took control of their town government.

MOVING THROUGH THE LANDSCAPE

One can see better how the communities matter when people speak of movement, of going for visits, vacations, and trips or of just "riding the roads." In recounting travels near and far, Indians progress from place to place, naming each one, sometimes producing a string of stories, each of which is "placed" in a particular community or has characters who are "located" by the communities they come from. The widely imagined nature of each of the communities provides sets of expectations about what usually, might, or almost never happens there that people use in their travels and that storytellers play off of or play against in their tales. Movement itself has a positive meaning, for it suggests life, vitality, connection to others. Even movement through space far from "home" is suggestive. When old friends returned from a long driving trip to the West in 1984, they were full of stories about what had happened at various places they had been—and many were incidents in which they had run into people who knew Indians they knew in Robeson County. New places were made meaningful by encounters with other people and made most vivid when connections to new people and places could be made through those they already knew.

Closer to home, travels in Robeson and nearby counties keep people in touch with one another. When a man said of his aging father, "He still gets out on the roads every day," he meant that his father still had vitality and interest in life. When I called an elderly Indian man to see whether I might talk with him, he said, "I'm afraid I can't do it. . . . I'm feeling poorly, and I don't do things like that anymore." Later I told one of the people who had urged me to see him, and he said, "Oh, he always says that. But he's okay, he gets out and goes every day." That is to say, he was strong and healthy enough to be independent in his movements.

While movement through space connotes well-being, personal strength, and the potential for wielding political power, the way people move may suggest whether they are confused and indirect or—what is more highly valued—straightforward and direct. Those who move through space should, ideally, move directly to a point in pursuit of a goal, and not spend all their time sheerly in motion. Of a woman who was notable on the political scene, one man who had worked with her said, "She'll drive from Harper's Ferry to Rowland and all the way around to Pembroke, when she could have come directly." A route like that would take one in a long southwesterly loop instead of straight into Pembroke. He also said that she would "confuse confusion." This woman was known for rambling oratory and confounding leaps of logic.

Politics heavily involves movement. Those who aspire or claim to be political leaders have to "get out on the road," have to move through the various communities strengthening old connections, making new ones, being personally "there," and showing involvement. One Indian man I had known well during the extremely politically active late 1960s said of a woman also active then, "We'd take money out of our pockets to give to her to lope the roads." She was supposed to be telling people about programs and getting them involved in a project. Movement through the peopled landscape gets things accomplished, puts them in gear, makes change on the social and political scene possible.

Fred Myers has said of the Pintupi, an Australian aboriginal people of the Western Desert, that "it is activity that creates places, giving significance to impervious matter" (1991:54). Although Pintupis clearly create different kinds of places with different sorts of activities, the same could be said for Lumbees. It is perhaps no accident that the connections between indigenous people and their lands are so intimate and so contested in both Australia and the United States. For Lumbees the connection is not a formalized one like the Dreaming, but it is certainly found informally in "historical, mythological, or contemporary" narratives (Myers

1991:54). Movement, for Robeson County Indians, is a metaphor for health, well-being, and connectedness, and folk history reminds them of the Henry Berry Lowry days when Whites tried unsuccessfully to curtail the movements of the band. The White people's failure is attributed to the band's defiance, resistance, and refusal to accept constraint, and to the larger community's support of the band. Movement may be less constrained today, but people are wary of anything that looks like an attempt to restrain them. To have freedom of movement may require a struggle, even violence, but that is part of the oral tradition, a familiar tale.

RECONCEIVING SHARED SPACE

It is not only Indians who use the term "community"—everyone in the South uses this term and treats the county as the major unit of geographic and political reference. In Robeson County, people of all "races" can point to communities largely inhabited by or dominated by one or another "race." Throughout the Carolinas, White, Black, and Indian communities are often to be seen associated with and sometimes named after churches or schools or even crossroads businesses. (As the "community school" is swallowed up by larger consolidated schools, however, the school may cease to be a focus for such communities.) But if the term "community" is commonly used among all the "races," what is meant by it and how it is used in the construction of group identity and political action is decidedly different for each "race."

Whites have placed importance on definiteness and the built environment—on communities named after merchants who run stores deemed to be at the heart of the community, on boundary lines surveyed for towns, on railroads that create or destroy communities. Indians and Blacks have lacked control over most of these matters, at least until very recently. For Blacks in Robeson County (most of whom are urban in the sense that they live in or just outside of towns), focal points are town communities with businesses that often serve Black people almost exclusively and with churches that are politically engaged. There are some predominantly Black rural communities, but they tend to look to the towns for leadership and activities to identify with. The Indian sense of community, by contrast, seems less heavily dependent either on the built environment or on the physical features of the land. Instead, the quality of human relations defines space. The focus is on places where "our people" are living. Church and school buildings get built where there are already Indian people—a reinforcement of community rather than a creation of community like that which so often occurred, in White cases, around a crossroads store or a new railroad stop.

At least some communities have persisted over a long time, even

though the characters imputed to them by Indians and by others, especially Whites, have changed. Although Prospect has long been considered important, it seems to have shifted from being "*the* center" to being
"*a* center" in rivalry with the upstart Pembroke, formerly "a rough town"
but now "the cultural and educational center of the Indian people."
Pembroke, now a town, used to be a densely Indian rural community
that Whites called Scuffletown. But whether town or country, center
or periphery, community as a place remains inextricably connected to
family, neighbors, and "our people."[9]

The way localized communities are conceived of by Indians also provides a view of the diversity of opinion, concern, and action among
Indian people generally. It is a way of acknowledging a multiplicity of
outlooks and ways of living in the world without reducing this diversity to "factionalism," as has too often been done. There are many ways
to be Indian in these communities—very "exposed" to other "races" or
not very exposed, culturally conservative or culturally progressive, "respectable" or "bad," "mean," or "tough," poor or well-off, landowning,
renting, sharecropping, or wage laboring, rural or "urban." A range of
possibilities and judgments about the communities are contained in say-
ings, stories, and descriptions of them and in the attitudes conveyed
about them. These possibilities, exemplified by the local areas, allow for
variety without threatening to deconstruct a more encompassing version of Indianness.[10] This permits both continuity and, simultaneously,
change. Some notions are shared, others subsumed and contested, but all
are negotiated as circumstances change. If this were not the case, they
would quickly cease to have emotional or cognitive relevance.

For people who had increasingly little control over their physical environment, who lost "ownership" of so much land, an orientation in
space centered on people makes sense. Social relations within the larger
community could more readily be controlled and enjoyed, could be
more predictable and satisfying than the inevitable frustrations and dis-
appointments connected with struggles over where the railroad should
go. For Indians at that time to have attempted to control railroad building and swamp draining would have been for them to try to win a card
game in which they were dealt no cards. They could disrupt the game
for a while, as the Lowry band did, but their resources were too scant to
make disruption a long-term strategy.

At the same time, vagueness and a certain amount of "invisibility" of
boundaries, of place, have been useful because it is difficult physically to
find people, to pinpoint Indian individuals in space, and difficult to place
people socially. Henry Berry Lowry and his band depended on their fluidity of movement within an amorphous space for their security and
their ability to "live off the land," just as modern Indians sometimes rely

on indirection from neighbors to avoid bill collectors, social workers, and even the odd anthropologist. Most White communities are plotted on maps, but most Indian and Black ones are not. Even when they are, the boundaries given on the maps are, to Indians, artificial and misleading, as in the case of Pembroke, where the community is so much larger than the town. Whites, however, like their communities more precisely located and closely defined.

This helps account for two quite different "stories" about Pembroke. The current White story is that Pembroke came into being in 1892 with the coming of one of the railroads. It discounts earlier discussions of "Scuffletown," a place that attracted White attention through Indian violence. The contemporary Indian story begins with "the settlement," a more acceptable term than "Scuffletown," and sees a definite continuity between this earlier community, long a rural entity, and the modern town of Pembroke, a formally White creation that Indians had to struggle to get control over. An intermediate proposal by Indians in 1885 to found "Oxendineville" has dropped out of both Indian and White folk history, so far as I can tell, but it speaks through its documents of an earlier attempt to shape space and create the sort of place Whites created, an attempt by Indians to sit down at the card table and be dealt a hand (Oxendineville 1885; see Blu 1994:286–87). They were denied, and it took more than half a century for Indians to take over the governing of Pembroke. For Indians, the ill-defined "communities" were places where power could be consolidated and exercised away from the penetrating Foucaultian "gaze" of more powerful Whites.

If Whites tended to focus on visible aspects of the landscape, or on creating visible aspects, Indians and Blacks concentrated on social aspects.[11] Both Indians and Blacks were "deceptive," keeping a lower profile than they might have liked in a far-from-ideal world. Both were nurtured and gained strength from their different kinds of low visibility to Whites. In a situation of unequal power and wealth, of unequal ability to control or affect the landscape, the unseen, the unmarked became a source of potential strength and resistance, an empowering counterconstruction.

HAVING AND SHARING A "HOME PLACE": SOME MORE GENERAL CONSIDERATIONS

Visually vague communities, then, are at the core of Robeson County Indians' ideas of "home place," which in turn are pivotal for their current sense of peoplehood, their ethnicity. Just as ethnic identity, if its emotional and practical relevance is to be maintained, must be constantly renewed and reconstructed as situations change, so, too, must senses of place change as circumstances do. Part of this change, a fairly large part of it in the Lumbee case, comes about because of contestation over place—where it shall be, whose it shall be, what kind it should be, what it should look like, smell like, provide, whether it should be maintained or cease to exist. These contests are familiar to anyone connected for long to a place in today's world. For Lumbees, arguments over place and space have come both from outside the group and from within it—from Whites and Blacks near and far, and from disagreements among Robeson Indians themselves, exemplified by "community" rivalries.

A sense of "home place" is problematical in the world today—it is a theoretical problem for social analysts trying to understand a postmodern world full of nationalisms, transnationals, and cosmopolites as well as a pressing political problem for people who disagree with one another over home place and who should control it. We have only to look at the fighting in Lebanon and India in the name of religions, at the breakup of Czechoslovakia and the old USSR in the name of more localized nationalisms, and at the disintegration and ethnocide rife in what used to be Yugoslavia to see some of the more dramatic political consequences of contestation over home place. Can the Robeson County situation help us at all to think about these larger and more highly charged instances?

Like Lebanon, some parts of India, and the former Yugoslavia, the territory of Robeson County is home to several distinctly different sorts of people, locally defined as "races" in older parlance, as "ethnic groups" in more recent terms. These different peoples share a single "home place," construct it differently, take different moral views of it, and have experienced vast changes in it and in their relations with each other over time. Bombarded as we are these days with vivid media images of the horrors of fighting in places that apparently used to possess some unity, it is perhaps well to remember that not everyone possesses a sense of home place, either positive or negative. Some people were simply born somewhere and have gone on to live and work somewhere else, and none of the places where they have lived or that they conjure up exists in their imaginations or in their experiences as all important or identity bestowing. They do not have a significant, emotional relationship to a place they designate "home," by which they mean something other than the place where their kinspeople happen to be.

On the other hand, some people (often known these days as transnationals) claim more than one home place. During World War II, for example, a despairing issei Japanese immigrant, asked whether his loyalties lay with Japan or America, told a young, uncomprehending U.S. military officer, "When your mother and your father are fighting, you don't want one of them to win, you want them both to stop fighting."[12] Home place, then, is where a person feels rooted, whether the roots are distant in time or recently sunk. This is one of the ties Clifford Geertz, Edward Shils, and others have called "primordial," a term many have mistakenly taken to refer to rootedness in the past rather than rootedness in strongly held, deeply felt emotions, which was its original sense. The emotional tie obviously may be concurrent with ties of kinship, marriage, or friendship, and it may be connected to relations of status and intellect as well. Often there is a nostalgic element to the emotion, or at least to the evocation of home place, both by those who claim it as home and those who do not. Nostalgia is frequently a strong element in current discussions about American Indian places.

Few home places are simple. Rarely do "a" people, "a" culture, and "a" society inhabit "a" place anymore, if they ever did. One group's home place may be another group's home place, too, which can be a terrible problem if the multiple claimants have different views of what should be done with the home place, how people should act while there, and who should be allowed to live there. In extreme forms, we get the horror of the Holocaust or of "ethnic cleansing." Even when a single group of people agrees that a place is their home place, they may violently oppose one another over what is to become of it, as we saw not too many years ago among some Mohawks of northern New York state and southern Canada, when one group supported a gambling enterprise on the reservation and another saw it as an abomination.

Alternatively, one group's home place may be a territory where other people live who do not see it as a home place but merely as a residence. Some people, for example, wish to reside in the United States and in other economically better-off countries of the world for economic rather than for patriotic or chauvinistic reasons.

Many problems arise in home places when claims of exclusivity are made about them. Some people claim prior or original or legal or moral rights to exclusive ownership, use, political sway, or economic dominion at the expense of the social and economic positions of other people who inhabit the same places. This sense of exclusivity can foster pernicious nationalisms and deadly policies of discrimination. Many places that are inhabited by a number of contesting groups (Jerusalem, for example), all with competing, historically impressive, and so far mutually exclusive claims, end up with states of siege and partisan warfare and pay a terrible price for zealotry among competitors.

Perhaps the small case of the Lumbees and their Black and White neighbors can illuminate a different sense of home place, one that is not (or not so far, for these things can change, sometimes seemingly overnight) based on exclusivity of use or ownership or habitation. No one I have heard or heard of has suggested that Indians and only Indians should live in Robeson County. Nor have the county's Blacks or Whites adopted that rhetorical or philosophical position. Yet for all three, the county or various portions of it are counted as one or another kind of home place. Indeed, for Indians, one of the values of Robeson County as a home place is that there are "others" (that is, non-Indians) present who validate the distinctiveness and reality of their Indianness. These others are people who "know who we are" (who are among the "wise," in Erving Goffman's terms), people who know how to behave respectfully toward Indians (if they are decent people and care to do that), people who can "appreciate our ways."

Although Lumbees have not tried to exclude non-Indians from Robeson County, they have sometimes tried to keep non-Indians from buying land in heavily Indian areas like Prospect. Indians want others to recognize them as Indians and to acknowledge their legitimate original position and status in the home place. They want, of course, more control over their own lives and destinies. The idioms about "race" relations that I heard from Indians during the heated political times of the late 1960s ranged from one of avowedly Christian sharing or forbearance ("We don't want to do to them what they've done to us") to a more aggressive version ("If they don't mess with us, we won't mess with them"), but all of them partook of a "live and let live" attitude.

Lumbee notions of home place do not conflict directly with their neighbors' notions in the matter of exclusivity, but they do differ in the way home place connects to ethnic identity, to perceived peoplehood as a whole. For Indians, "Robeson County" stands for the heart of their homeland, which includes portions of counties surrounding Robeson in both North and South Carolina, in much the way Pembroke as an Indian community encompasses a wider surrounding territory than Pembroke town alone, as defined by its legal limits. Members of the greater Lumbee-Cheraw-Tuscarora Indian population live in adjacent counties and in a number of urban areas as well, but for all of them, Robeson County represents home. It is a place where a country style and rhythm of life prevailed at least until recently and is still much in evidence despite industrial inroads. It is a place where personal knowledge and personal connections count for a lot, where the climate is damp from the swamps and the sky is a dominant feature of the flat land, and where food tastes "right," better than it does in other places. Food and its differences in taste, texture, proper preparation, and flavoring were sources of continual discussion, particularly among those who had been away and come home.

Had I been more attuned to multiple sensory experiences of place, such as the sounds of place so vibrantly depicted by Steven Feld (1982), I would have paid much closer attention to sound and to the smells and tastes of home, to the fine points of discussions about food, cooked and raw, made for family and given in exchange.[13] It is widely known that each area of the South has its own particular version of barbecue, and that particularity extends even more locally to families. Indians I spoke with asserted strongly that "real" barbecue, which in this area of North Carolina has nothing to do with the tomato-based sweetened sauce of the Texas version, had to be pork-based, in addition to having the right vinegar and hot red pepper spicing.

If home for Indians in Robeson County is the site of the major concentration of "our people," is importantly where "we belong," and includes the places where highly significant events of "our history" took place, then how does it differ from what home is to Blacks and Whites? For Whites, home seems to be centered on a home place that is a house or property to which one's family is or was importantly attached, whether as owner or tenant. That home place is, of course, embedded in its neighborhood and wider district and has a kind of generalized aura about it. Some White families have been in Robeson County for many generations and are deeply proud of that fact, but the home place association does not unite them in a sense of peoplehood, of strong group identity as White southerners or even as Robeson County White southerners (for class and ethnicity play dividing roles there), though perhaps for some the home place carries with it a sense of White Tarheel identity. (North Carolinians may refer to themselves as Tarheels just as people from Indiana may call themselves Hoosiers.) For Whites, the identification is at once more specific (familial) and more general (state compatriots).

For Blacks, the situation is different still. Certainly home place also means the place where family are or were located. Family reunions bring together often widely dispersed descendants in large numbers. Faye Harrison (1995) mentions that more than two hundred people attended a Black family reunion in Halifax County, North Carolina, in 1992. Such reunions can be considerably larger and can attract descendants from as far away as California (Walter A. Jackson, personal communication, 1993).

Yvonne V. Jones, working elsewhere in North Carolina, draws a distinction between family reunions and homecomings, which take place at churches rather than on farms, although they are not "religious ceremonies" (1980:58). The homecomings, she says, include broader kin networks and "affective ties attached to a specific locale," reminding people that there is a historical grounding for their relationships and that "regardless of the degree of kin connectedness," they are "all one people" (Jones 1980:62). She suggests that the homecomings can be thought of as an expression of "hamlet identity" in relation to other hamlets and notes that Black extended families use family reunions to compete locally for status and prestige (Jones 1980:58).

A more encompassing kind of homecoming is discussed by William Wiggins, Jr., in his study of emancipation celebrations (1987). He expands upon the various meanings of "home" in this context:

> Celebration fellowship is closely associated with the concept of home. . . . Home, the destination of these freedom pilgrimages, has numerous meanings. Physically, it is that domicile in which the celebrants grew up before moving away as adults. But, spiritually, terms like "down-home" refer to "a sense of place" shared by a particular group of people. Socially, "home" implies a much broader kinship system than the nuclear family; it is a "sentiment of corporateness," or a cultural concept which "reflects the intermingling of nuclear family members, other kinsmen, and non-kinsmen." (Wiggins 1987: 79–80; I have omitted his citations to other authors)

But no one of these particular homes stands metonymically for the whole people, for all African Americans. The emancipation celebrations commemorate the end of slavery in the United States and as such touch the historical traditions of the whole African American population, but they link that population to various "home" places (hence the varieties of communities in which the celebrations take place, as well as the number of different dates upon which the celebrations occur, as Wiggins [1987] well documents).

Lumbees, too, have both family reunions and homecomings that are associated with particular churches. Since 1970, they have also held a huge homecoming on Fourth of July weekend, located mostly in and around Pembroke, to celebrate and honor all Indians, living and dead, for whom Robeson County is home. A powwow is part of the celebration, attracting participants from a wide variety of Indian nations whose home places are scattered across the United States. For Lumbees, as for many other North American Indians (and, according to Owen Lynch [1996] and E. V. Daniel [1984], for at least some Asian Indians as well), an origin place or a place where one "belongs" is considered a vital part of personhood, as attached to one as an arm or a leg.

What sets Lumbees and other North American Indians apart from Blacks and Whites is that having a particular home place in the United States makes them a particular people; it is a fundamental part of their identity as a "nation," "tribe," or "group." A home place stands for the whole people, is synonymous with them. In the case at hand, Robeson County (or sometimes even Pembroke) and Lumbee Indian identity are one, even for those Lumbees who have never lived there. The strong sense of home place and the vital interconnection between localized life and the life of the group generates an image of diaspora when people migrate. For African Americans with family roots in North Carolina, attachment to Carolina places generates a subgroup, not a people. For Lumbees and other Native Americans, the attachment to a particular place or set of places is necessary, not optional, for their group identity. It defines them as particular peoples.

In the United States, American Indians are generally considered to be peoples with a special set of relations to federal and state governments. The issue of what a home place is and what sort of special connections indigenous people have to it has been and continues to be vital and repeatedly contested. Indian identities have seemed to hinge crucially on their retention or reconstruction of and access to a home place, perhaps because displacement was so common and so devastating, so politically beyond the control of most groups throughout their histories. Whether one's group has a reservation or not is still a vital distinguishing feature among contemporary Native Americans.

The reservation system is a product of struggle between Indians and Whites for primacy of place—for the right to inhabit and control place and space. It has brought with it a peculiar fixing of the relations between Indian people and their reserved lands. In order to maintain legal claims to the land, Indians have had to present themselves as having been in the same place, often for time out of mind (or at least since the first European or American documents locate them somewhere), and as having had an unchanging kind of connection to their landscape. Anything that bolsters that notion—ancient myths recounting places of emergence, religious rites as old as any memories or written records, ancestors buried there—counts as evidence of "real" Indian existence to governmental agencies and the popular media. Such claims and demonstrations may be justified, but they also speak strongly to White notions that Indians who change are not "really" Indian and that entitlement to property is embedded in the legal system of this country.

Such claims tend also to encourage a stereotyped view of "an" Indian people with "its" own culture and social organization located in "a" designated territory. Even when, as on some reservations, the territory is shared, the stereotype persists. It is a "premodern" view that contributes to the systematic skewing of relations between land and Indian peoples on reservations. Indians, for their part, need to make their claims convincing to federal or state legislators, lawyers, and policy implementers and are often forced to argue for their priority in time and stability in space in order to fit other Americans' ideas about Indianness, property, and rights.

Although nonreservation Indian peoples have faced a variety of other pressures, such as institutionalized racism in the Lumbee case, they have not had to cope with such narrow and systematically biased concerns as reservation Indians have had to deal with. Therefore, they may provide us with some better ideas of what an earlier, less systematically skewed relationship between Indian people and their land might have been. Classically, anthropologists and historians have looked to reservation Indians as people who carry on traditions (at least more than nonreservation Indians do), who know more about "ancient customs," who continue a "traditional" relationship to their land, and who thus provide the best window, even if not always a clear one, into the past. I propose that although this may be true for some areas of knowledge and social organization, for other matters — particularly Indian-land relationships — nonreservation people may offer better clues to the past. Perhaps the Lumbees and people like them can provide a glimpse, at a distance and through lenses not quite designed for our particular eyes, of possibly older forms of indigenous attachment to land.

This looking back has many difficulties and cannot be done straightforwardly, but the Lumbee kind of emphasis on people, on community, makes it easier to understand the many apparent movements of eastern Indians before and just after Europeans arrived. If eastern Indian notions about the land they lived on had been similar to those of, for example, the pueblo-dwelling Tewas of New Mexico, then their ability to cope with frequent and widespread movement and resettlement would be almost impossible to understand. According to Alfonso Ortiz (1969), Tewas see themselves as situated amid sacred mountains, springs, earth navels, and other highly visible or important places defining "the Tewa world." For a group like the Tewas, frequent and wide-ranging moves would, presumably, be entirely wrenching and destructive of basic worldview. (The Tewa worldview, in fact, fits nicely with their having lived in essentially the same place for many centuries.) But for a group that in earlier times embraced a Lumbee-like notion of place, population movements, whether chosen or forced, would be less disruptive, and society could more readily be reconstituted and settled in a new space.

By proposing a Lumbee-like construction of place as a model for understanding at least some eastern Indian history (and prehistory), in no way do I mean to suggest that Lumbees or the ancestors of any eastern Indians did not care about the land they lived on, that they were indifferent about where they resided, or that they were oblivious to the physical features of their environment. The emotional and cognitive attachment Robeson County Indians have to their geographical area is and has been extremely strong, but it is the combination of land and people together that makes the tie so compelling for them. A person has to know the land intimately to locate a community that is not visually marked.

NOTES

1. My debt to the many Indians of Robeson County who have been generous with their time and hospitality over the years is enormous and on-going. I name no names when I could have named dozens because I promised anonymity, in standard anthropological fashion. For their detailed comments and inspired commentaries on the manuscript for this chapter, I am deeply indebted to Keith H. Basso, Edward Casey, Steven Feld, Raymond J. DeMallie, Joan Lehn, Frank T. Miller, and, most of all, Clifford Geertz, who endured multiple versions and still managed fresh responses. For thoughtful comments and helpful suggestions on one part of the chapter or another, I thank Raymond D. Fogelson, Loretta Fowler, Charles O. Frake, Miriam Kahn, Owen M. Lynch, Geoffrey Mangum, Nancy Munn, and Kathleen Stewart. The standard disclaimer applies—any errors or misunderstandings are mine, not theirs.

2. I have systematically capitalized all three sets of people in Robeson County— Black, Indian, and White—in order to give them a textual equality despite the social and economic inequalities they continue to experience. Leaving one or two of the categories unmarked ("white," for example, is usually not capitalized) suggests that the unmarked category is the normal or standard category rather than the odd one, the exception. One has only to see male and Female as printed forms to understand the point.

3. In looking at these aspects of landscape, I am inspired by David M. Schneider's dictum to look at what is not done as well as what is done, at what is unmarked as well as marked, and by Keith Basso's landmark work on silence in Western Apache culture (1970b).

4. I use the term "Lumbee" here because most Native Americans in Robeson County designate themselves as Lumbees, although some people call themselves Lumbee-Cheraw, others Tuscarora, and a few prefer Cherokee. The groups are all intermarried and interlaced by bonds of kinship. For the sake of simplicity, I will mostly use the term "Indian" because that is the term all the groups of Native Americans in Robeson County use among themselves, a term that still unifies rather than divides.

5. There are disagreements about the origins of the name Pembroke. Dial and Eliades (1975:142–43) say, "How the new community acquired the name of Pembroke is disputed. A few people believe that it was named after the British town of Pembroke, but the great majority say it was named after Pembroke Jones, a railway official, and the evidence points to the latter explanation." Thomas (1982:230) is unequivocal: "Pembroke . . . received its name the way several towns did—from a railroad official (Pembroke Jones)."

6. The propensity of young, rural, southern men in general for violent demonstrations of manliness is well known and should not be considered uniquely Indian. But partly because Lumbee identity has hinged on the group's reputation and self-representation as a "mean" people, ready to fight at the hint of a slight or insult, hard and implacable in battle (see Blu 1980), this habit of violence and the testing of

prowess means even more for Indian youths, as more rides on it. John Gregory Peck has noted of young Lumbee men in the late 1960s that they were expected to drink heavily, to be a bit wild and unpredictable, and to fight when challenged or wronged (1972:68).

7. "Bad Indian" is highly nuanced language. It refers to the way Indians imagine that Whites view Indians—that as a category, Indians are "bad." It also suggests a fairly standard meaning reversal employed by Blacks whereby "bad" becomes "good." Further, in the instances mentioned, the Indians involved appeared to invoke jokingly not only the "usual" meanings given by Whites and Blacks but also an allusion to "meanness" (a testy independence of spirit) as a valued quality of their own Indianness (see Blu 1980:144–47).

8. Brenda Farnell, in her study of the Nakota (Assiniboine) people of Montana, discusses the "rich local knowledge of persons" that can be presumed by speakers and that results in, among other things, "the frequent use of pronouns and demonstratives in many contexts so that proper names of places and people are avoided whenever possible" (1990:145, 159). Indians in Robeson County do use proper names of places in conversations, but they assume the listener can mentally follow a route of travel between the places mentioned and will know the character of the land and people in the named places and in between. Unlike Nakotas, Lumbees do usually name a person they are discussing (the number of Lumbees is far greater than the number of Nakotas). Nevertheless, the problem of anaphoric reference mentioned by Farnell is daunting for a nonlocal anthropologist in Robeson County, because after a person is named the welter of pronoun references that often follows assumes just the same kind of "rich local knowledge of persons."

9. For further elaboration of the ethnohistory of these local communities, see Blu (1994).

10. For a widely shared set of notions about Indianness, see Blu (1980:134–68).

11. I want to make it clear that Lumbees do talk about their geographical area in other than "community" terms. Many times people mentioned the Lumbee, or Lumber, River, describing its sinuous and dangerous ways. Others talked about the beauty of tobacco fields in bloom or of golden, flue-cured tobacco leaves of the highest grade. People hunted over the land and fished the swamps and rivers (S. Marks 1991). But the communities defined the space of Robeson County most of all, identifying self and others in conversation, in storytelling, and in traveling about.

12. Paraphrased from Jeanne and James Houston's (1973) moving account of her family's internment during World War II.

13. Brett Williams (1988) notes that food (and gardens producing food) were important aspects of shared "Carolina culture" in the Washington, D.C., neighborhood where she worked. When people went "home" to the Carolinas for visits, they always returned with food that they distributed among family, neighbors, and friends in the city.

7

Pleasant Places, Past Times, and Sheltered Identity in Rural East Anglia

Charles O. Frake

East Anglia is the lost continent of Great Britain.
— *Len Deighton*, XPD

How, and why, is a sense of remoteness — of a place lost — maintained with regard to a region that has not, in any obvious way, been marginal to much of anything since Roman times? I argue here that a search for answers to this question tells us something both about my natives, in this case the English, in particular and also about the issues of place and identity in general.

To begin the search, consider first one of the less momentous events that marked the end of the nineteenth century in England. At that time, along with *Country Life* magazine, the Ancient Monuments Act, the Society for the Protection of Ancient Buildings, the National Trust for Places of Historic Interest and Natural Beauty, the British Naturalists' Association, the Society for the Promotion of Nature Reserves, the Society for Checking the Abuses of Public Advertising, the Commons Preservation Society, the National Footpaths Preservation Society, and the Society for the Preservation of the Wild Fauna of the Empire, there appeared the organization whose name suggested the title for this chapter: the Selbourne Society for the Protection of Birds, Plants and Pleasant Places.[1]

It is not the task here to explain why such organizations appeared with curious near-simultaneity at that moment of history, nor is it to argue that their appearance had great impact on subsequent history. Their appearance, as I said, was not momentous. It was, however, symbolic. At least in retrospect, we can see something very "English" in this joint concern with such things as plants, animals, footpaths, natural beauty, ancient monuments, and old buildings—all to be protected and preserved, not so much "as they are" but rather "as they were" in an imagined past of pleasant places. It is the "Englishness" of all this that I propose to explore. The terrain of this exploration comprises the region of England known as East Anglia, specifically the County of Norfolk, which, although part of a "lost continent" to Len Deighton, is to James Wentworth Day, a popular journalist, "the most English corner of all England" (P. Wright 1985: 68). But first, in the tradition of "ethnographic background," something must be said of these "English" and of this corner of their homeland.[2]

THE NATIVES AND THEIR PLACE

As subjects of anthropological investigation, the English are a rather troublesome tribe. They are easy enough to identify, and they know who they are. That's not the problem. The problem is that for anthropologists hungry for the taste of the exotic, the English seem to provide rather vapid fare (gastronomic metaphors somehow come to mind to an ethnographer in England). From the anthropologist's point of view, the English have no "culture," a failing that is very hard to explain to the English.[3] The English, an anthropologist might argue, have a restricted view of what "culture" really is. But so, in a complementary way, does the anthropologist. Anthropologists have long struggled to accord cultural dignity and intellectual interest to the strange practices of peoples of the world ignored by other disciplines. The struggle has been so successful, at least within anthropology, that culture, and therefore intellectual interest, has become tacitly identified with exotic practices. The height of culture for an anthropologist is not a Bach cantata; it is an asymmetrical circulating connubium. (It should be a well-executed conversational riposte in Toronto, Tulsa, or Tikopea.)

Every anthropologist would now deny this identification of "culture" with the exotic. But despite increasing interest in "the Western world," our practice still belies our denials.[4] Anthropologists now go to Europe in respectable numbers, but most head for the marginal, the rural, and the "ethnic" places. I decided to work in England, after long working with people as exotic as any anthropologist could desire, partly out of a perverse challenge. Could I make the English interesting? They are, after all, human in spite of their relatively central role in the world system. Still, I don't want to make them interesting by transforming them into some kind of exotic other. Much less do I want to make them interesting by transforming them into unwitting dupes of hegemonic oppression. I would like to make them interesting for the ways their lives inform what it is to be human in this world we all live in.

Yet despite these noble declarations, I seem to be sufficiently imbued with the anthropological habitus to have yearned for some bit of exotica. After all, I did pick a region of England that is rural, at least in local image. And that perhaps explains why, while reading a spy story to pass the time on a plane, I latched onto a characterization of my field site as a "lost continent." That, I must have subconsciously thought, might spark a bit of interest among my colleagues. The real reason this "lostness" is interesting, however, lies not in the factuality of it but in the image of it as both an outcome of and a contributor to local practices of constructing an identity for persons and their places.

East Anglia may be lost in the imagination of the English, but its inhabitants are, in everyone's mind, English to the core. They are not, in anyone's mind, "ethnic" or even "peculiar." They are sufficiently non-exotic to have never before, to my knowledge, attracted the attention of an ethnographer. The image of lostness may in fact be tied to the visible absence of ethnic minorities in rural East Anglia. My more cynical local friends tell me that this show of pure, white Englishness is, as much as the appeal of the countryside, what makes rural East Anglia such an attractive retirement area for British city dwellers. If one's place is "lost," perhaps all those foreigners and ethnics that one used to confront in London, Liverpool, and Manchester will not be able to find it. Of course one can be terrifyingly lost in a city or, outside England, in a wilderness. But romantic, poetic, pleasant lostness occurs in the rural English countryside, in a maze of narrow, hedged-lined roads obscured from but never too far from church, pub, or country house.

The image of ruralness associated with East Anglia has a firm historical foundation.[5] The water-powered industrial revolution of the eighteenth and early nineteenth centuries largely passed East Anglia by. This chalk and alluvial shelf jutting out into the North Sea was, the stock explanation goes, too flat and waterlogged for effective use of hydraulic power. But the absence of industry and its accompanying proletariat must also have been closely tied to the early capitalization of East Anglian agriculture. That created a farming system dependent on the existence of a landless class of cheap farm labor. East Anglia led the way, not only in England but in the world, toward capitalized, commercial, mechanized agriculture, controlled by investors and landowners, operated by a managerial class of resident "farmers," and worked by landless farm laborers.[6] As long as this system was profitable for farmers and landowners, there was little incentive to attract alternate sources of employment for farm workers.

This history of a prosperous, rural, but commercial economy extends well back into the Middle Ages. East Anglia was then a major center

Figure 7.1. A Pleasant Place: The northeast Norfolk landscape, looking inland from the North Sea coastal dunes. Drawing by Terence Loan.

of wool production and trade. Norwich, Norfolk's city, was second only to London in England. The profusion of medieval church towers that dot the skyline in any view over the landscape of Norfolk and Suffolk is testimony to the wealth possessed by landowners and merchants during that era (fig. 7.1).

After the postmedieval enclosure of farms and the capitalization of agriculture, the main source of wealth became the growing of grain, especially wheat. This rural economy has been an integral part of the world system since its beginnings. Prosperity was greatest at times of major European wars. The Napoleonic period, World War I, and World War II were the good times for farmers. In between, during most of the nineteenth century and the mid-twentieth, times were hard for farmers and farm workers. Since World War II, prosperity for farmers has been maintained by Common Market farm supports that encouraged a great expansion of grain and oil-seed fields, accomplished by the draining of wetlands and the appropriation of grazing land. These transformations of the real landscape have seriously threatened the image of the English countryside. Although farming is still by far the major source of wealth in East Anglia, the number of people engaged in farming is a very small percentage of the total population. For most of the rest, the land is not a source of wealth but a constituent of the ambience of their place, an ambience that contains their identities and inspires their lives.[7]

TALKING ABOUT PLACE

". . . I found myself in short in Thornton Lacey."
"It sounds like it," said Edmund.
". . . you would never be able to prove that it was *not* Thornton Lacey—for such it certainly was."
"You inquired then?"
"No, I never inquire. But I *told* a man mending a hedge that it was Thornton Lacey, and he agreed to it."
—*Jane Austen*, Mansfield Park

Not only are the English deficient as "natives" in the anthropological image but they also provide, in their talk, a special embarrassment to the ethnographer of place. One of the fundamental principles in the early days of cognitive anthropology was that if you wanted to know what was important to a people you had to find out what questions they asked of each other. "How're you two related?" "What's new?" "What do you do?" "What's happening?" As one of the alleged founders of this field once rashly advised ethnographers: "Look for query-rich settings" (Frake 1964). Unfortunately, English queries about place seem hardly more common now, at least in Norfolk, than in Jane Austen's time. True, one may sometimes hear inquiries about location from lost Londoners on holiday who have carelessly neglected to bring along their Ordnance Survey map or A–Z city plan. But the wait for a query about place of origin—the stock American get-acquainted ploy, "Where're yuh from?"—can be a long one. In marked contrast to American practice, one does not ask this of the English without seeming to cause a certain amount of understated discomfort.

There is, so far as I am aware, no real empirical evidence of the frequency of inquiries about place of origin in the discourse of the English, but the impression that one does not casually ask the provenance of someone one does not know well is certainly widespread. It is mentioned in humorous treatises on English-American differences: "Curiously, for people who identify so closely with region of origin, Brits refuse to tell outsiders where they're from. . . . [If you ask one] he freezes, tongue-tied. You have intruded somehow on private matters, and embarrassed him" (Walmsley 1987:82). An Englishman's place is sheltered, protected, secluded—a lost continent within which to hide the self. One does not intrude. We will return to this interactional peculiarity shortly.

The ethnographer's embarrassment is happily assuaged by the fact that the English do talk and write about place all the time and have been doing so for hundreds of years. It is, after all, their use of our language through all these years that has given the peculiarly English word "place" its rich semantic field, one that fills six three-column pages in the new edition of the *Oxford English Dictionary*. Its entry for "place" begins:

> Place has superseded OE. *stow* and (largely) *stede;* it answers to F. *lieu,* L. *locus,* as well as to F. *place,* and the senses are thus very numerous and difficult to arrange.

This characterization points up an etymological curiosity embedded in the English talk of place over the last nine hundred years since the conquest of England by French-speaking descendants of Norse-speaking Vikings. There are four sets of terms involved. First are the terms for the notion of "place," "location," "position," "site," and so forth, which are all forms of Romance origin (although, as the OED definition notes, the meaning correspondences are not the same as in their French sources).[8] These Romance forms did not add to the English language; they replaced Anglo-Saxon forms that now survive only in placenames.

Second are terms for the description or study of places, words such as those defined for us by Thomas Fuller in 1642 (II, vii, 75):

> Acquainted with Cosmography, treating the world in whole joynts; with Chorography, shredding it into countries; and with Topography, mincing it into particular places.

These are learned adoptions from Greek, another language rich in worlds for "place." Today, "cosmography" and "chorography" are obscure, even though the latter term does appear in several old guidebooks and local histories such as John Norden's early-seventeenth-century *Chorography of Norfolk* (Hood 1938). On the other hand, "topography," a nineteenth-century favorite, has survived as a well-known term today.[9] Almost every bookstore and library in East Anglia has shelves so labeled filled with guidebooks, travel descriptions, local histories, and racks of Ordnance Survey maps.

Third are terms that label kinds of "places," like "settlements," "villages," "hamlets," "lakes," "rivers," "steams," "creeks," "marshes," "fens," and so on, which present a mixed bag of Anglo-Saxon and Romance forms. Some are common throughout the English-speaking world, some, like "fen," "moor," and "mews," are peculiarly British (though well known everywhere to readers of British mystery novels), and some, like Norfolk's "broad," "carr," "staithe," and "loke," are associated with particular localities. Finally, there are names for individual places, names which in East Anglia and elsewhere in England are almost exclusively Anglo-Saxon (or in a few cases Saxonized Roman versions of earlier Celtic names). Neither Celtic precursors nor Anglo-Norman successors are recognized as having had a noticeable effect on the names that now fill the map of England, for the most part names already inscribed in the Domesday Book, William the Conqueror's inventory of the places and resources of his new land.[10]

NAMES FOR PLACES

I grew up in a neighborhood right next to a Black . . . right next to Harlem. . . . We called our little neighborhood White Harlem—cuz it sounded bad.
"Where're yuh from?"
"White Harlem."
"Heh!"
The real name was Morningside Heights.
— *George Carlin,* Occupation: Foole, *1973*

Discussions over what constitutes "place" have, as Keith Basso (1988) pointed out in a classic contribution, often overlooked a simple but universal attribute of places: places, like persons, have individual names. In fact, unlike persons, whose creation precedes naming, places come into being out of spaces by being named. All cultures not only label kinds of places, such as "settlements," "streams," "lakes," and "mountains," but they also name individual places like "Paris," "Bull Run," "Tahoe," and "Pinatubo." By finding what is named, one can quickly compile an inventory of local places with respect not only to their locations but also to their scope. For, unlike persons, whose phenomenal boundaries are (*pace* postmodern desconstructers of the self) relatively apparent, places can range from dimensionless points to infinite universes. The limits of a name serve, like a verbal fence, to enclose an individual place as a spatial self.

Peoples differ in how they mark off continuous spaces into bounded places. In Los Angeles, the same name attaches to a street for miles and miles regardless of interruptions by freeways, railroads, and airports. In London, each intersection and each bend seems to bring a new street name, a different place. Some Philippine peoples cut up rivers the way Londoners do streets. Americans, on the other hand, can get into political squabbles over which upstream branch continues the "same" river. Such a fight over the boundaries of a fluvial self occurred, I have been told by Rocky Mountain compatriots, in tracing the Colorado River (then the "Grand") to its "true" headwaters in the state of Colorado. The losing branch—the longer one, actually—became the Green, a river that arises in the rival state of Wyoming and joins the Colorado River in Utah, avoiding all but a tiny corner of Colorado. The state of Colorado, say its neighbors, stole a river and then renamed it for itself.

Names not only permit the demarcation of contiguous places but also reveal an organization of embedded places. This embedded structure, a universal feature of place naming, means that any given location can lay claim to a series of names. Where did I stay last summer? "Above Tom Plowman's shop," "on High Street," "in Stalham," "in North Norfolk," "in Norfolk," "in East Anglia," "in England," "in Britain," "in the UK," "in Europe," "overseas." Each of these answers truly names my location then. The answer I select says something about the degree of shared knowledge of place, and hence of mutual experience and common identity, that I accord to my interrogator. The recognition that places have parts shows up not only in the naming of parts, as in "Norfolk" and "North Norfolk," but also in the talk of parts as such. If places are thought of as bounded spaces, then one can envision both the whole place and parts of the place. On many early maps of England, places that appear only partially on the sheet are identified as "parts," for example, "Parte of Suffolk" on Saxton's 1574 map of Norfolk. Maybe that is the source of expressions like "not much excitement in these parts."

This way of referring to place is of some antiquity in English. In a prefeminist backlash of 1558, titled *The First Blast of the Trumpet against the Monstrous Regiment of Women,* John Knox (1558) wrote of a place where "women in those partes, were not tamed nor embased by consideration of their own sex and kind." The practice, common to part-whole terminologies, of naming the whole for a part is shared by placenames. This usage reveals a presumption of prominence of place. The use of "England" is a notorious example, one that irritates non-English inhabitants of the United Kingdom. Those who, like myself, speak of England *sensu stricto* often feel obliged to note the restriction explicitly.[11] A parallel case is offered by the use of "Holland" for the "Netherlands" by English (and German) speakers. Large cities often toponymically annex their politically independent suburbs in this way. The city named New York thus appropriates its whole state.

Places are also related to each other in a network of distance and direction. I could have answered the inquiry about my summer whereabouts with "about twelve miles northeast of Norwich." Locating a place in relation to another place is another way of according that place a presumption of greater prominence. A guide to Norfolk and Suffolk placenames called *Where's That?* (Walker n.d.) locates place by distance to the nearest more prominent place, thus revealing a hierarchy of place prominence. How do I find Stockton? The guide informs me that it is five miles northeast of Bungay. Great, so where's Bungay? Well, the guide warns me that "strangers may have to turn first to another page." I, knowing now that I am a stranger, do so, and find that Bungay is five miles west of Beccles, which yet another page puts twelve miles southwest of Yarmouth. And Yarmouth? The last page tells me it is twenty miles east of Norwich. That actually puts Stockton closer to Norwich than Yarmouth!

The guide, like a human conversationalist, attributes to the person inquiring about place the greatest degree of familiarity with local places that is consistent with the person's original inquiry. If someone doesn't know the whereabouts of an obscure place like Stockton, then the guide first assumes he or she knows the nearest less obscure place, Bungay. It then abandons that assumption as, step by step, each answer is met with new inquiries. The procedure efficiently sorts out us strangers.

There is more to the use of placenames than the formulation and demarcation of place. Sorting out strangers is another kind of work—very important work in East Anglian social encounters—done by placenames. Sounding "bad" in New York is another. In his landmark paper on the social entailments of using placenames, E. A. Schegloff (1972) explored various strategies exhibited in the selection and co-selection of alternative designations for the same location. George Carlin's "White Harlem" and "Morningside Heights" provide a choice example. Schegloff also pointed out, but did not fully explore, the use of placenames to formulate phenomena other than place. Occupation, for example:

A: You uh wha 'dijuh do, fer a living?
B: Ehm, I work inna driving school.
It turns out that B is, in fact, a messenger boy, not an instructor, in the school.
(Schegloff 1972:98)

A critical formulation to be worked out in any English social interaction is social class. In most of England this work is accomplished primarily by one's voice, sometimes inadvertently, often in quite a studied way. In Norfolk and Suffolk, and doubtless elsewhere as well, the marking of one's speech by localisms, an advantage in some contexts and a disadvantage in others, greatly compounds the difficulty of this work. The range of accents displayed, both by the same individual in different situations and by different individuals in the same family, can be quite impressive.[12] Backing up the import of accent are dress and demeanor. Using placenames also supports this work. In situations where one endeavors to bestow as high a class as possible upon oneself—these are, of course, not all situations; sometimes it is better to be bad—it is important to reveal one's badges of identity as subtly and unobtrusively as possible. It is vulgar, a mark of low class, not to do so. Provenance, marked by the name of one's home place, is commonly one of these badges. Some places rank better than others. If one comes from a posh place, it is rather unsightly to proclaim it; if your conversational partner comes from a common place, it is unkind to ask about it. Better not to ask or be asked at all. One does not intrude.

Names are not simply markers and delimiters of place, verbal signposts and fences along a conceptual road. Nor are they simply tokens used to negotiate and mark positions in social interaction. True, as with personal names, their denotative use does not depend on any meaning that can be read into the name. If I tell you I stayed in Stalham last summer, what you need to know is not what "Stalham" means or once might have meant, but what place it names. If you do not know, you do not ask, "What does it mean?" but "Where is it?" Nevertheless, the use of placenames implicates much more than their denotation. In their phonological forms and their semantic suggestiveness, names often become remarkable—worthy of a story—in their own right. For Western Apaches, the mere mention of a placename can tell a story (Basso 1988). Not only are Apache placenames semantically transparent but their meanings also constitute topographic descriptions that are powerfully evocative of incidents in well-known stories. The English language does not seem to have the capacity to pack so much semantic content into a single name. Nevertheless, English placenames are no more mere signposts than are those of any other language. It just takes more work, or at least a different kind of work, to make the verbal signposts more than simple markers of place. The inhabitants of the language's homeland have a long history of crafting noteworthy names for places.

England is famous for its quaint placenames oddly pronounced. Although seldom displaying Cotswaldian excesses such as Stow-on-Wold and Shipton-under-Wychwood, East Anglia contributes its share of toponymic curiosities. Remarkability in an English placename is best achieved with a suggestive but somewhat opaque meaning requiring a bit of imagination to discern. One does not expect in England a "Salt Lake City" next to a big salty lake. The semantic opacity of a placename is much like the patina on a flint tool. It covers the past of the place, hiding a story and a history. The decipherment of an English placename is rather like an archaeological dig. One strips away the deceptive superficial layers to get at the original meaning. The more stripping required, the more ancient, and thus the more interesting, the past.

Consider the North Norfolk place called "Great Hautbois." Conforming to a great English tradition, "Hautbois" is pronounced in a way only a local could know: "Hobbus." This pronunciation, locals insist, demonstrates that the name is not, despite appearances, originally French at all, but real English. Written guides to English placenames support this assertion by giving a derivation from Old English *hobb* + *wisce,* "meadow by a hummock." Old books and maps reveal a long history of variant spellings. The eleventh-century Domesday Book has "Hobuisse" and "Hobuist," Saxton's map of 1574 has "Hobbes," and Faden's map of 1797 has "Hautboys Vulgo Hobbies," implying that the current pronunciation was then seen as a vulgar corruption.[13] What matters now is that the place can be seen as having an authentic English past more ancient than the Norman intrusion of 1066. That is not the end to the Hautbois story, however. It must also be noted that Great Hautbois is a very tiny place, not much more than a ruined church and a Girl Guides camp (Norfolk Federation of Women's Institutes 1990). It does not even show on the current Ordnance Survey 1:50,000 map. Nearby "Little Hautbois," which is on the map, is actually larger and more frequented—it is at the entrance to a major air base.

Such games with "great" and "little" occur elsewhere in North Norfolk. "Great Walshingham" is smaller than "Little Walshingham" (which has been a major pilgrimage destination since medieval times); "Great Snoring" is smaller than "Little Snoring" (and neither, locals delight in telling visitors, has anything to do with noises made while sleeping; the names, they say, are tributes to a distant Viking ancestor named Snorri).[14] "Great Yarmouth" on the other hand, has no "Little" partner. The attribute seems to be a modern addition to the name of this port city, yet citizens assiduously use it in even the most causal references to their place. The "great" and "little" attribution also has more pretentious versions. Some places are "Magna" and "Parva." Suffolk has a case of "Inferior" and "Superior" attached to a place called "Rickinghall."

Other attributes are also popular. Being near any kind of water frequently commands mention everywhere in England, and since being near, if not immersed in, water is not uncommon in that country, the command provides a challenge to toponymic ingenuity. As mentionable water, the sea is best: "Holme-next-Sea," "Wells-next-the-Sea," "Caistor-on-Sea," "Ogmore-by-Sea," "Sea Palling," and, resorting, perhaps in desperation, to Latin, "Weston-Super-Mare." In absence of a sea, however, soggy land will do: the Cotswold hills have their "Moreton-by-Marsh"; Norfolk has its less quaintly phrased "Marsham" and "Fenside."

English placenames may be oddly pronounced and quaint, but they must be *English.* They may never be "foreign." England is not a place for the likes of a "Palo Alto," a "Los Gatos," or a "Santa Cruz"—upscale Anglo-American enclaves in northern California situated amid downscale, heavily Hispanic communities bearing names like "Mountain View," "Gilroy," and "Watsonville." Locals in Palo Alto not only acknowledge the Spanish origin of their placename but also know its meaning, and they can proudly show you a tall tree bearing a sign marking it as the authentic, original *palo alto* of Palo Alto. In Great Hautbois, on the other hand, not only is there no "high wood," there is also a denial of any French association whatsoever. Locals around (there are, actually, not many *in*) Great Hautbois take pains, in their pronunciation and their stories, to display the fundamental Englishness and (which is much the same thing) the deep antiquity of this Norfolk place.

East Anglia does have a number of placenames that locals consider to be "Danish" or "Viking." But the Norse invaders have, after a thousand years, been thoroughly acculturated as part of the "English Heritage."[15] The most noted heritage museum of England is devoted to glorifying the Viking period in York. In East Anglia, a placename ending in "-by," as opposed to the Anglo-Saxon "-ham," is proudly taken to indicate a Norse origin—for example, "Rollesby," "Clippesby," and "Filby," not far from "Ingham," "Stalham," and "Waxham."

On the other hand, the Norse who, as French-speaking Normans, conquered England several centuries later, had, in current views, little impact on placenames. In Norfolk, I have yet to hear any placename interpreted as being French in origin. The only example that the compiler of *A Popular Guide to Norfolk Place-Names* could come up with was a name that referred to the personal name of one of William the Conqueror's standard bearers. Even there, the spelling (Toney for "Toeni") does not make the reference completely transparent, and it is, after all, to a very old Frenchman (Rye 1991:8–9). Another case is instructive: it is said the second element of the South Norfolk village name "Kirby Cane" comes from another of William's knights who came from Caen in Normandy. To argue that an English form so seemingly transparent conceals a story in history is to make the name, albeit French in origin, very English indeed.[16]

In Norfolk, as everywhere else in the world, many kinds of spaces other than settlements become named as places. These names can, like village and town names, be used in ways that contribute to the construction and interpretation of ongoing social interaction. There is, of course, a rich coverage of topographic names for features such as rivers, lakes, marshes, woods, and dunes. Agricultural fields have a long history, diligently pursued locally, of individual names.[17] Residences, too, are commonly named—provided they are of the proper type. To have a residence name rather than a street number in one's address adds both prestige and a presumption of country life-style. It implies that one lives in a "cottage" in a village and not in a house or flat in a town or city. In Norfolk, my address was "92 High Street"; my landlord's mail went to "Goose Marsh Cottage."

Even better than living in a named "cottage" is living in a "hall." A hall is the traditional residence of the lord of the manor. It is named for the place, which is often the name of the original lord. Lord Gresham lived in Gresham Hall near Gresham village. Nowadays, a hall is as likely to be occupied by a real estate agent as by a squire, but the name of the hall does not change. As with boats, there seems to be a sentiment that a residence name belongs inalienably to the building regardless of who lives there.

Placenames, semantically empty as proper nouns, when used in what Certeau calls "the practice of everyday life," become "names that have ceased precisely to be proper. . . . A rich indetermination gives them, by means of a semantic rarefaction, the function of articulating a second, poetic geography on top of the geography of the literal, forbidden or permitted meaning. . . . They seem to be carried as emblems by the travellers they direct and simultaneously decorate." [18]

THE INSCRIPTION OF PLACE

Baile Beag/Ballybeg, County Donegal, Ireland, 1833:
OWEN: The captain is the man who actually makes the new map. George's task is to see that the place-names on this map are . . . correct. . . .
MANUS: . . . it's a bloody military operation, Owen. And what's Yolland's [George's] function? What's "incorrect" about the place-names we have here?
—Brian Friel, Translations

A standard feature in any East Anglian village store is a rack of Ordnance Survey maps for the local area. Bookstores in larger towns have these maps for all of Britain. This cartographic component of English culture has a long history, during which East Anglia was not slighted (Barringer 1989; Chubb 1928; Tyacke and Huddy 1980). Earlier mapping was sponsored by private investors, sometimes backed by the Royal Society. Notable county maps were Saxton's of 1571 and Faden's of 1797. Faden, who was the promoter, not the surveyor, sold his map by individual subscription and newspaper ads (fig. 7.2). The period of agricultural improvements and enclosures produced a large number of small mapping efforts covering individual estates. In 1791 the government set up an official mapping agency, the Ordnance Survey, headed by the Duke of Richmond in his role as Master of the King's Ordnance (he was perhaps motivated by a need to keep updating the surveys of his own estate, which increased from 1,100 acres to 17,000 acres during his tenure—this we learn from the current duke's foreword to the official history of the Survey [Owen and Pilbeam 1992]).

The Survey was charged with the mission of covering the kingdom with maps. It has done a good job. Although it is a government agency

A New Topographical Map of the
COUNTY OF NORFOLK
surveyed and measured in the years
1790, 91, 92, 93 and 94
By Tho. Donald, Tho. Milne
AND ASSISTANTS.

Planned from a scale of one inch to a statute mile.
Executed and published at the expense of the proprietor,
William Faden, Geographer to his Majesty, and to H. R. H.
the Prince of Wales.

In the above map are described all the seats of the nobility
and gentry, woods, parks, heaths, commons, rivers, great
and cross roads, marsh and fen lands, market towns, parishes,
villages, farms etc. Also the remains of Roman roads, camps
and other antiquities; embellished with plans of the towns
of Great Yarmouth, Lynn and Swaftham. The map is printed
on six sheets of the largest atlas papers. Price to subscribers is
Two Guineas and a half, in sheets; to non-subscribers it
will be three guineas.

Figure 7.2. Text from an advertisement in the Norfolk Chronicle,
19 August 1797.

with a military mission, the Survey has always been involved in the commercial aspects of map making; even before the Thatcher era, it was required to support itself by selling its maps to the public. Thus, what is on the maps depends much on public taste, public needs, and public political pressure. Cartographic power, as real as it is (Anderson 1991; Harley 1988), is not monolithic. The cartographic creation of place in Britain has been the outcome of the interplay of a complex of interests and pressures—one of which seems to have been a sincere concern "to get it right," a concern which reveals an underlying assumption that each place has a "correct" name to be discovered. In its history of inscribing placenames, the Ordnance Survey has gone to great lengths to demonstrate its commitment to toponymic, as well as topographic, accuracy. "Truth" in cartography, however, can be an illusive goal for all the familiar postmodern reasons.

Recording local names has caused difficulties for surveyors from the beginning. Regarding Faden's map, J. C. Barringer (1989:2) notes, "The Norfolk pronunciation clearly proved too much for the surveyor of the Aylsham area." But it was the colonial context of Celtic Ireland, where the Ordnance Survey began systematic mapping in the 1830s, that provided the greatest challenge to the aim of "correctly" recording placenames. The ensuing cultural and linguistic misunderstandings, as well as the political entailments of mapping, are wonderfully portrayed in Brian Friel's (1981) play *Translations*. In Ireland, the Survey developed a system of "Name Books" that was subsequently used by surveyors throughout Britain. In these books were listed the names for each place, the variant spellings, and the sources for each variant.

> The spelling of each name was, wherever possible, endorsed by written evidence as 'when taken down by word of mouth, errors are very liable to occur' and surveyors often pasted into the Name Books typed examples to support their recommendation. Almost anything seemed acceptable, from letter headings and local advertisements to extracts from Bradshaws' Railway Guides. . . . Names could be altered with the support of 'at least two good authorities' but important names tended to remain, even if they dropped out of general use and the maps tended to preserve some that would otherwise have faded from existence. . . . In making their recommendations, the Committee always abided by the long-stated principle that Ordnance Survey names should follow those in common use by the residents of an area, even if these were etymologically incorrect or suspect. (Owen and Pilbeam 1992:75)[19]

Ordnance Survey maps not only inscribed the official name in its "correct" spelling but also revealed the importance and significance of the place.

> The printing of names on the maps followed a careful hierarchy with the most important names written in the largest and boldest type. The typestyle used for each name gave further information. For example, if a Borough returned a member of Parliament, then its name was printed the same size as other Borough names but in bold type. Market towns were distinguished from ordinary towns in the same way. (Owen and Pilbeam 1992:75)

Antiquities, officially defined as features dating from before 1714 (the date of accession of George I), were marked as "Roman" by large Roman capitals (ROMAN ROAD) or as "Medieval" by Gothic lettering (𝔚𝔦𝔟𝔢𝔱𝔬𝔫 𝔅𝔯𝔦𝔡𝔤𝔢) (Owen and Pilbeam 1992:75, 152).

A glance at a Survey map, especially one in the small-scale 1:25,000 series, makes it appear that nothing is overlooked. Picking up at random from my desk sheet TG 22/32, Norfolk Broads (North), and beginning at the top righthand corner, I find a small triangle of blue for the sea, some pink for a sandy beach, a line marked MHW for Mean High Water, a seven-meter contour line (all that separates the rest of the map from the North Sea!), a gap through the dunes named "Cart Gap," and a road coded as "generally less than 4 meters wide" (generally much less!) that leads to "New Barn," "Green Farm," and "Whimpwell Green," with fourteen buildings including a "PO" (Post Office). Not far away is "Moat Farm" adjacent to a blue-bordered square labeled, in Gothic lettering to show its medieval antiquity, "𝔐𝔬𝔞𝔱." Convenient to the moat is perhaps the most sought-out symbol on Ordnance Survey maps, "PH" (Public House, i.e., a pub). It seems to be the only building at a place named "The Homestead." Then, isolated out in the middle of a field, is a church iconically coded to have a tower but no steeple. The isolation of churches and the nature of their towers, like the narrowness of roads, are critical constituents of the East Anglian countryside (Frake 1996). Then we come to "The Manor." We are now at the zero-meter contour line (we are heading inland from the coastal dunes, but we are going downhill) and not far from "Hempstead Marshes," "Commissioner's Drain," and "Ingham Poor's Allotment."

Since we have yet to traverse a full mile, we might as well imagine ourselves walking. That way we can at times depart from the narrow road and take a footpath marked on our map by a dotted line. We must take care, however, to find a *green* dotted line. Green dotted lines mark "Public Rights of Way (Not applicable to Scotland)." Even though we are definitely not in Scotland, it is often impossible to see that green dotted line or anything else resembling a path on the ground. A locally published walking guide for North Norfolk explains how this can happen: "Regretfully, as is usually the case, this delightful lane ends suddenly in a ploughed field; it has so obviously been scrubbed out by some thoughtless landowner whose lust for profit has overridden any sense of duty or responsibility for the environment. Walk through the field . . ." (Birch 1988:49). The back of the map, in fact, warns us: "Public rights of way shown on this map may not be evident on the ground."

Apparent on the ground or not, those dotted green lines on Ordnance Survey maps are diligently defended by the English (except for the landowner whose field is traversed by a line). The nineteenth-century National Footpaths Preservation Society, whose founding was among those listed at the beginning of this essay, has flourished; its members are now "The Ramblers." They can be spotted almost any weekend in rural England trekking across farmers' fields to secure public rights thought to be guaranteed since antiquity by those dotted green lines on Ordnance Survey maps. Even though the Survey map assures us that "public rights of way indicated by these symbols have been derived from Definitive Maps as amended by later enactments or instruments," it goes on, in bold print, to protect itself: **"The representation on this map of any road, track or path is no evidence of the existence of a right of way."**

Deciding after all to stay on the road, we pass Ingham Corner and come to a junction where we find a "Pit (dis)," the "Remains of Priory [Gothic print again] (Trinitarian)," and a school (now a private residence). Very strangely, not marked here with a PH is one of my favorite pubs in all of Norfolk. It is situated in a carefully restored building that goes back to Chaucer's time. The Ordnance Survey, whose maps miss not a single derelict windmill, ruined abbey, red telephone box, "tumulus," "moated site," or invisible footpath, does miss some things! Why it missed my pub I have no idea, but other omissions are interpretable. Their consideration leads into the realm of unofficial, everyday, practical knowledge tied to particular places.

LOCAL KNOWLEDGE

. . . a vessel bound northward . . . should proceed . . . until Blakeney church bears less than 238°.

. . . a vessel with local knowledge bound for The Wash, after passing Cromer (*Lat. 52° 56' N., Long. 1° 18' E.*) may, if of light draught and if the tide suits, proceed along the coast inside of Pollard.
—*North Sea Pilot III*

Maps and charts, by inscribing a place in official records, thereby open the place up. They make it accessible to all. They also improve the place to the official eye. They tidy it up, removing inconsistencies, fuzzy boundaries, and unimportant details. They make the place, all its parts and names, "correct." But the very nature of places, as known to locals in all their inconsistent, fuzzy, and trivial details, affords a built-in line of resistance to public inscription. We are talking naked reality here as well as veiled politics. It is the reality, for example, of that starkly real, unnegotiable world faced by a sailor offshore seeking shelter from a northwest gale. Frantically poring through the pilot book for this treacherous coastline, the sailor latches onto the entry for a nearby bay: "In N weather anchorage may be had in two coves on the N shore." After more instructions come the dreaded lines: "But local knowledge is necessary to avoid the dangers" (U.S. Department of Commerce 1977).[20]

Details—rocks, sandy shoals, kelp beds—unmappable in their tininess, inconsistency, and fluidity, can, nevertheless, become matters of life and death. Such dramas are well known on the Norfolk coast. The pilot book for this coast is studded with references to local knowledge and with bearings to churches whose recognition requires local knowledge. The church at Blakeney, commended as a landmark to the navigator, has, unlike any of the many others visible from offshore in this area, two towers. But the pilot book does not tell us that. (I leave the foregoing sentence from an earlier version of this chapter to stand as a telling example of careless ethnography. My old Norfolk friend Norman Peake, after reading it, gently pointed out my error: "Well, Charles," he said, "actually the pilot book is quite right in not mentioning that second tower on the church at Blakeney—because, I must tell you, it is not, and never has been, visible from the sea. It is obscured by the church roof." Local knowledge is full of tricks for those who presume to report it.)

As one rounds the northeast corner of Norfolk after passing Cromer, heading south, the book reassures the navigator by noting as easily visible landmarks a good number of village churches—those at Trimingham, Bacton, Walcott, Knapton, and Trunch. Then the letdown: "As all these churches have similar square towers they are liable to be confused" (United Kingdom 1960:199.) At this point it is good to keep in mind the local knowledge of a range alignment encoded in a verse I learned over a pint of Suffolk ale at the Ten Bells in Norwich:[21]

Gillingham, Trimingham, and Trunch
Three churches all in a bunch.

Happily, the Happisburg church can be spotted standing out atop what passes for a hill in these parts. That is good news, for at this point the navigator must take great care to avoid the dreaded Haisborough sand, over which floats a buoy marked "N. Haisbro." All three placenames are pronounced the same way: another bit of local knowledge, not for navigating but for telling sea stories at the Ten Bells.

It is the nature of seafaring that some critical knowledge must remain local. One cannot blame the pilot books for that (unless one is John Steinbeck—see his complaints in *Log from the Sea of Cortez*).[22] Yet the necessity for local knowledge in navigation does not deprive it of the possibility for strategic employment in other kinds of arenas, both economic and symbolic. Locals with this knowledge could sell it to others by piloting for them, or, in former, less upright times, they could withhold it from others, hoping to profit from the ensuing shipwrecks. Local knowledge also affords a symbolic protection from potential assailants. In past wars against the Dutch, French, and Germans there has been great fear of attacks along this exposed shore. In all these cases it is comforting to feel that one's local knowledge gives one some measure of control over outside forces.

The sea, in its navigation and its narratives, may provide prototypical exemplars of local knowledge, but everyday life on land also requires and exploits such knowledge in its maneuvering over both spatial and political terrains. This maneuvering, to use Clifford Geertz's (1983:167) characterization, is a craft of place, and like all such crafts it works "by the light of local knowledge." Just as nautical charts and pilot books contain many gaps, so do the detailed maps provided to the public by the Ordnance Survey. It is not simply a case of details too small to fit on the sheet (we have seen how even invisible footpaths are shown), or even a matter of occasional missing pubs. Early in my work, before I had acquired much local knowledge, I once thought I was lost—off the map—when, driving along a narrow, hedged-lined lane looking for a particular church, I suddenly found before me a cleared expanse surrounded by two rows of barbed wire, studded with machine-gun towers, filled with strange-looking space-age apparatuses, and marked with frightening warning signs. No mark of this on my map, no note of it in my guidebook. Could this be East Anglia? My "lost continent"?

Such military installations are common. Serving as a fixed aircraft carrier for the Royal Air Force and the United States Air Force has been a historic role of the East Anglian countryside since World War II. Some air bases are on the map, some are not. But the presence of all of them is locally obvious. Antennae intrude on the skyline, personnel become part of local life, and jets roar overhead. It is an unavoidable part of everyday life, but it has no place in the English image of the rural countryside as it is talked about, painted, or inscribed in books and on maps.[23]

Other intrusions on the image of the landscape are also missing from maps and guidebooks even when knowledge of them by anyone could in no way be considered a threat to anything except the image itself. There are, for example, mushroom-topped concrete towers periodically marring the otherwise bucolic landscape. The most radical of relativists would regard these silos as ugly. They provide, with local knowledge, great landmarks. But like ugly factories, waste dumps, junkyards, and the slaughterhouse in Stalham prominently signed "George Bush & Sons, Wholesale Butchers," they do not exist as places on the map.

Everyday knowledge of place is not just for filling in the gaps, the missing pubs, in official cartographic renditions of place. It fills a greater void in the renditions of space. It is, observes Michel de Certeau (1988: 127), like the architect in a poem by Morgenstein who

> Removed the spaces from the fence
> and built of them a residence.

The architect is accomplishing "a transformation of the void into a pleni-tude, of the in-between into an established place." Local knowledge ac-complishes such a transformation by telling stories. "What the map cuts up, the story cuts across" (Certeau 1988:127, 129). It creates places out of nothing. Margaret Rodman (1992:650), while mapping a Vanuatu vil-lage, experienced such a creation by a woman's stories about the birth sites of her children "Although I put an X on my map in the locations she pointed out, they were marked by nothing I could see in the land-scape. Yet for the old woman these memories were etched as clearly in the landscape as if they bore commemorative plaques."

There is power to this local knowledge that is part of everyday life. There is the counterpower of the everyday against the official, what Michael Herzfeld (1991), talking about time rather than place (which is much the same thing), calls the resistance of "social time" to official "monumental time." As in Herzfeld's Crete, a primary battlefield for the employment of this resistance in East Anglia is that surrounding govern-ment programs of preservation and restoration, especially as they conflict with the interests of local landowners and farmers. In East Anglia there are other battles, too. Outsiders, primarily tourists, often come into con-flict with locals. The power of local knowledge helps both to identify the outsider and to give the local the advantage. Much of this conflict stems from the tourist invasion of the Broads, an arena for both terres-trial and nautical local knowledge.

There is yet another realm for the employment of everyday knowl-edge, one in which it is the everyday world, not the official one, that is an instrument of exploitation. Local knowledge not only can empower by creating places out of official cracks, it can also disempower by ex-ploiting those who have fallen through the cracks—people who, in the view of others, have no place at all. They are known to locals, who have a place, as "travelers." Prototypically, "travelers" are Gypsies, but the term, in spite of its official recognition in the form of special school programs for them, is used very loosely. There are so-called "New-Age travelers." And there are people who are simply homeless. In rural Norfolk they fill the role of migrant workers for farmers needing cheap, temporary labor. A "traveler" is the ethnic identity assigned to someone who fills that role. A "traveler" has no place.

No place is where one finds the powerless. It is not to be confused with "nowhere," which, in East Anglia, is a place.

A NOWHERE PLACE

> But we lived in a fairy-tale place. In a lock-keeper's cottage, by a river, in the middle of the Fens. Far away from the wide world. . . . On those nights when my mother would be forced to tell me stories, it would seem that in our lock-keeper's cottage we were in the middle of nowhere. . . . A fairy-tale land, after all.
> — *Graham Swift,* Waterland

Once, during a long chat about the meaning of life, the state of the world, and the depressing East Anglian weather, a Norfolk friend suggested that I read William Morris's utopian vision of 1890 called *News from Nowhere*.[24] The book itself is not especially relevant to this discussion, but the appeal to this Norfolk man, who lives in a place called "Fenside," of a utopia named "Nowhere" struck a resonant chord. "Nowhere" pops up regularly in East Anglian talk about place. It receives lyrical expression in Graham Swift's (1983) account in *Waterland* of a boyhood in the East Anglian fens. It occurs as a local name for various out-of-the-way places such as underneath an old medieval bridge near the two-towered church at Blakeney. Jane Hales (n.d.:25) reports: "Most people hereabouts should know that underneath Wiveton stone bridge is Nowhere. . . . 'Why that's called Nowhere, that's above my know,' said a man at Glandford Mill further upstream."

I have yet to encounter a field named "Nowhere" in Norfolk, but I would be surprised if there were not one somewhere in East Anglia. Agricultural fields have names, and remoteness, of which "nowhere" is the ultimate expression, is a common theme; witness the fields named for faraway places—China, Siberia, Babylon, End of the World (Field 1989). These field names, like Graham Swift's prose, suggest Nebraska or even Wyoming. But one is in East Anglia in a cozy cottage, under a medieval bridge, or within a securely hedged little field. Remoteness, Deighton's "lost continent," is difficult to construct in East Anglia, but people try.

There is said to be another Norfolk place called "Nowhere." It is a part of the estuarian wetlands of the parish of Acle (Walker n.d.). It also seems to be located only in local knowledge; I have not been able to find it inscribed on any map or in any guidebook. In recent decades, far from being nowhere, this area has been the battleground of a fight to preserve the traditional marshland grazing economy from conversion to drained grainfields, a more profitable alternative only because of European Community farm subsidies (Ewans 1992). The placename "Nowhere" conjures up an image of nonthreatening past, contained within local knowledge, as a battle flag in this conflict of local interests. How does one construe a populous, open, flat, accessible area as Nowhere? By putting its buildings, its scenes, its stories into the past, a time now forever inaccessible except in nostalgic reconstructions. Like China, the past is a remote place.

AN IMPROVED PLACE

> By such improvements as I have suggested . . . you may give it a higher
> character. You may raise it into a place.
> —*Jane Austen*, Mansfield Park

In this passage Jane Austen is clearly poking fun at her character's improving talk. (The character is Henry Crawford, the same gentlemen who
"never inquires.") There can be too much of a good thing. But that "improvement" is a good thing for the English, then and now, there can be
no doubt. It is improvement that makes the place. Even "nature" needs
improvement to become, or be restored to, a "natural" place. The alternative to improvement is to let it go, to invite decay, spoilage, unruly
growth, untidiness. One's place can be "lost," but never should it be abandoned. "It is an English creed that all land requires human supervision.
Far from knowing best, nature needs vigilant guidance. . . . The prospect
of unmanaged wasteland is utterly repugnant" (Lowenthal 1991:218).
No search here for the American dream of "unspoiled wilderness"—an
oxymoron to the English.

These differences in the attitudes of the English and the Americans
about nature are, of course, not unrelated to the kinds of nature each
finds around them. The English do not have much in the way of untamed nature in their vicinity anyway. Not long ago it was thought that
the Norfolk Broads of East Anglia were a rare example of pure nature in
England. The Broads are lakelike widenings in the network of rivers and
channels that thread through the marshes and wetland woods ("carr")
of eastern Norfolk and northeastern Suffolk. They are billed as a natural wonderland, a boater's paradise, a bird watcher's dream. In the 1960s,
a masterful piece of geographical, geological, pedological, hydrographi-
cal, botanical, and historical analysis demonstrated conclusively that the
Broads, like the former inland lakes of Holland, were the product of peat
digging on a massive scale in the late Middle Ages when Norfolk was
heavily populated, poorly wooded, and fuel hungry. To find that one's
natural paradise was manmade would be a disaster in the United States.
Imagine the dismay of a backpacker in the Sierras upon discovering that
the pristine lake before her was in fact a reservoir built by Pacific Gas
and Electric. Not so in East Anglia. Even though they were published in
a technical monograph of the Royal Society of Geography, the results of
the Broads study became well known and accepted, so far as I can discern, without much comment almost immediately.[25]

The story of the origin of the Broads is now part of common knowledge. Most people I talk to express surprise that anyone could have
thought differently. It is only natural that the Broads were the product of
human activity. "The Broads are really very pleasant. Do you know how

they originated?" The Broads, like the rest of the countryside, have become part of history. When one sails on them, one is sailing through very
pleasant places, sheltered, like England, one's island, both by surrounding water and by stories that immerse one in a past of English accomplishments. It was improvement that raised the Broads, like an English
garden, out of raw nature into a place. Of course, one cannot relax. As it
does in a garden, it takes work, improving work, to keep the Broads from
becoming overgrown. This has been the fate of many Broadland areas
because of past neglect, pollution, and drainage. These areas must be restored to their prior, but not their original, state. They must be protected
both from natural decay and from human despoilment (Ewans 1992).

Improvement, then, is a good thing. But the banner of "improvement" can fly over quite antithetical agendas for action. This has been
true ever since the banner was first raised back in the times that informed
John Clare's poetry, John Constable's paintings, and Jane Austen's novels.
In that period a discourse emerged that has structured representations of
place down to the present, accommodating within its dialectic the enormous changes in ways of life that have marked the emergence, triumph,
and crisis of modern society in its English version. This discourse was
not, however, simply the product of imaginative novelists, inspired artists, and creative poets. Profound things were happening in the world of
the English at that time, things that, strangely, do not at first sight appear very clearly in the novels, poems, and paintings of the time.

> Artists remained indifferent to the spectacle of technical progress, environ-
> mental renewal and social unrest. . . . Landowners did not want pictures of
> new enclosures or new machines or new farmsteads and they certainly did
> not think of themselves as transforming the countryside. They were not in
> the business of revolutionizing rural society. On the contrary, they saw their
> role as pillars of stable communities and their efforts were devoted to secur-
> ing and perpetuating their position at the top of the social hierarchy. . . .
> Arguably, agrarian improvements were regarded at the time as restoring the
> order and composure attained in a classical golden age, dispelling the igno-
> rance and superstition that had supervened during the gothic middle ages.
> (Prince 1988:115–16)

Improvement could be interpreted not as leading to a new era, a new
kind of society, but as an intervention that returned one to the more
pleasant times of the past. Improvement reconstructed history.

The painters and poets of the seventeenth and eighteenth centuries
were not hiding anything from the landowners or, most certainly, from
the landless. The changes taking place were chronicled and praised by less
literary observers. In 1804, for example, Arthur Young published his *General View of the Agriculture of the County of Norfolk* as a report to the "Board
of Agriculture and Internal Improvement." It portrays, in the format of

objective observation, improvement as innovation: new tools, new crop-ping methods, new field layouts. It also documents what is happening to the poor: sometimes they are better off, sometimes worse. Norfolk leads the country in agricultural improvement. No nostalgia here. No preser-vation of the past. The landowners may have wanted nostalgic pictures in their halls and romantic novels in their libraries, but they wanted profits in their fields.

There were objections to improvement, both in nostalgic portrayal and in brutal deed. A poet of the time, John Clare, composed pieces such as *The Shepherd's Calendar* (1827) that at first glance seem to be rather simple pastoral verses. On closer inspection, they reveal themselves to be subtle yet powerful protests against the agricultural transformations occurring in Clare's home place (Barrell 1972). Agricultural improve-ment was neither a return to the past golden age nor a step to a better future. It was a move toward exploitation that was producing hardship and deprivation among masses of people. This message was carried more forcibly, with no pretense at poetic subtlety, by William Cobbet (1967 [1830]), who rode around the countryside in the early nineteenth cen-tury writing reports of what he saw. The painters, too, took some poetic hits. Here is an obscure one penned by the Reverend John Eagles in 1826 — not commendable poetry perhaps, but the point is clear:

> Learn this ye painters of dead stumps,
> Old barges, and canals, and pumps,
> Paint something fit to see, no view
> Near Brentford, Islington, or Kew
> Paint any thing, but what you do.

These lines appear as an epigraph in Francis Klingender's (1972) work on the industrial art of the nineteenth century — art depicting, sometimes as beautiful, sometimes as ugly, the changes in the real landscape. Such art did not have much of a future, at least locally in East Anglia.

Local paintings, local poetry, and books of local history continue to improve the visual reality of contemporary landscapes by ignoring the RAF installations, concrete silo towers, slaughterhouses, suburban housing tracts, and travelers' caravans. They attend only to old windmills, medieval churches, hedged roads, and gaff-rigged sailing barges (the famous Norfolk "wherry") — authentic constituents of the East Anglian countryside. I showed the Reverend Mr. Eagles's nineteenth-century verse to a Norfolk friend who was complaining about the plethora of unimaginative landscapes by local painters in an art show at the village church. He quickly composed a modern version:

> Learn this you painters of Grebe and Heron,
> Old windmills and wherrys, whereon the Broads they've long since gone.

Paint something fit to see,
That speaks of the 20th century,
Paint anything, a pylon, a parking lot, a dying tree.
Well maybe not—there's too much grief in everyday reality
And nostalgia is not the thing it used to be.

The notion of "improvement" as the restoring of a past that not only
was more pleasant and more sheltered but also is a part of heritage, a
component of identity, lives on today in opposition to the idea of "improvement" as progress, development, modernization, and urbanization.
National commentators like Patrick Wright portray the institutions of
preservation and reconstruction in British society, the flourishing successors to the nineteenth-century societies listed at the beginning of this
chapter, as tools of the conservation establishment.[26] He cites, in horror,
a rather comically extreme expression of the conservative view given by
Arthur Bryant in 1929 (P. Wright 1985:53): "And the spirit of the past—
that sweet and lovely breath of Conservatism—can scarcely touch him. It
is for modern Toryism to create a world of genial social hours and loved
places, upon which the conservative heart of Everyman can cast anchor."
Echoing Wright's lament, Robert Hewison (1987), in his *The Heritage Industry: Britain in a Climate of Decline,* warns that "a creeping takeover by
the past" is Britain's most dangerous enemy.

At the local level, at least in North Norfolk, the battle lines are drawn
somewhat differently. It is difficult to discern a stable front line with
the same troops always on one side. The preservation people are seen
to be at odds with the bastions of local conservatism, the local farmers.
The new outsiders, ex-urbanites and commuters, whether Conservative,
Labor, or something else in politics, see themselves as progressive and
forward-looking in the active defense of the countryside as "heritage."
They see the farmers as the enemies of the countryside, with no concern
to preserve anything. "They think the hedges, barns, and windmills belong to them!" The government, far from having the monolithic agenda
ascribed to it, is caught in between. Various branches and levels of it find
themselves at odds in particular conflicts, which are very local. They are
fights over particular places: who owns them, who defines them, who
uses them. Another place, another battle.

In North Norfolk, the bloodiest recent confrontation was the battle
of Waxham Barn. This is an old barn even by local standards. It has been
around, they say, in one form or another on this spot for some four hundred years. The farmer on whose land it was figured it had outlived its
usefulness. He applied for a permit to demolish it so he could replace it
with something more useful. The local agency, dominated by farmers,
approved. Nonfarmers, nonlocals, and, especially, county preservation
officials were appalled. "Why, that barn has got a hammer-beam roof!

There's no other like it in all England." Before the farmer could lift a sledge hammer, the county had bought the barn out from under him and embarked on a several-million-pound restoration project.

Now local farmers were appalled. "Two million pounds for a barn! The country's full of old barns with any kind of roof you could want. If it were up to me, I'd blow 'er up." (I was told this by a farmer at the fourteenth-century pub not marked on the map. We were deep into local knowledge). Even local preservationists, eager to save their fifteenth-century church (and every locality has one), were disturbed. In discourse everyone wants "improvement"; in practice people fight wars over what it means to improve a barn. The arguments are old and the images much the same: "I have heard a defence of Covent Garden against plans for development, which repeated in almost every particular the defence of the commons in the period of parliamentary enclosures," reports Raymond Williams (1985 [1973]:291), who goes on to say of two persistent images of this discourse, "Clearly the ideas of the country and the city have specific contents and histories, but just as clearly, at times, they are forms of isolation and identification of more general processes."

What one cannot fail to learn when trying to do ethnography in England is the horrible complexity of it all. It is very difficult to sort out the oppressors from the oppressed, the colonialist from the colonized, the improver from the degrader, the good guys from the bad guys. In some respects, when standing in the middle of a Norfolk field I am in the center of a busy, active world; in other respects, standing there I am on the periphery, in a marginal, lost, nowhere world. More typically, ethnographic places somehow, perhaps because of their greater strangeness, seem simpler. Their people are the oppressed, the colonized, the marginal—the good guys. Working in those kinds of places, anthropologists have begun to seek out the salient issues of exploitation and power in discourse and practice. This search seems harder when the places are more familiar, more like our home place. Whether or not our kinds of places are "really" more complex than other places or just seem that way to us, we must entertain the possibility that there are overlooked complexities still to uncover back in our second homes, the ethnographic places of the anthropologist's world. Perhaps all places should be seen as equally ethnographic and, like human language, equally complex and equally rich.[27]

As an anthropologist I have learned to find the English interesting. Even more remarkable, as a reader of novels, I have learned to find Jane Austen interesting. Having begun with Len Deighton, let me give the final word back to her. Her character Emma, in the novel of the same name, upon seeing "Abbey-Mill Farm, with meadows in front, and the river making a close and handsome curve around it," construes a place, an English place:

> It was a sweet view—sweet to the eye and the mind. English verdure, English culture, English comfort, seen under a sun bright, without being oppressive.

This construction remains firmly in English imagination and English discourse. It is a pleasant image, embedded in past times, of sheltered identity. It also mentions the weather.

NOTES

1. Selected from listings in Lowe (1989:114), Wright (1985:49–51), and Lowenthal (1985:104).

2. This study builds upon a previous exploration of these themes (Frake 1996). The references and acknowledgments listed there are relevant to this work as well.

3. "Within particular nations, those who most nearly resemble 'ourselves' appear to be 'people without culture'" (Rosaldo 1988:79).

4. For some recent complaints on this theme, see Rosaldo (1988), Keesing (1990), and Frake (1994).

5. The archaeologist Tom Williamson (1993:1) has claimed that "Norfolk is arguably the last truly rural county in south-eastern England."

6. Many "farmers," now and in the past, have owned the farms they operate, but precise statistics on landownership in England are difficult to come by. See Newby (1988), Barnes (1993), and Frake (1996).

7. The census for 1992 tells us that "East Anglia has the fastest growing population. . . . Despite this it remains the most thinly populated English region" (United Kingdom 1992:12). For more description and documentation of this economic and demographic history, see Riches (1967 [1937]), Newby (1978), Wade-Martins (1993), and Williamson (1993), as well as Frake (1996) and the references cited therein.

8. English translations of current French attempts to sort out place-related meanings are instructive in this regard; see, for example Certeau (1988:117–18) and Berdoulay (1989:124–25).

9. For Norfolk, see Blomefeld's (1805–1809) ten-volume classic, *An Essay Toward a Topographical History of the County of Norfolk,* Cooke's (1822) *A Topographical and Statistical Description of the County of Norfolk,* and Woodward, Ewing, and Turner's (1842) *The Norfolk Topographer's Manual.*

10. The phrasing here is intended to make it clear that I make no claims about the "real" sources of English placenames; my claims refer to the contemporary English discourse about placenames. This discourse is well documented in the many books on placenames, all of which seek the true, original meaning and original language of each name; the classic reference for England is Ekwall (1960), now in its fourth edition. For Norfolk there is Rye (1991).

11. See Newby (1988:5) as well as the discussion by Lowenthal (1991:209–10) in a paper whose title, "British National Identity and the English Landscape," displays the contrast.

12. East Anglians feel strongly not only that their speech is still distinctive in England but also that specific regions within East Anglia can be distinguished: "When my wife and I moved from East Suffolk to North Norfolk I was immediately struck by the difference in the people. There were even facial differences to be noted and more especially a different approach to life. . . . I did once live south of the river Stour for a year. They laughed at me when I went home and said that I had an Essex accent" (Hill 1990:18). The archaeologist and historian of Norfolk, Tom Williamson (1993:184), has described the county as "a land apart, distinct in the appearance of its landscape, and in the speech of most of its inhabitants, from London

and the South-East." Some sense of the linguistic realities behind these claims can be gained from Trudgill's professional studies (1974, 1990). Mardle's (1973) *Broad Norfolk* gives a unprofessional account of local speech forms and speech style. His pseudonym and title entail wordplays whose interpretation requires local knowledge. It is not only in rural pubs that one can witness multivocalic displays by the British—see the description in the *Economist* (1993) of Parliamentary sessions: "The hotchpotch of accent and language remains a fascinating testimony to the durability of the British class and regional chasms. In no country in the world can the personae of parliament be so type-cast by the inflection of their voices." The phrase "in no [other] country" is a predictable introduction to English descriptions of themselves (Frake 1996). In this case the statement may well not be literally true—there are plenty of multivocal parliaments in the world—but it is a true reflection of English attitudes about their speech, their classes, and their localisms.

13. Morris and Brown (1984) give the original Latin text of the Domesday Book for Norfolk with an English translation. Barringer (1989) reprints Faden's map. The story of Saxton's map is told by Tyacke and Huddy (1980).

14. Snorri is a venerable Norse name. I learned that when I turned to Jorge Luis Borges as an escape from working on this chapter: "In the course of my reading," says Borges, "I discovered another historical date. It happened in Iceland, in the thirteenth century of our era: in 1225, let us say. The historian and polygraph Snorri Sturlason, at his country house in Borgarfjord, wrote down, for the enlightenment of future generations, the details of the last exploit of the famous king Harald Sigurdarson, called the Implacable (Hardrada)." There is an English connection. Harald the Implacable, Borges says Snorri wrote, fought against King Harold of England at York. He lost (Borges 1967:180). Harold went on to be conquered by William of Normandy. We can imagine that much earlier, in 943, let us say, two other Norse Snorris, one great, the other little, each founded a village among the Saxons in the land of the North folk.

15. The Englishness of the Norse heritage was certified by Winston Churchill (1963 [1956]:82) himself in his usual style: "The blood-stream of these vigorous individualists [the Vikings], proud and successful men of the sword, mingled henceforward in the Island race. A vivifying, potent, lasting, and resurgent quality was added to the breed. . . . All through English history this strain continues to play a gleaming part."

16. Some inhabitants of a village called Trunch, shortly to be commemorated in verse, feel their peculiarly abrupt, monosyllabic placename is the only "Celtic" one in Norfolk.

17. See Field (1989) for a guide to Norfolk field names.

18. Certeau (1988:104–105). I have here reversed the order of his sentences.

19. Unfortunately the original Name Books for Norfolk County were destroyed by enemy action in 1940 (United Kingdom n.d).

20. Geertz's essay entitled "Local Knowledge" is about the law, whose practitioners do not, I believe, often use the phrase itself in their practice. Among seafarers, on the other hand, not only is local knowledge critical to the practice of their craft, but the phrase itself is an integral part of that practice. Its use at sea provides the prototypical meaning of "local knowledge." (During the seminar at which this paper was presented, Geertz informed us that he has since learned that lawyers who practice in the American South do, in fact, have a term for "local knowledge." They call it "home cookin'.")

21. Variants of this verse seem to have a long history. One, dating back to 1681, is cited by Hales and Bennett (1971:102).

22. Steinbeck and Rickets (1962 [1941]).

23. Harley (1988:289), in his discussion "Maps, Knowledge, and Power," notes that nuclear waste dumps are omitted from official USGS maps.

24. Morris's "Nowhere" is the name of Samuel Butler's earlier utopia, "Erewhon," spelled backward.

25. The report (Lambert et al. 1960) is one of those rare masterpieces of true science, both natural and human: it is clearly written and thoroughly documented with evidence gathered by painstaking research within a variety of disciplines. It adds a bit of solid truth to what we know of the world. I recommend reading it as an aspirin for postmodern headaches. Frake (1996) has more on the symbolic and political significance of the Broads.

26. The National Trust now has 2 percent of the English population as registered members; the Royal Society for the Protection of Birds has some 400,000 members (Rogers 1989:100).

27. See the recent work of John and Jean Comaroff (1992:158), who compare Raymond Williams's analysis of discourse, history, and power in England with their own in tribal South Africa: "In his study of *The Country and the City* in modern English literature, he notes that the rural-urban opposition served as a very general model for interpreting a radically changing social order. Inasmuch as this opposition lent itself to the expression of differing visions of English life, it evoked a complex discourse about society, production, class, and gender—a discourse, that is, about history. . . . It is not only in Africa that those caught up in the processes of radical change come to terms with their history by means of a suggestive opposition."

Afterword

Clifford Geertz

If you should look into the table of contents or, for that matter, into the index of a standard textbook or monograph in anthropology, you would not find there a category called "Place." You would find "Family," "Kinship," "Community," "Economy," "Language," "Gender," "Stratification," "Law," "Religion," "Art," "Culture," and "Social Structure," and sometimes "State," "Exchange," "Life Cycle," "Technology," or "Warfare." But even if a fair amount of attention is given to something called "the environment" or "the physical setting" (rainfall, vegetation, fauna, landforms), "place" as an analytical or descriptive concept, explicitly set out and formally developed, does not appear. Something that is a dimension of everyone's existence, the intensity of where we are, passes by anonymous and unremarked. It goes without saying.

There are a number of possible reasons for this. One is surely the simple ubiquity of place and the sense of place in human life. It is difficult to see what is always there. Whoever discovered water, it was not a fish. Also, the diffuseness of the term in ordinary language makes it hard to fix in the mind. The six three-column pages its definition takes up in the *Oxford English Dictionary* that Charles Frake mentions in chapter 7 is evidence enough that it is not a clear and distinct idea. But the invisibility of place has mainly to do with the fact that it is so difficult to free from subjectivities and occasions, immediate perceptions and instant cases. Like Love or Imagination, Place makes a poor abstraction. Separated from its materializations, it has little meaning.

It is for this reason, doubtless, that all the essays in this volume except Edward Casey's, which is an extended meditation on the scope and history of the concept of place as such, are sharply focused case studies: some Indians in the Southwest and the Southeast; some Papuans on the shore and in the hills; some voices in Appalachia and some mappings in East Anglia. The subject demands exactness, detail, the sort of care for the assumed and the unstated, for what is only felt or only enacted, that might best be called ethnographical tact. It is a patient art, and frequently a passive one. No one lines up people and asks them to define "place" and list three examples of it. No one really has a theory of it. No one imagines that it is some sort of data set to be sampled, ordered, tabulated, and manipulated. To study place, or, more exactly, some people or other's sense of place, it is necessary to hang around with them—to attend to them as experiencing subjects, as the responsive sorts of beings for whom, in Casey's words, "the world comes bedecked in places."

The advantage of this tight, drawn-in focus, of looking at things obsessively up close, is that the way person and place pour into each other comes into direct, here-it-is, think-about-it view. The inseparability of the lives the various peoples live and the settings in which they live them—what Basso calls their "interanimation"—can be shown, not merely asserted, and these studies are crowded with images of such inseparability: a spotted bull lingering at the end of an Apache funeral; stone peaks with their backs turned in anger toward a Papuan village; the "worked-out mouths of mines lying dark and gaping" on the sides of drab and junk-cluttered West Virginia hills; the "lift-up-over" sounds of hissing watercourses and crashing cataracts in the New Guinea rainforest; the definite-indefinite, half-visible communities of Indian North Carolina; the screened-out slaughterhouses, factories, and military bases of "improved" East Anglia. There is, even where the sense of place is embittered, conflictual, sorrowing, or—those English barns—a bit worked up, or even where things seem to be, as they seem to be everywhere, fragile, abrading, or sliding away, a pervading air of "we belong here" intimacy.

It is, in fact, this last matter, the sense of fragility and change, of some things clear and familiar threatening to end and others uncertain and unprepared for promising to begin—young Apaches finding their "wisdom" in school-taught skills rather than in old stories; Kaluli men abandoning classical song forms and Kaluli women taking them up; "painful hanging on [and] unthinkable leavings" in the "dying and degraded space" of West Virginia "hollers"; the industrialization of Lumbee life; the growing cosmopolitanism of Wamira; the romanticizing of East Anglia—that raises the question such determinedly local ethnography always raises and is meant to raise: Where does all this detail and nuance, example and episode, lead? What are those of us enclosed in a world where everybody seems to be on the move, displaced or disemplaced or merely restless, one whose iconography of place centers on airports, hotels, freeways, shopping malls, theme parks, street corners, and sports complexes, and one where almost every place is variously sensed, diversely valued, and, often enough, bitterly fought over supposed to learn from inquiries into "emotional landscapes," "sheltered identities," and "waterfalls of song"? Have we to do here with a world we have lost or with one, however enlarged, dispersed, deprovincialized, and remade it may be, in which we in fact still live?

For all the uprooting, the homelessness, the migrations, forced and voluntary, the dislocations of traditional relationships, the struggles over homelands, borders, and rights of recognition, for all the destructions of familiar landscapes and the manufacturings of new ones, and for all the loss of local stabilities and local originalities, the sense of place, and of the specificities of place, seems, however tense and darkened, barely diminished in the modern world. There may have been no *there* there for Stein in Oakland, but there surely is, and palpably, for those who now live there, more hazardously than she, block by block, project by project, as well as for those who contrive to escape, as she did, to elsewhere. (As Stein herself remarked in Paris, which, engaging it from her apartment, she made her village: "What good are roots if you can't take them with you?") The sort of hard attention just now starting to be given to such singular places as Trail Goes Down Between Two Hills, Where Earthquake Broke Open the Ground There, Devil's Fork Holler, Black Ankle, or the Norfolk Broads needs to be extended to the central sites of contemporary life. If the world is, as Casey argues, always already "a place-world to begin with," then there is nothing really that sets off his Topeka from Kahn's Inibuena, in this regard anyway, except a certain complexion of circumstance.

Such an extension of anthropological inquiry into the sense of place to the Bosavis and Cibicues of modern life, an extension that is already at least begun here in Frake's and Blu's and Stewart's essays and that hovers somewhere just over the horizon in the others—the rugby team T-shirts of Wamira, the waterfalls in Ulahi's head made into media consumables by Feld's CDs—represents less an alteration in our modes of attention than a development of them. All places, as Frake remarks, are equally ethnographic. What is needed in order to gain some understanding of how Japanese perceive fish markets, how Turks perceive Kreuzberg, or how Parisians perceive the Pantheon (to instance some cases upon which there has been some work) is the same sort of obsessive patience and passionate tact that is needed in order to gain such understanding of how Australian Aboriginals perceive their "estates" or kula partners their places of exchange.

The disaggregation of the worn, prefabricated units in terms of which we are used to thinking about the contemporary world (Asia, California, Sarajevo, the inner city, the Sahara, France, Silicon Valley, the Amazon, Hollywood, the Middle East) into configurations of particular places, particularly inhabited, is at least one of the ways—it is hardly the only one—in which the received procedures of small-scale ethnography can be brought to bear on the grand complexities that plague that world. It is not a matter of reducing large things to small, the United States to Middletown, General Motors to the shop floor. It is a matter of giving shape to things: exactness, force, intelligibility.

For it is still the case that no one lives in the world in general. Everybody, even the exiled, the drifting, the diasporic, or the perpetually moving, lives in some confined and limited stretch of it—"the world around here." The sense of interconnectedness imposed on us by the mass media, by rapid travel, and by long-distance communication obscures this more than a little. So does the featurelessness and interchangeability of so many of our public spaces, the standardization of so many of our products, and the routinization of so much of our daily existence. The banalities and distractions of the way we live now lead us, often enough, to lose sight of how much it matters just where we are and what it is like to be there. The ethnography of place is, if anything, more critical for those who are apt to imagine that all places are alike than for those who, listening to forests or experiencing stones, know better.

Anthropology, of the family, of law, of exchange, of ritual, of belief, of identity, has always had about it a sort of preludial quality, as if it marks the beginning of something that will reach far beyond the matters under immediate consideration. The anthropology of place, which can fairly be said to have been launched as a sustained and self-conscious enterprise in these pages (as a diffuse, unthematized concern, a sort of background continuo, it has, of course, been around much longer), has the same sort of air, the same kind of promise. One can only faintly imagine what sedulous and circumstantial inquiries like these into the Berlin of divisions and unitings, remembered pasts and suppressed ones, the Singapore of British swagger and officialism turned to Chinese push and discipline, or the Detroit of empty lots, screaming sirens, and boarded stores will bring. But one thing they will bring, if they are indeed ever done, is a grasp of what it means to be here rather than there, now rather than then, without which our understanding will be thin, general, surface, and incomplete.

References

Abu-Lughod, Lila, and Catherine Lutz
  1990   Introduction: Emotion, Discourse, and the Politics of Everyday Life. *In*
          Language and the Politics of Emotion, Catherine Lutz and Lila Abu-
          Lughod, eds., pp. 1–23. New York: Cambridge University Press.
Ackerman, Diane
  1990   A Natural History of the Senses. New York: Random House.
Agee, James, and Walker Evans
  1941   Let Us Now Praise Famous Men. Boston: Houghton Mifflin.
Aihoshi, Terry, and Margaret Rodman
  1992   Narratives of Place, Experience, and Identity. Session presented at the 91st
          annual meeting of the American Anthropological Association, San Fran-
          cisco.
Anderson, Benedict
  1983   Imagined Communities: Reflections on the Origin and Spread of Nation-
          alism. London: Verso.
  1991   Imagined Communities: Reflections on the Origin and Spread of Nation-
          alism. 2d ed. London: Verso.
Anglican Archives
  1936   Unreferenced Letter in the Anglican Archives. New Guinea Collection,
          University of Papua New Guinea Library, Port Moresby.
Appadurai, Arjun
  1988   Introduction: Place and Voice in Anthropological Theory. Cultural An-
          thropology 3(1):16–20.
  1992   Global Ethnoscapes: Notes and Queries for a Transnational Anthropology,
          In Recapturing Anthropology: Working in the Present, Richard Fox, ed.,
          pp. 191–210. Santa Fe, New Mexico: School of American Research Press.
Appadurai, Arjun, and Carol Breckenridge
  1988   Why Public Culture? Public Culture 1(1):5–9.
Ardery, Julia, ed.
  1983   Welcome the Traveler Home: Jim Garland's Story of the Kentucky Moun-
          tains. Lexington: University Press of Kentucky.
Aristotle
  1968   De Anima: Books II and III, trans. D. W. Hamlyn. Oxford: Clarendon Press.
  1983   Aristotle's Physics: Books III and IV, trans. E. Hussey. Oxford: Oxford Uni-
          versity Press.

Attali, Jacques
  1985   Noise: The Political Economy of Music. Minneapolis: University of Minnesota Press.
Augé, Marc
  1995   Non-Places: Introduction to an Anthropology of Supermodernity, trans. John Howe. London: Verso.
Bachelard, Gaston
  1964   The Poetics of Space, trans. M. Jolas. New York: Orion Press.
Bakhtin, Mikhail
  1979   Estetika slovesnogo tvorchestva (The Aesthetics of Verbal Creation). Moscow: S. G. Bocharov.
  1981   The Dialogic Imagination, trans. Caryl Emerson and Michael Holquist. Austin: University of Texas Press.
  1984   Problems of Dostoevsky's Poetics, trans. and ed. Caryl Emerson. Minneapolis: University of Minnesota Press.
  1986   Speech Genres and Other Late Essays. Austin: University of Texas Press.
Barnes, Pam
  1993   Norfolk Landowners since 1880. Norwich: Centre of East Anglian Studies, University of East Anglia.
Barrell, John
  1972   The Idea of Landscape and the Sense of Place, 1730–1840: An Approach to the Poetry of John Clare. Cambridge: Cambridge University Press.
Barringer, J. C.
  1989   Faden's Map of Norfolk. First printed 1797. Dereham, Norfolk: Larks Press.
Barthes, Roland
  1957   Mythologies. New York: Hill and Wang.
  1974   S/Z. New York: Farrar, Straus, and Giroux.
  1975   The Pleasure of the Text. New York: Hill and Wang.
Barton, Garry Lewis
  1992   The Life and Times of Henry Berry Lowry. 2d ed. Pembroke, North Carolina: Lumbee Publishing Company.
Barton, Lew
  1950   Prospect Shows the Signs of a Town in the Making. The Robesonian (Lumberton, North Carolina), September 12, p. 6.
Basso, Ellen B.
  1985   A Musical View of the Universe: Kalapalo Myth and Ritual Performances. Philadelphia: University of Pennsylvania Press.
Basso, Keith
  1966   The Gift of Changing Woman. Bureau of American Ethnology Bulletin 196. Washington, D.C.: Smithsonian Institution.
  1969   Western Apache Witchcraft. Anthropological Papers of the University of Arizona, 15. Tucson: University of Arizona Press.
  1970a The Cibecue Apache. New York: Holt, Rinehart and Winston.
  1970b "To Give Up on Words": Silence in Western Apache Culture. Southwestern Journal of Anthropology 26(3):213–30.
  1979   Portraits of the "Whiteman": Linguistic Play and Cultural Symbols among the Western Apache. Cambridge: Cambridge University Press.
  1984a Western Apache Place-Name Hierarchies. In Naming Systems, Elizabeth Tooker, ed., pp. 78–94. Washington, D.C.: 1980 Proceedings of the American Ethnological Society.

1984b   "Stalking with Stories": Names, Places, and Moral Narratives among the Western Apache. *In* Text, Play, and Story: The Construction and Reconstruction of Self and Society, Edward Bruner, ed., pp. 19–55. Washington, D.C.: 1983 Proceedings of the American Ethnological Society.

1988   "Speaking with Names": Language and Landscape among the Western Apache. Cultural Anthropology 3(2):99–130.

1991   Western Apache Language and Culture: Essays in Linguistic Anthropology. Tucson: University of Arizona Press.

Bauman, Richard

1977   Verbal Art as Performance. Prospect Heights, Illinois: Waveland Press.

1986   Story, Performance and Event: Contextual Studies in Oral Narrative. Cambridge: Cambridge University Press.

Bauman, Richard, and Charles Briggs

1990   Poetics and Performance as Critical Perspectives on Language and Social Life. Annual Review of Anthropology 19:59–88.

Bender, Barbara, ed.

1993   Landscape: Politics and Perspectives. Oxford: Berg.

Benjamin, Walter

1969   Illuminations: Essays and Reflections, ed. Hannah Arendt, trans. Harry Zohn. New York: Schocken Books.

1977   The Origin of German Tragic Drama, trans. John Osborne. London: New Left Books.

1978   Reflections: Essays, Aphorisms, Autobiographical Writings, trans. Edmund Jephcott. New York: Schocken Books.

Berdoulay, Vincent

1989   Place, Meaning, and Discourse in French Language Geography. *In* The Power of Place: Bringing Together Geographical and Sociological Imaginations, John A. Agnew and James S. Duncan, eds., pp. 124–39. London: Unwin Hyman.

Berger, Peter, Brigitte Berger, and Hansfried Kellner

1983   The Homeless Mind: Modernization and Consciousness. New York: Vintage Books.

Bergson, Henri

1988 [1908]   Matter and Memory. New York: Zone Books.

Berkeley, George

1934   An Essay Towards a New Theory of Vision. London: Dent.

Birch, Mel

1988   Historic Walks in Norfolk. Woolpit, Suffolk: Images Publications.

Blackwood, Beatrice

1935   Both Sides of Buka Passage. Oxford: Clarendon Press.

Blomefeld, Francis

1805–1809   An Essay toward a Topographical History of the County of Norfolk. 10 vols. London: W. Bulmer.

Blu, Karen I.

1980   The Lumbee Problem: The Making of an American Indian People. Cambridge: Cambridge University Press.

1994   "Reading Back" to Find Community: Lumbee Ethnohistory. *In* North American Indian Anthropology: Essays on Society and Culture, Raymond J. DeMallie and Alfonso Ortiz, eds., pp. 278–95. Norman: University of Oklahoma Press.

Boas, Franz
1934   Geographical Names of the Kwakiutl Indians. Columbia University Con-
        tributions to Anthropology, 20. New York: Columbia University Press.
Bodley, John H., ed.,
1988   Tribal Peoples and Development Issues: A Global Overview. Mountain
        View, California: Mayfield.
Borges, Jorge Luis
1967   A Personal Anthology. New York: Grove Press.
Bourdieu, Pierre
1977   Outline of a Theory of Practice, trans. R. Nice. Cambridge: Cambridge
        University Press.
Braudel, Fernand
1972   The Mediterranean and the Mediterranean World in the Age of Philip II,
        vol. 1, trans. S. Reynolds. New York: Harper.
Breuer, Joseph, and Sigmund Freud
1955   Studies in Hysteria, vol. 2 of the Standard Edition of the Complete Psycho-
        logical Works of Sigmund Freud, ed. J. Strachey. London: Hogarth.
Bruner, Jerome
1981   Review and Prospectus. In Universals of Human Thought: Some Afri-
        can Evidence, Barbara Lloyd and John Gay, eds., pp. 256–62. Cambridge:
        Cambridge University Press.
Bryant, Arthur
1929   The Spirit of Conservatism. London.
Burger, Julian
1990   The Gaia Atlas of First Peoples: A Future for the Indigenous World. Lon-
        don: Gaia Books.
Buttimer, Anne
1993   Geography and the Human Spirit. Baltimore: Johns Hopkins University
        Press.
Buttimer, Anne, and David Seamon, eds.
1980   The Human Experience of Space and Place. New York: St. Martin's Press.
Camus, Albert
1955   Noces suivi de l'eté. Paris: Editions Gallimard.
Carlin, George
1973   Occupation: Foole. LP. New York: Dead Sea Music and Little David
        Records.
Carmichael, David, Jane Hubert, Brian Reeves, and Audhild Schanche, eds.
1994   Sacred Sites, Sacred Places. London: Routledge.
Carpenter, Edmund
1960   Acoustic Space. In Explorations in Communications, Edmund Carpenter
        and Marshall McLuhan, eds., pp. 65–70. Boston: Beacon Press.
1971   The Eskimo Artist. In Anthropology and Art: Readings in Cross-Cultural
        Aesthetics, C. Otten, ed., pp. 163–71. Garden City, New York: Natural His-
        tory Press.
1973   Eskimo Realities. New York: Holt Rinehart and Winston.
1980   If Wittgenstein Had Been an Eskimo. Natural History 89(2):72–77.
Casey, Edward S.
1987   Remembering: A Phenomenological Study. Bloomington: Indiana Uni-
        versity Press.
1993   Getting Back into Place: Toward a Renewed Understanding of the Place-
        World. Bloomington: Indiana University Press.

1996   The Fate of Place: A Philosophical History. Berkeley: University of California Press.

Certeau, Michel de
1988   The Practice of Everyday Life. Berkeley: University of California Press.

Chambers, Ross
1991   Room for Maneuver: Reading (the) Oppositional (in) Narrative. Chicago: University of Chicago Press.

Chateaubriand, Francois Auguste René
1969 [1803] Voyages en Italie. Paris: Minard.

Chomsky, Noam
1965   Aspects of the Theory of Syntax. Cambridge, Massachusetts: MIT Press.

Chubb, T.
1928   A Descriptive List of the Printed Maps of Norfolk, 1574–1916. Norwich, U.K.: Jarrold & Sons.

Churchill, Winston
1963 [1956] The Birth of Britain. New York: Bantam.

Clare, John
1827   The Shepherd's Calendar. London: James Duncan.

Clifford, James
1983   Power and Dialogue in Ethnography: Marcel Griaule's Initiation. In Observers Observed: Essays on Ethnographic Fieldwork (History of Anthropology 1), George Stocking, ed., pp. 121–56. Madison: University of Wisconsin Press.

1986   On Ethnographic Allegory. In Writing Culture: The Poetics and Politics of Ethnography, James Clifford and George E. Marcus, eds., pp. 98–121. Berkeley: University of California Press.

1992   Travelling Cultures. In Cultural Studies, Lawrence Grossberg, Cary Nelson, and Paula Treichler, eds., pp. 96–116. New York: Routledge.

Cobbet, William
1967 [1830] Rural Rides. Harmondsworth, U.K.: Penguin.

Coles, Robert
1971   Migrants, Sharecroppers, and Mountaineers. Children of Crisis, vol. 2. Boston: Little, Brown/Atlantic Monthly.

Collingwood, R. G.
1932   An Essay on Philosophical Method. Oxford: Oxford University Press.

Comaroff, John, and Jean Comaroff
1992   Ethnography and the Historical Imagination. Boulder, Colorado: Westview Press.

Cooke, G. A.
1822   A Topographical and Statistical Description of the County of Norfolk. London: Sherwood, Neely, and Jones.

Cornford, F. M.
1957   Plato's Cosmology: The Timaeus of Plato Translated with a Running Commentary. New York: Liberal Arts Press.

Cosgrove, Denis E.
1984   Social Formation and Symbolic Landscape. London: Croon Helm.

Cultural Survival
1993   State of the Peoples: A Global Human Rights Report on Societies in Danger. Boston: Beacon Press.

Cunningham, Rodger
  1987   Apples on the Flood: The Southern Mountain Experience. Knoxville: University of Tennessee Press.
Cytowic, Richard
  1989   Synesthesia: A Union of the Senses. Berlin: Springer-Verlag.
Daniel, E. Valentine
  1984   Fluid Signs: Being a Person in the Tamil Way. Berkeley: University of California Press.
Daniel, Pete
  1985   Breaking the Land: The Transformation of Cotton, Tobacco, and Rice Cultures since 1880. Urbana: University of Illinois Press.
Deighton, Len
  1982   XPD. New York: Ballantine.
Deleuze, Gilles, and Felix Guattari
  1986   Nomadology, trans. B. Massumi. New York: Semiotexte.
  1991   A Thousand Plateaus. Minneapolis: University of Minnesota Press.
Deloria, Vine, Jr.
  1975   God Is Red. New York: Dell.
  1991   Sacred Lands and Religious Freedom. New York: Association on American Indian Affairs.
Derrida, Jacques
  1978   Writing and Difference, trans. Alan Bass. Chicago: University of Chicago Press.
Descartes, René,
  1985   Principles of Philosophy (1644). In The Philosophical Writings of Descartes, vol. 1, trans. J. Cootingham, R. Stoothoff, and D. Murdoch. Cambridge: Cambridge University Press.
Dial, Adolph L.
  1993   The Lumbee. New York: Chelsea House.
Dial, Adolph L., and David K. Eliades
  1975   The Only Land I Know: A History of the Lumbee Indians. San Francisco: Indian Historian Press.
Dinesen, Isak
  1979   Daguerreotypes and Other Essays, trans. P. Mitchell and W. Paden. Chicago: University of Chicago Press.
Duncan, James, and David Ley, eds.
  1993   Place/Culture/Representation. London: Routledge.
Durrell, Lawrence
  1969   Spirit of Place: Letters and Essays on Travel. New Haven, Connecticut: Leete's Island Books.
Durkheim, Emile
  1915   The Elementary Forms of the Religious Life, trans. J. F. Swain. New York: Macmillan.
Economist
  1993   Jolly Good Show. 326.7796, January 30, p. 55.
Ekwall, Eilert
  1960   The Concise Oxford Dictionary of English Place-Names. 4th ed. Oxford: Oxford University Press.
Eller, Ronald
  1982   Miners, Millhands, and Mountaineers: Industrialization of the Appalachian South, 1880–1930. Knoxville: University of Tennessee Press.

Entrikin, J. Nicholas
1989   Place, Region and Modernity. *In* The Power of Place, John A. Agnew and James S. Duncan, eds., pp. 30–43. London: Unwin Hyman.
1991   The Betweenness of Place: Toward a Geography of Modernity. Baltimore, Maryland: Johns Hopkins University Press.
Evans, W. McKee
1966   Ballots and Fence Rails: Reconstruction on the Lower Cape Fear. Chapel Hill: University of North Carolina Press.
1971   To Die Game: The Story of the Lowry Band, Indian Guerrillas of Reconstruction. Baton Rouge: Louisiana State University Press.
Ewans, E.
1992   The Battle for the Broads. Lavenham, Suffolk: Terence Dalton.
Fajans, Jane
1985   The Person in Social Context: The Social Character of Baining "Psychology." *In* Person, Self, and Experience, Geoffrey White and John Kirkpatrick, eds., pp. 367–97. Berkeley: University of California Press.
Farnell, Brenda
1990   Plains Indian Sign-Talk: Action and Discourse among the Nakota (Assiniboine) People of Montana. Ph.D. dissertation, Department of Anthropology, Indiana University.
Feld, Steven
1981   Music of the Kaluli. LP. Boroko, PNG: Institute of Papua New Guinea Studies.
1982   Sound and Sentiment: Birds, Weeping, Poetics, and Song in Kaluli Expression. Philadelphia: University of Pennsylvania Press.
1985   Kaluli Weeping and Song. LP. Kassel, Germany: Barenreiter Musicaphon.
1986   Orality and Consciousness. *In* The Oral and the Literate in Music, Yoshihiko Tokumaru and Osamu Yamaguti, eds., pp. 18–27. Tokyo: Academia Music.
1988   Aesthetics as Iconicity of Style, or, "Lift-Up-Over Sounding": Getting into the Kaluli Groove. Yearbook for Traditional Music 20:74–113.
1990   Sound and Sentiment: Birds, Weeping, Poetics, and Song in Kaluli Expression. 2d ed. Philadelphia: University of Pennsylvania Press.
1991   Voices of the Rainforest. CD/cassette. Salem, Massachusetts: Rykodisc.
1992   Voices of the Rainforest: "Imperialist Nostalgia" and the Politics of Music. Arena 99/100:164–77.
Field, John
1989   English Field Names: A Dictionary. Gloucester, U.K.: Sutton.
Finnegan, Ruth
1988   Literacy and Orality. Oxford: Basil Blackwell.
Foucault, Michel
1970   The Order of Things. London: Tavistock.
1979   Discipline and Punish: The Birth of the Prison. New York: Vintage Books.
1986   Of Other Spaces. Diacritics 16(1):22–27.
Frake, Charles O.
1964   Notes on Queries in Ethnography. American Anthropologist 66:132–45.
1980   How to Enter a Yakan House. *In* Language and Cultural Description, by Charles O. Frake, A. S. Dil, ed., pp. 214–32. Palo Alto, California: Stanford University Press.
1994   Cognitive Anthropology: An Origin Story. *In* The Remaking of Psycho-

logical Anthropology, M. M. Suárez-Orozco, G. Spindler, and L. Spindler, eds., pp. 244–53. Fort Worth, Texas: Harcourt Brace.

1996 A Church Too Far Near a Bridge Oddly Placed: The Cultural Construction of the Norfolk Countryside. *In* Redefining Nature: Ecology, Culture and Domestication, Roy Ellen and Katsuyoshi Fukui, eds., pp. 89–115. Oxford: Berg.

Friel, Brian

1981 Translations. London: Faber.

Fuller, Thomas

1642 The Holy State and the Profane State. London.

Geertz, Clifford

1973 The Interpretation of Cultures. New York: Basic Books.

1980 Negara: The Theatre State in Nineteenth-Century Bali. Princeton, New Jersey: Princeton University Press.

1983 Local Knowledge: Further Essays in Interpretive Anthropology. New York: Basic Books.

Gillison, Gillian

1993 Between Culture and Fantasy: A New Guinea Highlands Mythology. Chicago: University of Chicago Press.

Gitlin, Todd, and Nancy Hollander

1970 Uptown: Poor Whites in Chicago. New York: Harper and Row.

Gonzalez-Crussi, Frank

1989 The Five Senses. New York: Vintage.

Goodwin, Grenville

1939 Myths and Tales of the White Mountain Apache. Memoirs of the American Folklore Society, 33.

1942 The Social Organization of the Western Apache. Chicago: University of Chicago Press.

Gupta, Akhil, and James Ferguson

1992 Beyond "Culture": Space, Identity, and the Politics of Difference. Cultural Anthropology 7(1):6–23.

Gupta, Akhil, James Ferguson, and Roger Rouse, eds.

1992 Culture, Power, Place: Explorations in Critical Anthropology. Boulder, Colorado: Westview Press.

Hales, Jane

n.d. The East Wind: An Unusual Guide to Norfolk. Hunstanton, U.K.: Anglia Publications.

Hales, Jane, and William Bennett

1971 Looking at Norfolk. Wisbech, Cambridgeshire: Charles N. Veal.

Hallowell, A. Irving

1965 The History of Anthropology as an Anthropological Problem. Journal of the History of the Behavioral Sciences 1:24–38.

Harley, J. B.

1988 Maps, Knowledge, and Power. *In* The Iconography of the Landscape, Denis Cosgrove and Stephen Daniels, eds., pp. 277–312. Cambridge: Cambridge University Press.

Harrison, Faye V.

1995 "Give Me That Old Time Religion": The Genealogy and Cultural Politics of an Afro-Christian Celebration in Halifax County, North Carolina. *In* Religion in the Contemporary South: Diversity, Community, and Identity,

O. Kendall White, Jr., and Daryl White, eds., pp. 34–45. Southern Anthropological Society Proceedings, no. 28. Athens: University of Georgia Press.

Harvey, David
1989   The Condition of Postmodernity. New York: Blackwell.

Heany, Seamus
1980   The Sense of Place. In Preoccupations: Selected Prose 1968–1978, pp. 131–49. London: Faber and Faber.

Heelan, Patrick
1979   Space-Time and the Philosophy of Science. Berkeley: University of California Press.

Heidegger, Martin
1971   Poetry, Language, Thought. New York: Harper and Row.
1972   What Is Called Thinking? trans. J. Glenn Gray. New York: Harper and Row.
1977   Building Dwelling Thinking. In Martin Heidegger: Basic Writings, D. Krell, ed., pp. 319–39. New York: Harper and Row.

Hertz, Robert
1973 [1909]   The Pre-Eminence of the Right Hand: A Study in Religious Polarity. In Right and Left: Essays on Dual Symbolic Classification, R. Needham, ed., pp. 3–31. Chicago: University of Chicago Press.

Herzfeld, Michael
1991   A Place in History: Social and Monumental Time in a Cretan Town. Princeton, New Jersey: Princeton University Press.

Hewison, Robert
1987   The Heritage Industry: Britain in a Climate of Decline. London: Methuen.

Higgins, Kathleen Marie
1991   The Music of Our Lives. Philadelphia: Temple University Press.

Hill, David
1990   A Living in the Past: An East Anglian Venture in Antiques and Bygones. Woolpit, Suffolk: Images Publications.

Hirsch, Eric, and Michael O'Hanlon, eds.
1995   The Anthropology of Landscape: Perspectives on Space and Place. Oxford: Clarendon Press.

Hiss, Tony
1990   The Experience of Place. New York: Knopf.

Hood, Christobel M., ed.
1938   The Chorography of Norfolk: An Historicall and Chorographicall Description of Norffolck by John Norden (early 17th c.). Norwich: Jarrold & Sons.

Houston, Jeanne Wakatsuki, and James D. Houston
1973   Farewell to Manzanar: A True Story of Japanese American Experience During and After the World War II Internment. Boston: Houghton Mifflin.

Howes, David, ed.
1991   The Varieties of Sensory Experience: A Reader in the Anthropology of the Senses. Toronto: University of Toronto Press.

Husserl, Edmund
1958   Ideas. London: George Allen and Unwin.
1970   Logical Investigations, vol. 1, trans. J. N. Findlay. New York: Humanities.
1981   The World of the Living Present and the Constitution of the Surrounding World External to the Organism, trans. F. A. Elliston and L. Langsdorf. In Husserl: Shorter Works, F. Elliston and P. McCormick, eds., pp. 238–50. Notre Dame, Indiana: University of Notre Dame Press.

1982   Ideas Pertaining to a Pure Phenomenology and to a Phenomenological Philosophy, First Book (General Introduction to a Pure Phenomenology), trans. F. Kersten. The Hague: Nijhoff.

1989   Ideas Pertaining to a Pure Phenomenology and to a Phenomenological Philosophy, Second Book (Studies in the Phenomenology of Constitution), trans. R. Rojcewicz and A. Schuwer. Dordrecht: Kluwer.

Husserl, Edmund (assisted by L. Landgrebe)

1973   Experience and Judgment: Investigations in a Genealogy of Logic, trans. J. S. Churchill and K. Ameriks. Evanston, Illinois: Northwestern University Press.

Hymes, Dell

1975   Folklore's Nature and the Sun's Myth. Journal of American Folklore 88: 345–69.

1981   "In Vain I Tried to Tell You": Essays in Native American Ethnopoetics. Philadelphia: University of Pennsylvania Press.

1985   Language, Memory, and Selective Performance: Cultee's "Salmon's Myth" as Twice Told to Boas. Journal of American Folklore 98:391–434.

Idhe, Don

1976   Listening and Voice: A Phenomenology of Sound. Athens: Ohio University Press.

Jackson, John B.

1994   A Sense of Place, a Sense of Time. New Haven, Connecticut: Yale University Press.

Jackson, Michael

1989   Paths toward a Clearing. Bloomington: Indiana University Press.

Jackson, Peter

1989   Maps of Meaning. London: Routledge.

Johnson, Mark

1987   The Body in the Mind: The Bodily Basis of Meaning, Imagination, and Reason. Chicago: University of Chicago Press.

Jones, Yvonne V.

1980   Kinship Affiliation through Time: Black Homecomings and Family Reunions in a North Carolina County. Ethnohistory 27(1):49–66.

Jorgensen, Dan

1990   Placing the Past and Moving the Present: Myth and Contemporary History in Telefomin. Culture 10(2):47–56.

Kahn, Miriam

1984   Taro Irrigation in Wamira, Papua New Guinea: A Descriptive Account. Oceania 54:204–23.

1985   A Sabotaged Aqueduct: Sociopolitical Parameters of Agricultural Intensification in Lowland Papua New Guinea. In Prehistoric Intensive Agriculture in the Tropics, Ian S. Farrington, ed., pp. 683–98. Oxford: British Archaeological Reports, International Series 232.

1986   Always Hungry, Never Greedy: Food and the Expression of Gender in a Melanesian Society. Cambridge: Cambridge University Press.

1988   "Men Are Taro" (They Cannot Be Rice): Political Aspects of Food Choices in Wamira, Papua New Guinea. Food and Foodways 3(1, 2):41–57. Special Issue, Continuity and Change in Pacific Foodways, M. Kahn and L. Sexton, eds.

1990   Stone-Faced Ancestors: The Spatial Anchoring of Myth in Wamira, Papua New Guinea. Ethnology 29:51–66.

1992   Chiefs Who Fall Down and Get Washed Out to Sea: The Limitation of Museum Objects in the Representation of Ethnographic Reality. Paper presented at the 91st annual meeting of the American Anthropological Association, San Francisco.

Kant, Immanuel
1928 [1768] On the First Ground of the Distinction of Regions in Space, trans. J. Handyside. *In* Kant's Inaugural Dissertation and Early Writings on Space, pp. 19–29. Chicago: Open Court.
1950 [1787] The Critique of Pure Reason, trans. N. K. Smith. 2d ed. New York: Humanities Press.
1974 [1797] Anthropology from a Pragmatic Point of View, ed. and trans. M. Gregor. The Hague: Nijhoff.

Kapferer, Bruce
1988   Legends of People, Myths of State. Washington, D.C.: Smithsonian Institution Press.

Keesing, Roger
1990   Theories of Culture Revisited. Canberra Anthropology 13:46–60.

Keith, Michael, and Steve Pile, eds.
1993   Place and the Politics of Identity. London: Routledge.

Kelley, Klara, and Harris Francis
1994   Navajo Sacred Places. Bloomington: Indiana University Press.

Klingender, Francis D.
1972   Art and the Industrial Revolution. 2d ed., edited and revised by Arthur Elton. London: Paladin.

Knox, John
1558   The First Blast of the Trumpet against the Monstrous Regiment of Women. London.

Kripke, Saul
1980   Naming and Necessity. Cambridge: Harvard University Press.

Lambert, J. M., J. N. Jennings, C. T. Smith, Charles Green, and J. N. Hutchinson
1960   The Making of the Broads: A Reconsideration of Their Origin in the Light of New Evidence. RGS Research Series, no. 3. London: Royal Geographical Society.

Lawrence, Denise L., and Setha M. Low
1990   The Built Environment and Spatial Form. Annual Review of Anthropology 19:453–505.

Lawrence, Robert C.
1939   The State of Robeson. Lumberton, North Carolina: J. J. Little and Ives Company.

Leder, Drew
1990   The Absent Body. Chicago: University of Chicago Press.

Lefebvre, Henri
1991   The Production of Space, trans. D. Nicholson-Smith. Oxford: Blackwell.

Leibniz, Gottfried Wilhelm
1956   Philosophical Papers and Letters, vol. 2, ed. L. E. Loemaker. Chicago: University of Chicago Press.

Levin, David Michael
1985   The Body's Recollection of Being. London: Routledge & Kegan Paul.

Lévi-Strauss, Claude
1966   The Savage Mind. Chicago: University of Chicago Press.

Lévy-Bruhl, Lucien
  1978   The Notebooks on Primitive Mentality, trans. P. Riviere. New York:
          Harper and Row.
Locke, John
  1690   An Essay Concerning Human Understanding.
Louis, James
  1989   Landscape in Nineteenth Century Literature. *In* The Rural Idyll, G. E.
          Mingay, ed., pp. 61–76. London: Routledge.
Lowe, Philip
  1989   The Rural Idyll Defended. *In* The Rural Idyll, G. E. Mingay, ed., pp. 113–
          31. London: Routledge.
Lowenthal, David
  1985   The Past Is a Foreign Country. Cambridge: Cambridge University Press.
  1991   British National Identity and the English Landscape. Rural History 2(2):
          205–30.
Lynch, Owen M.
  1996   Contesting and Contested Identities: Mathura's Chaubes. *In* Narratives of
          Agency: Self-Making in China, India, and Japan, Wimal Dissanayake, ed.
          Minneapolis: University of Minnesota Press.
McCullers, Carson
  1967   The Heart Is a Lonely Hunter. Boston: Houghton Mifflin.
Malinowski, Bronislaw
  1922   Argonauts of the Western Pacific. London: Routledge.
Mardle, Jonathan
  1973   Broad Norfolk. Norwich, U.K.: Wensum.
Marks, Lawrence
  1978   The Unity of the Senses: Interrelations among the Modalities. New York:
          Academic Press.
Marks, Stuart A.
  1991   Southern Hunting in Black and White: Nature, History, and Ritual in a
          Carolina Community. Princeton, New Jersey: Princeton University Press.
Massey, Doreen
  1994   Space, Place, and Gender. Minneapolis: University of Minnesota Press.
Matthews, Gareth
  1982   The Varieties of Reference. Oxford: Oxford University Press.
Mauss, Marcel
  1979 [1935] Body Techniques. *In* Sociology and Psychology: Essays by Marcel
          Mauss, pp. 97–123. London: Routledge & Kegan Paul.
Merleau-Ponty, Maurice
  1962   Phenomenology of Perception, trans. C. Smith. New York: Humanities
          Press.
  1963   The Structure of Behavior. Boston: Beacon Press.
  1964a   The Primacy of Perception. Evanston, Illinois: Northwestern University
          Press.
  1964b   From Mauss to Claude Lévi-Strauss. *In* Signs, trans. R. McCleary, pp. 114–
          25. Evanston, Illinois: Northwestern University Press.
  1968   The Visible and the Invisible, trans. A. Lingis. Evanston, Illinois: North-
          western University Press.
Mitchell, Joseph
  1992   Up in the Old Hotel and Other Stories. New York: Pantheon Books.

Mitchell, W. J. T., ed.
1994   Landscape and Power. Chicago: University of Chicago Press.
Momaday, N. Scott
1974   Native American Attitudes to the Environment. *In* Seeing with a Native Eye: Essays on Native American Religion, W. Capps, ed., pp. 79–85. New York: Harper and Row.
1976   The Names. Tucson: University of Arizona Press.
Morris, John, and Philippa Brown, eds.
1984   Domesday Book: Norfolk. 2 vols. Chicester, U.K.: Phillimore.
Morris, William
1933 [1890] News from Nowhere, or, an Epoch of Rest, Being Some Chapters from a Utopian Romance. London: Longmans, Green and Company.
Mugerauer, Robert
1994   Interpretations on Behalf of Place: Environmental Displacements and Alternative Responses. Albany: State University of New York Press.
Munn, Nancy
1973   Walbiri Iconography: Graphic Representation and Cultural Symbolism in a Central Australian Society. Ithaca, New York: Cornell University Press.
1977   The Spatiotemporal Transformation of Gawa Canoes. Journal de la Société des Océanistes 33:39–53.
1986   The Fame of Gawa: A Symbolic Study of Value Transformation in a Massim (Papua New Guinea) Society. Cambridge: Cambridge University Press.
1990   Constructing Regional Worlds in Experience. Man 25:1–17.
Murdock, George Peter
1957   World Ethnographic Sample. American Anthropologist 59(4).
Myers, Fred R.
1991   Pintupi Country, Pintupi Self: Sentiment, Place, and Politics among Western Desert Aborigines. Berkeley: University of California Press.
Newby, Howard
1988   Country Life: A Social History of Rural England. London: Cardinal.
Newby, Howard, Collin Bell, David Rose, and Peter Saunders
1978   Property, Paternalism and Power: Class and Control in Rural England. London: Hutchinson.
Newton, Henry
1914   In Far New Guinea. Philadelphia: J. P. Lippincott.
Newton, Isaac
1687   Mathematical Principles of Natural Philosophy. London.
Nir, Dov
1990   Region as a Socio-Environmental System: An Introduction to a Systemic Regional Geography. GeoJournal Library Series, vol. 16, Wolf Tietze, ed. Boston: Kluwer Academic Publishers.
Norfolk Federation of Women's Institutes
1990   The Norfolk Village Book. Newbury, U.K.: Countryside Books.
Ochs, Elinor, and Bambi B. Schieffelin
1983   Acquiring Conversational Competence. London: Routledge & Kegan Paul.
1984   Language Acquisition and Socialization: Three Developmental Stories and Their Implications. *In* Culture Theory: Essays in Mind, Self, and Emotion, R. Schweder and R. Levine, eds., pp. 276–320. New York: Cambridge University Press.

Ohnuki-Tierney, Emiko
    1991   Embedding and Transforming Polytrope: The Monkey as Self in Japanese Culture. *In* Beyond Metaphor: The Theory of Tropes in Anthropology, James W. Fernandez, ed., pp. 158–89. Stanford, California: Stanford University Press.

Ong, Walter
    1982   Orality and Literacy. New York: Methuen.

Ortiz, Alfonso
    1969   The Tewa World: Space, Time, Being, and Becoming in a Pueblo Society. Chicago: University of Chicago Press.

Owen, Tim, and Elaine Pilbeam
    1992   Ordnance Survey: Map Makers to Britain since 1791. London: Her Majesty's Stationery Office.

Oxendineville, Act of Incorporation
    1885   An Act to Incorporate the Town of Oxendineville in the County of Robeson, January 21. North Carolina State Archives, Legislative Records of General Assembly, Legislative Papers, Engrossed Bills, 1885, Box 1144.

Pandya, Vishvajit
    1990   Movement and Space: Andamanese Cartography. American Ethnologist 17(4):775–97.

Papuan Annual Report
    1936–37 Papuan Annual Report. Victoria, Australia: Government Printer.

Parmentier, Richard J.
    1987   The Sacred Remains: Myth, History, and Polity in Belau. Chicago: University of Chicago Press.

Peck, John Gregory
    1972   Urban Station — Migration of the Lumbee Indians. Ph.D. dissertation, Department of Anthropology, University of North Carolina, Chapel Hill.

Prince, Hugh
    1988   Art and Agrarian Change. *In* The Iconography of the Landscape, Denis Cosgrove and Stephen Daniels, eds., pp. 98–118. Cambridge: Cambridge University Press.

Reed, T. V.
    1988   Unimagined Existence and the Fiction of the Real: Postmodernist Realism in *Let Us Now Praise Famous Men*. Representations 24:156–75.

Relph, Edward.
    1976   Place and Placelessness. London: Pion.

Richardson, Miles, ed.
    1984   Place: Experience and Symbol. Geoscience and Man, vol. 24. Baton Rouge: Department of Geography and Anthropology, Louisiana State University.

Riches, Naomi
    1967 [1937] The Agricultural Revolution in Norfolk. London: Frank Cass & Company.

Ricoeur, Paul
    1969   Le conflit des interpretations. Paris: Editions du Seuil.

Rodman, Margaret
    1985   Moving Houses: Residential Mobility and the Mobility of Residences in Longana, Vanuatu. American Anthropologist 87:56–72.
    1987   Masters of Tradition: Consequences of Customary Land Tenure in Longana, Vanuatu. Vancouver: University of British Columbia Press.

1992   Empowering Place: Multilocality and Multivocality. American Anthropologist 94(3):640–56.

Rogers, Alan
1989   A Planned Countryside. *In* The Rural Idyll, G. E. Mingay, ed., pp. 91–102. London: Routledge.

Rosaldo, Renato
1980   Ilongot Headhunting, 1883–1974: A Study in Society and History. Stanford: Stanford University Press.
1988   Ideology, Place, and People without Culture. Cultural Anthropology 3(1): 77–87.

Russell, Bertrand
1912   The Problems of Philosophy. London: Home University Library.

Ryden, Kent
1993   Mapping the Invisible Landscape: Folklore, Writing, and the Sense of Place. Iowa City: University of Iowa Press.

Rye, James
1991   A Popular Guide to Norfolk Place-Names. Dereham, Norfolk: Larks Press.

Salmond, Anne
1982   Theoretical Landscapes: On a Cross-Cultural Conception of Knowledge. *In* Semantic Anthropology, David Parkin, ed., pp. 65–87. London: Academic Press.

Sambursky, Samuel
1982   The Concept of Place in Late NeoPlatonism. Jerusalem: Israel Academy of Sciences and Humanities.

Santayana, George
1955   Skepticism and Animal Faith. New York: Dover.

Sartre, Jean-Paul
1965   The Philosophy of Jean-Paul Sartre, R. Cumming, ed. New York: Vintage Books.
1966   Being and Nothingness, trans. H. Barnes. New York: Washington Square Press.

Sataloff, Robert
1992   The Human Voice. Scientific American 267(6):108–15.

Schafer, R. Murray
1977   The Tuning of the World. New York: Knopf.
1985   Acoustic Space. *In* Dwelling, Place and Environment, D. Seamon and R. Mugerauer, eds., pp. 87–98. Dordrecht, Netherlands: M. Nijhoff.
1993   Voices of Tyranny, Temples of Silence. Indian River, Ontario: Arcana Editions.

Schegloff, E. A.
1972   Notes on Conversational Practice: Formulating Place. *In* Language and Social Context, P. P. Giglioli, ed., pp. 95–135. Middlesex, U.K.: Penguin.

Schieffelin, Bambi B.
1979   Getting It Together: An Ethnographic Perspective on the Study of the Acquisition of Communicative Competence. *In* Developmental Pragmatics, E. Ochs and B. B. Schieffelin, eds., pp. 73–108. New York: Academic Press.
1986   The Acquisition of Kaluli. *In* The Cross-Linguistic Study of Language Acquisition, D. Slobin, ed., pp. 525–93. Hillsdale, New Jersey: Erlbaum.

1990   The Give and Take of Everyday Life: Language Socialization of Kaluli Children. New York: Cambridge University Press.

Schieffelin, Edward L.
1976   The Sorrow of the Lonely and the Burning of the Dancers. New York: St. Martins Press.
1977   The Unseen Influence: Tranced Mediums as Historical Innovators. Journal de la Société des Océanistes 33(56–57):169–78.
1982   The *bau a* Ceremonial Hunting Lodge: An Alternative to Initiation. *In* Rituals of Manhood: Male Initiation in Papua New Guinea, G. Herdt, ed., pp. 155–200. Berkeley: University of California Press.
1984   The Retaliation of the Animals: On the Cultural Construction of the Past in Papua New Guinea. Bikmaus 5(4):1–14.
1985   Performance and the Cultural Construction of Reality. American Ethnologist 12(4):707–24.

Schieffelin, Edward L., and Robert Crittenden, eds.
1991   Like People You See in a Dream: First Contact in Six Papuan Societies. Stanford: Stanford University Press.

Schieffelin, Edward L., and Hiroyuki Kurita
1988   The Phantom Patrol: Reconciling Native Narratives and Colonial Documents in Reconstructing the History of Exploration in Papua New Guinea. Journal of Pacific History 23:52–69.

Schilder, Paul
1950   The Image and Appearance of the Human Body. New York: International Universities Press.

Schuster, Meinhard
1991   Aspects of the Aibom Concept of History. *In* Sepik Heritage: Tradition and Change in Papua New Guinea, Nancy Lutkehaus et al., eds., pp. 7–19. Durham, North Carolina: Carolina Academic Press.

Seamon, David
1979   A Geography of the Lifeworld: Movement, Rest, and Encounter. New York: St. Martins Press.

Seamon, David, ed.
1992   Dwelling, Seeing, and Building: Toward a Phenomenological Ecology. Albany: State University of New York Press.

Seamon, David, and Robert Mugerauer, eds.
1985   Dwelling, Place and Environment. Dordrecht, Netherlands: M. Nijhoff.

Shields, Rob
1991   Places on the Margin: Alternative Geographies of Modernity. London: Routledge Chapman Hall.

Shils, Edward A.
1981   Tradition. Chicago: University of Chicago Press.

Silver, Timothy
1990   A New Face on the Countryside: Indians, Colonists, and Slaves in South Atlantic Forests, 1500–1800. Cambridge: Cambridge University Press.

Soja, Edward W.
1989   Postmodern Geographies: The Reassertion of Space in Critical Social Theory. New York: Verso.

Sørum, Arve
1989   The Aesthetics of Spacetime: Temporality and Perception in New Guinea. Paper read at the annual meeting of the American Ethnological Society.

Spinoza, B.
    1949 [1677] Ethics, J. Gutman, ed. New York: Hafner.
Stanner, W. E. H.
    1965   Aboriginal Territorial Organization: Estate, Range, Domain, and Regime.
            Oceania 36:1–26.
Steinbeck, John, and E. F. Rickets
    1962 [1941] Log from the Sea of Cortez. New York: Viking Press.
Stewart, Kathleen
    1988   Nostalgia—A Polemic. Cultural Anthropology 3(3):227–41.
Stokes, Martin, ed.
    1994   Ethnicity, Identity and Music: The Musical Construction of Place. Oxford:
            Berg.
Stoller, Paul
    1989   The Taste of Ethnographic Things: The Senses in Anthropology. Philadel-
            phia: University of Pennsylvania Press.
Strathern, Andrew
    1975   Veiled Speech in Mount Hagen. In Political Language and Oratory in Tra-
            ditional Society, Maurice Bloch, ed., pp. 185–203. New York: Academic
            Press.
    1979   Men's House, Women's House: The Efficacy of Opposition, Reversal, and
            Pairing in the Melpa Amb Kor Cult. Journal of the Polynesian Society 88:
            37–51.
Strathern, Marilyn
    1988   The Gender of the Gift. Berkeley: University of California Press.
    1991   Partial Connections. Savage, Maryland: Rowman and Littlefield.
Straus, Erwin
    1963   The Primary World of Senses: A Vindication of Sensory Experience, trans.
            J. Needleman. Glencoe, Illinois: Free Press.
Swift, Graham
    1983   Waterland. London: Picador.
Taussig, Michael
    1991   Tactility and Distraction. Cultural Anthropology 6(2):147–53.
    1993   Mimesis and Alterity: A Particular History of the Senses. New York: Rout-
            ledge.
Tedlock, Dennis
    1972   On the Translation of Style in Oral Narrative, In Toward New Perspec-
            tives in Folklore, Américo Paredes and Richard Bauman, eds., pp. 114–33.
            Austin: University of Texas Press.
    1983   The Spoken Word and the Work of Interpretation. Philadelphia: Univer-
            sity of Pennsylvania Press.
Thomas, Maud
    1982   Away Down Home: A History of Robeson County, North Carolina. Lum-
            berton, North Carolina: Historic Robeson.
Tilley, Christopher
    1994   A Phenomenology of Landscape: Places, Paths and Monuments. Oxford:
            Berg.
Todorov, Tzvetan
    1984   Mikhail Bakhtin: The Dialogic Principle, trans. Wlad Godzich. Minne-
            apolis: University of Minnesota Press.
Toynbee, Arnold
    1947   A Study of History, vol. 1. New York: Oxford University Press.

Truax, Barry
  1984   Acoustic Communication. Norwood, New Jersey: Ablex.
Trudgill, David
  1974   The Social Differentiation of English in Norwich. Cambridge: Cambridge
          University Press.
  1990   The Dialects of England. Oxford: Blackwell.
Tuan, Yi-Fu
  1977   Space and Place: The Perspective of Experience. Minneapolis: University
          of Minnesota Press.
  1991   Language and the Making of Place: A Narrative-Descriptive Approach.
          Annals of the Association of American Geographers 81(4):684–96.
Turner, Frederick
  1989   Spirit of Place: The Making of an American Literary Landscape. San Fran-
          cisco: Sierra Club.
Tyacke, Sarah, and John Huddy
  1980   Christopher Saxton and Tudor Map-Making. London: British Library.
United Kingdom
  1960   North Sea Pilot, vol. 3. London: Hydrographic Department, Admiralty.
  1992   Regional Trends 27. London: Central Statistics Office.
  n.d.   Records of Ordnance Survey held at the Public Record Office. London:
          Public Records Office.
U.S. Department of Commerce
  1977   U.S. Coast Pilot, vol. 7. Washington, D.C.: United States Department of
          Commerce.
Urban, Greg
  1991   A Discourse-Centered Approach to Culture. Austin: University of Texas
          Press.
van Gennep, Arnold
  1960   The Rites of Passage, trans. M. B. Vizedom and G. L. Caffee. Chicago:
          University of Chicago Press.
Varela, Francisco, Evan Thompson, and Eleanor Rosch
  1991   The Embodied Mind: Cognitive Science and Human Experience. Cam-
          bridge, Massachusetts: MIT Press.
Vološinov, V. N.
  1986   Marxism and the Philosophy of Language, trans. Ladislav Matejka and I. R.
          Titunik. Cambridge, Massachusetts: Harvard University Press.
Wade-Martins, Peter, ed.
  1993   An Historical Atlas of Norfolk. Norwich, U.K.: Norfolk Museum Services.
Wagner, Roy
  1986   Symbols That Stand for Themselves. Chicago: University of Chicago Press.
Walker, Bob
  n.d.   Where's That? A Guide to Over 700 Norfolk Villages. Norwich, U.K.:
          Petersen Publicity.
Walmsley, Jane
  1986   Brit-Think, Ameri-Think: An Irreverent Guide to Understanding the
          Great Cultural Ocean that Divides Us. New York: Penguin.
Walter, E. V.
  1988   Placeways: A Theory of the Human Environment. Chapel Hill: University
          of North Carolina Press.
Wassmann, Jürg
  1991   The Nyaura Concepts of Space and Time. In Sepik Heritage: Tradition and

Change in Papua New Guinea, Nancy Lutkehaus et al., eds., pp. 23–35. Durham, North Carolina: Carolina Academic Press.

Weiner, James
1991 The Empty Place: Poetry, Space, and Being among the Foi of Papua New Guinea. Bloomington: University of Indiana Press.

Werner, Hans
1992 Soundscapes Akustische Landschaften: Eine klangökologische Spuren- suche. (TSNE vol. 1). Basel: Soundscape Newsletter, Europe Edition.

Whitehead, Alfred North
1925 Science and the Modern World. New York: Macmillan.

Wiggins, William H., Jr.
1987 O Freedom! Afro-American Emancipation Celebrations. Knoxville: Uni- versity of Tennessee Press.

Williams, Brett
1988 Upscaling Downtown: Stalled Gentrification in Washington, D.C. Ithaca, New York: Cornell University Press.

Williams, Raymond
1985 [1973] The Country and the City. London: The Hogarth Press.

Williamson, Tom
1993 The Origins of Norfolk. Manchester: Manchester University Press.

Woodward, Samuel, W. C. Ewing, and Dawson Turner.
1842 The Norfolk Topographer's Manual. London: Nichols and Son.

Wright, Gavin
1986 Old South, New South: Revolutions in the Southern Economy since the Civil War. New York: Basic Books.

Wright, Patrick
1985 On Living in an Old Country: The National Past in Contemporary Brit- ain. London: Verso.

Yoon, Hong-Key
1986 Maori Mind, Maori Land. New York: Peter Lang.

Young, Arthur
1804 General View of the Agriculture of the Country of Norfolk Drawn Up for the Consideration of the Board of Agriculture and Internal Improvement. London: B. McMillan.

Young, Michael
1971 Fighting with Food: Leadership, Values and Social Control in a Massim Society. Cambridge: Cambridge University Press.
1983a Magicians of Manumanua: Living Myth in Kalauna. Berkeley: University of California Press.
1983b "Our Name Is Women; We Are Bought with Limesticks and Limepots": An Analysis of an Autobiographical Narrative of a Kalauna Woman. Man (n.s.) 18:478–501.

Zizek, Slavoj
1991 For They Know Not What They Do: Enjoyment as a Political Factor. New York: New Left Books.

Zuckerkandl, Victor
1956 Sound and Symbol: Music and the External World. Bollingen Series, 44. Princeton, New Jersey: Princeton University Press.

Index

School of American Research
Advanced Seminar Series

PUBLISHED BY SAR PRESS

PUBLISHED BY CAMBRIDGE UNIVERSITY PRESS

DREAMING: ANTHROPOLOGICAL AND
PSYCHOLOGICAL INTERPRETATIONS
Barbara Tedlock, ed.

THE ANASAZI IN A CHANGING
ENVIRONMENT
George J. Gumerman, ed.

REGIONAL PERSPECTIVES ON THE OLMEC
Robert J. Sharer & David C. Grove, eds.

THE CHEMISTRY OF PREHISTORIC
HUMAN BONE
T. Douglas Price, ed.

THE EMERGENCE OF MODERN HUMANS:
BIOCULTURAL ADAPTATIONS IN THE
LATER PLEISTOCENE
Erik Trinkaus, ed.

THE ANTHROPOLOGY OF WAR
Jonathan Haas, ed.

THE EVOLUTION OF POLITICAL SYSTEMS
Steadman Upham, ed.

CLASSIC MAYA POLITICAL HISTORY:
HIEROGLYPHIC AND ARCHAEOLOGICAL
EVIDENCE
T. Patrick Culbert, ed.

TURKO-PERSIA IN HISTORICAL
PERSPECTIVE
Robert L. Canfield, ed.

CHIEFDOMS: POWER, ECONOMY, AND
IDEOLOGY
Timothy Earle, ed.

PUBLISHED BY UNIVERSITY OF CALIFORNIA PRESS

WRITING CULTURE: THE POETICS
AND POLITICS OF ETHNOGRAPHY
James Clifford &
George E. Marcus, eds.

Published by University of New Mexico Press

*Participants in the School of American Research advanced seminar
"Place, Expression, and Experience." Santa Fe, March–April 1993.*

*Seated: Steven Feld (left), Keith H. Basso. Standing (left to right):
Charles O. Frake, Karen I. Blu, Miriam Kahn, Edward S. Casey,
Kathleen C. Stewart, Clifford Geertz, Nancy Munn.*

DATE DUE

GAYLORD   PRINTED IN U.S.A.